NATIVE
AMERICAN
HISTORY

NATIVE AMERICAN HISTORY

A CHRONOLOGY OF THE VAST
ACHIEVEMENTS OF A CULTURE AND
THEIR LINKS TO WORLD EVENTS

JUDITH NIES

BALLANTINE BOOKS
NEW YORK

A Ballantine Book
Published by The Random House Publishing Group

Copyright © 1996 by Judith E. Nies

All rights reserved.

Published in the United States by Ballantine Books, an imprint of The Random House
Publishing Group, a division of Random House, Inc., New York, and simultaneously
in Canada by Random House of Canada Limited, Toronto.

Ballantine and colophon are registered trademarks of Random House, Inc

www.ballantinebooks.com

LIBRARY OF CONGRESS CATALOGING-IN-PUBLICATION DATA
Nies, Judith, 1941–
Native American history / by Judith Nies. — 1st ed.
p.   cm.
Includes bibliographical references.
ISBN 0-345-39350-3
1. Indians of North America—History.   2. Indians of North
America—Social life and customs.   I. Title.
E77.N56   1996
970.004'97—dc20   96-32659
                                             CIP

Text Design by Fritz Metsch
Cover design by Michelle T. Gengaro
Cover photo credits: Left column from top: © 1996 Donna DeCesare, Impact Visuals;
© 1995 Jerome Friar, Impact Visuals, © 1994 Kirk Condyles, Impact Visuals; David F. Barry,
Denver Public Library, Western History Department; The Granger Collection, New York.
Center photo: David F. Barry, Denver Public Library, Western History Department.
Right column from top: The Granger Collection, New York; © Archive Photos; © 1992
Rick Gerharter, Impact Visuals; Montana Historical Society, Helena; The Granger Collection.

Manufactured in the United States of America
First Edition: November 1996
11 13 15 17 19 18 16 14 12 10

Events do not happen in categories—economic, intellectual, military—they happen in sequence. When they are arranged in sequence as strictly as possible . . . cause and effect that may have been previously obscure, will often become clear, like secret ink.

BARBARA W. TUCHMAN
"PRACTICING HISTORY: SELECTED ESSAYS"

TABLE OF CONTENTS

ACKNOWLEDGMENTS

My research has been greatly aided by many people who pointed me in directions I might not have thought to go. My thanks to many of the members of the Harvard University Native American Program (1991–1993) whose lectures, discussions, and perspectives informed and enlightened me in ways I was not aware of at the time. Since part of the historical record exists in photographs rather than documents, my thanks to Andrew Connors at the Museum of American Art and Paula Fleming at the National Anthropological Archives in Washington, D.C. Special thanks to Sarah Flynn for help with photo research. Reference librarians have been wonderfully informative and I thank the Skidmore College Library, the Tozzer Library at Harvard University (Elizabeth Cherniack, Morris Fry, Gregory Finnegan), the Houghton rare book library at Harvard University, the Boston Public Library, the Schlesinger Library at Radcliffe College, the North Cambridge Public Library (Jessica Rabban), the Arizona State University Library Archives and the Brigham Young University Archives. Special thanks to Harvard doctoral candidates Gabrielle Tayac of the Piscataway community in Maryland and Athabascan Phyllis A. Fast of Alaska, now a professor at the University of Alaska, Fairbanks, who helped me conceptualize the beginning and end of this chronology, and advised me on matters of terminology and concepts. I take full responsibility for all mistakes. I must also thank Charlotte Sheedy and Regula Noetzli for their vision and encouragement. My thanks also to the Bunting Institute of Radcliffe College and the Yaddo Corporation for providing time and support.

INTRODUCTION

History is context. We choose our history by selecting certain events to include in the narrative. Those events take their meaning in relation to other events. And these narratives make up the myths of our culture—myths that are changing all the time. My idea for a chronology of Native American history grew out of the paradigm shift that resulted from the quincentenary celebration of Columbus's arrival in the western hemisphere in 1492. Like many people expecting a lively celebration of Columbus's heroism, courage, and mythic vision, my imagination was captured instead by the "view from the shore." The point of view presented by indigenous peoples was one of great native contributions and great European injustices. Their perspective changed the narrative of time and challenged the conventional myths of the Americas.

In colorful contradiction to centuries of national Columbus holidays and mainstream history texts, indigenous peoples throughout the hemisphere launched demonstrations to publicize the historical reality of the Arawak Indians and Columbus's genocidal search for gold. At the time Columbus landed on the island he dubbed Hispaniola in 1492 there were an estimated 30 million people in Mexico and the Caribbean Islands (Columbus's brother counted over one million male inhabitants in the Dominican Republic in the census he conducted to determine how many adult males should be bringing in gold for tribute) and another estimated 50 million in the U.S., Canada, and South America, many of whom lived in highly complex cultures with sophisticated knowledge of astronomy, agriculture, metalworking, weaving, geography, measurement of time.

America has been notably uninterested in the people who lived here before the European invasions of the fifteenth and sixteenth centuries. In the year A.D. 750, when London was still historically insignificant, the sixth-largest city in the world (including Constantinople and Alexandria) was Teotihuacán in the Mexico Valley, near what today is Mexico City. In the year 800 the Hohokam were irrigating the land that today is Phoenix and building seven-story apartment buildings at the same time the former barbarian Charlemagne was being crowned emperor of the Holy Roman Empire (which, to quote Voltaire, was neither holy nor Roman). The largest pyramid outside of Egypt was (and can still be seen today) in Cahokia, Illinois, near the confluence of the Missouri, Illinois, and Mississippi Rivers, a remnant of the great Mississippian civilization. The Mississippians left thousands of temple mounds and geometric earthworks along the lands of the Mississippi River valleys in settlement patterns so dense that when the Arkansas Archaeological Society recently put all 21,700 sites on a computerized map it showed a thoroughly settled state by the

NATIVE AMERICAN HISTORY

1300s. Albert Gallatin, Jefferson's secretary of the treasury, was the first to write about the great architectural marvels of the Mississippi Valley and the "mound builders." He was joined by Henry Brackenridge, an early explorer of the Ohio Valley as far south as Louisiana. "*An immense population has once been supported in this country,*" he observed about the thousands of geometrically arranged mounds that laced the South. But these were colonial Americans intent on land acquisition. Knowledge and exploration were in the service of real estate. American mythology required a virgin continent and "a vanished race." By 1950 over 90 percent of the archaeological marvels written about by Gallatin and Brackenridge had been declared valueless and lost to highways, railroads, farmlands, real estate development, shopping malls.

By 1992, however, a parallel narrative had been constructed by Native American writers. Their refusal to venerate Columbus's heroism and "discovery" raised a lot of questions: How can you "discover" a hemisphere that has over 70 million people? Why couldn't the European Christians "see" the Native peoples as fellow human beings? Is it true that Pilgrims in Plymouth, America's first permanent colony, survived their first winter only because of the instruction of an English-speaking Indian named Squanto? Did the principles of the Iroquois confederacy influence the drafters of the U.S. Constitution? How did the agricultural products of American Indians—corn, beans, squash—enrich the diet and health of Renaissance Europe? Were there great urban centers in America long before London or Paris were founded? Ultimately, the sputtering of Columbus's historic flame was best symbolized by the fate of the modern replicas of his boats. Instead of making triumphant entries into dozens of American harbors, the *Niña*, the *Pinta*, and the *Santa Maria* ended up marooned and bankrupt in New York, punctuation marks for the questions of America's new history.

Like many books, this chronology began as part of another project, a book on the contemporary strip-mining of Hopi and Navajo lands on Black Mesa in northern Arizona, and the U.S. government's removal of some 12,000 Navajo in what has become the largest Indian removal since the 1800s. To frame the political sequence of events, I constructed a chronology of the land dispute between the Hopi and Navajo along with a parallel chronology of the multinational energy companies' requests for coal-mining leases. I intended to include it as an appendix. But history is yesterday's politics. Soon I found myself researching the nineteenth century, when America's first Indian agents were renegotiating agreements the Navajo and Hopi had made with the Spanish in the seventeenth century; these in turn were based on dates of settlement, such as the year 1150 when the Hopi settled their first village on the Hopi mesas. Although the modern-day conflict has been structured in the language of the American legal system, certain larger questions presented themselves. Who are the Hopi? Where did they come from? And what about the Navajo? When did they migrate from Alaska to the American Southwest? How do we conceive of an America that didn't begin in 1620? The great Anasazi sites like Mesa Verde and Chaco Canyon testify to sophisticated agriculture, extensive trade routes, complicated architecture, urban planning, and complex religious and political systems. Their centralized population is estimated at somewhere around 200,000; yet they

2

still have not been included in the narrative of American history. Although there were only five Native American entries—Apache, Geronimo, Navajo, Chief Joseph, and Indian Summer—in the 5,000 names, dates, and concepts included in the *Dictionary of Cultural Literacy*, which purported to define all that a culturally literate American should know, most of us want to know more.

This chronology attempts to take Indian history out of the setting of anthropology and put it in the context of cultural history. I hope the reader might take from this a new sense of historical pattern, a larger framework in which to connect the jigsaw-puzzle pieces of history. It is meant for the general reader whose curiosity has been piqued by some of the new books about Native American history, as well as for the student, educator, or researcher looking for larger historical perspectives on the American experience. A chronology of Native American history offers the opportunity to bring together in a lively, exciting way material that has not been given historical or cultural connection before.

Because language reflects changing concepts, I have used a variety of terms interchangeably to refer to America's indigenous populations—"Indians," "Native Americans," "American Indians," "Native peoples," "indigenous peoples." The problem of clarity of terminology began with Columbus. He was lost. The people he met were not Indians because he was not in India. But for five centuries since Columbus the indigenous peoples of this hemisphere have been called "Indians." They are, in fact, many different peoples and many different nations with many different languages. Today the U.S. government recognizes more than 370 separate tribes or Indian peoples. Consequently, terminology is in flux. History, usage, and tradition have made "Indian" a widely used term. Indian peoples themselves often use the term "Indian," as in the Museum of the American Indian, the American Indian Movement (AIM), and the *American Indian Quarterly*. In the 1980s, "Native American" came into popular usage as a more historically appropriate term, but has recently fallen into disuse, since technically anyone born in North or South America is a "native" American. Alternatively, Indian people also use "Native," "Native Peoples," or "First Peoples." I have used different terms in different contexts, depending on how Indian writers use the same term on the page. (Oral use is somewhat different.) The important element to remember is that there is no single ethnic group called Indians; there are *hundreds of peoples* with distinct languages, religious beliefs, ceremonies, and cultural traditions. Using the term "Indian" is no more precise than using "European" to denote an Englishman.

For purposes of this book I have defined North America as Mexico and the United States up to the Canadian border, although in historical reality the borders were artificial. The organizing principle on the ground seems to have been watersheds and river systems. Population estimates for this area fluctuate wildly. Indian populations were dynamic and in constant motion, migrating from Mexico into the Southwest and up the Mississippi River system to Canada and back again; or from Alaska along the California coast and across the Southwest to the Atlantic coast. Shells from the Florida Keys have been found with the Cree in Canada; turquoise from the Southwest has been found in Natchez graves in Louisiana.

Trade routes laced the entire continent as far north as Hudson Bay, and a map of known Indian trade routes of the continental United States shows that no region was unsettled. Indian artifacts and archaeological ruins have been found throughout the United States. Sites of great architectural sophistication were located all along the river systems of Ohio, Kansas, Mississippi, Louisiana, Arkansas, Illinois, Alabama, Georgia, Texas, Oklahoma, and Wisconsin, as well as the Colorado Plateau region of the Southwest.

Population figures have been greatly revised over the past 10 years. Although all sites were not simultaneously occupied, population estimates at the time of Columbus range from 7 to 45 million people in South America; 7 to 30 million people in Mexico and the Caribbean islands; and one to 18 million people in the U.S. and Canada. Some revised estimates go as high as 110 million people in the entire western hemisphere. The variations are based on the interpretation of the numbers of settlements, the duration of settlement, the areas of land cultivated multiplied by the numbers of people they might have supported. I have used the more conservative of the revised estimates. About the only fact everyone agrees on is that there were far more people living in the Americas than was formerly believed or that our history books have told us.

In developing the two columns that make up the contextualized chronology, I have placed in the right-hand column Native American historical events as well as events that greatly affected Native America. In the left-hand column I have put world events or American governmental events that were outside Indian control but which framed the larger political and cultural environment in which Native peoples had to respond. Actions by the rulers of Spain, England, France, and Russia were distant but had particular impact on Native Americans. To use a recent example from the American political system, Indians were not allowed to vote until 1924, but they were expected to register for the draft for World War I. The problems of Indian veterans returning to their reservations after the war caused great dislocations and hardships while at the same time Indian tribes were without means to give political voice to their grievances. The Indians' belated right to vote is in the right-hand column; the war in the left.

Occasionally, certain events fall between the two columns. The first celebrity Indians in Europe were four Mohawk chiefs who agreed to accompany the English Indian agent to London in 1710. Although their historical visibility occurred in England, their historical impact stemmed from their later influence on Iroquois loyalty to England against the colonial Americans. I have placed the Mohawk visit of 1710 in the right-hand column.

Viewing global events with a focus on land issues, technology, population, and religion in conjunction with Native American history reveals the complex fabric of indigenous knowledge of agriculture, medicine, and astronomy that enriched Europe. It provides a unique perspective with which to explore America, an exploration we are still undertaking. In fact, some might say we are approaching the millennium by beginning the exploration of America's deeper history.

1

We locate events in relation to the birth of Jesus Christ—before his birth (B.C.) and after his birth (A.D.). This is not a universal time measurement. The Chinese started recording time over 4,300 years ago. Many Buddhist societies date the current year as 2585, counting from the year the historical Buddha was born in 560 B.C.* Recorded history actually begins about 5,000 years ago. In Mesopotamia texts from the city of Ur have been dated to 2800 B.C., which can also be calculated as 4,826 years ago (2,800 years, plus 30 years that Jesus lived, plus 1,996 years after his death). The Mayan calendar is based on the date 3372 B.C., which would be 5,368 years ago (or "Years Ago," as many contemporary archaeological texts refer to time "Before Present"). People around the globe have a very different sense of what time is and how it should be measured. (For a century after Europeans invented the watch, it only kept track of hours; the minute hand was not added until the seventeenth century.) Pope Gregory introduced our calendar, the Gregorian calendar, in 1582 to correct an error in the Julian calendar, which had fallen 10 days behind astronomically. Great Britain did not adopt the Gregorian calendar until 1752; Russia and Greek Orthodox countries didn't adopt it until 1918. It was finally adopted worldwide in 1950.

It has become standard in archaeological texts to measure time back from the present and say "30,000 Years Ago," or "Years Before Present." However, since I need to correlate with commonly accepted western dates measured by the Gregorian calendar, I have used B.C. and A.D. Occasionally I have also inserted the alternative measure to indicate another concept of time. For many Native Americans time is conceptually complex: mythical time, historical time, and personal time are all integrated within the same paradigm. Creation stories incorporate geological time and evolutionary time. The Mayas conceived of time as cyclical, and organized their calendar along three different intermeshing wheels. Some living Native American languages, like Hopi, have no tenses and all events take place in a continuous present. One Native American, whom I asked about this issue of time measurement, answered, "The question is, where do you place zero?"

Biblical time starts human history in the Middle East. In truth, if there was a "cradle of civilization" it was in Africa over a million years ago. If we start human

---

*There are two traditions of Buddhism. Theravadin, southern Buddhists, place the date of the birth of the historical Buddha, Siddhartha Gautama, at 560 B.C. Mahayana, northern Buddhists, place it at 460 B.C. Both agree that he lived for 80 years.

history at the moment we fashioned the first recognizable tools, our ancestral anthropoids (*Homo erectus, Australopithecus,* etc.) emerged somewhere in Africa over a million years ago. The evidence of our origins resides in archaeological findings—tools, hearth charcoal, remains of horticulture, bones, pottery, stone structures, cliff dwellings, cave drawings, flints, basketry, remnants of carved wood. History based on written documents roughly covers the past 5,000 years. Prehistory and history are the interrelated record of human beings; each requires the decoding of different symbols and materials.

The earliest human record in North America is hearth charcoal found on an island off the California coast, dated to 28,000 B.C. By 12,000 B.C. Stone Age sites were located all over North America in all the areas not covered by glaciers. Human fossil remains have been found in Mexico City dated to 10,000 B.C. At the same time the Sumerians were growing barley in Mesopotamia around 3000 B.C.— in the theoretical cradle of civilization between the Tigris and Euphrates Rivers— people in Mexico were growing maize and squash and had evolved a sophisticated horticulture with extensive irrigation canals. What is now Poverty Point in Louisiana is believed to have been first built sometime around 3000 B.C. Cotton was grown in Peru around 2500 B.C. And when Coronado arrived in Arizona in 1540, he was greeted by people in the area of the present-day pueblos wearing woven cotton.

28,000 B.C. TO 1 B.C.—
PREHISTORY AND HISTORY

WORLD HISTORY

28,000 B.C.
Stone Age residents left cave carvings, stone tools, and skeletons in the Dordogne region in southern France. In North Africa in the countries now known as Tunisia, Algeria, Morocco, inhabitants left stone hand axes. In Egypt the residents of this period constructed a 100-foot terrace. In Africa tools, points, and stone implements were fashioned by early inhabitants. Other sites with stone tools, scrapers, points, axes dating to this same time have been found in Palestine, China, Japan, Siberia, Russian Turkestan, Southeastern Asia, Brazil, Venezuela, and Oceania.

NATIVE AMERICAN HISTORY

28,000 B.C.
Earliest known date for inhabitants on California's coastline. California's early settlers left hearth charcoal on Santa Rosa Island, off the coast of California, attesting to inhabitants who lived along the California coast at least 30,000 years ago. Since only human beings light fires, and charcoal remains can be carbon-dated, hearth charcoal is the best evidence of the migration routes of our early ancestors. They followed several different migration routes along the California coast and inland into Central and South America. However, the California coastline from this era, still in the age of glaciers, is now 300 feet under the sea and the rare sites survive only on islands. (Brazilian rock shelters have also yielded hearth charcoal dating to 28,000 B.C.)

The **floor of the Bering Sea** emerged as dry land during the late Pleistocene glacial advances, approximately 28,000 B.C. to 10,000 B.C. Asian hunters followed big game herds migrating from Siberia into Alaska along this route. (See "The Bering Land Bridge or Berengia" on page 8.)

27,000 B.C.
Settlement in western Alaska. This date is based on the discovery of a tool

identified as a caribou scraper and dated to 27,000 B.C. This area, as well as the Yukon River drainage of central Alaska, was free from ice during this period, sealed off from the rest of the continent by western Canadian ice.

THE BERING LAND BRIDGE OR BERENGIA

During the period of the great glaciers, a subcontinent known as Berengia rose from the ocean and connected Siberia with Alaska. A flat land mass believed to have consisted of tundra, it expanded to almost 1,000 miles across, depending on glacial flow, or narrowed to 100 miles in width. Great herds of mammals crossed the bridge onto the North American continent, and hunters from Asia followed the game. Presently submerged under the Bering Sea*, Berengia was believed to have appeared and maintained itself during the period of the great glaciers, when ice caused the seas to lower. The human migrations took place over thousands of years. These early residents, sometimes called Paleo-Indians, traveled along the natural ice-free corridors that existed between glaciers. They hunted mastodons and other big game animals of the Ice Age, woolly mammoths, outsized bison, great stags. They also gathered wild plants and fished. Eventually they spread inland across North America, crossing to the Atlantic coast; they also migrated southward into Central and South America, where stone points from this era have been found in caves near the Strait of Magellan.

The migrations were regulated by ice. When the glaciers melted, the water contained in the ice flowed back into the seas and Berengia disappeared under the ocean. When temperatures dropped and the glaciers re-formed, Berengia reappeared. The last Ice Age ended only 10,000 years ago. However, as recently as 3000 B.C. Aleuts and Athabascans were still crossing the Bering Sea by means of dugout canoes and skin boats or walking across the ice in winter. Many of the people who migrated across the Bering Strait adapted so well to the Arctic climate they stayed. We know them as the peoples of modern-day Alaska, including Aleuts, Inuits, Yupiks, and Eskimos who live in the lands of the sub-Arctic Circle. The Eskimos are believed to have arrived as recently as 1,000 years ago. Although theory poses the idea that migration was consistently north to south, a somewhat more dynamic model seems to be accurate, with people migrating in both directions over thousands of years. The migration myths of some Alaska natives, for example, hold that their people originally "came from the south."

**The names of the Bering Sea and Berengia are of recent origin. Vitus Bering, a Danish navigator in the service of the Russian ruler Peter the Great, died during the 1741 expedition in which he crossed the Bering Sea and discovered Alaska for the Russians. His name was given to the sea and the strait, which is now a permanent body of water between Alaska and Russia.*

25,000 B.C.

Settlement in New Mexico. In the Sandia Mountains of New Mexico paleontologists have found tools which include worked flint and obsidian crafted into knives, scrapers, choppers, and spear points. Anthropologists named the human residents according to the name of the site where a particular tool was found, thus: Sandia, Clovis, Folsom, Plano, etc. The Clovis-era human was far more numerous than the Sandia, and Clovis stone points have been found in every state of the continental United States.

16,000 B.C.

The first art in the painted caves of Lascaux, France, reveals that prehistoric hunters could also draw and paint. Cave paintings in red and black show people hunting mammoths, big stags, bears, ibex, bison, tapirs, and rhinoceros-like animals. One figure of a bull is 16 feet wide and shows aspects of three-dimensional drawing techniques.

15,000–13,000 B.C.

The hall of bison in caves in Altamira, Spain, shows black bison, a red horse, deer and wild boars in a mural painting executed across a 45-foot cave ceiling. The prehistoric painters used red iron oxide and manganese to etch their paintings in rock.

12,000 B.C.

Paleo-Indians settled in all the unglaciated corners of both North and South America. They followed shoreline migration routes or inland routes between glaciers. The three different periods of glaciation affected not only coastline locations but climate, environment, habitat, vegetation, and animal life.

Western Hemisphere migration routes. These migration routes from 10,000 B.C. have been suggested by archaeological sites along these corridors. The absence of sites in California (except on islands) has been explained by the fact that during the glacial age the coastline was three hundred miles out to sea. This map suggests the variety and extensiveness of migration routes and illustrates why migration stories are central to Native American cosmologies. According to oral traditions, travelers went in both directions, not simply north to south.

11,000 B.C.

Colorado settled. The first Paleo-Indian site to be studied was at Linder-meier, Colorado, just south of the Wyoming border. These early Coloradoans lived a nomadic life based on collecting wild plants and hunting large game.

10,000 B.C.

Saugus, Massachusetts, settled. Hearth charcoal and stone tools of Paleo-Indian residents of Massachusetts were found in the excavation of what is now the Saugus Iron Works Historic Site. The Indians who had lived continuously for over 10,000 years at the site, which contained a rich vein of iron ore, disappeared within 50 years of the establishment of an industrial furnace in 1630 by the Massachusetts Bay Colony. The New England Iron Works, founded by the son of the colony's governor, John Winthrop, used the Indians as forced laborers. They were unable to survive in the suffocating heat, deafening noise, and flying streams of hot metal. The reconstructed iron works can be visited today as a National Park site.

10,000 B.C.

Mexico City settled. Human fossil remains found near the pyramids of Teotihuacán dated to 10,000 B.C.

10,000–7000 B.C.

The final Ice Age. The glaciers receded. Throughout North America, glaciers began to melt. Berengia disappeared under rising oceans. The melting marked the end of large-scale migrations from Siberia. Over the next 3,000 years climate changed dramatically, with corollary shifts in vegetation and habitat for big game species. Many of the big mammals gradually became extinct and Indian bands based on hunting big game like the woolly mammoths had to shift their settlement patterns. (Scholars debate whether or not the big mammals died out from climatic changes or overhunting by humans.) Paleontologists believe that as societies tried to replicate the growing of wild plants they became more sedentary and their economies more diversified.

9000 B.C.

In the valley between the Tigris and Euphrates Rivers permanent settlements began in the area later called Mesopotamia.

9000 B.C.

Beginnings of agriculture in Mexico. Inhabitants of south central Mexico in the Valley of Tehuacán began to experiment with a wild grass called *teosinte*. They kept seeds and began to germinate new strains of the grass, which eventually evolved into *maize*, or corn.

9000–8500 B.C.

Settlement sites throughout North America: Meadowcroft Rockshelter near Pittsburgh; Blackwater Draw, New Mexico (campsites and bison kills); Danger Cave, Utah (woven containers and grinding tools); Agate Basin, Wyoming (bison kills); Bonfire Shelter Site, Texas (bison kills); Olson Chobbock, Colorado; Lehner mammoth site, Arizona; Bull Brook, Ipswich, Massachusetts. The bones found in bison kill sites suggest that herds of bison were driven over a cliff or into an arroyo, surrounded, and killed. These bison belonged to the big mammals of the Ice Age and multiplied into enormous herds on the prairies as their natural predators—lions, bears, tigers—died out. The sites suggest a migration route down the California coast to southern California, across Arizona, New Mexico, and Texas; then heading north towards

Illinois and the Great Lakes, and across to the Atlantic coast.

8000 B.C.
World population estimated at five million people.

7000 B.C.
Extreme changes in North American climate and animal life. The Laurentide ice sheet retreated as far north as the Great Lakes. As the ice retreated the climate warmed, and flora and fauna changed. Mastodons, woolly mammoths, outsized bison, giant sloths, small prehistoric horses, and other great mammals of North America began to die out. As the ice sheets moved north, the tundra transformed into great grassland prairies. Evergreen (conifer) forests became deciduous with leaf-bearing hardwood trees. In the warming temperatures jungles developed in Mexico, and woodlands spread from the Atlantic coast inland to the Midwest.

6000 B.C.
In Iran and Soviet Turkestan people lived in permanent settlements and developed pottery-making techniques.

6000 B.C.
Settlement sites of this period in North America show a great variety of tools, trade goods, and burial relics. In Columbia River sites in Oregon archaeologists discovered diverse tools related to salmon fishing; in California many settlement sites were located around San Diego and Lake Mohave; in Michigan not far from Detroit archaeologists found tools such as scrapers, projectile points; in Utah archaeologists discovered sites with remains of wood, leather, fur and basketry. In the Great Basin area, where early residents lived in caves or rock shelters, archaeologists found basketry, sandals, the *atlatl* (a club or throwing stick), small stone points, digging sticks, smoking pipes, seashell ornaments, deer-hoof rattles, medicine bags, and bird-bone

whistles. Such artifacts reflected complex trade networks as well as a diverse economic life.

5500 B.C.
Southern California settled by people referred to as the Encinitas culture. Grinding stones and shell remains suggest an economy based on the sea and farming marine resources. In the San Diego area, the Encinitas tradition endured until 1000 B.C.

5000 B.C.
Events dating back to this period appeared on the Egyptian calendar. Earliest cities in Mesopotamia.

5000 B.C.
First cultivation of maize in Tehuacán Valley in central Mexico.

5000 B.C.
Arizona and New Mexico settled by the Cochise culture. They displayed a great knowledge of desert environment and the harvesting of wild plants and seeds. Seasonally migrating through the region, they built their homes in cliffs, caves, and desert valleys. They gathered and stored a wide variety of wild plants and were believed to lay the groundwork for the extensive agricultural development of later peoples of the same region.

4500 B.C.
First mounds built along lower Mississippi. Watson Brake settled near Monroe, Louisiana. This is the oldest circular monument discovered in North America.

4500 B.C.
Northern California settled. These first Californians built sturdy, semisubterranean earth lodges. As the climate warmed they shifted to lighter surface dwellings made of brush.

Inside the Whale House. The Whale House of the Chilkat Indians of coastal Alaska was a meetinghouse and repository of objects and art of the history of the tribe. Since Europeans only understood history as transmitted through written records based on a linear sense of time, they were often at a loss to comprehend the cyclical time of native cultures, in which thousands of years of migrations and history were passed on visually in symbols and pattern and through storytelling. Percy and Pond were former Alaskan gold prospectors who set up a photography studio in Juneau, Alaska. Sometime in 1895 they stumbled into a potlatch of a member of Chief Klart-Reech's Whale clan, in which the tribal member gave all his material goods away. They were made honorary members of the Chilkat tribe. The chief invited them into the Whale House where they took this extraordinary photo showing a house screen, elaborately carved boxes, masks, two guns, helmets, a ceremonial dance apron, and an enormous carved head. They sold the photo as a postcard which violated the sanctity of the Whale House.

4000 B.C.
Settlements at Kodiak Island, Alaska. The Ocean Bay Tradition. As the sea level stabilized, Aleut and Inuit hunters, who exploited mammals and fish in the area, created numerous tools and permanent sites to develop a marine-based economy. To the north at Onion Portage, Alaska, on the Kobuk River, settlers shifted to caribou hunting as a means of sustenance. This region was continually used as a major village or base camp in a central trade route for 5,000 years.

4000 B.C.
Hunters built permanent base camps at a location known as the Koster site in Illinois. Throughout the Midwest similar permanent hunting encampments of this era were found.

3500 B.C.
Sumerians settle on the site of the city of Babylon. Great floods in the Mesopotamian region.

3372 B.C.
The earliest date of the Mayan calendar, on which all later Mayan dates were based. No one knows what event took place at that time, but it is believed to relate to an astronomical calculation and marks a particular cycle of measured time. The Mayas of Mexico and Guatemala conceived of time in terms of cycles within cycles. The smallest measurement was a religious year of 260 days inside a secular year of 365 days. The Mayan civilization in Yucatán, Mexico, developed a complex but precise calendar that located time within large cycles like intermeshing wheels. They had a system of measuring time, based on precise knowledge gained from celestial observation, that was more accurate than the calendar later adopted by Pope Gregory. (Some Mayan documents placed the end of the world in the year 34,000.)

3000–2800 B.C.
The end of prehistory and the beginning of recorded history.

Commonly cited dates for beginning of Mesopotamia, the invention of writing with the clay tablets of Ur, the development of agriculture in Sumer with the cultivation of wheat and barley. The building of ziggurats, stepped pyramidal towers, began on the plain and spread south to Egypt where they evolved into pyramids. The culture of Mesopotamia spread south and stimulated the development of the Nile Valley. Other settlement sites of the same period were in Crete, along the Danube, in China, and in Palestine.

3000 B.C.

Beginning of astronomical observations in Egypt (in later centuries in Babylonia, India, and China). The classical Sumerian age in which astronomy and mathematical knowledge developed. Egypt introduced the calendar of 365 days. Sumerian cuneiform writing recorded legal and religious codes.

3000 B.C.

Extensive irrigation works developed along the Nile in Egypt. The Nile Valley where the ancient civilization flourished was 750 miles long and 13 miles wide, with little rainfall. The annual flood of the Nile and the elaborate irrigation works made its settlement and agricultural development possible.

2600 B.C.

Pyramids of Gizeh built in Egypt, followed by the Great Pyramid of Cheops. Cheops originally rose to a

3000 B.C.

Tehuacán Valley in Mexico occupied. Horticulture developed with extensive cultivation of maize (corn), squash, beans, and other crops. Archaeological records show villages developing in area that is today the Mexico basin, including Mexico City as well as lowland areas around Veracruz on the Gulf Coast. These early Mexicans built large buildings made from quarried stone, traded in jade, and made tools from obsidian, a volcanic glass which they shaped into weapons and sharp implements.

Southern California. In some areas of California the Encinitas culture, which was based on fishing, was replaced by a hunting culture which traded extensively in shells and obsidian. They were the ancestors of the modern Chumash of the Santa Barbara region.

Arizona and New Mexico horticulture began with the cultivation of maize, beans, and squash. Planting patterns show corn and beans planted together. (Beans put nitrogen back into the soil while corn takes it out.) Farming techniques were similar to those found in the Valley of Mexico. These are believed to be the ancestors of the later Hohokam and Mogollon peoples and the modern Pueblo peoples.

2600 B.C.

Southeast U.S. settlements were located largely in river valleys and based on fishing. Many sites show evidence of height of 481.4 feet and covered a base area of 13 acres. Its construction utilized plumb-lines, A-frame construction, and inexhaustible manpower.

long-distance trading, large population clusters, and more complex settlements.

In Peru, South America, there is evidence that cotton was cultivated.

2500 B.C.
The highland villages of the people called the Olmecs in Mexico ("Olmec" is an Aztec word which means "people of the region of rubber") continued to grow and claim larger tracts of land. As agricultural techniques, they employed both irrigation and terracing. Their influence may have spread north to the southwestern U.S. At the same time period, advanced horticultural techniques, more sophisticated tools, and better food storage (pottery) began to expand in the U.S. Southwest.

2500 B.C.
Archaic Indians developed sophisticated fishing techniques in Boston, Massachusetts. A basketry weir at the mouth of the Charles River was found during excavation for a modern subway. The weir had been used to trap the fish as the water flowed out of the river during the retreating tide. The weir, perfectly preserved in the river mud, was attributed to Archaic Indians who are believed to have used the Boston site as one of their summer camps. For thousands of years what is now Boston existed as a base camp or trading village.

2500 B.C.
In California Archaic Indians lived in permanent villages, buried their dead in mounds, and made shell ornaments and beads which were widely used in trade. They also made bowls, pipes, and baskets. They were the ancestors of the major indigenous cultures of the

Central Valley—the Yokuts, Miwok, Maidu, Wintun, and Ohlone.

Early pottery in Florida and Georgia. Plant fibers were used to strengthen the form. Their large pots and storage jars represented a major technical advance in the preparation and storage of food and contributed to the end of the Archaic tradition in which people moved continually among different sites. The ability to store food meant that people could grow surplus crops and establish permanent settlements.

2180 B.C.
End of Akkadian civilization in Mesopotamia. Trade flourished in Persian Gulf, Iran, Syria, and as far as the Indus Valley. Invasions by the Guti hordes from the Zagros brought the Akkadian dynasty to an end.

2060–1950 B.C.
Sumerian renaissance and the Dynasty of Ur. Babylonian mathematics reached its highest level. The Hanging Gardens of Babylon, a terraced tower temple, became one of the Seven Wonders of the ancient world.

2000 B.C.
The ancestors of the modern-day Inuit moved as far east as Greenland and established settlements. They developed unique hunting techniques and tools to survive in the remarkably harsh climate. Eventually they arrived in subarctic eastern Canada.

2000 B.C.
The first long-term settlements at Poverty Point, Louisiana. Evidence shows that the people who lived here began to save seeds gathered from the floodplain to plant the following spring. These early residents of the lower Mis-

sissippi Valley cultivated four agricultural crops: squash; sunflowers; mash elder, a berry-producing shrub; and chenpodium, a thick-leafed herb. (The last two are no longer cultivated.) They also created small votive objects of clams, falcons, and owls and made cooking pots of steatite brought from Alabama, Tennessee, and Georgia. The requirements of agriculture and storage of surplus crops transformed many hunting groups into more sedentary, horticultural societies and 500 years later produced great earthen architecture at Poverty Point. Up until this time evidence suggests that settlements moved every 30 or 40 years, after the soil was exhausted. (There is a museum at Poverty Point, located 55 miles west of Vicksburg, Mississippi, which displays some of the early artifacts found here.)

2000 B.C.

Great Lakes region. Inhabitants of this area mined copper and hammered it into a variety of tools and beads for trade.

2000 B.C.

Corn became a staple crop in Mexico. Olmec trade flourished. Horticulture became more sophisticated. In addition to corn the Mesoamericans (a term used to identify the advanced societies of central and southern Mexico and the Yucatán) developed experimental horticulture with other seeds and roots. They eventually produced beans, legumes, chili peppers, avocados, gourds, squash, cocoa, and, most important, cotton, which would serve as an important trade good. Over centuries of experimentation they would evolve a sophisticated horticulture which included crops unknown in Europe or the Middle

East, such as potatoes (originally developed in Peru), yams, sweet potatoes, chocolate, tapioca, vanilla, peanuts, and various varieties of peppers. After the fifteenth century A.D. these crops would eventually revolutionize European agriculture, and corn would eventually change world agriculture. (Today, corn is half of America's agricultural output.)

Despite the widespread impression that Native peoples lived by hunting—as late as the 1800s Justice John Marshall was saying that "all Indian sustenance comes from the forest"—the indigenous peoples of the Americas shaped their societies around agriculture and highly inventive horticultural techniques, which were often supplemented by fishing and hunting. The laborious processes involved in gathering and germinating roots and seeds, and finding ways to store foods, formed a crucial part of the knowledge and technologies of these early cultures.

1728 B.C.
Hammurabi, king of Babylonia, reunited the kingdom. Due to a shift in the course of the Euphrates River, Babylon became the capital of the empire. Hammurabi's Code, the most famous work of the period, defined criminal laws, lines of inheritance, medical procedures. Babylonian letters flourished; Akkadian was the common language.

1570–1320 B.C.
In Egypt priests under Akhenaten wrote a new religion based on Aten, a sun god, and consolidated a variety of cosmologies, myths, and rituals in a collection of religious documents of the Eighteenth Egyptian Dynasty. The Eighteenth Dynasty was the greatest of all Egyptian dynasties.

1500 B.C.
Greeks victorious at Troy. Led by King Agamemnon, the Greeks of Mycenae, Athens, Tiryns, and Thebes united in a joint war against the city-state of Troy in Asia Minor (Turkey). The Trojans held out for a long time against the Greek siege, but, according to legend, the Greeks won by means of the Trojan horse, made famous by Homer in the *Iliad*. This was the last war of Greek expansion as Greece itself was then invaded by Dorians from the north. (Archaeological dating of the destruction of the sixth level of Troy is 1193 B.C. Homer's Troy is 1101 B.C.)

1500 B.C.
Georgia and Florida Indians' pottery techniques improved to the production of fine fired earthenware ceramics.

1500 B.C.
Poverty Point mounds expanded in Louisiana. The first of the great Mississipian sites. It consists of six D-shaped concentric half circles approximately six feet high, opening to the river. The outermost ring is four-fifths of a mile in diameter. The innermost ring is 2,000 feet in diameter. On the circumference of the outermost ring is a mound 70 feet tall and approximately 700 feet square at its base, which is thought to have been in the shape of a falcon. One theory holds that Poverty Point was constructed by Olmec pioneers or settlers who migrated along the Gulf of Mexico into the Mississippi Valley and built monumental architecture similar to that found in Mexico, with the same design of temple platforms and enclosures forming sacred spaces but using earth instead of stone. They carried millions of baskets of earth to form the mounds, and were able to duplicate the geometric rings to almost exact measurements; modern aerial photography has shown at least five sites in the Mississippi floodplain which duplicate the configuration of Poverty Point's inner ring. Hundreds of smaller sites containing temple mounds and cultural characteristics similar to Poverty Point are located throughout the Mississippi Valley. These sites are generally referred to as the Mississippian culture and were mistakenly thought to be Spanish forts by the eighteenth-century Europeans who first saw them. The first American to write about Poverty Point was Henry Brackenridge of Pennsylvania,

who toured the sites of the mounds and in 1811 wrote a book on Louisiana's remarkable archaeology, *Views of Louisiana*. Unlike other early visitors, he did not mistake the antiquities for "Spanish forts": *"All these vestiges [mounds] invariably occupy the most eligible situations for towns or settlements; and on the Ohio and Mississippi, they are the most numerous and considerable. There is not a rising town or a farm . . . in whose vicinity some of them may not be found. . . . An immense population has once been supported in this country."* Poverty Point had at least 600 dwellings and an estimated population of 4,000 to 6,000.

1200 B.C.
Olmec civilization in Mexico. Centers at Chalcatzingo and La Venta.

750 B.C.
Temple mounds built in Ohio Valley by the Adena Hopewell peoples. These names refer to two peoples who coexisted and are now considered to be the same people. They are named for the owners of the lands where their first artifacts were found. (Adena is an estate near Chillicothe, Ohio, where 1906 archaeologists removed an array of burial artifacts; Hopewell is the name of a farmer who farmed "the old Hopewell place" a few miles away from Adena and where a rich find of grave goods was excavated. Hence the earlier residents became known as Adena Hopewell peoples.) Thousands of sites in the Ohio Valley eventually disproved the distinction between two peoples, although frequent references describe the earlier

753 B.C.
Traditional date for the founding of Rome. (The Romans called this year 1 a.u.c., *ab urbe condita*.)

Indians as Adena, later Indians as the Hopewell. The Adena Hopewell were a sophisticated culture with elaborately constructed ceremonial centers and an extraordinary trade network. Grave artifacts included elegantly finished sculpture and ceramic vessels, pipes with lively effigies of beavers and birds, jewelry of copper, silver, beadwork, mica, lead, and obsidian. The pipes were for smoking tobacco. Materials showed a vast trading network, with copper from Michigan, sharks' teeth from Florida, silver from Canada, lead from Wisconsin or Missouri, and mica from the Carolinas. There were thousands of Adena Hopewell sites spread throughout the rivers of Ohio and along the Missouri and its tributaries, with a few sites as far away as Kansas and the Florida Gulf Coast. They were farmers. They cleared forests, prepared fields, planted, cultivated, harvested, and stored at least seven different species of high-yield, high-nutrition seed crops. Their hilltop sites were different in purpose than the river sites and possibly were observatories. Oriented to the river, they spread among the river networks of the Mississippi drainage.

700 B.C.
Homer, a Greek poet/singer wrote down his best songs/poems about the heroes of the Trojan war. The oral narrative art form transformed into the written form of literature with the *Iliad* and the *Odyssey*. Greeks had learned the alphabet from the Phoenicians.

460 B.C.
Pericles in Athens. Golden Age of Greece. Greek philosophers flourish.

300 B.C.
Hohokam Indians began farming in the Gila and Salt Valleys of what is now Arizona. They began planting

beans for the first time and combining corn and beans in the same fields, following a similar horticultural practice found in Mexico. Their early settlements showed small villages with oblong rectangular pit houses, smooth pottery, and canal irrigation similar to Mesoamerican agriculture.

200 B.C.

Roman Empire at its height. Romans annex northern Greece, extending the empire around the Mediterranean. Cicero, a Roman poet, translated Plato and many of the Greek philosophers into Latin so that Greek ideas survived after the fall of Greece.

100 B.C.– CA. A.D. 100

The Dead Sea Scrolls stored in caves near the Dead Sea. Ancient scrolls written in Aramaic and Hebrew described the beliefs and history of different Jewish sects at this period.

100 B.C.

The Serpent Mound built by the Adena Hopewell Indians near the town of Locust Grove, Ohio. It is a huge raised earth effigy in the shape of an undulating serpent 1,254 feet long (four football fields in length) and in places 20 feet high, holding a globe or a comet in its mouth. The meaning and symbolism of the Serpent Mound are still unknown. The Serpent Mound was saved from urban renewal in the 1890s by Frederick Putnam of the Peabody Museum in Cambridge, who raised the money to save it. Thousands of other mounds, however, were destroyed.

In Kansas City the Adena Hopewell began to build a huge settlement and cultivated large fields of maize. Other great early Mississippian sites are at Etowah, Georgia; Spiro, Oklahoma; and Moundville, Alabama.

46 B.C.

Julius Caesar introduced the Julian calendar which provided for a year of 365 days, plus every fourth (leap) year, an additional day.

II

By definition a chronology is a description of linear time, a chain of discrete events. However, it must also include thematic developments such as plagues, migrations, religion, which take place over centuries. "Mesoamerica" is the term applied to Mexico and the Precolumbian cultures that radiated out from Mexico. The American Southwest—Texas, New Mexico, Arizona, Southern California—was part of Mesoamerica. In addition, recent scholarly research holds that the peoples of the Mississipian cultures who settled on the Mississippi and throughout the tributary rivers of the Mississippi, in the states now called Louisiana, Mississippi, Arkansas, Missouri, and Ohio, were also directly connected with the great sites of early Mexico, either through migration or direct colonization.

While barbarian hordes were swarming though Europe, causing what we call the European Dark Ages, the city of Teotihuacán rose to prominence in Mexico. With a population of 125,000 and the largest pyramids of the Americas, it became the center of a great civilization. By the year 300, when Christianity became the official religion of the Roman Empire and priests began to fill the posts of proconsuls in the greater Roman Empire, peoples called the Hohokam, the Anasazi, and Mogollon had settled thousands of sites in the U.S. Southwest. (Archaeologists estimate well over 50,000 Anasazi sites in northern Arizona and New Mexico, and southern Colorado and Utah.) By the year 500 they had left identifiable remains of their presence in architecture, canals, and pottery.

In the year 600 Cahokia, the great center of the Mississippian culture, was founded at the confluence of the Mississippi and Missouri Rivers, what is today Illinois. By the year 800 the Mississippi Valley showed widespread corn cultivation, with a variety of improved maize that previously had been grown only in Mexico. The Cahokia site expanded to encompass five square miles. Its central mound, which was also the home of its ruler, the Great Sun, had the largest pyramid base outside of Egypt. With a population that grew to 40,000 between the years 700 and 900, it was the largest urban center in what is now the United States, a record it held until 1800 when Philadelphia surpassed it.

In the area of present-day Phoenix, Arizona, in A.D. 800, at the same time Pope Leo was transforming a barbarian Frankish king into the Christian Emperor Charlemagne, leader of the so-called Holy Roman Empire, the Hohokam people were farming thousands of acres of desert and irrigating it with an intricate system of deep canals, laterals, and ditches. They were excellent engineers. One of their canals was over ten miles long with a perfectly engineered gradient, so that water flow flushed out silt and gravity did the work of distributing water. They used I-beam construction to build multiroom dwellings whose ruins can be seen in Phoenix today. (A map of the Hohokam canals along with the present-day canal system is on view in the main lobby of the Salt River Project in downtown Phoenix.)

From the approximate years 1000 to 1300 Anasazi communities flourished in New Mexico, southern Colorado, and northern Arizona. At Chaco Canyon, New Mexico, the Anasazi residents built Pueblo Bonito, considered the highest expression of Native American architecture in North America. A multistory building of 650 rooms constructed in a large D-shaped footprint, it was constructed out of sandstone blocks covered with a coat of mud plaster. Linked to it were two great circular kivas 63 feet in diameter, and 11 other buildings housing 2,000 rooms. Over 70 outlying settlement sites were connected by a complex road system. The Bureau of Land Management has surveyed the Chaco road system by aerial photography and identified over 500 miles of Anasazi roads, absolutely straight, 30 feet wide, excavated down to bedrock. It is believed that the roads were used to bring agricultural produce from the outlying areas. When the great pueblos were excavated, archaeologists found turquoise beads, small copper bells, and macaw feathers among the artifacts.

The population of North American Indians was believed to have reached its height between A.D. 1200 and 1300. Some estimates go as high as 110 million people in the Western Hemisphere at this time. In the 1300s the Mississippian sites began contracting and the large sites in the Southwest were abandoned. One theory for the decline is that an epidemic disease at this time spread throughout North America.

In Europe during the same period disease was the most profound influence of daily life. It affected every aspect of life—politics, economics, religion, government, culture, science. The bubonic plague broke out in 1347. Before it was over 20 million people in Europe had died. It spread as far as China and although estimates vary, it is also believed that one-third of the population of the Middle East and Asia died. But disease was not the only factor. The Spaniards who arrived in the Caribbean and in Mexico in the next century brought with them the medieval mind of Europe and a sense of economic purpose shaped by the gold and slave trades of Africa.

CA. 1 TO 1400 — MESOAMERICA AND THE GREATER SOUTHWEST

WORLD HISTORY

CA. *ANNO DOMINI* 1
Jesus Christ born in Judea, an outer province of the Roman Empire. (Probable date of birth 4 B.C.) His followers become known as Christians.

CA. 1
World population estimated at 300 million.

NATIVE AMERICAN HISTORY

CA. 1 (2,000 YEARS AGO)
City of Teotihuacán rose to prominence in the Mexico basin. Founded in the previous century, it was the first great civilization in central Mexico and was located in a great urban center. (See "Teotihuacán, City of the Gods" on page 34.) The name "Teotihaucán" is believed to mean "The Place of Those Who Have the Road of the Gods." Its great monuments were built in the first century in pyramid shapes. The Temple of the Sun and Temple of the Moon were built along a central axis called Avenue of the Dead. By the end of the first century its population was believed to be around 50,000 expanded by continuous migration of inhabitants from outlying villages into the city.

The pyramids of Teotihaucán were among the biggest in America. Its leaders had a sophisticated astronomical observatory and had developed a calendar that was more accurate than the one later adopted by Pope Gregory. Its enormous population was housed in one-story adobe houses built by the government. Teotihaucán ruled an area in the Valley of Mexico roughly the size of Sicily. Unlike the Romans, its leaders did not have the political systems or administrative bureaucracy to physically rule foreign lands. They did, however, exact tribute, and dominated the terms of trade. They invaded Guatemala and some Mayan cities including Tikal which eventually adopted their cult of war and human sacrifice. The influence of Teotihuacán was based on religion and trade which extended as far south as Honduras and as far north as the Mississippi Valley. They traded tools made with obsidian (a volcanic glass of great hardness which can be fashioned into blades or tools with a sharp edge); knives; cloth woven from cotton; ceramics including a tradeware called Thin Orange which was of elegant design and a bright terra cotta color; and other ritual paraphernalia related to religious ceremonies.

CA. 1
The Hohokam moved into sites along the Salt River in Arizona and began an irrigation farming system that is the basis of modern-day Phoenix.

30
Death of Jesus Christ. In the Roman province of Judea, the local Roman ruler, Pontius Pilate, ordered the leader of a small Jewish sect put to death for sedition. Jesus Christ's followers were known as Christians. For the next 30 years the Roman government treated Christianity as a legal religion, similar to other tolerated sects such as the Essenes, the Zealots, and the Pharisees, who had similar beliefs in apocalyptic traditions, baptism, and communion.

64
Rebellion in Rome. Emperor Nero begins persecution of Christians. Nero blamed the burning of Rome on the Christians because of their belief

in the second coming of Christ and worldwide conflagration. Nero's decree added to the Christian sect's visibility, and it continued to attract followers throughout the Roman Empire, despite persecution.

70

Revolt of the Jews in Judea against Rome. Jerusalem destroyed. The Essenes and the Zealots, two Jewish sects, took up arms against Rome and were annihilated.

100

By the end of the first century every major city in the Roman Empire had a Christian church headed by a male priest or bishop who was the only person authorized to interpret the teachings of Christ. Early Christian documents, such as those found among the Gnostic Gospels and the Dead Sea Scrolls, show that up until that time both men and women had been Christian spiritual leaders and there was no spiritual hierarchy.

100

People from Mesoamerica migrated north along several different routes and took up permanent residence in the Four Corners area of the Colorado Plateau (Utah, Colorado, Arizona, and New Mexico), the mountains of New Mexico, and central Arizona. They would become known as three distinct peoples, the Hohokam, the Mogollon, and the Anasazi. In the present-day Four Corners area over 50,000 sites have been identified as Anasazi sites, with two great centers at Chaco Canyon and Mesa Verde. The Anasazi who settled in the drainage area of the Little Colorado and San Juan River became known as Western Anasazi; those who settled on the Rio Grande and Chaco River were known as Eastern Anasazi. The mountain area of New Mexico was settled by the Mogollon, who became famous for their pottery (particularly the white on black Mimbres pottery). To the southwest along the Gila and Salt Rivers were the Hohokam, who would become known for their great irrigation canals and multistory pueblo buildings.

Eight stone images, Mimbres culture ca. 1000. The Mimbres peoples were a branch of the Mogollon peoples and lived between A.D. 200 and 1150 in an area of approximately 13,000 square miles in the southern regions of New Mexico. Their painted pottery is considered among the finest in the world. The lively figures and animated geometry of these stone images resemble the designs painted on Mimbres pots including the round heads, the thin arms in angular postures and the widely spaced facial features.

180

Death of Marcus Aurelius and beginning of the collapse of Roman economic and political systems. Anarchy among Roman soldiers. With the disintegration of the Empire, the Christian Church attracted greater numbers of followers and greater persecution. In Gaul Christians were imprisoned, beaten, pilloried, raped, stoned, impaled, thrown to wild beasts, torn by dogs, or drowned in the Rhône by Roman soldiers who were followers of Mithras, a sect of Zoroastrianism.

285
The Roman Empire divided in two with two capitals, East and West, with two Emperors. Diocletian in the east at Nicomedia; and Maximian in the west at Milan.

292
Emergence of the classic Maya civilization in the Yucatán lowlands of southern Mexico and Guatemala. Mayan culture is traditionally dated from 292, a "long count" date found in Tikal and based on the cyclical calendar of Mayan timekeeping.

312
Emperor Constantine (the Eastern emperor) became the first Christian emperor. Before Constantine went into battle with the Western emperor (Maxintius), he saw a flaming cross in the sky. He attributed his subsequent victory to the intervention of Christ; and accepted Christianity.

313
Edict of Milan restored to all Christians throughout the Roman Empire freedom of worship and restoration of their confiscated properties. Constantine proclaimed equal rights for all religions.

325
Council of Nicea. Christianity became the official religion of the Roman Empire. The Council was the first ecumenical (worldwide) council of the Church. Its purpose was to settle a point of theology. Priests in Constantinople became part of Constantine's court, wore elaborate costumes, and moved into positions formerly occupied by proconsuls of the Empire. Outlying Roman lands became known as dioceses of the Church; priests became bishops;

the bishop in Rome became known as *papa* or *pope*, then eventually pope. The Church in the East became known as the Orthodox Church; in the West, the Catholic Church. The concept of the territorial sovereignty of the Vatican had its roots in the supposed "Donation of Constantine," never verified, which was used to justify taking large tracts of land in Rome for the western Church.

337

Constantine was baptized a Catholic on his deathbed. His three sons succeeded him and began fighting with each other, and divided the Empire.

350

The Hohokam settled in several sites along the Gila and Salt River drainage in central Arizona. What is now Snaketown in Pinal County, Arizona, was a major early Hohokam site. They occupied it continuously until after 1100. The site included a well-constructed and lengthy canal system, clay figurines, stone bowls with sculptured surfaces, turquoise mosaics (similar to mosaics found at Teotihuacán), and a well-developed shell industry consisting of engraved and traded shells from both the Gulf and Pacific Coasts. This industry suggests a trade route from the Gulf of California through northern Mexico to the Gila-Salt drainage. The early Hohokam formed a northern frontier of Mesoamerican trade and reflected many of the same designs in pottery, shells, ceramics, and crafts. Although scholars still debate the early connections of the Hohokam with Mesoamerica, the *Smithsonian Handbook* suggests that *"if the present international border between Mexico and the United States were 150 miles further north, the ... Mesoameri-*

NATIVE AMERICAN HISTORY / 407

*can character of the Hohokam would
probably have been more readily recognized some time ago. The task now is not
to document more evidence of contact but
rather to understand the nature of these
relationships."*

382
Barbarian hordes from the Black Sea
region and Mongols from the Asian
steppes invaded the Roman Empire
from the Mediterranean to as far as
Britain. Emperor Theodosius I later
dealt with the Visigoths by agreeing to
"settle" them in the Balkans in exchange for a battalion of Visigoth soldiers for his army. The Roman army was
no longer made up of "soldier citizens,"
but of barbarian mercenaries. The Roman frontiers were largely defended by
barbarians fighting other barbarians.
The Roman legions began to evacuate
Britain after invasion by Picts and Scots.

400
The early Anasazi culture emerged in
northern Arizona and the Four Corners
area. The Anasazi sites all had similar
characteristics. They were centralized
sites surrounded by large cultivated fields
and one-story houses of multiroom dwellings. They had highly specialized agricultural systems that included growing
two crops a year of maize, beans, and
cotton. They used irrigation canals and
knew how to tap groundwater by digging
wells.

406
Gaul (France) overrun by successive
waves of Vandals, Alans, Suevi, and
Burgundians.

407
Britain overrun by successive invasions
of Jutes, Angles, and Saxons.

TEOTIHUACÁN, CITY OF THE GODS

Teotihuacán was the first great civilization to appear in central Mexico. It began sometime in the first century B.C. when the big population centers in the Mexico basin, Cuicuilco and Tlapacoya, were having internal difficulties. The rulers in Teotihuacán saw an opportunity to aggrandize at the expense of their neighbors. They did so through a combination of war and religion and forced thousands of residents of the Valley of Mexico out of their villages into the city, which had been constructed on a massive scale on a grid system. Then they planned enormous temples and monuments to institutionalize their rule. The largest monuments were designed and built in the first century and were based on Teotihuacán's location as a sacred site, a center of the cosmos.

By the end of the first century Teotihuacán's population was around 50,000. In succeeding centuries it continued to expand until, by A.D. 600, it was the sixth-largest city in the world, with a population well over 125,000. (Constantinople was the largest, with an estimated population of 500,000. Two Chinese cities, Changan and Lyang, were second and third; the Persian capital of Ctesiphon [near Baghdad] was fourth; Alexandria, Egypt, was fifth, with an estimated population of 200,000.) This enormous urban population was housed in one-story stone and adobe apartments, now believed to have been built by the central governing authority because of their uniformity of design and construction. Eventually Teotihuacán's rulers realized they had overcentralized the city and executed a planned repopulation of the Mexico Valley in order to better manage agricultural production and exploitation of natural resources.

Essential to the city's growth was the way its rulers exploited the attraction of its holy places and the prestige of its religion to establish the city as a crossroads of the cosmos. One interpretation of the meaning of the word Teotihuacán is "the place of those who have the road of the gods." The names Temple of the Sun, Avenue of the Dead, and Temple of the Moon were given to the sites by the Aztecs who settled there centuries later. (Temple of the Plumed Serpent is a name bestowed by archaeologists.) Although little is known about their belief systems—they did not have an alphabet and therefore left no texts or the equivalent of Egyptian papyrus scrolls— scholars believe that it was a religion based on sacred geography. Teotihuacán was the center of the universe, a supremely sacred site, a place where the gods emerged from the underworld, the sipapu.

Beneath the Temple of the Sun is a long cave, believed to have marked a place of emergence, the spot where humankind came into being and where the present cycle of time was born. This cave and subsequently the temple built over it were also the home of a powerful deity, the principal goddess of Teotihuacán, who was associated with corn and with agricultural plenty.

Until the 1960s scholars believed that the city was a theocracy, largely peaceful and agrarian. But later discoveries of the bones of hundreds of human sacrifices and murals showing the extraction of hearts from living victims altered that interpretation. The instruments used to cut out the hearts of their sacrifices (it was believed that a human being only rented the body in which the spirit was housed) were ritual knives made of obsidian, a volcanic glass of great hardness capable of holding an extremely sharp edge. These knives were a principal trade item along with cloth woven from cotton grown in the fertile valley; ceramics including a prized tradeware of elegant design and a bright terra cotta color known as Thin Orange; and other ritual paraphernalia associated with religious ceremonies.

The geographical area dominated by Teotihuacán in the basin of Mexico was probably not more than 10,000 square miles, about the size of Sicily. Its influence was economic, religious, and cultural, based on trade that extended as far south as Honduras and as far north as the Mississippi Valley. Unlike Rome, its leaders did not have the political systems or the administrative bureaucracy to physically rule foreign lands. They did, however, exact tribute and dominate the terms of trade. (After the Teotihuacáns invaded Guatemala, Mayan cities such as Tikal adopted Teotihuacán's cult of war and human sacrifice.)

It should be emphasized that there is still a great deal that is not known about Teotihuacán. As Berrin and Pasztory point out, the list of what is known is short:

1. Teotihuacán lasted over 700 years.
2. For most of that time everyone in the Valley of Mexico lived in one city organized on a grid plan—a pattern which did not exist before or after Teotihuacán in Mexico.
3. Its pyramids were among the biggest in America and were built in the beginning of the city's history, the first century.
4. Teotihuacán was laid out according to a newly devised astronomical orientation.
5. Permanent multifamily apartment compounds were built to house the population for the last 500 years of the city. The walls of many were painted with murals.
6. Its principal deity was a goddess.
7. The rulers did not glorify themselves in art.
8. Sometime around A.D. 750–800 it came to a cataclysmic end.

The destruction of Teotihuacán was deliberate, systematic, and ritual. The city was sacked, possibly by the Chichimecs, invaders from the north. Palaces were burned. Temples were reduced to rubble. Its destruction was so complete, it seemed that the intent of its destroyers was for the city not to arise again. It was never rebuilt, but a small population lived on in the ruins for another century. The Aztecs who occupied it centuries later viewed the earlier civilization with great respect. The Aztec awe regarding Teotihuacán was much like that of the medieval Europeans towards ancient Rome and Greece. Prior to Teotihuacán's ultimate destruction, its ruling elite fled north to the provincial city of Tula, where its leaders and artisans re-created the wonders of Teotihuacán. Tula became known as the capital of the Toltecs and flourished between A.D. 900 and 1100, repeating much of the culture and theocracy of the earlier city. It is believed that it was the Toltec inhabitants of Tula who traveled to outlying colonies and then by sea or land along the Gulf Coast into the Mississippi Valley.

410

Alaric the Visigoth sacked Rome. His brother went on to conquer Spain.

439

The Vandals took Carthage, a great Roman city in Tunisia.

452

Attila the Hun invaded Italy and reached the gates of Rome.

476

The official date of the end of the Roman Empire.

500

The Hohokam introduced ball courts, large oval courts similar to those found in Mesoamerica, for the playing of a game with a rubber ball.

520

First Benedictine monastery founded by St. Benedict in Monte Cassino, Italy, as a reaction to the worldly power of the popes and the lack of emphasis on spiritual life within the institutionalized Church.

590

Pope Gregory the Great the most influential person in Europe. He sent missionaries to convert the barbarians in England, France, and Germany and to convert the barbarian rulers of Europe into Christians under the control of Rome. He was largely successful. The Church of Rome replaced the Roman Empire as the cohesive force in western Europe. Many of the new barbarian kings recognized the primacy of Rome while evolving an elaborate theory of kingship and monarchy.

600

First settlers believed to have settled on the Red River site of Spiro, Oklahoma. The Red River runs from Louisiana into Arkansas and forms the border between the states of Oklahoma and Texas. Early Mississippians began a large center at Spiro which steadily expanded. They built magnificent truncated pyramids of earth around ceremonial plazas. Their burial mounds reveal sculpture, textiles, and ornaments. Their descendants, known as the Caddo Indians, were still there in 1542 when De Soto and his successor, Luis de Moscoso, came among them. Among the still-existing ruins are a two-mile-long, 200-foot-high ridge; a central ceremonial structure almost 600 feet long and 30 feet high (called Battle Place by recent archaeologists) with two raised platforms; as well as eight peripheral mounds.

603

First recorded mention of London as a city.

700-750

Teotihaucán, Mexico at its zenith and the sixth largest city in the world. By the eighth century Teotihuacán had a population of 200,000 and had become so overpopulated and its agricultural base so limited that its rulers mandated a forced emigration back into the countryside in the Valley of Mexico in order to increase agricultural production and exploit natural resources. A mapping project of the ruins carried out in the 1960s showed that Teotihuacán comprised 15 square miles of continuous structures organized in an urban grid system. Industrial zones were dedicated to the manufacture of ceramics and obsidian products. (See "Teotihuacán, City of the Gods" on page 34.)

Petroglyphs, Grand Canyon. These petroglyphs or drawings in stone are carved in the cliffs of the Grand Canyon. They represent shamans, hunters (upper right), historical events, star patterns, geographical directions, migration routes, and maps. The people called the Anasazi left thousands of petroglyphs throughout the Southwest.

750

Teotihuacán invaded and reduced to rubble. Sometime in the middle of the century Teotihuacán was invaded and came to a sudden and cataclysmic end. Its palaces were burned, its temples reduced to rubble. Its rulers fled to a small outlying provincial city on the Rio Tula where they began to re-create the temples and palaces and wonders of Teotihaucán. At about the same time the city of Cahokia in Illinois expanded along with other centers of the "Temple Mound builders" in the Mississippi Valley, enlarged by talented refugees from Teotihuacán.

Petroglyph, Canyon de Chelly. This road-runner was carved in stone over a thousand years ago. These rock drawings marked sites that were part of the histories of the ancestral clans of the present-day Hopi, Zuni, and Pueblo peoples. Elders and tribal priests from these tribes still visit these sites in pilgrimage to sites of former clan migrations.

750

Hohokam expanded their culture from central Arizona up the Verde and Agua Fria Rivers as far north as Flagstaff. These rivers served as major Hohokam migration routes. Speculation is that Hohokam expansion was a result of successful irrigation and agricultural techniques that produced large food surpluses enabling the population to increase. Hohokam expansion and contraction continued to 1300, when their centers declined. They are believed to be the ancestors of the present-day Pima and Papago.

750

Expansion of geometric patterns of mounds at Moundville, Alabama. Inhabitants laid out larger areas for agricultural development, principally of maize, and developed many truncated pyramids including a raised *sacra via* (sacred way) almost a mile long and 70 feet wide.

800

Tula became the new capital of the Toltec civilization in Mexico. Tula, located on the Rio Rosas and Rio Tula, 45 miles north of present-day Mexico City, became the new center of the Mesoamerican civilization and formed the cultural and historical bridge between the ancient Teotihuacán and the modern Aztecs who still ruled in Mexico at the time of Cortés (1519). The Nahuatl word "Toltecatl" was simplified to "Toltec" in English and referred to an inhabitant of Tollan, meaning "place of the reeds" in Nahuatl. "Tula" became the shortened version. Toltec also meant cosmopolitan as opposed to rustic, and skilled, particularly

in crafts. Historian Bernardino de Sahagun tells us that the Toltecs were "like the
inhabitants of Babylon, wise, learned,
experienced." They were supposed to
have been taller than other Indians and
sixteenth-century excavations attest to
this. They planted crops, composed poetry, appreciated the beauty of flowers,
played ball games in an enclosed court,
ate tortillas and other maize foods, en-
joyed beautiful pottery, wove fine cotton garments, and worried about the
future. They also worshiped deities
who required large amounts of human
blood from living victims. They fought
wars with gusto and even practiced
cannibalism.

With a population of 50,000, Tula
became known as the New Teotihuacán and over three centuries after
its downfall was still revered by the
Aztecs.

825–1000
**Athabascan peoples from Alaska mi-
grated into the Pacific Northwest and
Southwest.** Because of cataclysmic
volcanic eruptions in Alaska that caused
significant climate changes there and
in northern Canada, Athabascans began moving south along separate migration routes. One group migrated
along the coastline into what is now
the Washington and Vancouver area
and became the Pacific Coast Athabascan (including the Chasta Costa,
Tutuni, Galice, Hupa, Kato). The other
group followed the inland migration
route into the Great Basin and down
into what is now Arizona and New
Mexico, where they later divided into
two linguistically distinct people, the
Navajo and the Apache (Jicarilla, Mescalero, Chiricahua, Western Apache).

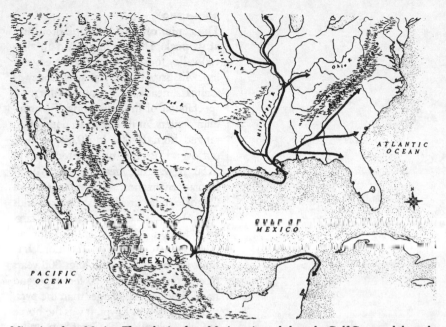

Migrations from Mexico. The colonists from Mexico migrated along the Gulf Coast and through-out the river systems of the Mississippi watershed. They left thousands of temple mounds in the form of truncated pyramids and a system of terraced farmlands similar to those found in Mexico. They built with earth rather than stone and grew maize, beans, and squash as well as a variety of other agricultural products. American scholars have rejected the idea of Mexican colonization on the basis that Mexican civilization was not powerful enough to generate such an expansion.

800
Pope Leo III crowned Charlemagne, king of the barbarian Franks, emperor of the new Holy Roman Empire. The pope wanted the right to choose the emperor and to guide the new Euro-pean political configuration known as the Holy Roman Empire, which would eventually be ruled by the Hapsburg monarchy, descendants of the Visigoths.

Sometimes referred to as the South-western Athabascan or Apachean peoples, they settled areas adjacent to the Anasazi.

800
Mogollon people in Arizona began producing Mimbres pottery, a very high quality ceramic with elegant black on white designs.

900–1250

The center of the Mississipian culture at its peak. The site located in an alluvial valley four miles east of the edge of the Mississippi River, at what today is Cahokia, near East St. Louis, is the most spectacular of the remaining Mississippian centers. At its height its population ranged from 10,000 to 40,000, spread out over 15 square miles. From 750 to 1150 it was the heart of the Mississippian civilization. All that remains of Cahokia today are 19 platform mounds surrounding a central plaza. The largest, "Monks Mound," named for an eighteenth-century French monastery built on top of it, is still, after 800 years of erosion, more than 90 feet high and has an earthen base larger than the pyramids of Gizeh in Egypt. It was the home of Cahokia's ruler, the Great Sun, and is believed to have been built according to strict principles of mathematics and astronomy. Cahokia also replicated a solar observatory of Mesoamerican origin composed of 48 posts set in a circle and coordinated with the equinoxes and solstices in A.D. 1000. (It has since been restored and mistakenly referred to as "Woodhenge.")

Cahokia is believed to have been settled by Toltec colonists as early as 600, and gained prominence as a major religious and commercial center between 700 and 900, when the turmoil at Teotihuacán caused the Great Sun there to send forth those of his people he couldn't protect (according to a story passed in the oral tradition of the Natchez). (See "The Natchez Tradition" on page 43.)

The Mississippian civilization was so named because its culture spread along the Mississippi, Ohio, and Tennessee

THE NATCHEZ TRADITION

About A.D. 800, a strong Mesoamerican influence appeared in the Mississippi Valley and spread throughout the Mississippi River system, including the culture of corn cultivation and the building of truncated pyramids or "platform mounds" in the Mexican style. The Natchez Indian tradition attributes this influence to actual colonization from Mesoamerica.

In 1758 Antoine Simon Le Page du Pratz, a Louisiana Frenchman, published the traditional story of how the Natchez came to the lands the French called Louisiana, told to him by the "Keeper" or priest of the Natchez temple:

Before we came into this land we lived yonder under the sun [pointing with his finger nearly southwest, by which I understood that he meant Mexico]; we lived in a fine country where the earth is always pleasant; there our Suns had their abode, and our nation maintained itself for a long time against the ancients of the country, who conquered some of our villages in the plains but never could force us from the mountains. Our nation extended itself along the great water [the Gulf of Mexico] where this large river [the Mississippi] loses itself; but as our enemies were become very numerous, and very wicked, our Suns sent some of their subjects who lived near this river, to examine whether we could retire into the country through which it flowed. The country on the east side of the river being found extremely pleasant, the Great Sun, upon the return of those who had examined it, ordered all his subjects who lived in the plains, and who still defended themselves against the antients (sic) of the country, to remove into this land, here to build a temple, and to preserve the eternal fire.

The Natchez survived as one of the most powerful of the Mississippi nations until the 1720s when the French put down a rebellion by destroying all the Natchez villages and selling most of the Natchez people, including the Great Sun, into slavery in the Caribbean.

Rivers and other tributaries of the Mississippi. Other great Mississipian sites are located in Arkansas and Oklahoma and include Ocumulgee, Spiro, Etowah, and Moundville. Over its 400-year history Cahokia created and maintained a great trading network which extended from Canada to the Gulf of Mexico and included trade goods made of copper, obsidian, mica, crystal, gold, silver, and conch shells. In 1988 the United Nations designated the site as a location of global importance. The

Chaco Canyon. Chaco Canyon with its pueblos of six hundred and fifty rooms and five hundred miles of graded roads is considered the highest expression of Native architecture in the continental United States.

Cahokia Mounds Museum Society commented:

"When Cahokia Mounds was designated a United Nations World Heritage Site, it was formally recognized as an irreplaceable property of international significance. Cahokia Mounds belongs to an elite group of cultural and natural landmarks of special importance in the history of mankind."

919

Roof beams were cut for Pueblo Bonito. Considered the highest expression of Native American architecture, Pueblo Bonito at Chaco Canyon, New Mexico, was constructed in several phases by the Anasazi people. Built out of sandstone blocks overlaid by a coat of mud plaster, Pueblo Bonito at first rose three stories and contained over 100 rooms. For almost a century construction was halted. Then in 1019 a second phase began, which was completed in 1067. The scale and speed of construction implied thousands of laborers. Seven other great pueblos were built in addition to Pueblo Bonito. Roof beams were cut from forests as far as 75 miles away and transported on foot, as the Anasazi did not have the wheel or any domesticated animals. The lower walls were almost three feet thick to support the five-story construction. Pueblo Bonito itself was enlarged to 650 rooms. The front plaza held two great kivas for community religious functions; one kiva was 63 feet in diameter, with murals on the interior walls. Eleven other connecting structures contained over 2,000 rooms. Artifacts found there included turquoise beads, small copper bells, macaw feathers.

987

The god Quetzalcoatl was banished from Tula. Quetzalcoatl was the god of the Toltecs (and later the Aztecs) and was represented as a plumed serpent. Tradition holds that it was at this time that many Toltecs arrived at various centers in the U.S. and at Chichén Itzá in the Yucatán, where worship of the plumed serpent continued.

1066

William of Normandy invaded England and conquered King Harold at the Battle of Hastings. He is named William the Conqueror and crowned king.

1073

Beginning of construction of pueblos at Mesa Verde in southwestern Colorado.

1100-1300

Mesa Verde at its height. The settlement in southern Colorado reached its largest population. The largest of its dwellings, called the Cliff Palace, contained some 220 rooms and 23 kivas and housed as many as 350 people. By 1300 it had been abandoned. Its residents migrated to the Hopi/Zuni areas and to the Rio Grande pueblos to the southeast. Before the invasions of Coronado in 1540 there were over 100 pueblos in the Rio Grande area, believed to be populated by the descendants of Mesa Verde.

1110-1158

Tula was overrun by invaders, probably Chichimec raiders from the north, and its temples and palaces burned to the ground. The Toltec tradition has a chronicle, *La Historia Tolteca* or *Ixtlilochitl*, which tells the story of a band of travelers called the Toltecas, who knew sophisticated architecture, irrigation systems, and agricultural methods, and whose mission it was to travel and spread the knowledge and highly developed religion of the Toltecs. During the years of Tula's decline some Toltecas were sent south into the Yucatán where they influenced the development of the Maya and turned Uxmal and Chichén Itzá into cities very similar to Tula in architecture and design; others went north along the Gulf Coast into what is now Texas and Louisiana and along the Mississippi River and into its tributaries. Some headed through the American Southwest, leaving behind centers with large irrigation systems, sophisticated agriculture, excellent quality pottery, specialized skills such as cotton cultivation and weaving, and a highly intricate religion. These Toltec travelers are believed to have directly shaped and influenced the development of the Hohokam societies in the Gila and Salt River drainage (Arizona); the Anasazi of the San Juan, Little Colorado, Chaco River, and Rio Grande River drainage (New Mexico, Colorado, Utah, Arizona); and the Mogollon of New Mexico.

1119–1180
Chaco Canyon peoples built an elaborate road system. Over 500 miles of road carved into rock in order to link outlying communities to the central site at Pueblo Bonito. Over 70 outlying settlements up to 100 miles away were linked by a road network comprising hundreds of miles. The roads were absolutely straight, excavated down to bedrock, and 30 feet wide. Using aerial photography, the Bureau of Land Management has estimated that over 500

miles of Anasazi roads were connected to the Chaco Canyon pueblo. Each of the settlements (called outliers) was organized on the same preplanned design as Pueblo Bonito—a great kiva, a multistory central house, and outlying agricultural fields.

1125

Hohokam at its height. The present-day site of Phoenix, Arizona, was settled as early as 300 B.C. and expanded greatly around A.D. 800. The site was located in the heart of the Sonora Desert at the confluence of three rivers—the Salt, Verde, and Gila—and with over 300 days of sun per year produced a rich agricultural yield. The Hohokam built hundreds of miles of canals to irrigate their fields of maize, beans, squash, and cotton. Skilled farmers and excellent engineers, they constructed an intricate irrigation system of deep canals, laterals, and ditches. One of their canals was over 10 miles long with a perfectly engineered gradient so that water flow flushed out silt, and gravity did the work of distributing water. (Its route is still used today although it has been lined with concrete.) They used I-beam construction to build multi-room pueblo dwellings whose ruins can be seen in Phoenix today. Casa Grande, a late Hohokam settlement to the south of Phoenix, has a massive building four stories high with 11 rooms and walls that in places are five feet thick. Another Hohokam settlement, Snaketown, was an important trading center with Mesoamerica as well as with the Mogollon and the Anasazi.

Three hundred years before Europeans invented the technique of etching, Hohokam etched designs in shells by

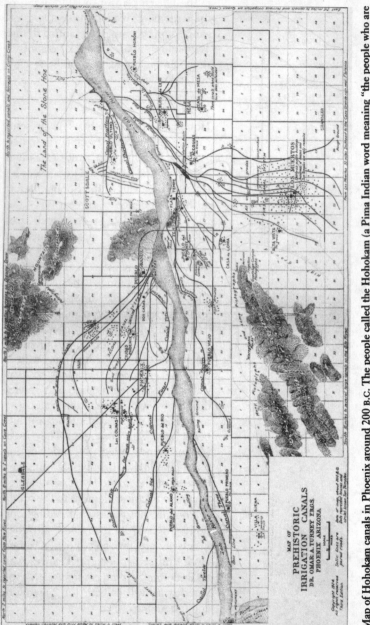

Map of Hohokam canals in Phoenix around 200 B.C. The people called the Hohokam (a Pima Indian word meaning "the people who are gone") came into the valley that is present-day Phoenix sometime around 300 B.C. They were knowledgeable engineers and built hundreds of miles of irrigation canals on the south and north banks of the Salt River. Careful maintenance kept the system in operation for over a thousand years. Its design as well as some of the actual canals formed the basis of the present-day water system for Phoenix. Today the Salt River has so many dams on it that it is a barely visible trickle in downtown Phoenix.

applying an acid solution made from the juice of the giant saguaro cactus. They also had fine pottery, stone bowls, copper bells, mirrors, and abundant ball courts identical in size and construction to those found in Mesoamerican sites.

Sometime around 1350 the canals and the fields were abandoned. Archaeologists speculate that the abandonment was brought on by a drop in the water table, a long-lasting drought, toxic salinization of the soil because of salt buildup from centuries of irrigation, or the collapse of the supporting Toltec culture to the south.

Phoenix was reinvented in 1867 when an out-of-work prospector and his Apache guide dug out the old Hohokam canals and found that the ancient irrigation system still worked. Soon they were leasing farmland in the desert and selling water rights. Today's irrigation system exactly parallels the old Hohokam canal system. (An electrified map comparing the two systems can be seen in the museum of the central offices of the Salt River Project in downtown Phoenix.) The Pima and Papago are the modern-day descendants of the Hohokam. "Hohokam" is a Pima word meaning "the people who are gone."

1132

City of Texcoco founded in the Mexico Valley, one of the city-states that four centuries later would ally itself with the Spanish conquistador, Cortés. **Archaeological surveys of the Mexico Valley during this period show dense settlement: 700 different sites including 10 towns; 19 large villages; 100 small villages; and 555 tiny hamlets.**

1175

The village of Awatovi settled on Antelope Mesa near the present location of Hopi mesas. Now a ruin, it was believed to have been originally settled by Anasazi from another site near Winslow.

1189–1192

The Third Crusade. The third of a series of papal-inspired wars to reclaim the Holy Land from the infidels, this crusade was led by Frederick Barbarossa of Germany, King Richard I of England, and King Philip II of France. It ended with the captivity of Richard and a heavy ransom. Although there were subsequent European military invasions of the Near East, it ended the golden age of crusades.

1200

Construction of Great House at Casa Grande, Arizona, a Hohokam building of unknown purpose. Built with pueblo-style architecture with walls up to five feet thick. This century marks the end of the Hohokam sites.

1204

Constantinople sacked by the Christian Crusaders, the first capture of Constantinople in history and the most violent looting of the city. The Fourth Crusade and the sack of Constantinople discredited the pope, shocked Europe, and ended the Crusades. It also opened Europe to the advance of the Turks and the Ottoman empire.

1300

Native American population in North and Central America reached its peak. The population of Mexico was believed to be over 30 million; of North America between 12 and 15 million; and South America, over 20 million. The Delawares migrated from west to east. The Mississippians withdrew southward. Onondaga culture in what is now upstate New York began to show marked change. Apachean peoples began to break into separate tribes of Navajo and Apache. The decline in population during this century is coincident with the Black Death in Europe and Asia and one theory holds that there may also have been a plague or epidemic in the Western Hemisphere at the same time.

1325

The traditional date for the founding of the Aztec city, Tenochtitlán, in the Valley of Mexico at the "place of the cactus in the rock." The Aztecs were originally the Mexicas, a *"rude and landless"* tribe of mercenaries who came down from the north into the Mexico basin. They worked as mercenary soldiers for the competing city-states around Lake Texcoco and called themselves Aztecs for Aztlan, their legendary homeland in the north. Their god of war, Huitzilopochtli, told them that when they saw an eagle standing on a cactus growing out of a rock, their journey would end. There they should stop and build their city, and name it Tenochtitlán, the "place of the cactus in the rock." Their story says that their ancestors wandered for years without finding such a sign or a site, but in 1325 in the swamps and marshy islands of Lake Texcoco, a site so unattractive that no one else wanted it, they saw a cactus growing out of a rock with an eagle standing nearby. There they began to build a city. They filled in the swamps; they dug canals to irrigate fields; they constructed an aqueduct to bring fresh water from a mainland spring four miles away. Throughout the islands they dug canals to serve as the city's principal arteries of transportation and commerce. Tenochtitlán took shape quickly and

1332

The height of the Mandingo Empire in West Africa. A center of gold trade, it was the source of the precious metal that made its way up through the Sahara into Arab trade routes and then to Europe. The Arab traveler Ibn Ba Tuta crossed the Sahara and later wrote a description of his visit to the Mandingo Empire.

1347

First outbreak of bubonic plague in Europe. Over 20 million Europeans died. One-third of the world's population is believed to have died. The bubonic plague was spread by rats and fleas that lived on rats. Historians believe it first occurred somewhere in central Asia and spread along the caravan routes. Medicine was one aspect of medieval life still unshaped by Christian doctrine and described (because of Arab influences) largely in terms of astrology. The cause of the plague was attributed variously to poisoned air, thick sulfurous mists, stagnant lakes, and a malign conjunction of the planets. In 1348, when Philip VI asked the medical faculty of the University of Paris for a report on its origins, the official cause was deemed to be "a triple conjunction of Saturn, Jupiter, and Mars in the 40th degree of Aquarius which occurred on March 20, 1345." This explanation was copied by scribes, translated from Latin, and accepted everywhere.

1378

The Great Church Schism. Two popes were elected: one in Rome; one in Avignon, France. It lasted for the next 39 years, until 1417.

soon it was in competition with neighboring city-states for land and resources and trade.

1347

Tlatelolco, a companion city to Tenochtitlán, founded on Lake Texcoco. It would become the site of the Aztecs' famous trading market.

THE BLACK DEATH

"In October 1347, two months after the fall of Calais, Genoese trading ships put into the harbor of Messina in Sicily with dead and dying men at the oars. The ships had come from the Black Sea port of Caffa (now Feodosiya) in the Crimea, where the Genoese maintained a trading post. The diseased sailors showed strange black swellings about the size of an egg or an apple in the armpits and groin. The swellings oozed blood and pus and were followed by spreading boils and black blotches on the skin from internal bleeding. . . . So lethal was the disease that cases were known of persons going to bed well and dying before they woke, of doctors catching the illness at a bedside and dying before the patient. So rapidly did it spread from one to another that to a French physician, Simon de Covino, it seemed as if one sick person 'could infect the whole world.' "

BARBARA W. TUCHMAN, *A Distant Mirror*

1390

Traditional founding date of the League of Haudenosaunee. The five Iroquois-speaking tribes—Seneca, Oneida, Onondaga, Mohawk, and Cayuga—of Ontario and upper New York State joined together to form a confederacy to keep the peace among themselves and to deal with trade and relations with other tribes. According to legend, the vision of a confederacy belonged to Deganawidah, a Huron boy born in what is now Ontario. Warfare between the tribes was constant because clan members were obliged by honor to seek a death for any death caused by someone outside their clan. The oath of blood revenge applied even if death were accidental. Deganawidah traveled with Hiawatha, an Iroquois warrior and great orator, to all the different tribes to explain the idea of confederacy. When the Onondaga nation (near present-day Syracuse) refused to join, Deganawidah made Onondaga the seat of the new Iroquois confederacy so that they would have to participate.

Women played a powerful political role under the new confederacy. They chose the delegates to the central council from the 49 lineages from the five nations, a lineage which was hereditary and passed on only through the mother's line. Women held their own councils and advised the central council. They had the power to veto war or to modify decisions about relations with other nations. Although the Iroquois confederacy waged war with surrounding nations, they kept the peace among their own nations for almost 300 years until rivalries with the French and English broke it apart. Scholars debate whether the principles of the Iroquois confederacy and its methods of operation influenced the drafters of the Albany Plan of Union and the subsequent U.S. Constitution. (See "Deganawidah, the Peacemaker, and the Iroquois Confederacy" on page 55.)

1394
Birthdate of Prince Henry the Navigator of Portugal. He was a great explorer and patron of cartography, who spurred exploration of Africa and the New World.

1398
Casa Grande, the last Hohokam settlement, destroyed by Apache raiders. By this time the Navajo and Apache had separated into two distinct linguistic groups. The Navajo called themselves Diné, or People of the Earth's Surface (Navajo was a name later given to them by the Spanish). They settled land bounded by four sacred mountains in New Mexico known as "Dinetah." This would be the historic land claimed by the Navajo. The Apache moved into the mountains of Arizona and New Mexico.

DEGANAWIDAH, THE PEACEMAKER, AND THE IROQUOIS CONFEDERACY

This is to be strong of mind, O chiefs: Carry no anger and hold no grudges. Think not forever of yourselves, O chiefs, nor of your own generations. Think of continuing generations of our families, think of our grandchildren and of those yet unborn, whose faces are coming from beneath the ground.

—from the words of the Peacemaker

The traditional date of origin for the Haudenosaunee, later known as the Iroquois confederacy, is 1390. Eight Iroquoian nations claimed the northern part of the northeastern forest, extending from the mouth of the St. Lawrence River to the middle of the Great Lakes. The nations were the Huron, Erie, Mohawk, Seneca, Oneida, Cayuga, Onondaga, and Susquehanna. Later (in the 1700s) the Tuscarora, an Iroquoian speaking group from North Carolina, moved north to escape the English slave trade and became part of the confederacy. The Huron and the Erie were dispersed after a series of wars with the Mohawk in the 1600s; the Susquehanna were allied with the Iroquois, but not a part of the confederacy itself, although the confederacy held authority over Susquehanna (called Susquehannock in Pennsylvania) lands and negotiated land cessions on their behalf with white settlers in New York, Pennsylvania, and Ohio.

As legend has it, the Peacemaker was born into the Huron tribe sometime in the 1300s. At the time of his birth portents of destruction were so powerful that twice his parents tried to kill him, leaving him in an icy river to drown. But he survived and grew up into a strong young man who had great visions expressed in dreams, a magic power called orenda, the force of the Great Spirit that unites all things.

Intertribal warfare was constant among the tribes of the Northeast, and Huron torture of prisoners was legendary. One day as the Peacemaker watched the torture of a Mohawk warrior—forced to run between two lines of Huron warriors who first struck him with clubs, then slashed him with knives, then poured red-hot coals on his head and built a fire at his feet—the Peacemaker thought, What a waste of life! This constant warring and torturing between tribes must stop. He had had a dream in which he saw a great pine tree that grew so tall, its tip pierced the sky and reached into the world of the Great Spirit. Its roots were the eight great tribes of the Iroquois. On the top sat an eagle.

He believed that the dream foretold a stop to warfare. The tribes must join together and establish a peace. But when the Peacemaker tried to explain his plan and vision he stuttered so badly that no one understood him. So, filled with the power of orenda, he took a birchbark canoe and paddled east down many lakes and streams until he entered the country of the Mohawk. There sitting outside a bark lodge deep in the forest was Hiawatha. Hiawatha was an Onondaga and an eloquent orator. He listened patiently while the Peacemaker told him the vision in his dream.

"How do you propose to accomplish the Great Peace?" asked Hiawatha.

"We are all branches of the one tree of Life," answered the Peacemaker. "But we must unite the roots, the five tribes in a league to establish the peace." The Peace he described was not simply an absence of war, but a dynamic interrelationship which would form the foundation of law and justice among tribes. The two men began traveling together from tribe to tribe, Hiawatha, the eloquent orator, whose name meant "he makes rivers," explaining the idea of a confederation of tribes preserving the Great Peace; and Deganawidah, the Peacemaker, whose name meant "two rivers flowing together," developing the organizational details of how the tribes would actually work together in the league he had in mind.

So was formed the League of the Iroquois, the Confederation of Five Nations, also more recently called the Haudenosaunee. The Huron, Deganawidah's original tribe, were defeated in a disastrous war with the Iroquois confederation and became known as the Wyandot. The Erie and the Susquehanna were also defeated and dispersed by war, the Erie taking refuge with the Seneca and the Susquehanna with the Oneida.

By 1570 the Iroquois confederacy had developed into a sophisticated political organization. The central council was formed of 50 sachems, or chiefs, from all five tribes. The sachems were chosen by the women of families possessing hereditary chieftanship rights. The women exercised the right of initiative, referendum, and recall. A sachem served for life, and the one who replaced him took his name. The central council met in Onondaga country whenever it was necessary to settle matters affecting all tribes — trade with other tribes, defense, war against encroaching tribes, boundary issues. Each tribe had one vote, each chief could speak as long as he wanted, each decision had to be unanimous. If the vote was not unanimous, the matter was discussed until all tribes were in agreement. The Onondaga served as "keepers of the fire."

For close to three centuries the League survived, keeping the peace among the tribes who were members. In the 1700s the (misnamed) French and Indian Wars splintered its unity and the War for American Independence finally tore it apart. Although the Peacemaker and Hiawatha survived only in the myths and legends of many tribes (Longfellow took the name for his poem "Hiawatha" from the myths of the Ojibwa/Chippewa) the Haudenosaunee has resurfaced and is undergoing a revival, active not only within its own tribes but in the United Nations and other international organizations concerned with issues of sovereignty and human rights.

Many scholars believe that the framers of the U.S. Constitution were familiar with the League, and that its principles of confederation influenced thinkers such as Benjamin Franklin on the creation of a federal system for the United States.

III

1400s — The Mississippians and Hispaniola

In March of 1493 Christopher Columbus wrote from aboard ship to his patrons and sponsors, the king and queen of Spain:

Most Christian and lofty and powerful sovereigns:

That eternal God who has given Your Highnesses so many victories now gave you the greatest one that to this day He has ever given any prince.

I come from the Indies with the armada Your Highnesses gave me, to which [place] I traveled in thirty-three days after departing from your kingdoms ... I found innumerable people and very many islands, of which I took possession in Your Highnesses' name, by royal crier and with Your Highnesses' royal banner unfurled, and it was not contradicted. . . . I have found many other [islands] . . . [which] like these others are so extremely fertile, that even if I were able to express it, it would not be a marvel were it to be disbelieved.

The breezes [are] most temperate, the trees and fruits and grasses are extremely beautiful and very different from ours; the rivers and harbors are so abundant and of such extreme excellence when compared to those of Christian lands that it is a marvel. All these islands are densely populated with the best people under the sun: they have neither ill-will nor treachery.

The "discovery" of America is a misnomer. The arrival of the Spanish in the lands that came to be known as the Americas was an invasion, not a discovery. And the invasion went quickly. The pattern was established at the beginning. Once he arrived on Hispaniola, Columbus immediately began gathering Arawaks—"the best people under the sun, with neither ill-will nor treachery"—to take back to Spain to sell in the slave markets. He had his brother do a census to determine how many male inhabitants over 14 could provide tribute. (Over a million.) He found the source of gold used in an ornament given to him by one of the local Native Indian chiefs, or *caciques*, and immediately impressed Arawak men to work the mines. If they didn't produce the requisite amount, a hand or a foot was cut off. The brutality of the Spaniards, these sons of Visigoths, was so extreme one of the accompanying priests called it a "fierce and unnatural cruelty."
Estimates hold that Hispaniola, present-day Dominican Republic and Haiti, had

between three and four million inhabitants. Other estimates go as high as seven million. It was organized into five principal areas, with a *cacique*, or chief, for each region. The model for exploitation of other cultures had been formed in the Spanish and Portuguese slave trade along the coast of Africa. The Portuguese were the first to gain access to West Africa (1433) and the African Gold Coast. At first they traded only for gold, but by 1441 they had begun the trade in slaves. The primary slave buyers were in the Islamic states and the primary slave markets were in Spain. From the first, gold and slaves were linked.

Unlike Africans, however, the inhabitants of the Western Hemisphere had no immunities to the diseases that the Europeans brought with them. They began to die by the tens of thousands. Village after village of Arawaks was swept by epidemics of measles, chicken pox, scarlet fever, or smallpox. The epidemics did more than kill people; they shattered political cohesion and disoriented established rituals and cosmologies. Native shamans had no cure for these murderous afflictions; their leaders were powerless in the face of such massive death. By 1520, less than 30 years from the time that Columbus wrote his letter to the Spanish king and queen, three million Arawaks had died. In Puerto Rico, the island Columbus visited on his next voyage (with 17 ships and a thousand colonists and soldiers), 180,000 natives died in three years. Without natives to do the work, the Spanish could not support themselves or realize the profit they expected to extract from their new colonies. They increased their suppression of the survivors, and one chronicler speculated that the natives died in such numbers because they did not want to live in a world controlled by such evil. Within a few decades the Spanish supplemented the declining indigenous peoples with African slaves in chains.

In addition, Spanish violence and cruelty was incomprehensible to the natives: "*[The Spaniards] made bets as to who would slit a man in two, or cut off his head at one blow; or they opened up his bowels. They tore the babies from their mothers' breast by their feet, and dashed their heads against the rocks . . . They spitted the bodies of other babes, together with their mothers and all who were before them, on their swords . . . [They hanged Indians] by thirteen's, in honor and reverence for our Redeemer and the twelve Apostles, they put wood underneath and, with fire, they burned the Indians alive. . . . I saw all the above things . . . All these did my own eyes witness,*" wrote Fray Bartolome de Las Casas, the Spanish priest who came to the New World for land and ended by writing the famous *Historia de las Indias*, a history of the land Columbus mistakenly called India.

The Arawaks revolted. In 1498 Columbus was replaced as governor of the Indies and his titles revoked. He was sent back to Spain in chains to stand trial for the unchecked destruction of the native population and their subsequent revolt. His trial ended in a brief imprisonment, appeal, and exoneration. Several years later he made his fourth and last voyage to the Indies, and ended up shipwrecked off the coast of Jamaica. He died in obscurity in Spain. In 1498 Vasco da Gama sailed around the southern tip of Africa and up the east coast to finally reach India, making it clear in Europe that Columbus had not discovered part of India.

At the same time that attention was focused on the islands of the Caribbean, every river valley in the continental United States was inhabited by Native peoples. Most grew corn and had fairly sophisticated horticultural practices which were supplemented by hunting. The Mississippian cultures, spread out among all the rivers and tributaries of the Mississippi basin, were still strong even though their great centers like Cahokia had passed their height.

1400s — THE MISSISSIPPIANS
AND HISPANIOLA

WORLD HISTORY

1410
First translation of Ptolemy's *Geography* appeared in Toledo and revived the notion that the earth was round. Toledo was the greatest intellectual center of Europe, where Moslem traditions, rather than Christian scholarship prevailed. Arab works on mathematics, astronomy, philosophy, and medicine were kept in the great libraries of Toledo and translated into Latin.

1419
Prince Henry of Portugal sent expeditions west to explore the Madeira

NATIVE AMERICAN HISTORY

1400
The population of the Mississippi River system began to decline. Mississippian sites existed as far north as Wisconsin. The Sioux, for example, were originally a Mississippian people who had inhabited the lower Ohio and Mississippi Valleys. They referred to themselves as *Dah-Kota*, meaning "alliance of friends." Sometime in the 1400s they were dispersed and fragmented by unknown causes, and they moved north to Wisconsin and northern Minnesota.

1400
The Aztec city-state of Tenochtitlán arose as the preeminent city in the central Mexico basin dominating much older and more established cities.

Islands. The sphericity of the earth was widely accepted in scientific circles in Toledo, and it revived the idea of reaching Asia by sailing westward. Prince Henry issued settlement permits for colonists to settle on Madeira. The island was heavily forested. Within 40 years the island had been stripped of its forests and the settlers were growing sugar cane, sending 70,000 pounds of sugar back annually to Portugal.

1431

Joan of Arc burned at the stake in Rouen, France. A mystic and a visionary, she was a heroine of the Hundred Years' War, successfully leading French troops against the English. After Charles VII was crowned, she was turned over to an ecclesiastical court, tried as a heretic, and publicly burned. (In 1920 she was canonized as a saint in the Roman Catholic Church.)

1432–1434

Prince Henry sent another expedition to explore the Azores. After 10 years of effort the Portuguese explorer, Joao Diaz, rounded Cape Bojador, opening West Africa to the gold trade and slave raiding.

1428

Itzcoatl became ruler of the Aztecs and led the city-state of Tenochtitlán to great wealth and military power. With his nephew and royal counselor, Tlacaelel, he built up the island city and a neighboring one called Tlatelolco, constructing great works of temples and roads and great public squares. Ambitious and driven, he built causeways of hewn stone across Lake Texcoco in all four directions, connecting the city-state with other islands and with the mainland. He also put up to 100,000 men under arms, conquering tribes as far south as Guatemala.

1438

The height of Itzcoatl's rule of the Aztecs and the revision of official Aztec history to align the Aztecs with the Toltec tradition. Itzcoatl and his advisors decided that their people needed a new version of history, one that was worthy of their greatness and the scale of their conquests. He ordered all books written by previous rulers to be burned. An informant of Sahagun later wrote of this event: *"They preserved an account of their history, but later it was burned, during the reign of Itzcoatl. The lords of Mexico decreed it, the lords of Mexico declared: 'It is not fitting that our people should know these pictures . . . for these pictures are full of lies.' "*

The new history of Tenochtitlán claimed that the Aztecs were descended from the Toltec nobility of Tula and like the Toltecs the Aztecs were superb artisans, devout worshipers, and skillful tradesmen. They also superimposed one of the gods of the Toltec religion, Quetzalcoatl, onto their own religion and placed the Aztec god, Huitzilopochtli, at the same level as the ancient Toltec god. (According to mythology, at some point before the city of Tula was abandoned, Quetzalcoatl departed eastward, promising that someday he would return from beyond the sea.) The new Aztec god had to be constantly fed precious food—human blood. The source of all life, the sun, would die without human blood. The practice of live sacrifice raised warfare to a mystical plane, whereby the Aztec warriors, "the people of the sun," were required to take live captives for future sacrifice. This ritual aspect of warfare would prove the Aztecs' downfall in war with the Spaniards, who believed in war as annihilation.

The great wealth of Tenochtitlán was largely due to Itzcoatl's conquests and strategic alliances with two other city-states of the Mexico Valley, Texcoco and Tlacopán. The population of the city is believed to have been at least 250,000, with thousands more in outlying settlements. The city-state had beautiful gardens, great palaces, and a vigorous social, religious, economic, and political structure. Itzcoatl's nephew, Tlacaelel, also a skillful leader, was believed to have completely recodified the judicial structure as well as the laws governing the trading class, *pochtecas*, or traveling merchants.

1440
Itzcoatl's death. Tlacaelel remained as royal advisor to the new Aztec king Axayacatl. The city continued to expand and Tlacaelel reorganized the judicial system, the army, and the protocol of the royal court. A large botanical garden was built in the center of the city, a garden so grand that Europeans who later saw it called it a "wonderment." Its ceremonial center boasted more than 25 major pyramids of various heights, surmounted by temples dedicated to a pantheon of deities. There were arsenals for military stores; monasteries for the priests who served in the temples; workshops for goldsmiths and feather workers; schools for the professions. Beautiful gardens of roses and tropical flowers adorned the houses of the elite; royal aviaries housed thousands of rare birds; canals laced the island.

1441
Portugal began the slave trade from West Africa. They took slaves from Africa and sold them in Spain and Lisbon, primarily to Arab buyers.

MISSISSIPPIANS AND THE CULTURE
OF THE GREAT SUNS

In the 1400s the most densely populated regions of North America were the Pacific Northwest coast and the Trans-Mississippi West, which extended from the Great Lakes to the Gulf of Mexico and from the Appalachian chain in the East as far west as Kansas. The Mississippians (an approximate term) were a people oriented to rivers, which provided them with fish, fertile floodplains for their fields, water, a transportation system, and a connection to the underworld of their cosmology. Their ancestry went back thousands of years to Poverty Point, Louisiana, 1500 B.C., and as European documents attest, they were still flourishing well into the 1500s. The people of the Trans-Mississippi region are known in American documents as the Adena people (700 B.C. to A.D. 200), the Hopewell people (A.D. 200 to 700, as in the "old Hopewell farm" where a rich archaeological grave site was excavated, and more recently as the Adena/Hopewell peoples), and after A.D. 700, as the Mississippians. Objects found in grave sites include obsidian from the Black Hills, copper from the Great Lakes, shells from the Atlantic and Gulf Coasts, mica from the Appalachians, silver ornaments and pottery designs from Mexico; these attest to a great trading network. But the foundation of their culture was believed to be religious rather than commercial.

They left behind extraordinary flattop earthwork pyramids which were so carefully arranged in mathematically precise geometric clusters that the ratio of measurements among the mounds, plazas, houses, causeways, and ball courts was duplicated in hundreds of related settlements all along their river systems. From Wisconsin to Louisiana they also built effigy mounds or "geoforms" in the shape of serpents, bears, panthers, and birds. The function of the sculptural earthworks is not certain, but they are believed to represent supernatural beings or the ancestors of clans in the Mississippian social system. (One theory about why the Native peoples in America never domesticated animals is they believed themselves to be part of the chain of creation in which all living beings, from insects to birds to humans, were equal links.)

Architectural historians now believe that the significance of the geometric precision of the mounds lay in the relationships between the buildings and surrounding spaces, which replicated the Mississippians' cosmology. The axis of the site related to sunrise and sunset, to solstices and equinoxes, to the plane of the earth, to fire and water in the world below, and fire and sun in the world above.

Many of the objects found in Mississippian sites show Mesoamerican connections: pottery representations of human sacrifice, stylized skulls, bones, or weeping eyes in sculptures and masks. The religious life of the Mississippians seemed to include sun worship, sacred fires, ceremonial ball games, and the ritual enlargement of their temples upon the death of their ruler, called the Great Sun. He lived in a large house built on top of the central temple and when he died he and his retainers, who accompanied him to the next world, were put in a log bier on the top of the mound and cremated. A new layer of earth was added to the top and sides of the mound, and a new house prepared for the next Great Sun. A sacred fire of logs arranged in a star shape was tended continuously and was symbolic of the sun, the life-giving force. (Some contemporary pueblos, which also have Mesoamerican traditions, still have a sun priest whose job it is to greet the sun every day.)

Only a few eighteenth-century Americans (among them Albert Gallatin, Henry Brackenridge, Thomas Jefferson) were able to invest the ubiquitous mounds with meaning. Gallatin proposed the mound builders had migrated from Mexico, bringing corn and horticultural techniques with them. Botanist William Bartram, who visited Yuchi and Creek Indian villages in the 1700s, made the connection between the ceremonial courtyards, ball fields, and winter council houses found among contemporary Creek, Cherokee, and Chickasaw settlements, and suggested that they might be the constructions of the Mississippian descendants. Of one Yuchi settlement along the Chattahoochee River in Georgia, Bartram wrote that its design and layout were exceptionally well planned and that it was "the largest, most compact and best situated Indian town I ever saw: the habitations are large and neatly built; the walls of the house are constructed of a wooden frame, then lathed and plastered inside and out with a reddish well-tempered clay or mortar, which gives them the appearance of red brick walls, and these houses are neatly covered or roofed with cypress bark or shingles of that tree. The town appeared to be populous and thriving, full of youth and young children . . ."

We know from thousands of sites that the Mississippians lived in the areas that today include Florida, Georgia, North and South Carolina, Alabama, Mississippi, Louisiana, Arkansas, Missouri, Oklahoma, Kansas, Iowa, Illinois, Indiana, Ohio, Wisconsin, and Michigan, and also north of the Great Lakes. Aside from information about grave goods and burial customs derived from archaeological digs, what we know about how the Mississippians lived comes from a few accounts by early Europeans.

Chroniclers from De Soto's 1539 expedition through what is now Florida, Georgia, Alabama, Tennessee, and Oklahoma described the lush and extensive agricultural fields of the Coosa kingdom, spread across Georgia, Alabama, and Tennessee, which took two weeks to cross. They saw hundreds of settlements with temples and houses and fertile gardens laid out in identical geometrical designs. They told of the Great Sun of the Coosas being carried out on a stretcher to meet De Soto, accompanied by a thousand men in great feathered headdresses.

Almost 200 years later, beginning in 1718, Frenchman Antoine Le Page du Pratz spent a total of four years among the Natchez. A trained architect and engineer, Le Page drew a site plan of their "Grand Village" on the bluffs of St. Catherine's Creek in the vicinity of present-day Natchez, Mississippi. The central ceremonial site for nine surrounding villages, it had two temples at the south end of the ceremonial plaza flanking the great temple of the Great Sun, the paramount chief also known as the Tattooed Serpent. When the Tattooed Serpent died in 1725 Le Page drew sketches of the burial ceremony, depicting the ritual strangling of the chief's wives and retainers and his cremation and burial on the top of the temple mound.

Le Page also described the rectangular dwellings of ordinary people, the rigid class structure organized around sun worship, and the carefully laid-out agricultural fields in the floodplains in which individual families tended gardens of corn, beans, and pumpkins, and also worked larger communal gardens. The religious classes lived separately in large residences and climbed the flattop earth temple mounds by stairways cut into the earth with log-reinforced steps. The war chief and head priest were selected from the brothers of the Great Sun. A temple guardian, or "keeper of the temple" resided at the sun temple, tending a perpetual fire of hickory logs. Carved and painted wooden bird *effigies decorated the roof. Within two years of Le Page's final visit, the Natchez people were conquered in battles with the French, who then sold most of them, including the Great Sun, into slavery in the Caribbean. Some survivors went to live with the Cherokee and took on mystical stature as the last representatives of the Southeast's Mississippian heritage.*

Sometime in the 1400s there was a great reduction in population among the Mississippians, probably caused by disease, crop failure, and/or political strife.

1450
Pope Nicholas V authorized the Portuguese to *"attack, subject, and reduce to perpetual slavery the Saracens, pagans, and other enemies of Christ southward from Cape Bajador . . . including all the coast of Guinea."*

1453
The end of the Hundred Years' War between England and France. France succeeded in driving the English off the continent and capturing all English territory. In England modern English developed from Middle English. In France the country was in ruins, the nobility decimated, but the monarchy strengthened.

1456
In Germany Gutenberg, who introduced movable type into Europe, produced the first printed Bible.

1458
Death of Axayacatl. Assumption of Moctezuma I as ruler.

1469
Death of Moctezuma I.

1474
Queen Isabella succeeded to the throne of Castile in Spain. Five years later (1479) her husband Ferdinand succeeded to the thrones of Aragon,

Catalonia, and Valencia. Ferdinand and Isabella then represented the most powerful royal house in Europe. By royal decree they deprived many of their landed aristocracy and rival barons of many of their rights, possessions, and lands.

1478

Ferdinand and Isabella instituted the Spanish Inquisition, a quasi-religious and civil court, in coordination with the pope and the Spanish Catholic Church. Under the joint direction of Church and State, it persecuted all religious and ethnic minorities, particularly Jews and Moors, and confiscated their properties. The Crown and the Church divided their lands between them.

1481

Death of Tlacaelel. He had remained as chief advisor to the Aztec kings since 1438 when his uncle Itzacoatl brought him to power. One of the great "what if's" of history is what would have happened if a king as brilliant and visionary as Tlacaelel had held power when Cortés arrived in Mexico. After Tlacaelel's death, Aztec rulers continued the policy of constant warfare against all the other city-states around the lake, but without his parallel strategy of building alliances. The Aztec generals maintained military readiness with up to 100,000 men under arms and, as the most powerful and dominant city-state, saw little need for allies. Some of the other city-states, such as Tlexcala, engaged in an almost perpetual state of war with Tenochtitlán over the capturing of its citizens as human sacrifices. Forty years later they would become Cortés's indispensable allies and spies.

1483

Christopher Columbus, an Italian sailor, traveled to the court of the king of Portugal to request financing for an expedition to the west to reach India. His request was turned down.

1486

The *Malleus Maleficarum* published in Germany by two Catholic priests. It described the *"step-by-step instruction on the arrest, torture, conviction and execution of witches."* An inquisition for northern Europe, which unlike Spain had few Jews or Moors, it provided a religious pretext by which Church and State could take land from specific groups. The *Malleus* went through 28 editions between 1486 and 1600 and was accepted by both Catholics and Protestants as the authoritative source on satanism and sorcery. Over the next two centuries it spread throughout all of Europe and resulted in the eventual death of an estimated three million "witches"—widows, midwives, healers, or women who lived alone. One theory holds that as a result of the eradication of midwives' knowledge of birth control and midwifery, the 1600s and 1700s saw a population increase which far outstripped the agricultural capacity of Europe.

1486

Franciscan monks presented Columbus's request for financing to the Spanish court a second time. It was rejected.

1492

Spain conquered Granada, the last Moorish stronghold, and ended 700 years of war between Christian Spain

1492

The paramount chief of the Arawaks, Guacanagari, rescued the crew and cargo of the *Santa Maria* when it went and the Islamic Moors. The Inquisition then expelled all the Moors, along with 200,000 Jews, and confiscated all their properties. (Those who did not leave had to become Catholics.) After 700 years of fighting the "infidels," Spain had become devoted to holy wars. New venues for this fanaticism and intolerance would be the Crusades of the next century and the conquest of the New World.

1492

Columbus's project of a westward route to India was presented a third time at court and approved. He was given the titles of admiral and "governor of territories to be discovered" and three ships. He was also given letters to take to the Great Kahn of China, assuming he would reach the same destination as Marco Polo.

aground on a coral reef off the north coast of a Caribbean island now comprising the Dominican Republic and Haiti. Guacanagari was one of five paramount chiefs and ruled over a district along the northern coast.

The island called Hispaniola by the Spanish held a population of at least three million Arawaks organized into five separate chiefdoms. (Some estimates of the Arawak population in 1492 go as high as six or seven million.) The Arawaks (sometimes called Tainos by anthropologists) were skilled boat builders and navigators, conducting trade throughout the Greater Antilles (Puerto Rico, Hispaniola, Jamaica, Cuba) and Lesser Antilles (Trinidad, Grenada, Martinique, Guadeloupe). All of the Caribbean Islands were populated by migrants from South America and perhaps Mesoamerica. They spoke a variety of Arawak and Carib dialects. The Arawaks had developed a highly complex agricultural and trading society. Their agriculture produced crops three times a year. Their chief staple was manioc (also called cassava, a root vegetable) supplemented by yams or sweet potatoes. They also grew the combination of maize, beans, and squashes familiar throughout Mesoamerica. They had ball courts and played the game the Spanish called *bata*, but which was similar to the Mesoamerican game. Columbus, believing he was in India, called the Arawaks *los indios*, or Indians.

Guacanagari gave Columbus gifts of a mask, plates, a belt, and objects of gold including a golden head ornament. Among the Arawaks, trading was ritualized, a way of expressing friendship, avoiding disputes, or ensuring peace. Gifts were not tribute, but a form of interaction. (*"Of anything they have, if it be asked for, they never say no, but do rather invite the person to accept it, and show as much lovingness as though they would give their hearts,"* wrote Columbus of the Arawaks.) Columbus gave the chief a red cape and decided that the chief had recognized the Europeans' superiority and was offering his submission to Spain.

1493
Columbus returned to Spain with two dozen captured Arawaks and declared he had found India. The king and queen gave him 17 ships, 1,200 colonists, 300 soldiers, and 34 horses and assorted animals for a second expedition.

1493
Pope Alexander VI publishes papal bull dividing the New World between Spain and Portugal.

1494–1559
Beginning of the Italian Wars between France and Spain for control of Italy. The French king Charles VIII invaded Florence and Rome. Pope

1493
Because of their cruelty, the Spaniards remaining on Hispaniola were killed by the Arawaks. Arawaks had destroyed the fort that Columbus had built on Hispaniola, named La Navidad, and killed all the Spanish men. When Columbus returned, Guacanagari told him of the cruel and violent behavior by the Spanish soldiers left behind. The Spanish had enslaved Arawak men and put them to work panning for gold or working in mines in the mountains. Columbus reacted with even greater repression. Soldiers invaded villages with mastiffs and rounded up whole populations. The inhabitants were either killed or shipped to the slave market in Spain. Those who resisted had their ears or noses cut off. Some were burned alive; others were hanged. Columbus ordered every Arawak over the age of 14 to pay a tribute of a hawk's bell of gold every three months. Many Arawaks soon became ill from strange diseases. Columbus rounded up 500 Arawaks for his return voyage to sell in the slave markets in Seville, Spain.

Alexander VI had to take refuge in Castel Sant'Angelo. In 1495 Charles became king of Naples.

1495

Syphilis epidemic spread from Naples all over Europe by French soldiers.

1495–1496

Disease devastated island populations. Wherever the Spaniards landed, epidemics broke out which were uncontrolled and incurable. These were believed to be variations of measles, smallpox, scarlet fever, and other diseases for which the native populations had no immunities. In Puerto Rico tens of thousands died. Among the Arawaks famine and disease killed with unimaginable speed. The declining numbers of the Arawaks only intensified the extraordinary cruelty of the Spaniards, who insisted that the Arawaks work to supply the colonists and soldiers with food. Many Arawaks killed themselves and their children rather than submit to the Spanish. (*"Some threw themselves from high cliffs down precipices; others jumped into the sea,"* wrote Girolamo Benzoni.) Others organized what would become a 20-year resistance fought in the mountains. A Theodore De Bry engraving of the period shows the Arawaks defending a mountainous location against Spanish soldiers in full armor on horseback. It would take less than five decades for the Spanish to make the Arawak population virtually extinct and to replace them and their labor with black slaves brought in chains from Africa.

1497

John Cabot, an Italian explorer (Giovanni Caboto) in the service of the English Crown, and his son Sebastian reached the east coast of North America.

1498

Savonarola burned at the stake in Florence for preaching against the excesses of the Borgia pope, calling him "an infidel, a heretic, no longer a Christian." The pope, Alexander VI, had seven children, several mistresses, one of whom was publicly acknowledged, and enormous personal wealth drawn from revenues from bishoprics in Spain and abbeys in Italy. He appointed 43 cardinals, charging each one 130,000 ducats for the red hat. His reign (1492–1508) included unexplained poisonings and violent deaths, including that of his own son, who was found floating in the Tiber River with nine stab wounds. He annulled the marriages of his daughter twice in order to marry her to more powerful Italian princes. Although Savonarola was excommunicated, imprisoned, tortured, then hanged and burned, others took up his cry. It is said that the excesses of Alexander VI, formerly Rodrigo Borgia, brought the Catholic Church to its lowest point and provoked the Protestant secession throughout Europe.

1498

Vasco da Gama, a Portuguese sailor, discovered the actual sea route from Portugal to India, rounding the Cape of Good Hope and reaching the coast of India at Malabar.

1499

Columbus arrested by the new governor of the Indies, Francisco de Bobadillas, put in chains, and returned to Spain to be tried in royal court for cruelty. Columbus never regained his titles and, under Bobadillas, direct royal control of the Caribbean islands was instituted.

1498

Bartolomew Columbus's census listed 1,100,000 male natives in half of Hispaniola. Columbus removed as governor of the Indies.

The Spanish ship 600 Carib Indians to Spain to be sold into slavery.

IV

1 5 0 0 s — I N V A S I O N   B Y
E U R O P E A N S

Far from settling a virgin continent, Europeans, from the very beginning, moved into preexisting Indian villages and followed Indian trade routes into new territories using Indian guides. Without Indian villages, it's entirely possible there could have been no successful European settlements. From the moment of contact, the appearance of white men raised complex choices for native leaders. What the natives did not realize until it was too late was that European Christianity made it impossible for the Europeans to view the Indians in a way that allowed a fair or equitable negotiation. They saw Indians as savages, as a people without a culture, valuable only as a source of slave labor.

It is ludicrous to imagine that the Indians understood what the Spanish were saying when they read them the *Requerimiento* in Spanish: "We ask and require you . . . to acknowledge the Church and the ruler as superior of the whole world and the high priest called the Pope. . . ." If they didn't submit, the Spanish warned them, "We shall take you and your wives and your children and shall make slaves of them . . . and we shall take away your goods and shall do you all the harm and damage we can." And they did.

Often by the time Indian leaders realized that they did not understand European thinking and their only hope lay in war—war was too late. Some, like the Tlexcalas of Mexico, who allied themselves with Cortés and thought they could put the Spanish horses and guns into service against their greatest enemy, the city-state of Tenochtitlán, met the same fate as the Aztecs they helped to defeat. Soon they, too, were slaves on Spanish *encomiendas*. As Alvin Josephy has written, "The Europeans saw no reason to apply rules of honor to people they considered savages."

The century began with Columbus's fourth and final voyage (he had been rehabilitated after his trial in Seville) in which he was shipwrecked off the coast of Jamaica. But Spain's rulers knew they had found a New World and put in place the administrative apparatus to govern it. The capital of New Spain was at first in Havana, Cuba, then in Mexico City. In 1519 Hernando Cortés ignored the governor's orders to explore the mainland of Mexico and instead decided to conquer it. His victory has been reevaluated in light of recent scholarship about the epidemic diseases that ravaged the city of Tenochtitlán. Indeed, disease is the shadow figure that accompanied the Europeans in all their contacts with Native peoples: Cortés in Mexico; De Soto in Florida, Georgia, Alabama, and Mississippi; Coronado in Arizona and New Mexico. Ninety percent of the populations they encountered were believed to have been eliminated by epidemics of measles, chicken pox, and smallpox to which the natives had no immunities. In sixteenth-century Mexico millions of people died, deaths in such numbers it is difficult to comprehend. They were replaced by black slaves, shipped in chains from Africa to the European colonies. (Over 10 million Africans were shipped to the plantations of the New World with another two to three million dying en route.)

While the Spanish invaded from the south, dominating the Caribbean, the Gulf Coast, and the American Southwest as far as California, the French invaded from the north. By the end of the 1500s France was entrenched in what is now Canada, had mapped the entire Mississippi Valley, and established a few settlements of French Huguenots on the Carolina coast. In 1588, after England and the Netherlands had defeated the Spanish Armada, they began to plan colonies on the Atlantic Coast in the areas of New England and New Amsterdam (New York). The destruction of the Armada marked the end of Spanish ascendancy and the beginning of English domination in the New World. Gold and silver from the New World had already changed the system of coinage, created the banking houses of Italy, and enlarged the monetary system of Europe. This gave rise to a new mercantile class, capital formation, and the emergence of modern banking, which in turn created a new sense of nationalism and national identities.

Native leaders were facing an enemy, the true nature of which they had only dimly begun to comprehend. Every 20 years the Spanish ripped open a larger tear in an ancient fabric. The descendants of the great Mississippian cultures—the Timcua, the Calusa, the Coosa, the Mobile, the Natchez, the Caddo—who even at the time of De Soto were still constructing temple mounds, were virtually wiped out within the century, devastated by a combination of guns, epidemics, and slavery. But their cultures lived on in oral traditions, in recovered artwork, and in place names and archaeological remains that insist on telling their story.

1500s — INVASION BY

EUROPEANS

WORLD HISTORY

1500
Beginning of the period in Europe known as High Renaissance.

1500
World population estimated at 400 million.

1500
Spanish royal decree made Indians of the New World "vassals of the Crown." The *encomienda* system instituted. In order to pay off the conquistadors without depleting the royal treasury, the Spanish Crown gave land grants along with the labor of the "Indian vassals" who lived on them. In return for a specified number of Indian laborers, the Spaniards were expected to protect and instruct them in Christianity. That same year Columbus was put on trial in Spain for excessive cruelty toward the natives. The court exonerated him and gave him permission and backing for a fourth voyage.

1501
The Council of the Indies established. Columbus's successors began exploration of mainland Mexico, Florida, and the Gulf Coast. Spanish settlers introduce African slaves into Hispaniola.

NATIVE AMERICAN HISTORY

1500
Inuits of Greenland see Portuguese explorer Gaspar Corte-Real and his party on their way to Labrador. A year later Corte-Real kidnapped more than 50 Indians from the northeast Atlantic Coast and took them back to Lisbon.

1502

Bartolome de Las Casas, a Catholic priest, arrived in Hispaniola to accumulate lands for the Church. Although a conservative, he underwent a conversion on behalf of treating the natives humanely and became a powerful voice on the side of the Indians. It is from his writings that we know Columbus ordered the decapitation of an entire group of Arawaks who were innocent of any offense.

1502

Moctezuma II ascends the throne at Tenochtitlán at age 22.

1503

The Abenakis and Pasamaquoddy of Maine began to trade with English fishermen who made regular trips to fish the waters off the Atlantic coast. Micmacs, Malacites, Penobscots, and other groups who lived along the northeast Atlantic Coast traded furs and food for metal tools, kettles, and cloth. Unknown diseases soon began to appear among their villages. The English fishermen frequently had a sideline in the slave trade and kidnapped Indians to sell as slaves. As a consequence, the Abenakis became very wary of trade with Europeans and would only trade from boats off the shore. They would not let the Europeans land.

1504

America named after Vespucci's second voyage. Amerigo Vespucci, a Florentine living in Seville, took a second voyage to the New World in the service of Portugal. In *Mundus Novas*, an account of his two voyages, he proposed that these lands were not part of Asia but a new world. It led a noted geographer, Martin Waldseemüller, to propose (in 1507) calling the New World after him—America.

1504

The natives on Jamaica found the shipwrecked Columbus off their coast. He had gone as far south as Honduras in his fourth and final voyage. This time the Crown awarded him no land grant and no Indian vassals. He returned to Spain and died two years later.

1504

Venice sent ambassadors to the sultan of Turkey proposing the construction of a canal across the Isthmus of Suez to open trade routes with East Africa and India.

1506

Machiavelli created the Florentine militia, the first national army in Italy.

1506-1518

The Huron and the Iroquois along the St. Lawrence River in Canada began trading with French fishermen. Over a million natives occupied what is now Canada. Approximately a third were located on the Pacific Coast (the Pacific Northwest Indians) where they lived along ocean bays and river valleys and had a highly developed culture; the other two-thirds of the Canadian native population were concentrated in the east along the St. Lawrence River and the Great Lakes region. (The Neutral and Petan were agricultural peoples with fixed villages. The Cree and Micmac bands to the north were residential bands of extended families. The Inuit, who occupied regions of Hudson Bay north of the treeline, lived in snow houses [igloos] in winter and sod huts or skin tents in summer. They gathered in large bands during the winter and separated into smaller ones in the summer.) The Huron and Iroquois lived in palisaded villages surrounded by fields of corn, beans, squash, and tobacco. The Huron, known to be great traders, controlled the trade networks as far as the Great Lakes. The French eventually established trading relations with the Huron and all their trading partners, including the Inuit and Cree in the far north.

1508-1512

Michelangelo painted the Sistine Chapel in Rome for Pope Julius II. (The Last Judgement was added in 1534–1541.)

1509

Beginning of the slave trade directly from Africa to the New World with slave markets set up in Haiti (Hispaniola).

1512

In Rome Pope Julius II issued a decree on the humanity of the Indians. As a result of the debate in Hispaniola and in Spain, the pope declared that Indians were descended from Adam and Eve. The Fifth Lateran Council in Rome later issued the dogma of the "Immortality of the Soul" and declared Indians *did* have souls.

1512

Attempts at reform in Spain. Law of Burgos. The *Requerimiento*. The new reforms outlawed Indian slavery among certain populations. The Law of Burgos ordered the owners of large tracts of land, *encomiendas*, to improve the treatment of their Indians. The *Requerimiento*, which

1508-1511

Genocide in the West Indies. The native populations of the West Indies were decimated by disease, warfare, and slave labor. Tens of thousands died. The entire Carib population of the Lesser Antilles was exterminated. The Arawaks of Hispaniola died by the hundreds of thousands.

1511

Debate on the humanity of the Indians. Father Antonio de Montesinos shocked the Spanish community on Hispaniola with his sermon on the Indians' humanity, asking: "*Are these Indians not men? Do they not have rational souls?*" The issue was taken up and seriously debated by clerics in Spain. Bartolome de Las Casas began to write *Destruction of the Indies*, in which he chronicled the Spanish conquistadors' extraordinary cruelty toward Native Americans.

the conquistadors were required to read in Spanish to the Indians before attacking or enslaving them, outlined the conditions under which the Spanish could legally invade, enslave, or exploit Indians.

1512
Spanish Crown gave Ponce de Leon, governor of Puerto Rico, permission to explore Florida.

1513
Doctrine of Discovery extended. Vasco Nuñez de Balboa crossed the Isthmus of Panama, observed the Pacific Ocean, and then claimed to have "discovered" it in the name of Spain. The *Doctrine of Discovery* was a legal fiction based on the pope's division of all lands in the Western Hemisphere between Spain and Portugal and used to justify the idea that all lands in the Americas belonged to the European nations that discovered, claimed, or conquered them. Balboa was the first to apply it to oceans.

1513
In Italy Machiavelli wrote *Il Principe* on the cultivation and exercise of power (it was published after his death in 1532). Italy's artistic and intellectual primacy was acknowledged throughout Europe. Politically though, it was weak because of its division into five warring states: Venice, Milan, Florence, the papal states, and the Kingdom of Italy. France, Spain, and Germany all had ambitions in Italy, which led to a century of shifting alliances and wars.

1513
Portuguese explorer Jorge Alvarez reached Canton, China, in the first European ship to reach China.

1513
Calusas of Florida successfully drove Ponce de Leon away. Ponce de Leon had accompanied Columbus on his second voyage in 1493 and had been a leader of the suppression of the Arawaks on Hispaniola. By the time he got to Florida word had spread among the Calusas of the strange and brutal behavior of the men "with houses on water." So when Ponce de Leon's ships appeared in their bay, what is today Fort Myers, they gathered all their warriors in 80 war canoes and drove them off. Unfortunately, Ponce de Leon had glimpsed their kingdom and went back to Puerto Rico to plan another invasion.

The Calusas were the dominant tribe of southwestern Florida and inheritors of the Mississippian civilization. They were traders and skilled in long-distance sea travel, using seagoing canoes lashed together with a sail and holding up to 50 men. They traded with other Indian coastal towns in the Florida Keys, the Bahamas, and Cuba. They built their capital city, Calos, in the geometric design of the temple mound cities, using a base of huge shell mounds. Their trading center and ceremonial center of Key Marco was an elaborately engineered site intersected by nine canals which led to its center. It had three lagoons connected by a canal leading to a central pyramid mound. On its summit was the temple and home of its paramount chief, known in Spanish documents as Carlos I. Modern infrared photography has revealed numerous canals dug along the coast for trade and transportation, including a long waterway that bisected present-day Pine Island. They were an ocean-oriented people who farmed the sea using lagoon systems for oyster beds and holding pens for sea turtles and other fish. In 1895 a team of archaeologists found an enormous cache of sophisticated wood carvings, tools, bowls, clubs, and other ceremonial artifacts, perfectly preserved by the mud of the swamp in which they had been deposited. In the late 1500s, after repeated Spanish invasions, the Calusas deserted Key Marco and disappeared into the Everglades or the other 50 tributary towns that formed their domain.

1515

Bartolome de Las Casas, a Catholic priest, began writing his *Historia de las Indias*, a book documenting Spanish behavior in the New World. It was one of the primary accounts of the cruelty of the Spaniards toward the Arawaks. He had acquired estates and Indian slaves in Hispaniola, but underwent a conversion and became a fiery defender of the Indians. He later (1517) went to Spain to argue before Charles I (later Charles V as Holy Roman Emperor) on behalf of Indians.

1517

Revolt against the Catholic Church. Martin Luther, an Augustinian monk in Erfurt, Germany, tacked his Ninety-Five Theses against the abuse of

1517

First Spanish expedition to the coast of Mexico. An expedition from Cuba reached the Yucatán peninsula, where they encountered Nuahtl-speaking na-

Church authority on the door of the Wittenberg Cathedral, beginning the Reformation in Germany. Luther particularly objected to the pope's sale of indulgences and his involvement in worldly politics. Luther's act coincided with new critical scholarship on the weaknesses of basic ecclesiastical writings and the rise of nationalist feeling in Germany and England precipitated by the growth of a middle class and a capitalist economy. The gold and silver that Spain brought into Europe from the New World had changed the monetary system of Europe, helping to create a class where wealth consisted of money rather than land. Luther's reforms called for German control of the German Church, thus supporting new nationalist feelings. Frederick III of Germany gave Luther protection after the Church ordered his excommunication and arrest.

tives of mainland Mexico. They sighted *"a large town standing two leagues back from the coast . . . We had never seen so large a town in Cuba or Hispaniola,"* wrote one of the members of the expedition, Bernal Diaz del Castillo. Castillo later published his account of the conquest of the Aztecs.

It was on these earlier expeditions that the adventurers found formerly shipwrecked Spaniards like Aguilar who had gone to live with the coastal Indians and had learned the native language and eventually agreed to act as translators. (One of them refused to leave his new Indian family.) Aguilar also described the new foods he had eaten which included chocolate, peanuts, sweet potatoes, tortillas, turkeys, tomatoes, vanilla, and green beans.

1518
The population of Native peoples in Central Mexico at this time estimated at 25 million by Borah and Cook.

1519–1521
Beginning of the destruction of the Aztec empire. Hernando Cortés and 400 Spaniards landed on the Yucatán coast. How did a handful of Spaniards defeat an empire of 200,000 Aztecs with 50,000 men at arms? New scholarship discards old theories of Cortés burning the boats, Moctezuma's mistaking him for the god Quetzalcoatl, and indecision and paralysis among the Aztec generals. New explanations include disease, alliances with the Tlaxcalas and other anti-Aztec Indians, and two entirely different conceptions of war between the Spanish and Aztecs which worked to the Aztec's ultimate downfall.

THE AZTEC EMPIRE

The city of Tenochtitlán was built on an island in Lake Texcoco (near present-day Mexico City) with many gardens and pyramids and canals. There is no doubt that when the Spaniards arrived, they knew they had come to a great civilization. Bernal Diaz del Castillo, a member of the expedition, wrote: "When we saw so many cities and villages built in the water and other great towns on dry land and that straight and level causeway going towards Mexico [Tenochtitlán] we were amazed and said that it was like the enchantments . . . of Amandis, on account of the great towers and cues [pyramids] and buildings rising from the water all built of masonry. . . . We turned to look at the great marketplace and the crowds of people that were in it. . . . Some of the soldiers among us who had been in many parts of the world, in Constantinople, and all over Italy and in Rome, said that so large a marketplace and so full of people and so well regulated and arranged, they had never beheld before . . . I do not know how to describe it seeing things as we did that had never been heard of or seen before, not even dreamed about."

Moctezuma II had ruled in Tenochtitlán since 1502. It was the year of One Reed in the Aztec calendar, a year in which prophecy held that the god-hero Quetzalcoatl would return from the east clothed in the sacred color white. Information came from the Yucatán coast of men who arrived in "houses on water" who rode "great stags" (horses) who were "very white like chalk" and who had yellow hair. Moctezuma sent his ambassadors to inquire who these men were. Cortés ordered the ambassadors shackled and forced them to watch as his men fired a cannon which blew a tree apart on the shore. Cortés had acquired a valuable translator and mistress, Malintzin, whom the Spaniards called La Malinche, a native who had learned Spanish from one of the shipwrecked survivors and who also knew several of the local languages. She was able to instruct Cortés in the politics of the city-states of the Mexico Valley and to tell him about Moctezuma's numerous enemies. The disaffected city-states hated the Aztec soldiers, who stole their children as slaves or sacrifices, and bitterly resented the wealth the Aztecs extorted from them in tribute. Cortés was able to pose as a liberator to the enemies of Tenochtitlán.

He first made an alliance with the powerful city-state of the Tlaxcalas and with them gained entrance to Tenochtitlán. Moctezuma, borne on a litter and accompanied by a retinue of nobles and war chiefs in colorful feathered headdresses and gold ornaments, went out on the great causeway to greet the Spaniards. Cortés told the emperor he had come in peace. Moctezuma welcomed him, gave Cortés gifts, and his men a palace to stay in. One of the Aztecs later described the procession of the Spaniards into the city: "They came in battle array, as conquerors, and the dust rose in whirlwinds on the roads. Their spears glinted in the sun, and their pennons fluttered like bats. They made a loud clamor as they marched, for their coats of mail and their weapons clashed and rattled. Some of them were dressed in glistening iron from head to foot; they terrified everyone who saw them. Their dogs came with them, running ahead of the column. They raised their muzzles high; they lifted their muzzles to the wind. They raced on before with saliva dripping from their jaws."

Moctezuma showed his guest the splendor of his city and invited his guests to attend its festivities. The Spaniards quickly tired of being tourists. They wanted gold. Pedro de

Alvarado, Cortés's chief lieutenant, massacred all 600 celebrants during their religious ceremony. This account (from oral histories collected by Bernardino de Sahagun 20 years after the conquest) describes the Spaniards' treachery at a dance and celebration where the natives were unarmed. First the Spanish soldiers locked the doors so no one could escape: "They attacked the man who was drumming and cut off his arms. Then they cut off his head, and it rolled across the floor. They attacked all the celebrants, stabbing them, spearing them, striking them with their swords. They attacked some of them from behind and these fell instantly to the ground with their entrails hanging out. . . . Some attempted to run away, but their intestines dragged as they ran; they seemed to tangle their feet in their own entrails. No matter how they tried to save themselves, they could find no escape."

The Aztecs mobilized their army and besieged the Spanish within the city. Cortés took Moctezuma hostage. Cut off from their Tlaxcala allies, Cortés and his men were forced to abandon the city, escaping via a causeway at night, weighed down with gold they had looted, many of them drowning. According to an Aztec version of events: "The canal was filled, crammed with them. Those who came along behind walked over on men, on corpses. . . . And when the Spanish thus disappeared, we thought they had gone for good, nevermore to return."

Moctezuma was killed in the fighting. The Aztecs could have obliterated the Spanish at this juncture, but a war of annihilation was a foreign concept to them. They fought wars for tribute and to take live captives. Two-thirds of the Spanish troops had died. The Aztecs thought the Spaniards were gone forever.

The Aztecs chose a new king, Cuitlahuac, to succeed Moctezuma. His generals organized to fight. The Spanish were not to be allowed back into the city under any circumstances. The Aztecs believed the Spanish had been vanquished. But the Spanish had left behind a great weapon, one against which the Aztecs had no defense. Disease. "But about that time that the Spaniards had fled from Mexico . . . there came a great sickness, a pestilence, the smallpox . . . it spread over the people with great destruction of men. It caused great misery. . . . The brave Mexican warriors were indeed weakened by it. It was after all this had happened that the Spaniards came back."

Cortés and his surviving troops spent a year recuperating with the Tlaxcalas. In the meantime, another Aztec city-state, Texcoco, had decided to ally with Tlaxcala against Tenochtitlán. Their leaders mistakenly believed they could harness the guns and horses of the Spanish to their purpose. A new campaign was devised against Tenochtitlán, whereby they would attack the city from the water and Cortés would mount his guns on boats. In 1521 a four-month siege began of Tenochtitlán, already struck by plague.

An Aztec account described the epidemic inside the city: "It lasted for seventy days, striking everywhere in the city and killing a vast number of our people. Sores erupted on our faces, our breasts, our bellies: we were covered with agonizing sores from head to foot. The illness was so dreadful that no one could walk or move. The sick were so utterly helpless that they could only lie on their beds like corpses, unable to move their limbs or even their heads. They could not lie facedown or roll from one side to the other. If they did move their bodies, they screamed with pain."

The new king was among the casualties of the plague. Starvation broke out because they could not get supplies into the city. After four months of siege, during which thousands died, the Aztecs sent another newly appointed king to surrender. Tenochtitlán was subjugated. More than 24,000 Aztecs were killed. It is believed that almost all the nobility of Tenochtitlán perished. Cortés established himself as the new ruler of Mexico. His former allies, the Tlaxcalas and the Texcocos, also succumbed to epidemics. They eventually became "vassals of the Crown." The city of Tenochtitlán was systematically looted and destroyed, and the Aztec empire disintegrated.

1519
Fernando Magellan in the service of Spain commanded the first exploratory voyage around the world.

1519
Charles I of Spain became Holy Roman Emperor, Charles V, after electors of the Holy Roman Empire chose him as emperor. His vast Spanish holdings, combined with those of the Hapsburgs, made Spain the preeminent power of Europe. He issued an edict prohibiting any new Catholic reforms. The Catholic Church redoubled its efforts to send missionaries to the New World under the patronage of Spanish kings. The missionaries were to convert the natives, establish land grants, and amass riches for the Church. As Catholicism prospered in the Americas, the papacy grew rich and powerful again.

1520
Martin Luther publicly burned the papal bull condemning him. Beginning of Lutheran doctrine, Lutheran Church, and the spread of the Reformation.

1519
The first phase of Cortés's conquest. First battle of Tenochtitlán. (See "The Aztec Empire" on page 82.) The city of Tenochtitlán was built on a lake (near present-day Mexico City) with many gardens and pyramids and canals. There is no doubt that the Spaniards knew they had come to a great civilization. Cortés made an alliance with the Tlaxcalas and gained entrance to Tenochtitlán easily. Cortés eventually took Moctezuma hostage and looted his palace of gold and treasure. The Aztec generals mobilized their armies and besieged the Spanish within the city. Cut off from their Tlaxcala allies, Cortés and his men were forced to abandon the city. They escaped via a causeway, weighed down with gold they had looted. Although the Aztecs could have obliterated the Spanish at this juncture, they did not because a war of annihilation was a foreign concept. War had ritual purpose. If the Aztecs could not take a man alive, they hit him on the back of the head so that he died like a prisoner rather than a warrior. Two-thirds of the Spanish troops were lost.

1520
Beginning of 14-year Arawak rebellion on Hispaniola. An Arawak rebel, Guayocuya, called Enrique by the Spanish, took to the mountains and for the next

Luther believed in justification by faith alone, which made Catholic priests unnecessary intermediaries between the individual and God, and questioned the infallibility of the pope. He was excommunicated in 1521.

1520
Chocolate from Mexico was introduced into Spain.

1521–1529
Wars between France and Spain over Italy continue.

1521
Spanish Crown established New Spain in what is now Mexico and declared control of all Indian subjects as far south as Guatemala.

decade led hundreds of Arawak rebels in harassing the Spanish authorities. After 14 years of fighting, Guayocuya and his followers were granted land on which to live without having to give tribute to a Spanish overseer.

1521
The second battle of Tenochtitlán. Plague raged throughout the city. (See "The Aztec Empire" on page 82.) The Aztecs chose a new king, Cuitlahuac, to succeed Moctezuma. His generals organized to fight. The Aztecs believed the Spanish had been vanquished. Cortés and his surviving troops spent the year recuperating with the Tlaxcalas and gained another ally in the city-state Texcoco. A new campaign was devised against Tenochtitlán, whereby Cortés mounted his guns on boats and attacked the city from the water. After a four-month siege, the Aztecs surrendered. The real cause of the surrender was the plague epidemic that had broken out in the city after the Spanish left. The new king had died as had thousands of soldiers. A new Aztec king was appointed and sent to surrender. Tenochtitlán was subjugated. More than 24,000 Aztecs were killed. It was believed that almost all the nobility of Tenochtitlán perished. Cortés established himself as the new ruler of Mexico, and the city of Tenochtitlán was systematically looted and destroyed.

1521
Calusas mounted strategic resistance to Ponce de Leon's second expedition. Death of Ponce de Leon. Spurred on

Eagle Warriors dance at Tesuque Pueblo. These Eagle dancers at Tesuque Pueblo, New Mexico, bear a certain resemblance to life-size ceramic figures of Aztec warriors wearing wings and beaked masks that were unearthed in archaeological ruins near Mexico City. The eagle was the symbol of Aztec greatness and continues to be the center of ceremonies in many pueblos where the eagle is viewed as a messenger to the spirit world.

by the stories of Cortés's successes, Ponce de Leon mounted a second expedition against the Calusas. He landed at Carlos Bay with 200 Spanish soldiers and settlers to establish a colony. The aged Calusa chieftain, known in Spanish documents as Carlos I, allowed them to build a settlement while he assembled a huge force of Calusa warriors. After the Spanish had established their settlement Carlos I directed his warriors in a surprise attack with weapons that included poisoned darts and arrows. Although many Calusas were killed, Ponce de Leon sustained a poisoned arrow wound in the thigh. He ordered a retreat back to Havana, where he died from the infected arrow wound. The legend of the Calusas grew in the Spanish mind, particularly after Spanish ships blown off course in the Straits of Florida were wrecked in storms on the Calusa coast. The Calusas were believed to horde large amounts of Spanish gold as well as prisoners, both men and women.

1522
Martin Luther introduced public worship with the liturgy in German rather than Latin. Reformation spread.

1522
Another large-scale slave rebellion broke out in Hispaniola.

1523
Portuguese expelled from their settlement in China.

1523–1524
The Narragansett and Delaware Indians encountered Verrazano as he traveled along the Atlantic Coast. France had hired him to survey the eastern coast of the United States. His narrative is the earliest known firsthand description of the people of the Atlantic Coast. Of the Wampanoag of Massachusetts he wrote: *"They are the most beautiful and have the most civil customs that we have encountered on this voyage . . . Their women are . . . very gracious . . . of attractive manner and pleasant appearance."* The Narragansetts, who had had no previous contact with Europeans, were particularly friendly. He reported that in trade they "prized . . . little bells, blue crystals, and other trinkets to put in the ear or around the neck. They did not appreciate cloth of silk or gold." The Indians of the Maine coast, who had previous experience with kidnappings and European violence, were less friendly.

1525
Three of Cortés's letters published in Spain describing his conquest. He emphasized that the Aztecs had taken him for a god.

1527

Rome plundered by Spanish and German mercenaries of Emperor Charles V. Even by standards of pillage of the day, destruction was judged to be horrible. The indecisive pope, Giulio de Medici (Clement VII) had changed sides mid-war. Charles V had him imprisoned. Four thousand inhabitants were killed; many art treasures were looted.

1528

Timcua Indians of Florida successfully resisted 400 Spanish settlers who wanted to start a new colony in Tampa Bay. Already familiar with the nature of Spanish explorers, the Timcua, who controlled much of the area of Florida around Tampa, fought and harassed the Spanish, who were under the leadership of Panfilo de Narvaez. They succeeded in sending a quarter of the group back to their ships. But the others escaped and continued on to the north, where they were attacked by other Indian people. At Apalachee Bay the Spanish could endure no more. They killed their horses and constructed small boats from the hides and tree limbs, subsisting on horseflesh. They hoped to reach Mexico but were shipwrecked near Galveston, Texas.

1528–1536

Cabeza de Vaca's myth of the seven cities of gold. Two survivors of the Narvaez party, Cabeza de Vaca and a black slave named Estevanico, survived and lived for six years among the Karankawa and Atakapa Indians of the Texas coast, where they were treated as healers and holy men, possibly because of the color of their skin. They walked across Texas, following existing Indian trade routes, and eventually met up with Yaqui Indians who guided them south through the Sonora Desert into Mexico. They reached Mexico City in 1536. De Vaca, who had been the king's accountant on the Narvaez expedition, wrote an account of their journey, and to ingratiate himself with the Crown he invented sightings of cities of gold, which they had never seen, in the American Southwest. It was his account that led to the Coronado expedition into New Mexico three years later searching for the "seven cities of Cibola."

1529

Bernardino de Sahagun started his Franciscan mission in Mexico and began to compile the first history of the Aztecs. Called the father of ethnography, Sahagun trained native Mexicans to write down the oral histories of Aztec life, religion, and beliefs before the arrival of Cortés. He taught the Mexican natives to translate from Nahuatl to Spanish and then wrote down the accounts in a multivolume work, now called the *Florentine Codex* or *A General History of the Things of New Spain*. It is from Sahagun's early histories that the Aztec version of Cortés's invasion survived.

1531

Guadalupe, the black Virgin Mary, appeared to an Indian acolyte, named Juan Diego by the Spanish, near Mexico City. In his vision she was a mestizo. The day of the Virgin of Guadalupe is celebrated on December 12.

1531

The Yaqui Indians of northern Mexico repel a party of Spanish soldiers on a

slaving mission. Nuño de Guzman explored the Sea of Cortés. At the northernmost end the Yaquis warned him not to proceed further. In the ensuing battle the Spanish were driven back.

1533

Pope excommunicated King Henry VIII of England after secret marriage to Anne Boleyn. After the pope refused an annullment of Henry's previous marriage to Catherine of Aragon, Henry divorced her and remarried without the pope's permission. The pope then excommunicated the King.

1534

King Henry VIII confiscated all the properties of the Church and under the Act of Supremacy named himself Supreme Head of the Church in England. Beginning of the English Reformation.

1534

Micmac Indians established friendly relations with Frenchman Jacques Cartier on his first voyage to the coast of Labrador.

1535

Second voyage of Jacques Cartier down the St. Lawrence Seaway to Quebec and Montreal. He established friendly relations with Chief Donnacona of the St. Lawrence Iroquois from the village of Stadacona (now Quebec) and exchanged European goods for furs. Two sons of the chief, Domagaya and Taignoagny, accompanied Cartier back to France.

1535–1541

Iroquois traded with the French. For the next six years the Iroquois Chief Donnacona's sons guided Cartier throughout the St. Lawrence River region, meeting with the Iroquois and Algonquian-speaking peoples of the region. The agricultural town of Hochelaga (present-day Montreal), occupied by 1,500 to 3,500 people, traded with Cartier. When many of his crew developed scurvy from vitamin C deficiency the Iroquois taught them how to brew white cedar tea, which was rich in vitamin C. (Although 25 of his men had already died the rest recovered.) Cartier later took Donnacona and nine of his chiefs to France where they were presented to King Francis I. Donnacona told the French king about a kingdom to the west of the Huron said to be rich in gold and silver and inhabited by white men. (Some historians think that the Huron and Iroquoian trade routes had brought news of the Spanish in Mexico.) As a result, Francis I, decided to establish a French settlement on the St. Lawrence and challenge Spanish claims to North America. The Iroquois chief died in France.

1536
Royal College of Santa Cruz founded in Mexico.

1537
Pope Paul III declared Indians could become Christians and were worthy of conversion.

1537
Slaves on Hispaniola organized another rebellion.

1539
The Zuni killed Estevanico, the black slave and survivor of the Narvaez expedition, sent ahead by Coronado as reconnaissance. The Zuni recognized that he was not a true medicine man and that he was carrying a rattle from an enemy nation. A Franciscan friar named Marcos de Niza, traveling behind Estevanico, returned to Mexico saying that the Zuni had killed Estevanico and that the region of the Zuni pueblos had wealth greater than the Aztecs or Incas. Coronado immediately planned a major expedition into the region of northern Mexico that today is Arizona and New Mexico.

1539

Timcua, Appalachia, Coosa, Mobile, Natchez, and Tonkawa fight invasion of Hernando De Soto through southeastern United States. A member of Pizarro's army in the earlier conquest of the Inca Empire in Peru, De Soto had been given license by the king of Spain to "conquer, pacify, and people" the lands known as *La Florida*—Florida, Georgia, South Carolina, Tennessee, Alabama, Mississippi, Louisiana. De Soto's expedition marked the first and last European chronicle of the Mississippian civilization in the southeastern United States. Within three decades after his expedition, disease had devastated the entire region.

The Timcua lived on Florida's west coast, in hundreds of towns lining the rivers. Their chiefdoms were among the inheritors of the Mississippian civilization: they carried on the ancient traditions of mound building and of paying religious honor to the sun. The homes of the chiefs were on top of the carefully sculpted mounds. The Timcua had large plazas for ceremonies, cleared playing fields for ball games, and carefully tended agricultural fields.

De Soto and his army cut a path of destruction through this ancient world from Florida to Texas. When De Soto unfurled the Spanish flag at Acuera and read, in Spanish, the *Requerimiento*, the Timcua chief ordered his men to battle. With an army of 600 soldiers with guns, 100 servants, 200 horses, herds of pack animals and trained attack dogs, De Soto won the day. He immediately seized Timcua men and women to be slaves and servants, plundered food supplies, and looted burial sites. He moved on to the country of the

Apalachees, a rich agricultural chiefdom at the site of present-day Tallahassee. He spent six months there and then continued into Georgia and South Carolina.

1540

De Soto encountered the Creek town of Cofitachequi. When he reached the Muskokean-speaking village at what is now Camden, South Carolina, he asked for food stores and whatever treasure they posessed. The village was ruled by an elderly woman chieftain who was sent into hiding in a distant village. Her niece presented De Soto with a string of freshwater pearls, hundreds of bushels of corn, and mica. The Spaniards dug up a great temple mound looking for more pearls, which they had learned were buried with the dead. De Soto took the niece with him to safeguard his passage through the country. (She eventually escaped.)

De Soto then crossed the Appalachian mountains and entered the **kingdom of the Coosas in what is now Georgia, Alabama, and Tennessee.** The Spaniards were amazed by the rich agricultural fields and the architectural design of the Coosa villages, with their great temple mounds and geometrically arranged houses. In Spanish documents it was reported that the Coosas' paramount chief was carried out to greet De Soto on a litter, accompanied by a thousand men in great feathered headdresses. The chief escorted the Spaniards into the Coosa capital on the Coosawattee River in northwestern Georgia, where the Spaniards stayed for a month. The Coosa chieftain escorted De Soto the length of the province, showing him hundreds of Coosa tributory towns, and finally directing him into another region. Stories of the Coosas, their feathered headdresses, their lush and fertile countryside would become legendary in Spain.

De Soto moved on to the territory of another great Mississippian chiefdom, the Mobiles in Alabama. However, word about the Spaniards had spread in advance and **all the chiefs of the Mobile nation gathered for war in the fortified town of what is now Mobile, Alabama.** When De Soto read the *Requerimiento,* a Mobile warrior came out and replied for the chiefs: *"Who are these thieves and vagabonds who keep shouting come forth . . . come forth . . . No one can endure longer the insolence of these demons, and it is therefore only right that they die today, torn into pieces for their infamy, and that in this way amends be given to their wickedness and tyranny."* De Soto immediately had the messenger killed, whereupon thousands of Mobile warriors poured out of the town to do battle. They were great fighters and the Spaniards were forced to retreat and advance several times, but De Soto's guns carried the day. He then had the entire city burned to the ground. One Spaniard observed, *"they [the Mobiles] fought as though they wanted to die."* Spanish accounts say the number of Mobile deaths ranged from 2,500 to 11,000. The number of Spanish losses is not known. De Soto had to rest for a month before advancing on Chickasaw territory, where he stayed the winter in abandoned Chickasaw towns, harassed by constant Chickasaw attacks, while his wounded recovered.

Zuni water jar. This Zuni ceramic pot was made in the 1800s but is decorated in an ancient Anasazi pattern of bold black on white geometric designs, widely spaced and placed within an overall diamond pattern. The Zuni, who trace their history to a specific clan that migrated from Mesa Verde, continue to make splendid ceramic pots using ancient designs. (The Zuni also still commemorate the killing of Estevanico, Coronado's advance messenger.)

1540

Francisco Vasquez de Coronado was given license by the Spanish Crown to mount an expedition into the American Southwest to locate the "seven cities of gold." The stories told by Cabeza de Vaca and Estevanico of great cities of gold to the north had been taken seriously. Coronado was given an army of 300 soldiers, 900 Mexican Indian "allies and slaves," 1,000 horses, 500 mules, and hundreds of domesticated animals. Four Franciscan friars accompanied the expedition. When Coronado first encountered the Zuni in Arizona, they drew a line of cornmeal on the ground and told him to go no further. He invaded the Zuni pueblos. After much fighting the Zuni were defeated.

1540

Hopi pueblo of Awatovi encounter the Spanish. The Franciscan priest accompanying the Spanish expedition described the Hopi territory as having "twenty thousand souls" wearing finely woven cotton garments and making a flat bread from blue corn. The Hopi sent them north to the Grand Canyon, where Coronado's lieutenant de Cardenas was the first European to see the Grand Canyon. Coronado and the main expedition continued east toward the pueblos of the Rio Grande.

1541

John Calvin introduced the Reformation in Switzerland, and organized Geneva, Switzerland, as a theocratic state based on the principles of Calvinism. Protestant refugees from England and France poured into Geneva.

1541

The Tigeux rebellion—Kuaua pueblo revolted in New Mexico. There were approximately 90 pueblos along the Rio Grande area of New Mexico at the time of Coronado's expedition, with connections back to the great centers of Chaco Canyon and Mesa Verde. The Kuaua pueblo in Tigeux province, near what is now Bernalillo, New Mexico, became Coronado's winter headquarters. Of Tiwa origin—"Kuaua" is a Tiwa word meaning "sacred evergreen"—the Kuaua had an extensive pueblo on a beautiful site overlooking the Rio Grande River. Their intricate religion was based on ancient dances and days of celebration and their kivas had painted murals on the interior. Castenada, a Franciscan priest, later described them: *"We visited a good many of these pueblos. They are all well built with straight well-squared walls. Their houses are three, five, even seven stories high, with many windows and terraces. The men spin and weave and the women cook, build houses and keep them in good repair. They dress in garments of cotton cloth, and the women wear shawls of many colors. They are quiet, peaceful people of good appearance and excellent physique, alert and intelligent. . . . We saw no maimed or deformed people among them. The men and women alike are excellent swimmers. They are also expert in the art of painting and are good fishermen. They live in complete equality, neither exercising authority nor demanding obedience."*

When Coronado arrived, he ordered the Indians to vacate their homes, provide his men with food, and give him any valuables they might possess. His men treated the villagers with inquisitorial brutality. In the winter of 1540–41 the Kuaua people revolted against the Spanish soldiers. Other pueblos of Tigeux province joined in the rebellion. Kuaua was virtually destroyed and later abandoned. Perhaps because of the haste in which its people left, it is the only pueblo in the Southwest in which painted kiva murals have survived. The Kuaua pueblo can be visited today at the (ironically named) Coronado National Monument at Bernalillo, New Mexico, a national park site.

1541–1542
Natchez nation invaded. De Soto reached the Mississippi River and crossed into the kingdom of the Natchez, another inheritor of the Mississippian culture. The paramount chief and spiritual head, Quigaltam, the Great Sun of the Natchez, was carried out to meet De Soto on a litter. Treated as a god, he was always carried so his feet would not touch the ground. His head was flattened according to Natchez custom and tattoos of black, red, and blue designs were etched all over his body.

1542
De Soto died. The Natchez were spared the worst of De Soto's excesses because he became suddenly ill of an unknown disease and died. He was succeeded by Luis de Moscoso, who continued the journey as far as Texas, then turned around and took the Mississippi River back to the Gulf of Mexico.

1542
Coronado returned to Mexico empty-handed. It is said that Coronado's guide, a Pawnee and a slave, deliberately led him in circles around the empty plains of Kansas, knowing there were no cities of gold to be found anywhere. All that Coronado found were the dwellings of the Wichita Indians. Coronado had the guide killed and turned back. In the pueblos his invasion left behind horses and sheep, the begin-

ning of the use of wool and weaving on flat looms. After Coronado's return to Mexico he was sent back to Spain, where he stood trial for mismanagement of his army and cruelty to Native peoples.

1542–1543
Tonkawa confederacy in eastern Texas was the last stop in the De Soto expedition. Natchez war canoes harassed De Soto's survivors all the way down the Mississippi to the Gulf of Mexico. The Tonkawa Indians of Texas showed the Spanish turquoise stones and cotton shawls traded from the Rio Grande pueblos. Luis de Moscoso found these of little value and turned the expedition back to the Mississippi River, where the Spanish built barges to sail toward the Gulf of Mexico. Pursued by 100 Natchez war canoes, the Spanish had to kill their horses to lighten their load. They reached Mexico in 1543. Since they had not found gold, they had no way to give meaning to or to describe what they *had* found and the trip was considered a failure. They had actually encountered the ancient Mississippian cultures still managed by priests or sacred chiefs linked to the Great Sun. The Mississippian culture nations are known today as the Creek, Cherokee, Natchez, Chickasaw, and Choctaw.

1542–1543
Jacques Cartier unsuccessfully searched for precious metals in Canada. His relationships with the Stadacona Iroquois began to deteriorate. Efforts to start a French settlement failed. He made new alliances.

1543
The Portuguese landed in Japan and brought firearms.

1544
Silver was discovered in Potosi, Peru. Eighty-five percent of the silver that entered Europe over the next century came from this site. The Spanish imported 6,000 African slaves to work the mines. Because silver was more practical for daily transactions, it changed Europe from a barter to a true money economy. Monetary value superseded land as a basis for wealth. Within 50 years royal customs agents in Seville recorded 16,000 tons of silver from Potosi, valued at $2 billion in today's dollars.

1551
Emperor Charles V founded the national University of Mexico. He also sponsored a traveling exhibit of gold objects from Mexico and then had them melted down for coins to finance the expansion of his army.

1553
The potato described for the first time in Europe in Pedro de Leon's *Chronicle of Peru*.

1555
An Aztec dictionary published in Spain. Tobacco from America introduced in Spain for the first time.

1556–1598
King Philip II succeeded to the Spanish throne. His father, Charles V, abdicated, assigning Spain to his son and the Holy Roman Empire to his brother, Ferdinand. Charles then retired to the

monastery of Yuste. Spain was the richest nation in Europe. Philip II vigorously supported catholicism, the Inquisition, and the papacy.

1559–1577

The Spanish Inquisition established the first Papal Index of Forbidden Books, which prohibited any books on native cultures. The order expressly decreed that officials in New Spain must destroy any writing *"in any language . . . concerning the superstitions and way of life that these Indians had."* **All writings on pre-Columbian cultures were to be delivered to the Spanish Crown.**

1560

Bernardino de Sahagun's work on Mesoamerican culture and Aztec history jeopardized in Spain. A Franciscan priest, Sahagun had worked for 30 years training natives in the Mexico Valley to record oral histories in the Nahuatl language and to take down accounts of life as it was lived among the Aztecs before the Spanish arrived. He trained others to translate from Nahuatl to Spanish and to write in manuscript form in a series of volumes, *A General History of the Things of New Spain*. The material formed a different portrait of the Spanish from the official version the Church and the Crown had constructed.

Here is a Nahuatl description of the Spanish reaction when they found Aztec gold: *"They picked up the gold and fingered it like monkeys; they seemed to be transported by joy, as if their hearts were illumined and made new. The truth is that they longed and lusted for gold. Their bodies swelled with greed, and their hunger was ravenous;*

they hungered like pigs for that gold. . . .
The Spaniards grinned like little beasts
and patted each other with delight."

The governor of the Indies was sym-
pathetic to Sahagun's work and made
no immediate effort to censor his efforts, but the long-term future of the
project was in doubt.

1560

The demise of the Coosa reported.
Epidemics in the Southeast. A second
Spanish expedition under Tristan de
Luna tried to retrace De Soto's route.
Expecting to find a wealthy kingdom
like the one described by De Soto's
chronicles, he found only ruin. Instead
of towns of 500 houses, he found 50.
The fields were left untended. Everywhere on the same route he found only
deserted settlements, temple mounds in
decay, cornfields overgrown.

A sick Spanish slave left behind by
De Soto had spread an epidemic
which had swept through the Coosa
towns and decimated the population.
Historians believe that a series of epidemics virtually wiped out the Southeastern tribes in this period in a matter
of decades.

1562

The French settled in South Caro-
lina. French Huguenots, escaping the
persecution in France, settled in the
Carolinas.

1563

A general outbreak of plague in Eu-
rope. Over 20,000 people killed in
London among a total population of
66,000.

1563

At Fort Caroline, a French artist,
Jacques Le Moyne drew some of the
first representations of South Carolina
Indians.

1564

Spain launched an expedition to the Philippines from Mexico's Pacific Coast. Began annual trade to the Philippines and settled Manila.

1565

The town of St. Augustine founded in Florida by Spanish. It was their first permanent settlement on mainland U.S. It was established in order to attack the French Huguenot settlements up the coast.

1565

Sir John Hawkins, a slave trader, introduced sweet potatoes and tobacco into England. Queen Elizabeth was one of the investors in his slave ventures.

1566

Spanish destroyed the French settlements in Florida and the Carolina coast.

1566

Spanish turned their attention to the Calusa Indians. The third Calusa resistance to the Spanish. After defeating the French Huguenots, the commander of Ft. Augustine, Pedro Menendez de Aviles, requested license to invade the Calusas. The new Calusa leader was Carlos II, 25 years old, the son of Carlos I. When Menendez sailed into the harbor, the Calusas had been greatly weakened by disease. Carlos II negotiated with Menendez, agreed to accept a Jesuit missionary, and suggested that the agreement be honored in Calusa custom by Menendez's marriage to his sister. While Menendez returned to Havana with his Calusa wife and had her baptized Dona Antonia, the Calusas made fun of the missionaries and refused to convert. Menendez returned. Under the guise of a false negotiation, the Spaniard seized the young chieftain along with 20 of his warriors and had them all beheaded. Then Menendez selected another chieftain, but no one obeyed him and Menendez eventually had him killed for insubordination. The Calusas retaliated for the Spanish execution of their real chieftain by burning their capital to the ground and abandoning the island. Without the food and labor of the Calusas, the Spanish couldn't survive, and they later abandoned the area. Disease eventually accomplished what Menendez could not. Surviving bands of Calusas joined with migrant Creeks (originally called Muskokees) and became the Seminole Indian nation of Florida.

1568
Spanish Crown ordered review of military tactics in New Spain. Too many natives were dying. Labor was scarce. Menendez's request to exterminate the entire Calusa nation denied.

1570
Japan opened the port of Nagasaki to overseas trade.

1570
Mission established in Maryland on Chesapeake Bay by seven Spanish Jesuits guided by a converted Indian (called Don Luis Valasco by the Spanish). They were all killed by Powhatan or Piscataway residents.

1571
An office of the Inquisition moved to New Spain and set up offices in Mexico City. It concentrated on deviant Spaniards rather than Indians.

1577
Spanish Crown issued a royal decree enforcing the 1559 papal Inquisition order for all books and writing on Indian societies existing in New Spain to be sent to Seville.

1577
The work of Sahagun pronounced illegal. Inquisition demanded all pre-Columbian works in existence in New Spain. The governor of the Indies, who had protected Sahagun's work, was

replaced by an Inquisition governor who was unsympathetic. When he protested the destruction of his life's work, Sahagun was excommunicated. Technically abiding by the new law, Sahagun translated one copy (13 volumes) of his work from Nahuatl into Spanish and gave the copy of A *General History of the Things of New Spain* to Father Seguera, a Franciscan general commissioner, supposedly to take to Spain and the Inquisition. The manuscript never arrived in Spain but ended up in a library in Florence, Italy, and survived under the name the *Florentine Codex*. (Although the work was translated into French and Italian, the full English translation was not completed until 1985.)

1578-1579

Sir Francis Drake sailed the *Golden Hind*, harbored near San Francisco. He explored the California coast and encountered peoples like the coastal Miwok, who had more than 170 villages.

1580

An English fisherman at St. Johns, Newfoundland, recorded seeing dozens of Indian villages that had been abandoned, either because of disease or slaving raids. Over 500 European vessels a year · fished off Newfoundland and Georges Bank, making North American fisheries a big European industry. French fishermen reported that it took less than 10 days to sail from St. Malo, France, to Georges Bank.

1582

Pope Gregory XIII introduced the Gregorian calendar to correct an error in the Julian calendar which had fallen 10 days behind astronomically.

(Great Britain did not adopt it until 1752; Russia and the Greek Orthodox countries adopted it in 1917; it was adopted worldwide in 1950.)

1584
Dutch trading post established at Archangel, Russia.

1585
Sir Walter Raleigh supported an English colony on Roanoke Island in North Carolina to be called Virginia after the Virgin Queen, Elizabeth I. After two unsuccessful scouting expeditions and violent encounters with the Secotan Indians, Raleigh planned a third expedition of 118 men, women, and children under the leadership of John White, an artist-explorer, to settle on the Chesapeake.

1587
Spain at war with England and the Netherlands. England constructed a fleet of war. King Philip II of Spain formed the "invincible" Spanish Armada to invade Protestant England.

1587
North Carolina Indians introduce the English to corn. The ship carrying the colonists set in at Roanoke Island. Thomas Hariot, a member of the first Roanoke expedition, gave England its first description of maize in his book, *A briefe and true report of the new found land of Virginia*. "A graine of marvelous great increase," he reported about the fields of corn the Algonquians grew. He also was impressed with the Indians' methods of fishing. *"Ther was never seene among us soe cunninge a way to take fish."* John White gave England its first drawings of North Carolina Algonquians, including a drawing of the Indians fishing at night with a fire on the bottom of the dugout canoe to attract fish. White and Hariot returned to England, leaving the settlers to manage while they arranged for another boat and supplies.

1588

The Spanish Armada of 132 vessels with 3,165 cannons was defeated in the English Channel by the English and the Dutch fleets and then destroyed by a storm off the Hebrides. In terms of a shift in geopolitical fortunes, it ranked with the Greek defeat at Marathon. England would replace Spain as the dominant power in Europe and the New World.

1588

The French king, Henry III, began policy of granting fur-trade monopolies in Canada. Indian beaver pelts were in great demand in France. The fur trade greatly expanded. Henry III was also deeply involved in the wars of religion in France in which persecution of French Catholics alternated with persecution of French Protestants.

1590

Roanoke, the lost colony. Because of the war between England and Spain and Sir Walter Raleigh's loss of favor at court, it took John White three years to raise additional money for supplies and a ship for the Virginia colony. He did not return to Roanoke until almost four years later. When he got there all 117 settlers had vanished, leaving behind only words CRO and CROATOAN carved on some trees. One theory is that they had gone to the outer-island Indian village of Croatoan on what is now Cape Hatteras, but they were never found.

1596

Tomatoes introduced in England.

1590–1598

Rio Grande pueblos invaded by Spanish from Mexico coming up through the Rio Grande Valley. Juan de Onate was appointed governor of New Mexico. Apache and Pueblo peoples drove them back, but in 1598, the Spanish established a colony at San Juan Pueblo in northern New Mexico. Onate mounted several expeditions to the Rio Grande pueblos.

Acoma Pueblo or Aku, Sky City. Situated on a 400-foot-high mesa, Acoma was almost impenetrable to outsiders until 1598 when the new Spanish viceroy wanted to establish the northern boundary of New Spain. Don Juan de Onate set off a siege in which 800 Acoma Indians died, 570 were put on trial, and all males over 14 were mutilated by having a hand or foot cut off. This early morning scene shows the terraced adobe houses with their ovens for bread baking and meat and vegetables hung on racks to dry in the sun.

1597
Rebellion of the Guale Indians of the Georgia coast against the Spanish and the Spanish mission system.

1598
England and France replaced Spain as the preeminent European powers. England defeated a second Spanish Armada. Henry IV of France, a Protestant who converted to Catholicism, issued the **Edict of Nantes** establishing religious toleration and ending the wars of religion in France.

1598
Acoma resistance to Juan de Zaldivar. The Spanish siege of Acoma pueblo in New Mexico ended in subjugation of the pueblos. New Mexico governor Juan de Onate was determined to conquer the pueblos and consolidate his rule of New Mexico. He sent his soldiers under Zaldivar to Acoma to obtain Indian submission to the Spanish crown. An accidental exchange between the soldiers and the Indians set off a siege in which Zaldivar died along with 800 Acoma Indians; 570 were put on trial afterward. Two Hopi visitors had their right hands cut off and were sent home to the Hopi mesas as a lesson of the consequences of resisting the Spanish Crown. Women between the ages of 12

to 25 were indentured to 20 years of servitude at the Spanish capital at San Juan. All males over 14 were mutilated. In the plazas of other pueblos, males over 12 had one foot chopped off. Onate was later tried for excessive cruelty.

V

1 6 0 0 s — E c o l o g i c a l

R e v o l u t i o n s

The myth of "frontier America" was formulated by the historian Frederick Jackson Turner in the late 1800s. His hypothesis, which became a crucial narrative of American history, held that America was a virgin continent in which civilization (the Europeans) encountered savagery (the Indians). This metaphysical encounter took place on "the frontier," a locale that moved from east to west in a line parallel to the Atlantic Coast. According to Turner, it was this frontier experience, not European urban traditions, that shaped America's unique character.

Even a quick look at the pattern of European invasion in the 1600s shows that Turner's frontier theory was a fiction. Europeans invaded from every direction at once. The Spanish came up from the south, conquering Florida and Mexico and then moving into the American Southwest by 1540. They invaded the Pueblo peoples of what is now New Mexico and founded their regional capital in Santa Fe, New Mexico in 1609. The French invaded from the north, moving down from Canada along the St. Lawrence Seaway into Lake Champlain and then down the Mississippi River. The French settlement of Quebec was founded on the site of the old Iroquois village of Stadacona in 1608. France also in 1673 sent Joliet and Marquette down the Mississippi River to establish trading posts and to claim all lands on either side of the river as Louisiana, named for King Louis XIV. (The capital of Louisiana was moved to New Orleans to forestall any English settlement and to prevent the Spanish from advancing from Florida.) In the east, along the Atlantic Coast, the English negotiated with the Powhatans for lands in Virginia in 1607 on the site that became known as Jamestown (after King James I) and with the Wampanoags in Massachusetts in 1621 for the lands that became Plymouth. The Dutch, who were formidable traders and sailers, established themselves in Manhattan in 1626 in the city they called New Amsterdam. They traveled up the Hudson River, named the lands of the Hudson Valley "New Netherlands," and established Fort Orange (named for the Dutch Prince of Orange) at Albany. By the late 1700s the Russians were sailing down coastal Alaska, the Pacific Northwest, and into California.

The practice of drawing up treaties with "sovereign Indian nations" began with the need to substantiate European land claims. The traditional boundaries among Indian nations became the basis for one European power's land claims against another. New Spain, New France, New England, New Netherlands, New Sweden were all based on alliances with the Indian inhabitants, many of whom quickly learned the distinctions among the identities of the "white tribes from across the great lake." The European powers' territories were, in fact, based on the aboriginal land rights of their Indian allies (usually mentioned in European documents as "subjects") but who actually controlled the territory on the ground. The Indians had to choose their European allies carefully. From a European point of view, the 1600s might be characterized by the struggle to convert Indian allies in order to claim their lands. Although the Europeans were impressed with the skills and mastery among the Indians they saw—"ther was never seene among us soe cunninge a way to take fish," Thomas Hariot wrote in 1590 of North Carolina Indians who fished at night with a fire in the bottom of a dugout canoe (in a book published in England as A *briefe and true report of the new found land of Virginia*)—they were the products of medieval beliefs. They saw the people of the New World as savages, without religion or government or culture, even though these savages might know how to produce two agricultural crops a year.

The European invaders varied among themselves as much as the Indian nations did, so that the realities of contact were very different in different places. The only constant seemed to be disease: the Europeans, regardless of nationality, carried diseases against which the Indians had no immunities. Wherever the Europeans— whether Catholic or Protestant—made contact, epidemics of smallpox, measles, typhoid, chicken pox, or scarlet fever, soon followed.

The Indians, however, were quite human and quite humane. Although most traditional accounts of American history begin in 1620 with the landing of the Pilgrims in Plymouth, Massachusetts, historians rarely mention Squanto (Tisquantum), the English-speaking Patuxet Indian who taught the survivors of the first winter how to survive their second. Recruited by Chief Massasoit to help the Pilgrims, Squanto was seen by the English as God's "specialle instrument" to confirm their divine mission. The English subsequently rewrote their own history, crediting their survival not to Massasoit's generosity or Squanto's skill in teaching them how to plant crops and build shelter, but to the power of written documents (the Mayflower Compact), God's will, and their innate European superiority. They mistranslated the French word "*sauvage*," which meant "wild" or "of the wilderness," into "savage" and forgot that "the savages" had instructed them *in their own English language* on how to farm and fish and construct shelter. Like the old Aztec ruler Itzcoatl, who burned all the Mexicas' history books so that the Aztecs would have a new and glorious history linking them to the Toltecs, the English colonists ignored the real cultural exchange that took place, and attributed all their political and social influences back to the glorious days of Greece and Rome. Within a century, cultural propinquity and the relations with the intact Indian nations of the 1600s were forgotten.

America became a "virgin land," the "great green breast" of the New World. In *The Founders of America*, historian Francis Jennings wrote about America's need for a mythology and the mythic quality of Turner's frontier theory as well as about the problems arising from substituting the concept of the frontier for real history: "*Turner, like most English-speaking historians, adopted the point of view of the sixteenth and seventeenth century English invaders. For them, as a wit has observed,*

God was an Englishman. They [the English] held themselves to be possessed of qualities superior to all other peoples, even such as Frenchmen. . . . They conceived the natives of America as natural candidates for subjection. Their object was to 'reduce' the Indians 'to civility' which in plainer terms meant conquering them. Turner adopted this point of view so completely that he waved aside the entire human population of North America by word magic. In his writings the land became simply wilderness, more specifically 'free land,' which a disciple correctly translated into 'land free to be taken.' . . . [The Indians] as wilderness creatures lacked the humanity of persons with civil government who were the only civilized peoples and, by inference, the only truly human persons."

A look at the 1600s reveals that the "American wilderness" was a highly complex ecology of peoples, cultures, wildlife, and trade. The intricate pattern of relationships between all living things and their environments began to undergo fundamental and radical changes

1600s—Ecological
Revolutions

WORLD HISTORY

NATIVE AMERICAN HISTORY

1600

Juan Onate colonized New Mexico for Spain under the *encomienda* system. Pueblo villages and their inhabitants were commended to the care of Spaniards, who "protected" them in exchange for tribute or head tax that Indian men were to pay in labor or products.

1600

Spanish kidnapped Apaches, Navajos, and Utes who lived near Spanish colonies in New Mexico to use as slave labor or household servants. The Spanish governors also sold kidnapped Apaches and Navajos to the silver-mining camps in the south. They used Pueblo warriors on their slave-raiding forays to capture other Indians. Since Spanish law forbade Indians from riding horses, the Pueblo men were recognizable because they were on foot. The Navajos (who called themselves Diné, the People) got their name from the Spanish who called them Apaches de Navajos. Although linguistically connected, the Apaches and Navajos had become distinct groups by the fifteenth century. The source of the resentment between Navajos and Apaches on the one hand and Pueblo peoples on the other stems from the actions of different Pueblo warriors in the service of Spanish governors. Spanish kidnapping, particularly of Navajos, continued until the early 1900s. The U.S. government built on these longstanding hostilities by later using Navajo policemen against the Hopi in the early 1900s.

1601

Elizabethan Poor Law in England. This famous law charged Church parishes with being responsible for the poor. It also regulated vagrancy, apprenticeship, and the definition of paupers. Eventually poor people, charged as felons, were shipped to English colonies as indentured servants or forced laborers.

1602

The Dutch East India Company formed, the first modern public company to sell and trade shares.

1602

Bartolomew Gosnold crossed from England to what is now New England and explored the coast.

1602–1603

Sebastian Vizcaino explored the California coast for the Spanish.

1603

French explorers began active fur trading along the St. Lawrence Seaway in Canada and established an outpost at Tadoussac.

1603

Samuel de Champlain made contact with the Algonquian-speaking and Iroquois tribes, and explored the New England coast as far south as Cape Cod.

1604

A trading agreement entered into between a band of Canadian Micmac and the French formed the basis of French claims to all Canadian provinces controlled by the Micmac. The Micmac (who are called Pasamaquoddy in Maine) controlled what is now Nova Scotia, Prince Edward Island, much of New Brunswick, and the Gaspé Peninsula of Quebec. Led by their chieftain, Membertou, the Micmac established trade with the French at Port Royal, a site on the Bay of Fundy. Membertou eventually converted to Christianity and the Micmac became "allies" of the French, thus substantiating France's claims to their lands.

1606

The English king, James I, chartered the London Virginia Company, a trading corporation with the economic mission of settling a permanent colony in what is now Virginia, which would send agricultural and other products back to England. The colony, called Jamestown, was the first permanent English settlement in North America.

1606

Warfare broke out between the Spanish and the Indians in New Mexico involving the Navajo, Jemez, and other Pueblo peoples. The Indians captured herds of Spanish horses and began trading them.

1607

Chief Wahunsonacock and Indians of the Powhatan confederacy assisted the English in Jamestown, Virginia. The Powhatan Indians were an Algonquian-speaking confederacy of tribes, which included the Pamunkey Indians. Their territory extended from what is now Washington, D.C., to North Carolina, the area designated as Virginia by England. Their paramount chief was Wahunsonacock, referred to as Powhatan by the English. He presided over 30 tribes extending from the Potomac River in Maryland to Albemarle Sound in South Carolina. He lived upriver near Richmond and received John Smith, the Jamestown governor, with great courtesy. In the first winter the chief did not let his uninvited guests die from starvation. The aged (he was over 70) chief's 10-year-old daughter, Pocahontas, was among those who took the starving settlers gifts of corn, fish, and wild game. The gifts were misunderstood and unappreciated by their English guests, who believed the natives were paying tribute to their European superiority. George Percy, one of the settlers, recorded that when daily English rations were reduced to a can of barley "sodden in water" for five men, they were saved by the food supplied by the Indians. He mistakenly thanked God who "put the terror in the sauvages' hearts" so that they "relieve us with victuals, as bread, corn, fish, and flesh in great plenty." The settlers were also introduced to Indian tobacco, the crop that would eventually make the colony rich.

1608

British ships returning to Jamestown colony with supplies caught on fire. Everything was lost.

1608

Samuel de Champlain founded the settlement of Quebec for France.

1608

John Smith asked Powhatan for his submission to the English Crown and to provide the settlers with an annual tribute of corn. Powhatan and his chiefs had already learned a few things about European kings, slave catchers, and traders. He quickly realized that although the English were a valuable source of weapons, metal for knives, and other trade goods, they were not going to be easy neighbors. When John Smith and his men took corn from villages along the river by force, Powhatan ordered him captured and brought to him. The popular, but unverified, story of John Smith being saved from death by the 12-year-old princess Pocahontas surfaced in John Smith's old age as he was writing his memoirs, at which time he gave several accounts of being saved from death by Indian maidens. Pocahontas supposedly saved him by declaring the right of a chief's offspring to a prisoner's labor in lieu of his death. (See "Powhatan of Virginia" on page 119.)

1608

The Iroquois nation welcomed Champlain and agreed to a French trading post on the site of the former Iroquois village of Stadacona. The site would be known to the French as Quebec. The Iroquois village of Hochelaga would later become the site of Montreal. Champlain expanded trading relations with different Algonquian-speaking tribes, making agreements to buy furs in exchange for metals, knives, and other European trade goods. From the beginning the French pattern differed significantly from the English in that it was based on trading posts and allied Christian missions attached to existing Indian villages rather than colonies of permanent settlers. It was why many of the Indian villages allied themselves with France in the subsequent wars between England and France in the New World.

1609

Spain declared Santa Fe the new capital of the province of New Mexico.

1609

In Italy Galileo perfected an astronomical telescope, invented earlier in the Netherlands. He revealed the results of his first telescopic observations of celestial phenomena which included the finding that the moon shines from reflected light.

1609

Full-scale war broke out between the Powhatan and the English in Virginia. John Smith was back in England because of an accidental injury. More settlers had arrived, but they tended to be sons of English gentry, unused to hard labor. They wanted the lands that the Indians had already cleared for themselves. They drove the Powhatan off their fields, burned their villages, and captured them as slaves. The Powhatan retaliated. Chief Powhatan tried to preserve the peace, but he failed.

1609

Champlain aided the Algonquians and the Montagnais of Canada in their war against the Mohawks of what is now upper New York State and Vermont. He gave them guns, powder, and supplies. This changed Indian patterns of warfare and established the superiority of European guns.

1609

Henry Hudson, sailing for the Netherlands, claimed what is now New York for the Netherlands, and opened the fur trade for the Dutch. He traded furs for alcohol. The Manhattan, the Hackensack, the Munsee, Mohican, and Lenape (Delaware) Indian nations living along the Hudson River continued to trade furs for European goods.

1609

The Spanish Crown gave land grants around Santa Fe and encouraged the establishment of Catholic missions in the pueblos. Ongoing wars between the Spanish, the Pueblo peoples, and the Navajo continued. The Spanish encouraged active slave trade, particularly in Navajo women and children. The practice continued until the early 1900s.

1609

A Huron delegation visited Champlain in Quebec City in order to buy guns. The St. Lawrence Iroquois encountered by Jacques Cartier had disappeared from the region and had been replaced by the Huron. The Huron wanted weapons from Champlain in exchange for furs, in order to mount a war against the Lake Champlain Iroquois. Champlain recognized ·

the value of a strong French-allied Huron nation against the English-allied Iroquois. He not only sold them muskets, but joined them in the successful raid. (He joined other raids in 1610 and 1615 and skillfully played one Huron band off against another to enlarge French control.) As a result of the warfare and Champlain's sale of guns to the Huron, the tribes of the Iroquois confederacy stayed south of the St. Lawrence River basin.

1610

The English king appointed Lord de la Warr (Lord Delaware, also called Sir Thomas West) the new governor of Jamestown, Virginia.

1610

Lord Delaware stayed in Jamestown less than a year but named the body of water to the north Delaware Bay and called the Indians living in that area, the Lenape, the Delaware Indians.

1611

Completion of the translation of the King James version of the Bible in England. It had been the full-time occupation of 47 scholars since King James I authorized it in 1604. The Protestant version of the Bible, it was officially adopted by the Church of England.

1612

The Iroquois expanded their trade with Dutch traders on the Hudson River. They traded furs and food for metal tools, knives, and guns for hunting, changing the traditional economy of the region. Iroquois men began to hunt full-time for fur-bearing animals.

1612

The Powhatan taught the English to cultivate tobacco, which they planted as an export crop.

POWHATAN OF VIRGINIA

The language-family of tribes that inhabited the eastern seaboard from Canada to Georgia were known as Algonquians. In the late 1500s one of their chiefs, Wahunsonacock, in what is now Virginia, brought under his control a population of some 13,000 people in 30 tribes and 200 villages in an area that extended from the Potomac in Maryland to what are now the cities of Richmond and Fredericksburg, Virginia. His headquarters were at Powhatan at the falls of the James River (present site of Richmond). "Powhatan" means "falls of the river." The alliance of tribes thus became known as the Powhatan confederacy, and Wahunsonacock, as paramount chief, became known to the English as "the Powhatan," or simply "Powhatan."

In 1607 English ships arrived and unloaded 105 English colonists at the mouth of the James River, not simply for trade, but to establish a permanent colony. They called their settlement Jamestown and soon their governor, Captain John Smith, went upriver to meet with Powhatan and other leaders of the confederacy. Smith wanted corn and land.

On January 12, 1608, Smith's boat reached the small village of Werawocomoco, his men having to pull the barge through waist-deep water of the frozen river. The Indians put them up and fed them bread, turkey, venison. They then marched by foot to Powhatan's village, a large compound of longhouses enclosed by a log palisade, housing over a thousand people. Powhatan, who received him in his longhouse, which was over a hundred feet long, wore a headdress of feathers, many necklaces of shells, and a robe decorated with beaded shell designs of a man and white-tailed deer. (The famous "Powhatan's robe" has survived.) Two of Smith's company, with the aid of interpreters who had learned the language from previous trading encounters, recorded the meeting.

Powhatan told Smith he did not have corn to give him and that he doubted the Englishman's purpose: "Yet some doubt I have of your coming hither, that makes me not so kindly seek to relieve you as I would. For many do inform me your coming is not for trade, but to invade my people and possess my country, who do not dare come to bring you corn, seeing you thus armed with your men. To cheer us of this fear, leave aboard your weapons. For here they are needless, we being all friends and forever Powhatans."

But Captain Smith refused to give up his weapons and eventually negotiated 10 "measures of corn" and a piece of land in exchange for a copper kettle. Half of the colonists died in the first year. In a pattern that would be repeated in Plymouth, the Powhatan saved them with donations of food and taught them to fertilize their fields with seaweed; to plant corn, beans, pumpkins, squash; to bake clams and beans and corn in a hole in the ground. For the first time, they smoked a strange native leaf called tobacco and discovered the export crop that would eventually make the colony rich. In exchange the colonists wanted more and more of the Indians' land.

In 1608 John Smith was captured in battle after settlers had a series of skirmishes with neighboring tribes. No one knows the truth of the well-known story of Smith being saved from death by one of Wahunsonacock's daughters, Pocahontas. Smith's first writings of his experiences in Virginia made no mention of having been threatened by Powhatan or saved by the daughter. Not until 16 years later when he was writing his memoirs did he tell the story for the first time. Pocahontas died in England before she could tell her version.

As the London stock company financing the colony made profit from tobacco, more and more colonists came, and instead of trading for new land or clearing the forest themselves, they drove the Powhatans off their fields, burned their villages, and tried to capture the Indians as slaves. Fighting intensified and the Indians came close to annihilating the British. In 1613 the English in desperation captured Pocahontas and offered to ransom her for all the English prisoners held by the Powhatans. Although the Indians released their prisoners, the English continued to hold Pocahontas. They claimed she did not want to leave. While a captive she was baptized a Christian, instructed in English, and although already married, was supposedly in love with one of her English captors and teachers, John Rolfe.

In 1614, weary of the fighting and wanting to see his daughter again, Wahunsonacock finally agreed to peace terms. When he was told of the proposed marriage of Pocahontas and John Rolfe, which would seal the peace, he is supposed to have asked her: "Is this what you wish? To marry a coat-wearing man? One who is stealing our land to plant tobacco on it? Are you sure you are not being tricked?"

Two years later John Rolfe and Pocahontas went to England, accompanied by a group of Powhatans which included Tomocomo, a trusted aide to Chief Powhatan. The old chief had instructed him to count the people in England. In London Pocahontas was a sensation, presented at court as Lady Rebecca, and had her portrait painted in English finery. But on her way back to Jamestown in 1617 she became ill and died, and was buried in an unmarked grave in Graveshead, England, on the river Thames. Years later her son, Thomas Rolfe, returned to Virginia, became a wealthy tobacco planter, and founded one of Virginia's most "aristocratic" families.

Powhatan died the following year, 1618, after hearing Tomocomo's report of the number of people in England: "Count the stars in the sky, the leaves on the trees, and the sand upon the seashore . . ." Powhatan's death initiated two decades of warfare between the Powhatans and the colonists, which ended in 1644 with the destruction of the Powhatan confederacy.

1613

Pocahontas kidnapped by the English. In four years of intermittent fighting the Powhatan almost, but not quite, annihilated the English. Tobacco had become so popular in London that more settlers came and claimed larger tracts of Indian lands for tobacco fields. Each new settler was given 3 acres. Fighting was constant, and the war between the Jamestown settlers and the Powhatan Indians escalated. Both sides held prisoners. In retaliation for the killing of white colonists, the English soldiers kidnapped Pocahontas, the daughter of the chief. The English offered to return her in exchange for *all* the English prisoners held by the Powhatan. The chief agreed. Although the Indians released their captives, the English did not release Pocahontas, claiming that she did not want to leave. During her captivity, she had converted to Christianity, was baptized by a minister of the Church of England, and took the name Rebecca. Although she was already married to a Powhatan husband, she announced she would marry one of her English captors and teachers, widower John Rolfe. (See "Powhatan of Virginia" on page 119.)

1613
French and the Micmac took control of Newfoundland. French armed the Micmacs against the Beothuk and offered them bounties for Beothuk scalps. In Newfoundland the Beothuk Indians had killed 37 French fishermen after a Frenchman shot one of their tribesmen. The Beothuk population was soon extinct and the French and the Micmacs controlled Newfoundland.

1614
In the Netherlands the Dutch king chartered the United New Netherlands Trading Company to colonize New York, and authorized a year-round trading post on the upper Hudson River at what would later be Fort Orange (Albany). The Dutch began developing their fur trade in North America.

1614
Wahunsonacock (Powhatan) finally agreed to the marriage of his daughter Pocahontas to John Rolfe and arranged peace terms with the Jamestown settlers. On April 5, 1614, Pocahontas married John Rolfe. Powhatan did not attend the wedding, although his brother did.

1614
John Smith took an exploratory voyage along the northern Atlantic Coast and used, for the first time, the term

"New England," reporting: *"The Countrie of the Massachusets is the Paradise of all those parts: for, heere are many Iles all planted with corne; groves, mulberries, salvage (sic) gardens, and good harbors. . . . The Sea Coast as you passe, shewes you all along large corne fields, and great troupes of well proportioned people."*

1614

Tisquantum (also called Squanto), a Patuxet, was one of 24 New England coastal Indians kidnapped by English sea captain Thomas Hunt and sold in the slave market of Malaga, Spain. Ransomed by monks, he worked in a monastery for three years and then escaped to England, where he worked for a wealthy merchant, John Slaney. Slaney instructed him in English, which he learned fluently, and in 1619 arranged for his return to North America via Newfoundland fishermen.

1615

France sent the first Jesuit missionaries to New France.

1615

Pocahontas, now called Rebecca Rolfe, gave birth to an infant son, Thomas.

1615

The Huron villagers of Huronia welcomed Samuel de Champlain, leader of New France, as their guest. The Huron numbered some 30,000 people living in villages of up to 3,500 people in the Lake Huron region, called Huronia, near Lake Simcoe. They lived in longhouses and had extensive agriculture, which included fields of corn, beans, squash, sunflowers, and some tobacco. The Huron chiefs had reached a satisfactory agreement with Champlain about trading relations, particularly fur, and the European trade goods he would supply in return. The Huron, middlemen in the fur trade, were renowned for their extensive trade networks, which went as far west as Minnesota and intersected larger networks in the Mississippi Valley as far south as the Gulf states, lands which the French eventually claimed as part of their empire. In the alliance with Champlain these trading networks were able to circulate manufactured goods, metal knives, cloth, guns, and other items as far north as the Cree in James Bay and as far west as the Sioux in Minnesota. Champlain joined the Huron on a raid against the Onondaga Iroquois in New York State.

1615–1649
The French-Huron trading empire at its height. The Huron traders profited by buying the furs from many different bands and taking them to the French trading centers in Quebec City, Trois-Rivières, or Montreal. In return the Huron had to agree to accept French Catholic missionaries in their villages. They also had to prevent the aggressive tribes of the Five Nations of the Iroquois confederacy from gaining trade access to the rich hunting lands of the western interior.

1616
John Rolfe and Pocahontas/Lady Rebecca visited England. Pocahontas, "the right-thinking savage," was presented to the king of England, shown off in the best circles, and had her portrait painted in the style of an English lady. The purpose of the trip was to build economic and political support for the Jamestown colony. Rolfe presented his wife, "the Powhatan princess," to English clergy, royalty, and merchants.

1616–1619
A smallpox epidemic ravaged coastal New England Indians from Massachusetts to Maine, killing off entire tribes. Squanto returned from Europe. The disease was believed to have been spread by European fishermen who had established temporary stations on the coast to process their catches. The Native peoples had no immunities and no experience in dealing with the disease. Many who might have recovered

1616
British East India Company began trading in Persia (Iran). Commercial relations began when a representative of the English Muscovy Company reached Persia overland from Russia.

1618–1648
The Thirty Years' War in Europe. Largely a generalized conflict of Catholic Europe against Protestant Europe, it led ultimately to the end of the Hapsburg domination, the crippling of the Holy Roman Empire, the devastation of Germany, and the emergence of France as the leading power in Europe.

1619
The first African slaves sent to Jamestown and the Virginia colony.

died of starvation or dehydration because no one knew how to nurse them through the illness.

1617
Pocahontas died in England. On her way to take the boat back to Virginia she developed a disease (possibly pneumonia or smallpox) and died quickly. She was 22. Pocahontas's infant son, Thomas Rolfe, remained in England for 19 years and then returned to Virginia, where he became a wealthy tobacco plantation owner.

1618
Powhatan died. The First Powhatan War against the English. Powhatan's brother, Opechancanough, who was much more militant against the English, assumed leadership of the Powhatan tribal confederation. His accession marked the beginning of 25 years of increasing hostilities between the Powhatan and the English settlers. The new Jamestown governor assigned 50 acres of land to every person who attracted one more settler to the colony, ignoring that these were lands which belonged to the Powhatan.

1619
The English colonists in Jamestown founded a school for Indian children in order to convert them to Christianity. Like the Spanish, the English wanted the Indians to declare submission to the Crown and the Church of England and to work for free. By 1620 there were over 1,000 English colonists in Jamestown who asserted their right to

the Powhatan lands. The problem of labor was solved by importing African slaves.

1619

Squanto returned to the site of his own village of Patuxet to find it deserted. He traveled to a neighboring Wampanoag village, met with Chief Massasoit, and joined a village that had survived the smallpox epidemic. The Wampanoags had also been greatly weakened by the epidemic, although their powerful neighbors, the Narragansetts, had been spared. Squanto met with the Wampanoag *sachem*, or leader, Massasoit, who was interested to hear about what Squanto had seen in England, the source of all the traders and fishermen who had been landing on their shores. (A Plymouth settler, Edward Winslow, visited the interior in 1621 and described what Squanto might have seen: *"the late great mortalitie which fell in al these parts aboute three years before the coming of the English, wherin thousands of them dyed; they not being able to burie one another, ther sculs and bones were found in many places lying still above the ground, where their houses and dwellings had been; a very sad spectackle to behould."*)

1620

A group of English religious separatists living in Leiden, Holland, decided to go to the New World to start a new religious community. Unlike the Jamestown colonists, whose purpose was economic, the Leiden colonists wanted to create a Christian community. Known as Pilgrims, they obtained a land patent from the London Company and set out for what should have been northern Virginia. They began in

1620–1621

"Welcome Englishmen" were the first words the Pilgrims heard when their first Indian greeted them after they arrived at Plymouth harbor. On December 21, 1620, a party from the *Mayflower*, which had been blown off course, went ashore, marched inland, and discovered lands that had been cleared and planted. Finding a freshwater brook on the southern shore of the harbor, they staked off lots for every member of the colony and then

Rotterdam, changed boats in Plymouth, England, and landed in Massachusetts.

1620-1639

Struggle for the Valtelline Pass in the Alps, the most important communications link between the Hapsburg possessions in Italy and Austria. Spain, Austria, and the Swiss Confederation fought for 20 years over this pass as part of the Thirty Years' War. Spain eventually won.

mounted a cannon. Their first Indian visitor was Samoset, an Abenaki, who spoke a little English. By spring of 1621, 50 of the 102 colonists had died from scurvy, pneumonia, or tuberculosis.

MASSASOIT

The land that would become known as Massachusetts was home to the Massachusett, the Pawtucket, the Nipmuck, and the Wampanoag Indians. Chief among the Wampanoag was the sachem Massasoit, also known as Usamquin or Yellow Feather. He ruled over eight large villages and 30 lesser villages. On December 21, 1620, Massasoit heard of a "house floating on water" that had come into the harbor the Patuxet called "Little Bay." One hundred and two people got out of the floating house (the Mayflower), mounted a cannon, and staked out lots at the mouth of a freshwater brook. Unused to the harsh cold of a Massachusetts winter, and with food supplies running low, many of them soon became sick, died, and were buried in the woods.

Massasoit then sent an Abenaki Indian from Maine who spoke some English and had spent time trading with the English fishermen and traders. "Welcome Englishmen," Samoset said when he walked into their little settlement, a greeting that shocked the Pilgrims. Massasoit then sent Squanto, a bilingual Patuxet Indian, whose English was fluent. Squanto had spent time in England (the result of kidnapping and slavery) and had told Massasoit about the size of London and the country the English came from. Squanto's people, the Patuxet, had been completely wiped out in the recent epidemic that had swept the coastal Indians of New England.

By spring 50 of the colonists had died, including their governor. Massasoit took pity on them. He told Squanto to teach them how to plant corn—20 acres, enough to feed the survivors—and how to build shelter. Squanto acted as their teacher, interpreter, and negotiator. He showed them how to put traps in the stream to catch fish and how to build adequate shelter for the winter. By summer none of the Pilgrims' barley or peas had come up; but all of the corn and squash and pumpkins they had been directed to plant by Squanto had yielded a rich harvest.

In 1621 Massasoit met with his English visitors, accompanied by 60 warriors, to negotiate a treaty. They signed a mutual peace agreement whereby each pledged to help the other if they were attacked by a third party. It is likely that the "third party" was the Narragansetts of what is now Rhode Island, who were encroaching on Wampanoag lands. He should have feared his new allies. The Peace Treaty of 1621 had a lasting influence on subsequent relations between the colonists and the

Wampanoag. It established legal practices and attitudes which would be fleshed out by legislation and court action. The treaty assured Indians that they could gain equal justice, but that justice would be English in form, substance, and execution. Native custom and law governing land use ceased to be valid.

Massasoit, despite great provocation, was determined to preserve the peace. He sent his two sons, Wamsutta and Metacomet, to the colonists' school so they would know how to deal with the English. The colonists named Wamsutta "Alexander" and Metacomet "Philip." Metacomet later became famous as King Philip. It was largely because of Massasoit's good offices that the Pilgrims wrote back to England of the peace and safety with which they walked in the Massachusetts woods. Consequently, in the next two decades 20,000 English men and women came to see for themselves.

John Winthrop, who came in 1630, expressed the colony's attitude toward the lands belonging to native inhabitants: "That which lies comon & hath never been replenished or subdued, is free to any that possesse & improve it . . . As for the Natives in New England, they enclose noe land, neither have any setled habytation, nor any tame Cattle to improve the Land by, & soe have noe other but a naturall Right to those Countries. Soe as if we leave them sufficient for their use wee may lawfully take the rest, there being more than enought for them & us."

When Massasoit died in 1661 his son Wamsutta/Alexander was named chief. The Plymouth militia captured Wamsutta and took him to Plymouth under guard to declare loyalty to the Crown of England and the government of New Plymouth. Alexander was told he was to pay a hundred pounds a year and five wolves' heads in tribute. After being released, he immediately fell sick and died on the way home. The Indians believed he had been poisoned. Metacomet/Philip took over and to him fell the burden of the new colonial order. In the 40 years from the day that Massasoit had sent Squanto to teach the white settlers how to survive their first winter, the settlers had come to outnumber the Wampanoag. Between 1630 and 1643 over 20,000 English arrived in New England. By 1660 another 15,000 had come. Massasoit had originally hoped to use the English as allies against the Narragansetts, but the English had become his people's greatest enemy. His son Metacomet/Philip was determined to fight the English.

1621

The Dutch chartered the Dutch West India Company and gave it a monopoly of trade in Africa and America.

1621

Massasoit greeted the Pilgrims and negotiated a peace agreement, using Squanto as his translator. The Wampanoag chief met with the English visitors. Massasoit (also called Usamquin or Yellow Feather) was the paramount chief of the tribes in the region. He ruled over eight large villages and thirty smaller ones. Massasoit arrived at the first meeting with 60 warriors whose faces were painted black, red, yellow, or white. His own face was painted "mulberry." Governor John Carver presented the chief with a pair of knives, a copper chain, bisquits and a "pot of strong water." With Squanto as interpreter the governor and Massasoït pledged themselves not to "doe hurte" to one another. The peace treaty between the English and the Wampanoag pledged that each side agreed to help the other in the event of an attack by a third party.

At Massasoit's urging, Squanto took on the role of diplomat, translator, and instructor to the English Pilgrims. The Pilgrims saw Squanto as *a speciall instrumente sent of God for their good beyond their expectation.*

In October of 1621 Massasoit invited the Pilgrims to join in the Wampanoag's annual harvest ceremony, which became the holiday of Thanksgiving. (Europeans in America would celebrate Thanksgiving in October until 1863, when President Lincoln moved it to November.)

1621–1660
More than 40,000 English colonists arrived in Massachusetts Bay. Land conflicts escalated. Settlers came from England at the rate of a thousand a year, encouraged by reports of the friendly relations the Pilgrims had with Massasoit. The Crown chartered the Massachusetts Bay Colony. Massasoit "sold" a large tract of land to the new settlers and new settlements sprang up in Lynn, Watertown, Salem, Roxbury, Boston. However, since the concept of private property and exclusive use was unknown to the Indians, trouble began when Wampanoags continued to hunt and fish on land they had "sold." *"Did we not buy this [land],"* asked Captain Miles Standish about a tract he had pur-

chased near Bridgewater, *"for seven coats, eight hoes, nine hatchets, ten yards of cotton cloth, twenty knives, and four moose skins? Now it is ours. No one has the right to trespass upon our property."* Massasoit responded: *"What is this you call property? [The Earth] belongs to everybody and is for the use of all. How then can one man say it belongs to him only?"* Indians understood land payment as a gift or as a rental fee for land use, but could not conceive of private land ownership. The concept of individual transferrable title to land was the prime source of misunderstanding between whites and Indians. The court in Plymouth then translated the debate into legal terms and adopted the following resolution: *"Voted, that the Earth is the Lord's and the fulness thereof; Voted, that the Earth is given to the Saints; Voted, that we are the Saints."*

1621

Spanish governor gave ranchers in New Mexico permission to employ Pueblo men on horseback. The *encomienda* system brought new Spanish settlers into bitter conflict with the Church over control of Indian labor. When Pueblo men on horseback escaped, horses escaped with them. The Apaches stole horses from the Pueblos and learned to fight on horseback. As the use of horses spread, the Apaches and Navajos became raiders against Spanish settlements and Pueblo towns.

1622

Powhatan uprising against the Jamestown colony. Jamestown burned. In England it was called the First Virginia War. Opechancanough and his chiefs decided it was time to move against the land-hungry colonists. In the ensuing uprising more than 350 English colonists were killed, more than one-third of the colony, others were pushed off their lands, and Jamestown burned to the ground. The English Crown, when it heard the news, took direct control of Jamestown, guaranteeing aid and protection to settlers. The royal British Virginia Company ordered the extermination of all the Powhatans and forbade the making of peace on any terms. The Powhatan uprisings lasted for 10 years with many deaths among the Indians, colonists, soldiers, and allied tribes. The Chickaminy nation, an ally of the Powhatan, was virtually wiped out by English soldiers. John Smith, back in England, viewing the situation strategically, observed correctly that the war *"will be good for the Plantation, because we have just cause to destroy them by all means possible."* Another colonist reflected: *"[We are] now set at liberty by the treacherous violence of Sauvages ... [We can] enjoy their cultivated places ... and [possess] the fruits of others' labours. Now their cleared grounds in all their villages (which are situated in the fruitfullest places of the land) shall be inhabited by us, whereas heretofore the grubbing of woods was the greatest labour."* ("Grubbing" was the clearing of woods for farmland.) Although the Powhatans fought strategically and with discipline, disease and demographics were against them.

1623
English settlements established at Dover and Portsmouth, New Hampshire, and at Casco Bay and Saco Bay, Maine. Cape Ann (Gloucester, Massachusetts) settled. The new settlements

were organized under the charter of the Council of New England.

1623
The infamous English-Powhatan peace conference. The English invited the Powhatan leaders to a peace conference (which Opechancanough did not attend). At the end they served glasses of wine, which were poisoned, and proposed a toast to "eternal friendship." The Indians drank. Those who didn't die immediately were shot by English soldiers. The war went on for another nine years, with the Powhatan refusing to attend another negotiation. When peace came in 1632 it was accompanied by a massive colonial expansion that the Indians couldn't stop. The Powhatans were squeezed off their rich lands into small parts of their former homeland. When John Smith first arrived, there had been about 30,000 Powhatan and allied Indians in the area. By 1669 only 2,000 remained—decimated by warfare, disease, and migration.

1624
Cardinal Richelieu made chief minister to Louis XIII of France. He promoted concentration of power in the monarchy, supported France's expansionist aims in America, and helped to make France the dominant power in Europe. France moved to take over Spanish settlements in the Caribbean. Guadeloupe, Martinique, Tortuga, St. Martins, St. Barthélemy, St. Croix, St. Lucia, and Grenada were all occupied by French settlers.

1624
Following the First Virginia War (Powhatan Uprising), James I of En-

1624
Dutch West India Company built Fort Orange. The company had been established by the Dutch in 1621 to develop trade routes and the fur trade in the New World. They founded Fort Orange at what today is Albany, and claimed much of New York State as New Netherlands. The hostilities that subsequently developed between the Huron and the Iroquois were largely surrogate wars between France and the Netherlands.

gland revoked the charter of the London Virginia Company and made it a royal company with a governor appointed by the Crown.

1626

Peter Minuit, governor of New Netherlands, traded 60 Dutch guilders worth of goods (supposedly worth $24) to the Shinnecock Indians for the island of Manhattan and named it New Amsterdam. He later had to buy it again from the Reckgawawanc, another Manhattan band, which claimed hunting rights to the island. The Dutch West India Company also established settlements that year in Connecticut, New Jersey, Delaware, and Pennsylvania.

1627

Carib slaves introduced into Virginia. The English brought Carib Indians from the West Indies to Jamestown to use as substitute slave labor for the disappearing Powhatan. Many of the Carib Indians escaped and took refuge in the Powhatan villages.

1627

Company of New France, also known as the Company of the Hundred Associates, chartered by French Crown. Organized by Richelieu, it was granted all lands between Florida and the Arctic Circle and given a monopoly in all trade except for cod and whaling. Its mission was to expand the fur trade with Indians.

1628

England sent John Endecott and 50 colonists to settle in Salem, Massachusetts. The Council of New England changed its name to the Massachusetts Bay Company.

1629–1633

Spanish soldiers accompanied missionaries to Acoma, Hopi, and Zuni pueblos. The western Pueblos were forced to accept Spanish missionaries and missions in which Indian labor was used to support the mission. The Spanish Crown in concert with the Church used religious missions as a means by which a few priests could control much larger populations. Activist priests used Indian labor to build Catholic churches in the Indian pueblos, hauling building supplies from more than a hundred miles away, and forced the Indians to be laborers and agricultural workers to sustain the life of the mission. After 20 years in the eastern pueblos of the Rio Grande, the Spanish turned west to the Zuni and to the pueblos in Hopi country. Although the missionaries were always accompanied by military guards, the Zuni religious leaders were so opposed to the Catholic priests and their suppression of Zuni religion that they began to organize a military opposition.

1630

Massachusetts Bay Colony founded, with 1,000 colonists arriving in 17 ships from England. Ten years after the Pilgrims had arrived in Plymouth, the Puritans, led by John Winthrop, received a charter from the Crown to settle the area known as Massachusetts Bay. Believing that it was their mission from God to found a perfect Christian society, a "City on the Hill," they formed a covenant among themselves to live a perfect Christian life. The colony functioned as a theocracy. One of the most powerful men of the colony was minister Cotton Mather. His view of the native inhabitants, which prevailed, was that they were the "accursed seed of Canaan" sent by Satan. He believed that the epidemic diseases which ravaged the Indians were God's way of killing Satan's children and clearing the land for His true children, the English.

1630–1642
The Great Migration from England to Massachusetts. Over 16,000 English settlers left England for the Bay Colony because of discontent with the Anglican church or government of Charles I.

1631
James Bay Region explored by the English. James Bay, a southern inlet of Hudson Bay and home of the Cree and Inuit, was explored by Thomas James and Luke Fox of England.

1632
Publication of chronicles of Bernal Diaz del Castillo in Spain. *The True Story of the Conquest of New Spain* was the first published account of the conquest of the Aztecs by one of Cortés's soldiers. Diaz del Castillo was a conquistador who went to Cuba in 1517 and participated in two preliminary explorations of the Mexican coast before joining Cortés's expedition in 1519. He survived the first invasion of Moctezuma's city, Tenochtitlán, and participated in the subsequent buildup of a second army and Cortés's triumph. He retired to an *encomienda* in Guatemala and wrote his vivid memoirs in his seventies. They were not published until more than 50 years after his death.

1632
Galileo published his *Dialogue Concerning Two World Systems*, openly supporting the theory of Copernicus

1632
Truce in Virginia. Negotiations with the Pamunkey and Chickahominy Indians in central Virginia brought a brief peace. Despite the treaties, English settlers continued to encroach on Indian lands and used Indian slaves on their tobacco plantations. Resistance continued among the Powhatan.

that the earth and other planets rotated around the sun. It put him in opposition to the Church doctrine that the sun rotated around the earth.

1633

The Inquisition arrested Galileo for his heliocentric theory, which contradicted papal doctrine that the sun revolved around the earth. Galileo refused to recant. He was sentenced to house arrest, where he remained until his death in 1642. It wasn't until 1992 that the Vatican acknowledged its mistake.

1634

Maryland founded. The colony was a plantation grant to George Calvert, later Lord Baltimore, in 1632. The British Crown had granted Calvert land in Newfoundland which he did not like. He received instead the colony of Maryland. Calvert was given the right to collect taxes, make land

1633

Zuni revolt against the Spanish. The Zuni revolt had been four years in the making. Zuni warriors killed all the Spanish soldiers and two of the four Catholic missionaries. In the face of Spanish reprisals, the Zuni retreated to the top of Corn Mesa, where some stayed as long as 10 years.

1633–1635

Smallpox and other epidemics spread throughout the colonies of New France, New England, and New Netherlands. Over 10,000 Huron died. Some French Jesuit missionaries told the Huron that if they were baptized as Catholics they would be spared: if they weren't, they would come down with disease. Indian oral histories hold that the missionaries also gave the unbaptized Huron blankets that came from smallpox victims, to ensure that their predictions came true.

1633

Massachusetts Colony established a policy of a centralized government to deal with Indian issues.

grants, create manors, appoint ministers, and found churches. Calvert, a Catholic, died before he could travel to his plantation and his sons sent two ships with 20 gentlemen (Catholics) and 200 laborers (Protestants) to found the first settlement at St. Mary's.

1634
French explorers reached Michigan.

1635
The beginning of the so-called Beaver Wars between the Huron and the Iroquois. Fur—beaver, ermine, mink, fox—became one of the main items on the Huron traders' intertribal circuit. As middlemen, the Huron bought furs from many allied tribes and sold them to the French, who seemed to have a limitless demand for fur. (Beaver was used to make hats in Europe and was in great demand.) The French control of the Huron trading network became a great annoyance to the Dutch at Fort Orange, who were effectively excluded from the fur trade.

The Dutch enlisted members of the Iroquois confederacy—whose lands already had been hunted out of fur-bearing animals—to gain access to the rich fur trade of the interior. The Iroquois bands were to fight the Huron and undercut the French. The Mohawk (Iroquois), supplied with guns and ammunition by the Dutch, enlisted the Seneca as allies, and planned a great raid on Huronia. These raids became known as the Beaver Wars.

1636
Harvard College founded to train ministers. Increase Mather was its first president.

1636
Roger Williams, minister at Salem, founded Rhode Island because of the Massachusetts Bay Colony's treament of Indians. He had publicly said that

the colony had illegally expropriated tribal lands because it had no legal charter. He was expelled from Salem for opposing theocracy. Urging a humane policy toward the Narragansett Indians in Rhode Island, he insisted that settlers buy land from Indians. In Providence he organized a government in which Church and State were separate.

1636-1637

Pequot War under Sassacus against New England colonists. Massachusetts and Connecticut went to war against the Pequots. The two most powerful Native peoples in southern New England were the Pequots of the Connecticut Valley and the Narragansetts of Rhode Island, traditionally enemies. Both Massachusetts and Connecticut colonists wanted Pequot lands, which were strategically important because they controlled access to the Connecticut River and the rich Connecticut Valley. In 1634 Indians of unknown tribal affiliation killed slave hunter John Stone of Massachusetts and eight of his companions hunting for Indian slaves. The Puritans of Massachusetts Bay used Stone's death as an excuse to claim jurisdiction over the Pequots and their lands. The Pequots attacked settlers in Connecticut who also had designs on Pequot lands. The governor of Massachusetts Bay Colony organized a military force to punish the Indians. On May 26, 1637, 90 white men under Captain John Mason with 200 Mohegan and Narragansett allies launched a surprise attack and set fire to the Pequot fort at the mouth of the Mystic River, killing over 700 men, women, and children. Puritan minister Cotton Mather wrote: It was a terrible sight *"to see them thus frying in ye fyer . . . and horrible was ye stinck and sente thereof; but ye victory seemed a sweete sacrifice, and they gave prayse thereof to God."* Connecticut obtained legal grounds for claiming "rights of conquest" to Pequot lands and surviving persons. (In the 1990s Pequot descendants, whose reservation is near Norwich, Connecticut, run one of the largest and most profitable gambling casinos in the country at Ledyard.)

1636–1640
The Iroquois and Huron Wars. The Beaver Wars developed into full-fledged war between the Iroquois and Huron. Fueled by the Dutch and French, a state of perpetual war persisted among the two most powerful Indian nations in the St. Lawrence region. In 1639 a smallpox epidemic reduced the population of Huronia from 20,000 to 10,000, drastically affecting their morale and fighting capabilities. The epidemic also affected other Algonquian-speaking nations. The Iroquois invaded Huronia.

1637
In Africa the Dutch took Elmina from Portugal and built many forts on the West African Gold Coast.

1637
The Ute of the Great Basin acquired the horse. In the lands of Utah and Colorado the Spaniards of New Mexico sent slaving parties into Ute country to raid villages and capture slaves to take back to Spanish settlements in New Mexico. In the process, many of the kidnapped Ute escaped, taking with them Spanish horses. Their possession of horses subsequently made the Ute one of the most powerful nations of the Great Basin. In time, use of the the horse would spread throughout the Great Basin and change the culture of the Plains.

NATIVE AMERICAN HISTORY / 1640

1638

New Sweden founded along the Delaware Bay. Sweden claimed land in what is now Delaware and maintained a trading post there until 1655.

1638

Beginning of Great Peace in Japan (1638–1864). Under the military shoguns the capital was moved from Kyoto to Edo (Tokyo). Power of the Buddhist establishment was curbed by the emergence of a military aristocracy (samurai), and a four-class social system—warrior, farmer, artisan, merchant—took hold. The shoguns outlawed travel abroad, and foreigners were excluded from Japan. The policy remained in effect for two centuries.

1638

The English Puritans established the first Indian reservation in Connecticut. The English forced an agreement on the Quinnipiacs (Wappingers) of New Haven, Connecticut, taking most of their lands and leaving them only 1,200 acres of their original lands as a reservation. Under the terms of the agreement the Indians were subject to the jurisdiction of an English agent; could not sell or leave their lands or receive "foreign" Indians; could not buy guns, powder, or whiskey; and had to accept Christianity and reject their traditional spiritual beliefs, which Puritans believed were the teachings of Satan. The circumstances of the negotiation are unknown.

1639

The Taos Indians of New Mexico abandoned their pueblo and traveled to Kansas with Spanish horses. They fled from the Spanish to western Kansas where they built another pueblo. The Taos took Spanish horses with them and introduced horses to the Kiowa, Comanche, Wichita and other southern Plains Indians.

1640

The Dakota migration from northern Minnesota into the Great Plains. The Plains Indians (later so well known to Hollywood) originated in Minnesota and did not exist as a horse culture until the seventeenth century. Following an intertribal dispute, Dakota bands from Minnesota split from their allied tribes and began a series of migrations which took them as far west as the Rocky Mountains and south into the Great Plains. There they began to use the

139

horse and adopted a buffalo-hunting culture. The Rocky Mountain bands became known to the Europeans as Assiniboine; the Great Plains bands as Dakota or Sioux. The Dakota and Assiniboine both spoke a Siouan language.

1640

Floral patterns entered the beadwork of Northeast Indians through Catholic (Ursuline) nuns in Canada, who taught Huron and other Indian converts embroidery and European floral design. The designs traveled west and became part of Indian beadwork.

1640

New Netherlands' governor, Willem Kieft, warred against surrounding tribes of Esopus, Wappinger, and Manhattan, and had to hire English mercenaries for protection.

1641

Insurrection in Ireland against English rule. Massacre of the Protestants in Ulster. The resulting friction between the king and Parliament led to an English civil war. The Parliament, which had been struggling for greater powers against the monarchy, refused to raise the taxes to finance an army to put down the Irish rebellion. The House of Commons passed instead the document known as the "Grand Remonstrance," a summary of all their grievances against the king's reign.

1642–1648

Civil War in England and Scotland. The Stuart monarchy was overthrown by the forces of Parliament as a result of a war between the Parliament's soldiers

1641

The Five Nations of the Iroquois confederacy tried to make peace with the French, and agreed to negotiate with the Huron to gain greater access to furs. The French refused to deal with them because it would divert trade to the Dutch in New York.

1641–1642

Civil war among the Spanish in New Mexico. The resulting division of loyalties was devastating to the Pueblos and other Indians, who got caught on both sides.

1642

The first dictionary of a Native American language, Roger Williams's Algonquian-English dictionary, is published in London.

and the king's army over constitutional rights and governmental authority. The king was supported by the Anglican clergy, the peasantry, and the gentry; Parliament was supported by the middle classes, the merchants, and many nobles. The two sides were known as Cavaliers (royalists) and the Roundheads (parliamentarians). The king's army was decisively defeated in 1646 and the monarchy abolished for a time.

1643

Beginning of the reign of Louis XIV in France. He believed in absolute monarchy and the divine right of kings. His extravagance and reckless spending helped to wreck France's finances and weaken its settlements in America.

1642

Montreal founded by the French. Constructed at the site of the former Iroquois village of Hochelaga, it began as a Jesuit mission and developed into an important military outpost and center of the French fur-trading empire in North America. **Increasing Iroquois attacks on the French and on Huron trading parties began to disrupt the fur trade.**

1642

Maryland defeated the Susquehannocks. Lord Calvert's settlers took Susquehannock lands in Maryland, failed to abide by agreements, and put down the increasingly violent resistance with their superior weapons.

1643

Susquehannocks, with Swedish help, defeated Lord Calvert's Maryland settlers. The Susquehannocks appealed to the Swedish settlement on the Delaware Bay to supply them with guns and powder. With the help of Swedish guns the Susquehannocks forced the Maryland settlers off their lands. The turmoil of the English civil war prevented English support for Maryland colonists.

1643-1701

The Iroquois Wars. The Mohawks signed a treaty with the Dutch and began 60 years of war against the French-allied tribes. The first battle was fought near the mouth of the Richelieu River in Quebec where the Huron attacked the Iroquois. The Mohawk, along with the other members of the Iroquois confederacy, had signed a treaty with the Dutch to secure a steady source of firearms, knives, axes, cloth, beads, and guns and powder. They planned a larger campaign against the Huron and the entire French-Huron trading network. The Iroquois would subsequently defeat not only the Huron, but the Tobacco, Neutral, Illinois, Susquehannock, and Erie. The wars would move as far west as Michigan.

1644

Beginning of the Qing (Manchu) dynasty in China, the last dynasty of the Chinese emperors. The Qing forces had been called from Manchuria to put down a rebellion. Instead they seized control. The Manchu line lasted until 1912.

1644

The second uprising of the Powhatans in Virginia. Opechancanough, now old, but implacable in his hatred of the English, was carried onto the battlefield on a litter. He wanted to die a warrior's death rather than submit to the English. The English had continued to expand north into Maryland, west into the land of the Rappahannock, and south of the James River into the Carolinas and Georgia. After two years of fighting, the two parties finally negotiated a treaty defining a boundary between the Indians and the settlers. But the sheer numbers of the English settlers overwhelmed the Powhatans. Although the Powhatans abided by their agreement to become subject to the rule of the colonial Virginia courts and provide an annual tribute of beaver pelts, by 1649 settlers disregarded the provisions of the agreement and moved further into lands guaranteed to the Powhatans.

1646

Massachusetts encouraged John Eliot to translate the Bible into Algonquian languages. The English Protestant colonies had no organized religious effort in the same way the Catholic French and Spanish did. John Eliot, a Puritan minister, translated the Bible into Algonquian and tried to convert Massachusetts Indians to Protestant Christianity. Recent Indian family histories hold that in addition to translating the Bible, John Eliot sired a number of their ancestors during his visits to Natick.

1649
Execution of King Charles I in England. Commonwealth proclaimed. Oliver Cromwell, as the leader of the parliamentarians, made head of state. Cromwell ordered the massacre of Irish civilians in Drogheda, Ireland.

1649
The victory of the Iroquois over the Huron. Mohawk invasion of Huronia around Lake Simcoe and the dispersal of the Huron. In the winter of 1649–1650 over a thousand Mohawk warriers along with their Seneca allies descended on Huronia. Although there had been previous raids by the Seneca, the Huron had never seen a raid on this scale and never before with firearms. The Huron were weakened by both disease and Christianity. To a degree, the destruction of the Huron had been prepared by the French. The French Jesuit missions divided the Huron into rival factions, pitting the traditionalists against the Catholic converts. The French supplied firearms only to those Huron who had converted to Catholicism. Epidemic diseases had reduced the Huron population by the thousands. In less than 10 years the Huron had been reduced to a fraction of their previous strength.

When the combined Mohawk and Seneca forces descended onto the Huron villages, the demoralized Huron were unable to sustain the fight. They broke up into bands and scattered among other Iroquoian tribes between Lake Erie and Lake Ontario, suffering terrible casualties from exposure, deprivation, and continuing raids from the victorious Iroquois. Many ended as an adopted village of the Seneca; some moved west and joined other villages. The Neutral nation was almost wiped

1650

World population estimated at 500 million.

1650

Slave trade from Africa to New World colonies greatly expanded. Portugal, Spain, and England were joined by slave ships from France, Denmark, and American colonials. The main slave markets were in Haiti (Hispaniola), Brazil, and other islands of the West Indies. In the next 150 years more than 10 million Africans were shipped to the Americas as slaves.

1651

Navigation Acts passed by the English Parliament to control trade between England and the colonies. The laws were aimed at the Dutch and provided for high tariffs on any goods sold in the colonies not transported in English boats. These laws, amended and expanded in many versions over the next century, ultimately caused great resentment between the American colonial government and the English Parliament and led to the revolt of the colonies.

1652

Cape Town, South Africa, founded by the Dutch as a supply station for ships of the Dutch East India Company. It was the first permanent white settlement in South Africa.

out along with the Erie. The Iroquois then sent colonies of their own into the broad peninsula between Lakes Huron, Erie, and Ontario. By 1650 much of the Huron trading empire had been infiltrated by the Iroquois confederacy, and the French position greatly weakened.

1650

The Apache of the Zuni Mountains began open warfare with the Spanish.

1650

Iroquois massacre of the Nipissing peoples near Lake Nipissing, Ontario.

1652

Maine annexed to the area known as Massachusetts. Despite an appeal to the English Parliament, Maine was decreed to be part of the Massachusetts Bay Colony and under the jurisdiction of the Massachusetts General Court.

1653

First and only written constitution in English history. Cromwell was given broad powers. Parliament passed Act of Satisfaction, proclaiming the rebellion in Ireland ended. More than 8,000 Irish deported to the Caribbean as indentured laborers.

1654

Iroquois expansion and trade wars of the Great Lakes region. After the defeat of the Huron, the well-armed Iroquois confederacy continued their expansionist wars to the west. They attacked the Chippewa, the confederated tribes of the Illinois, and the Ottawa, and pushed these nations into what is now Michigan and Wisconsin. The ongoing trade wars of the Great Lakes region pushed additional tribes even farther west. The Shawnee separated from other Algonquian-speaking groups such as the Sauk and the Fox and migrated into the Ohio River Valley. The Cheyenne, who lived in southern Ontario, began to migrate westward, eventually reaching Montana and the Dakotas, where they adopted many aspects of the Plains culture. The Huron fled their lands. By 1654 almost the entire lower Michigan peninsula was uninhabited because of intertribal wars.

1655

The Dutch were the first Europeans to secure limited trading rights in China. (The British obtained trading privileges in 1670.)

1655

The Ojibwa attacked the Iroquois near Sault Ste. Marie, Michigan.

1655

The Timcua Rebellion in Florida against the Spanish. The end of the Timcua nation. For a hundred years the Timcua of northern Florida had experienced hard times at the hands of the Spanish. After De Soto's disastrous raids, the Spanish increased their military presence, and in 1609 installed the first of a series of missions among the northern Florida Indians. Between 1613 and 1617 a violent epidemic reduced the Timcuan population by more than half. Dependent on Spanish trade goods, the Timcua fell completely under Catholic mission control, a system which destroyed their own economy and culture. Greatly weakened by the brutal labor demands, the population was again reduced by half when a second epidemic struck in 1655. The Timcua, furious over the corruption among colonial officials who traded away goods and supplies meant for the Timcua laborers, followed the call of a Timcua chief, called Lucas Menendez by the Spanish, to resist and rebel. The Spanish had trained and armed a Timcua militia, in constant expectation of an English invasion. Instead, the Timcua militia followed Menendez and turned against the Spanish. In the uprising that followed the Timcua killed all soldiers and civilians at the San Pedro mission. When the Spanish retaliated with a huge force of soldiers drawn from other missions, they overwhelmed the Timcua forces. Menendez and 11 of his followers were paraded through mission towns and publicly hanged. Other leaders were sentenced to forced labor while many of the remaining Timcua were either relocated or sold into slavery to serve the needs of the

Spanish empire. The Timcua as a nation ceased to exist. Remnants of the Timcua became part of the Seminoles of Florida.

1656

French Jesuit mission founded in Onondaga, New York. In an effort to gain preeminence with the French, the Onondagas—the third tribe of the Iroquois Five Nations—invited the French to establish a mission in their village. They thought favored status would result in more guns. Four French Jesuits and 50 retainers set up a new mission in Onondaga. Then an epidemic broke out and within two years more than 500 children and as many adults had died. Baptism provided no immunities. Factions of Christianized Iroquois worked against traditionals, and the cohesion of Onondaga was greatly weakened.

1656

The Iroquois decimated the Erie tribe in the Lake Erie region.

1658

Mohawks destroyed the French mission near Onondaga. The Mohawks, the most intransigent Iroquois opponents of French missions and Christianity, marched on Onondaga and destroyed the French mission. Forewarned, the French personnel had fled; the Onondagas did not resist. The Mohawks then became "the head and Leaders" of the Iroquois League.

1658

The Esopus Indians of Hudson Valley rose up against New Netherlands. Initially successful in their rebellion, the Esopus were defeated when the Dutch hired

Mohawk warriors to aid Dutch troops to defeat and disperse the resisters. The refugees scattered to other tribes; some descendants survived into the twentieth century near Kingston, New York.

1659
Ten thousand Florida Indians died of measles.

1659–1660
French traders Des Groseilliers and Radisson traded furs near Hudson Bay for the first time. Former *coureurs de bois* (literally "runners of the woods," Frenchmen who went into the interior Indian villages to trade directly with tribes far from the missions and trading posts), they returned from Hudson Bay with a cargo of the finest quality furs, which they expected would bring their fortune. Instead, they were fined by the French Hudson's Bay Company in Quebec for having traded without the requisite license. In retaliation they went to London and obtained a charter from the English, under the name Rupert's Land Company, to conduct fur trading at posts or "factories" around the rim of Hudson Bay. The company's posts attracted bands of hunting Cree, who settled nearby, providing food, crafting equipment like snowshoes, and trading furs. The French, who often married Cree wives, proved to have greater endurance and better trading networks than the English in Hudson Bay. In 1670 the English chartered their own Hudson's Bay Company.

1660
Restoration of the monarchy in England. Charles II was restored to the English throne by Parliament.

1661

Louis XIV, age 18, began personal rule in France following the death of Cardinal Mazarin who had ruled during his minority. Louis was an absolute monarch who ruled without consulting parlement or the Estates General. Following reports about the native chieftains in New France, such as the Natchez leader who was called the Great Sun, Louis designated himself the "Sun King." At a time when Indian tribes had ritual baths or sweat lodges, Louis XIV built Versailles (begun in 1661 with 1300 rooms), the greatest palace in Europe, without plumbing of any kind.

1661

The Chippewa-Sioux Wars and the beginning of the Plains Sioux. The Chippewa (Ojibwa) who lived in the upper Great Lakes region were pushed west by colonial expansion of the French and English and by bands of Iroquois raiders. The Chippewa invaded Sioux territory in what is now Minnesota. After years of fighting, the Sioux moved farther west to the Plains, where they adopted the buffalo-hunting horse culture for which they are known in U.S. history. Before this time, the Sioux had been a settled horticultural people living in the woodlands of Minnesota.

As they migrated west they broke into three groups with distinct but mutually intelligible dialects of the Sioux language: the Santee, Yankton, and Teton. The Santee stayed in Minnesota as agricultural people. The Yankton moved west to the Dakotas, but combined agriculture with hunting. The Teton Sioux moved into the Upper Plains of Montana and the Dakotas and were renowned as great fighters, wanderers, and buffalo hunters. They had seven subgroups: Hunkpapa, Two Kettle, Sans Arc, Blackfoot, Miniconjou, Oglala, Brulé. The last two were the most formidable and were at the center of the wars on the northern Plains in the 1800s.

1661

Georgia Indians rose up and attacked Spanish missions. The Spanish missions north of the Savannah River were subsequently abandoned.

1661

Pueblo religions in New Mexico suppressed. Raid of Pueblo kivas and the burning of kachina masks. The Spanish governor ordered soldiers to raid the sacred kivas (underground ceremonial rooms) of many Pueblo Indian villages. They burned hundreds of kachina masks and religious objects, outlawed ceremonial dances, and attempted to eradicate Pueblo religions.

1661
Massasoit, the leader of the Wampanoag in Massachusetts, died. His two sons, Metacomet and Wamsutta, who had been sent to colony schools to learn English, succeeded to leadership. Wamsutta, the older of the two, became *sachem*. He was forced to chose whether to agree to English demands for more land or organize a resistance.

1661
John Eliot's Bible translated into Algonquian published in its first American edition. It was financed by the Corporation for Propagating the Gospel in New England.

1662
Wamsutta died after a peace council with the governor of Massachusetts. Metacomet, who became chief, believed Wamsutta had been poisoned. Forced to acknowledge himself a subject of the English Crown and of the governor of New Plymouth, Metacomet promised not to dispose of any lands without the authority of the governor and to pay a hundred pounds a year in tribute. Metacomet began to organize the Nipmucks, Sakonnets, Pocassets, Nausets, Parnets, and Narragansetts for a general uprising.

1663–1667
War between England and the Netherlands known as the Second English-Dutch War. Dutch monopoly of the slave trade assumed by the English.

1663

King of England gave a royal charter to eight proprietors for the land area known as Carolina lying between Virginia and Florida (present-day Georgia and North and South Carolina). The grant also included the Bahamas. Political philosopher John Locke wrote a constitution which seemed more feudal than the political liberalism he became famous for.

1663

Louis XIV's finance minister Colbert dissolved the Company of New France and instead formed the colony of New France with Quebec as its capital and a royal governor. Louis XIV's extravagances led France into greater debt.

1664–1667

As a result of victories in the Second English-Dutch War, Britain annexed all the Netherlands' colonies in Connecticut, Delaware, and New Jersey. The English Duke of York forced Peter Stuyvesant to surrender in New Amsterdam, and he renamed the village for himself as New York. Fort Orange surrendered to Britain and was renamed for the Duke of Albany.

1664

The English continued the Dutch policy of supplying the Iroquois confederacy with weapons to help them carry on their trade wars with the interior Indian nations allied with the French. These nations were at a disadvantage because the French were reluctant to arm their trading partners before they had converted to Christianity.

1664

Second Esopus uprising, this time against the English. Continuing Dutch policies, the English hired the Mohawks to fight the Esopus all along the Hudson River. Survivors scattered and took refuge with other tribes.

1664

Spanish in New Mexico issued laws restricting the Pueblos' freedom to trade and associate. Because the Apache were believed to be obtaining their horses and supplies from trade with the Pueblo peoples, the governor of New Mexico issued an edict stating that no "foreign" Indians would be allowed inside the pueblos except during restricted times. The policy was an attempt to prevent Apache-Pueblo trading. The Apache continued to be effective and disciplined raiders and constantly harassed the Spanish.

1665

Sir Isaac Newton discovered the laws of gravity, calculus, and variations in the light spectrum.

1665

The Iroquois Wars reduced the French population of traders and missionaries in New France to less than 2,000. The constant Iroquois expansion threatened the very survival of the French in New France.

1666

French troops destroyed Tionontoguen near Canajoharie, New York, as part of the Iroquois Wars. De Tracy burned Mohawk villages.

1667

England and the Netherlands declared war on France to counter Louis XIV's claim to the Spanish Netherlands in the Belgian provinces.

1668

Triple Alliance formed by England, the Netherlands, and Sweden against France. England's Charles II signed a secret treaty with Louis XIV within a year and Louis then concentrated his forces against the Dutch.

1668

Des Groseilliers sailed from England to Hudson Bay and wintered there at Charles Fort; Fathers Claude Dablon and Jacques Marquette founded a mission at Sault Ste. Marie in what is now Michigan.

1669

The "Praying Indians" of eastern Massachusetts were induced to join an attack on the Mohawks of western Massachusetts and the New York border. John Eliot had established Natick, Massachusetts, on the Charles River as a native village for "praying Indians," those who worshipped according to the catechism or Bible. He had the Bible translated into Algonquian. Natick also had the first Indian church in New England. The military expedition against the Mohawks was a failure.

1670

Charles Town, South Carolina, founded, as an English colony, named after King Charles II.

1670

English Crown chartered Hudson's Bay Company in Canada.

1670

China gave England limited trading rights.

1671

A French trading post was set up to compete with the English Hudson's Bay Company and its first "factory" processed furs. Father Marquette founded Mission St. Ignace at Michilimackinac; de Saint-Lusson officially claimed the entire Northwest and Canada for France.

1672-1678

Third Dutch War. France declared war against the Netherlands and invaded. William of Orange saved the country by opening the dikes around Amsterdam and the French were flooded out. Louis XIV wanted to expand French lands and commerce at Dutch expense.

1673
Louisiana Territory explored. Louis Joliet, a trader, and Father Jacques Marquette claimed the lands around the Mississippi River for the French. They canoed down the Fox and Wisconsin Rivers to the Mississippi and continued as far south as its confluence with the Arkansas River.

1673
The governor of New France, Count Frontenac, founded Fort Frontenac on Lake Ontario and offered protection to some of the Indian allies of the French.

1675–1676
King Philip's War. Metacomet's (called Philip by the white settlers) organized uprising against the constantly expansionist Massachusetts colonists was prematurely triggered by the shooting of an Indian by a settler. Philip and his Indian coalition, which included Wampanoags, Narragansetts, Nipmucks, Mohegans, and Podunks attacked 52 out of 90 towns in Massachusetts and Rhode Island, completely destroying 12. Deerfield, Massachusetts, was set aflame by Indians; Lancaster, Massachusetts, was burned to the ground after all the men were killed and the women and children taken prisoner.

Like the Powhatan in Virginia, Metacomet/Philip's Indian coalition almost prevailed, but ammunition for their guns was in the hands of the English, and once they had used up their ammunition store they were unable to replace it. The English raised an army with conscripts from every town and village. Every male over 14 was expected to serve in the local militia. Puritan ministers exhorted their parishioners to volunteer for the militia in order to "exterminate the savage Canaanites." The Narragansetts were slaughtered outside

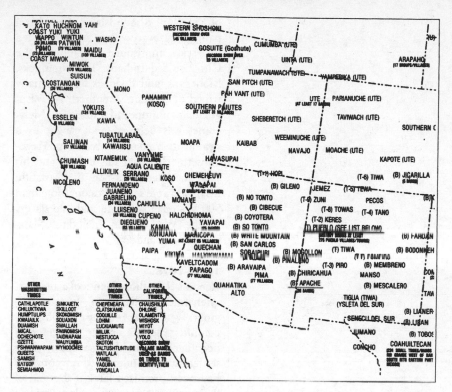

Arizona and New Mexico Pueblos. Historical records reveal some 275 Pueblo villages and towns.

Partial List of Pueblos

Hopi	Keres	Tewa
*Awatovı	Acoma	Nambe
Homolovı	Cochıtı	*Pojoaque
Hotevilla	Calısteo	San Idlefonso
Jeddıto	Laguna	San Juan
Kiskakobi	San Crıspobal	Santa Clara
Kuchaptuvela	San Filipe	Teseque
Mishongnovi	San Lazaro	Isleta
Moenkapi	San Marcos	Pıcurıus
Orabi	Santa Ana	Taos
Polacca	Santa Domongo	
Sıchomovı	Zia	
Shipalovı		
Shungopovı		
Tanalca		
Walpi		

*Former pueblos

of Kingston, Rhode Island. The Wampanoags in every village were rounded up and imprisoned, including the Christianized Indians. The Nipmucks, Mohegans, and Podunks were virtually wiped out, opening southern New England to unimpeded expansion. Metacomet was betrayed and caught in a swamp in Swansea in southern Massachusetts. His head was cut off and his skull mounted on a pole in Plymouth; his hands were sent to Boston. More than 500 Wampanoags were sold into slavery in the West Indies, including Metacomet's wife and son.

1675–1676

Bacon's Rebellion: Nanticoke and Susquehannock villages in western Virginia were attacked by land-hungry colonists despite peace agreements negotiated with the governor. The settlers, former indentured servants who had been promised land at the end of their seven-year service, also attacked royal troops who were sent out to put down the rebellion.

1680

Successful Pueblo rebellion. The Pueblo villages of New Mexico rose up against the Spanish in a coordinated revolt and succeeded in driving the Spanish out of New Mexico for the next 20 years. After Popé and 46 other traditional Pueblo religious leaders had been arrested and publicly whipped for "idolatry" by the Spanish, they determined to revolt. Popé claimed he had been visited by the spirit world and given a holy message to rid his homeland of the Spanish. At the time there were more than 60 Rio Grande villages. (In the 1500s there had been more than 90.)

Butterfly maiden from Santa Clara Pueblo. The Butterfly dance is done in October at the end of the ceremonial year. Some say that in addition to celebrating the harvest it also commemorates the victory over the Spanish in 1680. The dance is performed by the women's societies of the pueblos and is part of a ceremonial cycle of dances that begins with the winter solstice on December 21st. The plant on either side of this woman's tablita headdress represents corn, the basic crop and the one which signals a successful harvest and a plentiful winter.

Runners were sent to all the pueblos with knotted cords, which measured the days until the revolt was to take place. Although the Spanish were warned by informers, the leaders pushed up the date of the uprising and succeeded in surprising the greatly outnumbered Spanish. The revolt began at the Taos pueblo on August 10, 1680, and spread quickly to the other pueblos. Spanish missionaries were thrown off cliffs; Spanish functionaries were killed. In all, 21 priests and 400 Spanish were killed by the Pueblo Indians. The resistance leaders eliminated the Spanish presence from New Mexico. Crosses and rosaries were destroyed or burned. The names of Christian dieties were forbidden. The Spanish language was outlawed. Records of the Spanish government were burned in the Santa Fe plaza. Plants introduced from Europe, like peach trees, were pulled from the ground. The successful uprising is still celebrated in many pueblos every year with a ceremonial dance.

1680–1684
The Indians of Guale (coastal Georgia), the Yamasee, rebelled against the Spanish. With English backing and ammunition they began raiding Georgia's other Indian tribes, particularly the Yuchis, to capture and sell slaves to the English. In the process the Spanish lost control of Georgia.

1680
South Carolina settlers, with Shawnee allies, destroyed the Westos Indians.

1681
The French Crown chartered Compagnie de la Baie d'Hudson to compete with English Hudson's Bay Company.

1681

The English Crown gave William Penn a land grant of 48,000 square miles and a charter for a Quaker colony in the lands that would become known as Pennsylvania.

1682–1689

Frenchman La Salle cruised down the Mississippi River to its mouth and took possession of the entire Mississippi Valley for France, naming it Louisiana for Louis XIV. La Salle established a French colony at the mouth of the river (in the vicinity of New Orleans) to control the fur trade and to establish a base from which to attack Spain. He returned to France and in the next five years led four unsuccessful expeditions with hundreds of men and supplies but could not locate the mouth of the Mississippi or his colony. On his last voyage, when a storm blew his ship off course and he landed in Texas, he was murdered by his crew. The colony he left behind was wiped out by a Chickasaw raid.

1682

The English Hudson's Bay Company, was managed by French *coureurs de bois*. It expanded from one post to three.

1685

The Edict of Nantes revoked by Louis XIV ending toleration of Protestants in France. Thousands of French Huguenots emigrated to New York, Virginia, and South Carolina.

1686

French aggression in New France. The French intercepted a large trading

1682–1683

Lenape (Delaware) Indians made an agreement and treaty of friendship with William Penn to permit a colony in the area of present-day Philadelphia. The Treaty of Shackamaxon permitted Penn to purchase the territories that would become southeastern Pennsylvania.

1682

First captivity narrative published. Mary Rowlandson of Deerfield, Massachusetts, published the narrative of her captivity among the Indians. It started a new and popular literary genre that was used to justify taking Indian lands and imposing the harshest treatment on the "savages."

party from Albany (intending to go on to Michilimackinac) and confiscated its goods; French seized all but one of Hudson Bay English posts.

1687
Western Indian allies and French destroy four Seneca villages between Seneca Lake and Genessee River, New York.

1687
The Iroquois massacre the Miami Indians near what is now Chicago, Illinois.

1689–1697
King William's Wars in Europe. After William of Orange became the king of England (1689) the major European powers (England, the Netherlands, Spain, Austria) allied to oppose the expansionism of Louis XIV.

1689
Peter the Great became czar of Russia. As a young man he had studied in the Netherlands and became determined to transform Russia, where 80 percent of the Russian people where serfs, into a modern European power. He created a new city on the Baltic, St. Petersburg. He also initiated land reforms, administrative changes, and a series of expansionist wars.

1689–1697
King William's Wars in America. These were a series of wars fought between the English, the French, and their respective Indian allies for control of the colonial lands in North America. These were also known as the French and Indian Wars in America. In general the Iroquois tribes sided with the English; the Algonquian tribes with the French.

1691
Jacques Le Tort's expedition from Burlington, New Jersey, along the Susquehanna, Allegheny, Ohio, Mississippi, and Missouri Rivers. He reported making contact with more than 40 Native peoples.

1691
Virginia banished English who married Indians, blacks, or anyone of mixed ancestry.

1692

Witch trials in Salem, Massachusetts, ended with 14 women, five men, two dogs, and a cat being condemned to death by hanging. The judge, Samuel Sewall, went on to become Chief Justice of the Massachusetts Supreme Court. These trials were the New World expression of the witchcraft hysteria that had spread across Europe in the preceeding two centuries.

1696

Peter the Great sent 50 young Russians to England, Holland, and Venice to study shipbuilding and fortifications. He himself, traveling under the alias of Peter Michailoff, traveled for a year and a half in Prussia, Holland, England, and Vienna to study European ways.

1698

Court of Versailles became the model for European courts.

1692–1696

Spanish military commander Diego de Vargas given the mission of reconquering of the Pueblos. Many Pueblo peoples migrated to the West rather than live under Spanish rule. They went to live with the Hopi in Arizona or with small Navajo bands on the northern Arizona and New Mexico borders. Many other pueblos were destroyed or abandoned. Only 19 of more than 60 pre-revolt Rio Grande villages survived. Anti-Spanish feeling was so strong that in 1700 the Hopi razed the village of Awatovi and killed all its adult male inhabitants rather than accept a Spanish mission. When the Spanish came back to the Pueblos they did not reintroduce the *encomienda* system. However, the Pueblos still lived under constant encroachment by the Spanish for forced labor, tribute, and religious suppression.

1692

Spaniards "reconquered" Pueblo Indians and restored Santa Fe as their capital in New Mexico.

1695

First Pima revolt against the Spanish in Arizona and New Mexico.

1696

The French burned an Onondaga village near Manlius, New York.

The village of Walpi. The site of the Hopi village of Walpi sits at the tip of a mesa with a narrow bridgelike road of natural rock connecting it to the larger mesa and a set of steps carved into the rock to reach the desert floor and Hopi farm plots some five hundred feet below. The village looks much the same today as it must have looked in the 1500s when some of Coronado's men first saw it.

1699

French forces under d'Iberville built Fort Maurepas at Biloxi, Mississippi, to enforce French claims to Louisiana and to forestall English occupation of the lower Mississippi. A French Franciscan mission was founded at Cahokia in what is now Illinois.

VI

1 7 0 0 s — L A N D   C E S S I O N S

"The world of culture and nature," poet Gary Snyder writes, *"is almost a shadow world now, and the insubstantial world of political jurisdictions and rarefied economies is what passes for reality. We can regain some small sense of that old membership by discovering the original lineaments of our land."*

In the 1700s Native American peoples still lived in their original habitats, defined by rivers, river valleys, mountain elevations, watersheds, mountain ranges, deserts, canyons, and natural land forms. Corn was cultivated almost everywhere in North America, where weather allowed at least 140 consecutive growing days. Europeans learned a lot of agricultural techniques from Native peoples, like using fish as fertilizer in planting corn. Although villages were located along rivers or other water sources, they used the resources of larger unpopulated land areas with great skill and knowledge. Virgin forests were important to Indian villages hundreds of miles distant, because there hunters found seasonal game and fish; craftsmen found clay for pots, and trees for dugout canoes; medicine women found plants for dyes, and herbs for healing. The Pueblo Indians at Acoma, for example, carried roof timbers from forests 75 miles distant. For Native Americans there was no such thing as wilderness. For the Europeans, who brought the medieval mind of Europe with them, the forest was wild, uncivilized, uninhabited, and unproductive.

In the 1700s the Native American peoples of North America and Canada were primarily influenced by having to choose between alliances with France and England; and secondarily by the variety of local and regional governmental entities taking their lands—by agreements, by treaties, by land cessions, by theft. There was also a larger cultural interchange in which accounts of travel among the aboriginal peoples of the New World were published with great success in Europe. These in turn influenced the writings of Enlightenment philosophers, like Rousseau and Locke, who used the concept of "man in nature" to structure a new framework within which to examine the assumptions, the limitations, and the hypocrisies of European monarchy.

While the geopolitical struggle was between France and England, the local struggle was between Indian nations allied with either the French or the British. Many Indian nations sided with the French against the British because they perceived the French as the lesser evil: the French seemed primarily interested in trade, with widely dispersed trading posts and missions; while the English seemed land-hungry, intent on settling the land with endless numbers of colonists. After the French lost the Seven Years' War in Europe (called the French and Indian

War in America), many Indian nations tried to remain neutral in the subsequent war between Britain and her colonies. The issue of Indian neutrality was one of the prime considerations in the deliberations of the colonists as to whether or not to declare independence from Britain or to seek conciliation. If, for example, the nations allied in the Iroquois confederacy continued to support the British, it meant a formidable enemy against the colonies.

By the end of the 1700s the former colonies had become the United States of America and Native peoples of both coasts had been decimated by war, removal, slavery, disease, economic deprivation, and missionary excesses. In many areas Indian populations had been reduced by two-thirds. Among intact Indian nations, like the Cherokee, pressures mounted to remove them from their lands so that the lands could be made available to white settlers. The next great region of conquest was the area known then as the Great Northwest, lands in Ohio, Indiana, Illinois and the Great Lakes region. These were claimed by land companies from Virginia, Massachusetts, New York, and Connecticut. By 1800 over 300,000 settlers had moved into the multi-tribal hunting grounds of the Shawnee and the allied tribes of the Northwest confederacy. These regions soon became the states of Kentucky, Tennessee, and eventually Ohio, Indiana, Illinois, Michigan, and Minnesota. The native inhabitants were pressured to cede vast amounts of land, and land-hungry settlers did not abide by the agreements their governments had negotiated with tribal leaders.

Although tens of thousands of Indians disappeared, many survived, abandoning villages and merging with other tribes, and sustaining the knowledge of the land through oral traditions and in historical narratives connected to rivers and mountains, as well as to the immense and multiple Indian ruins and temple mounds that laced the entire Mississippi River system. Albert Gallatin, at one time a senator from Pennsylvania, a leader of Thomas Jefferson's Democratic Republicans, and minister to France and England, traveled throughout the Old Northwest Territory and wrote several books about the Indians and their extraordinary artifacts. As Jefferson's secretary of the treasury he sponsored the first major study of the mounds, although the final work was not published until 1848. (*Ancient Monuments of the Mississippi Valley* by George Squier and Edwin Davis. It was the first publication of the newly established Smithsonian Institution.) Although the white mythology of the 1700s was so dismissive of Indian culture that most of the white settlers called the temple mounds "Spanish forts" because they could not credit such immense geometrical and precise structures to a non-European source, there were a small group of men, which included Thomas Jefferson and George Washington and Andrew Jackson's father-in-law, all of whom had excavated temple mounds, who knew that this "virgin land" contained a vast history.

1 7 0 0 s — L A N D   C E S S I O N S

WORLD HISTORY

1700s
In Europe the 1700s were known as the Age of Enlightenment. The new intellectual movements, rooted in the scientific movement and devoted to rationalism, emerged in France and spread through Europe and to America.

NATIVE AMERICAN HISTORY

1700
Migration to the Plains. Many of the tribes that acquired horses migrated to the Plains, particularly the Comanches (the southern Plains) and the Siouan-speaking peoples of Minnesota (the northern Plains).

1700
Hopis in the Southwest massacred all male villagers of Awatovi because they were friendly with Spanish priests and had agreed to allow the return of a Spanish mission. The Spanish priests, from either the Jesuit or Franciscan orders, oversaw life at the mission, using Indian labor to build the churches and to tend the fields that supported the economy of the mission. The resulting political and economic control was in direct opposition to the traditional leadership of the Hopi villages, which was chosen by birth, clan, and family. The Hopi, who had absorbed many peoples from the Rio Grande pueblos before the rebellion of 1680, wanted no Spanish intrusion. According to Hopi history, men from the other villages agreed to enter Awatovi at night during preparations for a religious festival. While all the Awatovi men were in the kivas, ceremonial rooms dug down into the earth, Hopi men pulled up the ladders

and set fire to the buildings. After killing all the adult men, they destroyed the village and kivas and settled the women and children in other villages. The ruins of Awatovi remain on Antelope Mesa a few miles beyond the site of the present-day Hopi villages. The ferocity of the destruction reveals the determination of the Hopi to resist Spanish control.

1701–1714

The War of Spanish Succession in Europe. These were a series of genealogical wars among the major European powers over who would succeed to the throne of Charles II, the childless Spanish Hapsburg king. The three lines of succession were Louis XIV of France, Leopold I of Germany, and a Bavarian prince. In America these wars among France, England, and Spain were called Queen Anne's War (1702–1713), and centered on conflict between the English and French in the northeast and the English and Spanish in the southeast.

1701

The French king reversed his expansionist policies in America and made the decision to close down forts farther to the west and to limit further fur-trading licenses. A depleted royal treasury, a glut on the European fur market, and Jesuit complaints led to the king's decision.

1701

The Iroquois Wars (1641–1701) came to a close. Peace councils took place at three political centers: Onondaga, New York, headquarters of the Five Nations of the Iroquois confederacy; Albany, New York, where British authorities presided over negotiations between the Iroquois and the Ottawa; and Montreal, Canada, where the French and their more than 20 Indian allied tribes made a comprehensive peace agreement with the Iroquois confederacy. The outcome was a peace agreement between all the Iroquois tribes and the French (and all their Indian allies). The final council in Montreal was attended by leaders of the Ottawa, Huron, Missisauga, Nipissing, Algonquin, Temiscaming, Ojibwa, Potawatomi (who also represented the Sauk), Menominee, Winnebago, Mesquackie, Mascouten, Miami, Illinois, Kickapoo, Indians of the French missions at Sault Ste. Marie, Abenaki, Onondaga, Seneca, Oneida, and Cayuga. Geographically they represented lands as far away as Wisconsin and Minnesota. The Mohawk did not participate but later added their consent. As a result of the agreements of 1701, the Iroquois were allowed to hunt in the north-south corridor along Lake Champlain into Canada; while the Ottawa could travel peacefully through Iroquois lands to trade at Albany. All Five Nations of the Iroquois adopted an official policy of neutrality between the French in New France and the British in their English colonies. When the Iroquois wars were over, only two widely separated groups retained the name "Huron": one group near Quebec and another at Detroit. The Detroit Huron community would eventually be called Wyandot by the British.

1701

The French concentrated their new missions in Michigan and Illinois. Antoine de Cadillac founded Fort Pontchartrain at Detroit. French contacts with Indians in the Great Lakes region focused on two widely separated locales, the new mission villages of Illinois Indians on the Mississippi River near the mouth of the Kaskaskia River (present-day Utica, Illinois) and Detroit, Michigan, where they built a fort and trading post. With the idea of spearheading French fur trade in the southern regions around the Ohio River, Antoine de Cadillac invited tribes from the Upper Great Lakes to settle in the vicinity of the fort in order to associate with French traders. Villages of Huron and Ottawa came from the Straits of Mackinac; Potawatomi and Miami came from the St. Joseph River; Sauk, Mesquackie (Fox), and Mascouten came from the Green Bay area of Wisconsin; Missisauga and Ojibwa (later called Chippewa) came from northern Lake Huron. More than 6,000 Indians settled in the Detroit area. (Ottawa Chief Pontiac was born in the Ottawa village on the Canadian shore opposite Detroit.)

1701

The Iroquois adopted a policy of neutrality toward the French and the British, and strengthened their own internal government. The Iroquois also concentrated authority in the central council of the Iroquois confederacy, choosing one chief from the 49 chiefs of the Five Nations as spokesperson, in order to deal more effectively with the Europeans. They also negotiated trade agreements with the Ottawa (in Michigan and Ohio), the Ojibwa (Chippewa in Wisconsin, Minnesota, Ontario), and French-allied tribes of the Illinois confederacy (Illinois). These agreements remained in place until the 1740s.

1701

The Susquehannocks in Pennsylvania negotiated with William Penn for trade agreements and cession of lands in their valley. Penn promise to treat the Indians fairly and pledged that the Quakers would maintain a special relationship with the Susquehannocks.

1703-1704

A French mission was founded in Illinois at the junction of the Kaskaskia and Mississippi Rivers near present-day Utica, Illinois. It was also the home of the Illinois confederacy. The Illinois Indians became the most staunch allies of the French—through intermarriage, Christianization, and commerce. In 1703 they numbered over 6,000;· by 1763 their numbers would be reduced to 2,000. Disease, alcohol, and factionalization were compounded by the constant raiding and warfare of the anti-French tribes, particularly the Iroquois, the Mesquackie, the Sauk, and the Dakota.

1704

English raided Spanish missions in Georgia attacking the Indians of Guale (Georgia). With Creek and Cherokee allies, the English attacked missions from the Savannah River to St. Augustine, depopulating the entire area and causing Indian migrations north. The Spanish refused to protect their "mission Indians" and as a result the Spanish mission system was destroyed in Florida. The Apalachee Indians of northwest Florida were almost completely destroyed, with the remnants joining the Creeks and the Seminoles. The Yamasee migrated farther south.

1708

English traders in the Carolinas seized between 10,000 to 12,000 mission Indians, many of them Yamasee who had been part of the Spanish mission system, and sold them into slavery in the West Indies.

1710

Four Mohawk leaders agreed to accompany English agents to London where they had their portraits painted, and met with Queen Anne. They were the first celebrity Indians in Europe. One of them was Chief Hendrick, uncle of Joseph Brant and staunch British ally until his death in 1755.

1710

Treaty at Conestoga between Pennsylvania and the Iroquois League. The Iroquois League claimed lands in western New York, Pennsylvania, Kentucky, and Ohio. The Iroquois agreed to mediate land disputes among Pennsylvania settlers and the resident Indians of Pennsylvania, particularly the Delaware and the Susquehannock.

1711

Mobile, Alabama, made the capital of French Louisiana. The territory, named for King Louis, encompassed a corridor of land over a thousand miles wide both east and west of the Mississippi River from the Gulf Coast to

Canada. The British and French were in constant dispute over the lands to the east of the Mississippi that bordered the British colonies.

1712

Rhineland and Ulster religious persecutions result in large-scale European immigration to Pennsylvania.

1712–1736

The beginning of the Fox Wars. The French commandant in Detroit, Dubuisson, along with his Huron and Ottawa allies massacred several hundred Masquackies (Fox) who had been harassing the Illinois Indians. (Some estimates say as many as 1,000 men, women, children were killed.) Surviving Mesquackie returned to their kin in Wisconsin and gathered allies (the Sauk, Mascouten, Kickapoo, and Dakota). They subsequently made the Great Lakes waterways dangerous for the French and all their Indian allies. The French embarked on a war of extermination that lasted two decades, while the Fox regrouped continually in different locations with new allies. These raids with different sets of allies on both sides became known as the Fox Wars in the western Great Lakes, and went on inconclusively for 25 years. The only constant players were the Fox and the French. As a consequence many groups moved away from Fort Detroit, although they continued to trade with the French. Only the Huron and Potawatomi remained close by. The Ottawa moved to the opposite shore to what is now Ontario.

1712

The Tuscarora Wars fought against the English slave traders in North Carolina. The Tuscaroras migrated to New York to become the sixth nation of the Iroquois confederacy. The

Tuscarora, an Iroquoian-speaking nation living in North Carolina, went to war against the English over their excessively cruel trading practices. English traders sold goods on credit in the fall, expecting to be paid back in the spring after hunting season. If the hunting season was bad and the debt was not paid, the trader seized the man's wife and children and sold them as slaves to the West Indies. Outraged, the Tuscarora went to war against the English in North Carolina. Within a year the Tuscarora were largely defeated. The Oneida invited the Tuscarora to become members of the Iroquois confederacy and they began migrating north.

1713

Treaty of Utrecht marked the formal end of Queen Anne's War in America and the War of Spanish Succession in Europe. In Europe Louis XIV's grandson, Philip of Anjou, became the new king of Spain. France ceded to Britain some territories in the New World, including Nova Scotia and Hudson Bay Territory. Spain ceded Gibraltar to England and the *asiento*, or the contract for supplying Spanish colonies in the Americas with slaves. **The English slave trade greatly expanded.**

1714

Witch trials abolished in Prussia.

1715

Louis XIV died. His five-year-old grandson succeeded him. France in severe financial distress because of constant wars. Under a Bourbon regent, France made new alliances with England and the Netherlands.

1713

The Micmac and Maliseet refused to recognize the authority of the English. One provision of the Treaty of Utrecht was the transfer of certain Canadian lands from the French to the English. The Micmac and Maliseet in Canada, who inhabited those lands, refused to recognize that their homelands had now become English. The Iroquois of the Canadian border region also refused to recognize terms of the treaty that removed them from French control and placed them under English governance.

1715

Anne, a Powhatan tribal leader, called Queen Anne by the English, addressed the Virginia legislature and set out the interests of her people in the Virginia colony. Queen Anne was the leader of the Pamunkey from 1706 to 1718. She complained that the English surveyors surveyed more Indian lands than had actually been purchased; she complained about the liquor sold to her people; and she suggested that in light of the impoverishment of her people at the hands of Virginians the Pamunkey should not have to pay their annual tribute. The governor of Virginia, with the agreement of the Virginia Assembly, agreed to forgive the tribute if she would send her son to the college of William and Mary, which she did. The land and liquor issues were harder to resolve, and she never gave up trying to negotiate new compromises with the Virginia governor.

1715
Yamasee War in Georgia. The Yamasees of Georgia allied with the Creek and other small coastal nations to rise up against the British slavers and their practice of collecting trading debts by capturing Yamasee families and selling them into slavery. Within a year the Yamasees were defeated. Many left Georgia and migrated into Florida to become part of the Seminole nation. Others migrated into central Georgia and Alabama to join the Creek confederacy.

1717
France gave Scottish financier John Law a 25-year monopoly on trade and government in Louisiana on the condition he send at least 9,000 people, white and black, to settle the region and develop economic growth.

1717
Delaware bands were pushed westward into western Pennsylvania and the Ohio Valley. Iroquois *sachems* made agreements with the settlers in Pennsylvania and their colonial Indian commissioners (one Indian commissioner for Pennsylvania was Benjamin Franklin) to manage land sales and to negotiate with various Indian tribes. The result was that the Delaware, who lived on what were claimed as Iroquois lands, were pushed west. The Shawnee

and the Delaware refused to recognize Iroquois authority over their lands in Ohio and Kentucky.

1718
New Orleans founded near the mouth of the Mississippi and later made the new capital of French Louisiana.

1718
William Penn died in England. His successors in Pennsylvania, including his son, did not honor his commitments to deal honorably with the Indians.

1720
John Law's Mississippi Company caused a financial panic in France. It was a speculative scheme to sell stock in the Company of Mississippi. But there were few settlers, little trade and no economic growth. The price of the stock rose rapidly, then collapsed, creating a problem for the French Crown, which had backed it. The collapse of the "Mississippi Bubble" ruined many French investors.

1722
The Tuscarora joined the Iroquois confederacy. The Five Nations became the Six Nations of the Iroquois League. One of several waves of refugee peoples to move out of the southern states, the Tuscarora settled in lands that are now upstate New York and became the sixth nation in the Iroquois League. Since the 49 chiefs of the Five Nations did not want to give up their positions or create new Tuscarora chiefs, and their traditional laws of governance limited the number to 49, the Oneida chiefs spoke for the Tuscarora in council sessions.

1724

Teaching of Christianity banned by imperial edict in China. All Christian missionaries expelled.

1725

Peter the Great of Russia crowned his wife, Catherine, czarina. She succeeded him upon his death the same year.

1727

Quakers in England demanded the abolition of slavery.

1728

Vitus Bering's voyage through the Bering Strait. A Danish navigator in

1724–1729

The Natchez revolt under the Great Sun on the lower Mississippi River. French destruction of the Natchez nation. The Great Sun sold into slavery. The Natchez nation, a direct descendant of the ancient Mississippian culture, resisted the attempts of the local French commander on the French plantation in their territory to impose new taxes and to confiscate lands in its central village, Natchez. This led to a series of rebellions against the French culminating in 1729 with the killing of some 200 French on the Natchez plantation. The French determined to exterminate them. In a series of raids conducted with the help of Choctaw allies, the Great Sun, the central sacred chieftain, was captured along with 480 other Natchez prisoners. They were sold into slavery in the Caribbean. Other Natchez survivors were given refuge and protection by the Chickasaws. (This led to war between the Chickasaws on one side and the Choctaws and French on the other.) The Natchez nation ceased to exist. Information about the customs and beliefs of the Natchez nation survived in France with the later publication of Antoine Le Page du Pratz's book. (See "Mississippians and the Culture of the Great Suns" on page 64.)

service of Peter the Great, he gave his name to the strait and the Bering Sea.

1729
The English Crown divided Carolina into two colonies, North and South Carolina.

1730
Fox Indians massacred by the French and French-allied Indians as they trekked eastward seeking sanctuary among Iroquois (the Seneca). More than 400 Fox were killed and another 500 sold into slavery.

1731
English factory workers prohibited from emigrating to America.

1733
English founded the colony of Georgia as a buffer between Spanish-owned lands in Florida and the Carolinas. James Oglethorpe its first governor.

1734
Lafitau's study of Iroquois customs published in France with illustrations. The account of Iroquois social and governmental organization influenced French writers in their philosophical deliberations about the nature of man and government.

1734
The French defeated by the Fox and their allies, the Sauk, in battle of Butte des Morts. It marked the opening of peace negotiations between the French and the Fox.

1736–1739
Chickasaw resistance against the French along the lower Mississippi.

1737
End of the Fox Wars. The French commander, Beauharnois, made peace

with Fox (Mesquackie) after the defeat of 1734 and under pressure from his other Indian allies. The remaining Mesquackie and Sauk reestablished villages on the east bank of the Mississippi at the mouth of the Wisconsin River, present-day Prairie du Chien. French trade with these tribes resumed with the building of Fort Marin in 1738. Other Fox settled in Iowa.

1737

The "Walking Purchase" took Delaware lands and caused the removal of thousands of Lenape Indians from Pennsylvania. Thomas Penn, the son of the colony's founder, William Penn, "discovered" a treaty signed by three Delaware (also called Lenape) chiefs, ceding to Penn's father all of the Delaware lands around the forks of the Delaware River, west of Neshaminy Creek in Pennsylvania "as far as a man can go in a day and a half." At the time the Lenape occupied lands scattered over southern New York, New Jersey, Delaware, Maryland, and Pennsylvania. After gaining agreement from several Delaware chiefs as to how this treaty should be honored and the distance determined, the colonists selected their three best athletes and offered money and land to the one who could travel the greatest distance. The runners trained for nine days and colonists cleared trees and brush from the path they were to follow. From the sidelines Lenape called out to the runners to walk, not run. Two out of the three runners died en route from dehydration and prostration. The third covered 65 miles in a day and a half, securing approximately 1,200 square miles of intensively used Indian lands. The embittered Delawares refused to move. The Iroquois League, however, which had agreed to mediate the land disputes between white Pennsylvania and its Indian population, was called in to mediate. Historians question the authenticity of the treaty (which subsequently disappeared).

1738

Gaultier de la Verendrye made the first recorded visit to the Mandan Indians in North Dakota, although *coureurs de bois* had preceded him. Early European accounts describe the Mandans as being especially light-skinned, with blue eyes, and with great dignity and bearing. (They were virtually wiped out by smallpox epidemics in the 1830s.) Various folktales attributed Welsh or Viking ancestry to the Mandans.

1740-1748

The War of Austrian Succession in Europe. In America it was called King George's War (1744-1748). It was the third of the so-called French and Indian Wars, which were fought between the French and English in America with various Indian allies.

1741

The explorer Vitus Bering made a voyage to mainland Alaska. The Russians opened trade with Alaska natives for sea otter pelts. The Russian system was to enslave entire villages of women in order to force the men to hunt furs for them.

1742

Iroquois League enforced Pennsylvania's land claims from the Walking Purchase. Acceding to Pennsylvania's wishes, Onondaga Chief Cannastego decided the mediation in favor of Pennsylvania and ordered the Lenapes off their land. It is believed that the Iroquois did not want to go to war over these lands. (Another theory is that the chief was bribed.) The Delawares/ Lenapes were forced to settle in refugee areas in western Pennsylvania, one of which was called Wyoming. A Moravian missionary in 1748 reported seeing Indian refugees from the lands of the Delawares (Piscataways, Shawnees, Mahicans, Nanticokes) on their way to Pennsylvania's refugee areas "carrying the bones of their dead in their arms so they would not have to leave them behind."

1742
Great Lakes Indians shifted trade from the French to the British. When the French adopted a policy of auctioning trading posts to the highest bidder, they pushed up the cost of goods. The Indians in turn began to go to British traders, who often had lower prices and a better supply of quality hatchets, knives, kettles, and guns.

1744
Robert Clive, the first British governor of India, arrived in Madras as a clerk for the British East India Company. He eventually defeated the French in the south of India, conquered the native rulers of Bengal, and became British governor of all India.

1744
The Russian fur trade was extended to the Aleutian Islands.

1744-1748
King George's War, the American phase of the War of Austrian Succession in Europe.

1747
Huron uprising against the French, "the conspiracy of Nicholas." A Huron leader named Orontony, called Nicholas by the French, resented French trading practices and organized a series of attacks on French traders in Michigan, culminating with the killing of five of them on their way back to Detroit. At the same time the pro-British Miami Indians made a successful attack on the French fort at St. Phillipe (now Fort Wayne). Following this uprising, the Huron and Miami both moved eastward, leaving Michigan for the Ohio Valley. There they encountered Pennsylvania merchants who had already penetrated the French trading territory of northwest Ohio.

1748
In France Montesquieu published *The Spirit of Laws,* articulating the separation of governmental powers that influenced the drafters of the U.S. Constitution.

1749
First colonial Ohio settlements. French commandant Celeron de Blainville toured the Ohio tribes, demanding the expulsion of Pennsylvania traders. He was rebuffed.

1750
World population estimated at 800 million.

1750–1850
Industrial Revolution began in England. The economic shift from agriculture and cottage-industry to the use of machinery for production radically changed England. The privatization of the commons—which prohibited landless rural agricultural workers from

1750
Moor's Indian Charity school founded in Connecticut. It was later moved to Hanover, New Hampshire, when Presbyterian ministers in Scotland offered to raise money for the education of the Indians. It was later named Dartmouth College.

1750
The Ohio Company of Virginia formed by a group of Virginians and a

grazing livestock on common lands—forced huge rural populations off the land and into the cities. The accompanying invention of the steam engine, the flying shuttle, the spinning jenny, and the power loom all contributed to the rise of urban textile factories and the total dependence of workers on their industrial employers. The industrial system spread to France, Germany, and America.

1751
First volume of the French *Encyclopédie* published in Paris. A French encyclopedia of science, arts, and trades which eventually comprised 35 volumes, it was a major effort in the consolidation of European knowledge and an important tool in spreading the ideas of the Enlightenment. Edited by Diderot, it contained articles by all the major French thinkers—Rousseau, Voltaire, Montesquieu, Quesnay and others. They subsequently became known as the Encyclopedists. In the American colonies possession of the *Encyclopédie* was a mark of intellectual leadership.

number of wealthy Englishmen. Its purpose was to open rich new lands in the Ohio Valley for development. These lands were already populated by hundreds of Indian villages and were also claimed by land companies in Massachusetts and New York as well as Englishmen seeking a charter from the Crown.

1752
Virginia's treaty at Logstown (now Ambridge, Pennsylvania) with local tribes residing in Ohio country. Virginia, Pennsylvania, New York, and Massachusetts all had designs on the lands in the Ohio Valley. Virginia was the first to make a local treaty through its land company, the Virginia Ohio Company.

1752
Miami Indians in Ohio fighting on the side of the British were defeated by French and Ottawa allies. French

troops in alliance with the Ottawa captured British traders at Pickawillany (near present-day Piqua, Ohio, on the banks of the Great Miami River) and "made a broth" out of the local Miami leader known as La Demoiselle. With the destruction of Pickawillany, the Miami Indians returned to their former residence on the Wabash River and to their alliance with the French. It was a prelude to the Seven Years' War, which would become known in America as the fourth French and Indian War.

1753
The French expelled colonial Pennsylvania traders from the lands of Ohio Valley by virtue of their treaties with local Indian peoples.

1753
The governor of Virginia sent George Washington, a young surveyor, to enforce the Virginia claim in Ohio and to expel the French from the lands Virginia claimed there. Washington and the Virginia militia were attacked and defeated by French-allied Indians.

1753
Benjamin Franklin, one of Pennsylvania's Indian representatives, met with Ohio Indians in Pennsylvania regarding lands in Ohio. At the treaty council at Carlisle, Pennsylvania, with the Ohio Indians (Delawares, Shawnees, Wyandots) and Iroquois League representatives, the Onondaga chief and the Mohawk chief recounted the origins of the Great Law of Peace and the League of Haudenosaunee. Franklin presented a wampum belt to the Indians. His letters repeatedly made reference to the Great Council at Onondaga and how

the Six Nations educated their leaders. He began to contemplate a political instrument of unity for the colonies based on some of the ideas of the Iroquois confederacy. Writing to a friend he said: *"It would be a strange thing . . . if Six Nations of ignorant savages should be capable of forming a scheme for such a union, and be able to execute it in such a manner as that it has subsisted for ages and appears indissoluble; and yet, that a like union should be impracticable for ten or a dozen English colonies, to whom it is more necessary . . . and who cannot be supposed to want an equal understanding of their interests."*

1754–1760
The French and Indian War. (The American phase of the Seven Years' War in Europe 1756–63).

France joined Austria against Prussia and England. This war led to the loss of most of France's colonial empire in North America.

1754
The first iron rolling mill developed in England.

1754
The Albany Congress and the presentation of Franklin's Albany Plan of Union.

At the outset of the fourth French and Indian War, a meeting of all the colonial Indian commissioners and the *sachems* of the Iroquois confederacy was convened in Albany. Anticipating war with the French, the English colonists urgently needed at least the neutrality, if not the support, of the Iroquois tribes and their vast network of allies. Chief Hendrick of the Mohawk had requested that colonies organize themselves with one spokesman, so that the Indians did not have to meet separately with each Indian commissioner from each colony. To that end, Benjamin Franklin had drafted the Albany Plan of Union, in which each colony retained its own constitution, but would send representatives to a central council. **Debates on the plan, he wrote, "went on daily, hand in hand with the Indian business."** (See "The Iroquois Confederacy and Its Influence on the U.S. Constitution" on page 184.) The

Albany Plan, which borrowed many of the principles of the Iroquois confederacy—individual autonomy of the colonies except in issues of trade and foreign relations which affected all—was adopted by the commissioners but was not subsequently ratified by the colonies. However, it did form the basis of the Articles of Confederation of 1777, which Franklin also helped to draft, and which in turned formed the basis for the U.S. Constitution in 1789.

1754–1763

The French and Indian War in America paralleled the Seven Years' War in Europe. The war occurred primarily in two theaters, western Pennsylvania and the New York–Canada corridor along Lake Champlain. Indian military assistance to the French came from almost every section of the Great Lakes region, including Pennsylvania and upper New York State. French and Indian forces secured initial victories on the New York frontier, capturing Fort Oswego on Lake Ontario in 1756 and Fort William Henry in 1757. Both were retaken by the British in 1759. The British were eventually able to control the war, despite being outnumbered on the ground, because they could control sea trade and prevent French merchant ships from landing with supplies and ammunition to resupply French troops. Both France and England used Indian warriors as surrogates for European troops. Indians fought on both sides of this struggle, but primarily with the French, largely because they perceived the war as a contest between French fur-trading interests and British colonial settlers' land-owning interests. The English were more aggressive than the French about taking Indian lands; they exhibited every intention of taking over the whole country rather than being content with the French system of widely separated military and trading posts; and British officials, unlike most (but not all) of the French, displayed a contempt and dislike of Indians. Consequently, most Indian nations fought on the losing side, a political reality that would greatly affect their post-war agreements with the English. A key alliance during this period was that of the British Indian superintendent, William Johnson, with the Iroquois leaders.

1754
The opening battle of the war between the French and British in America was fought at Fort Duquesne/Fort Pitt. The war began as a fight between the British and the French in western Pennsylvania for control of the Ohio Valley. Virginia claimed it for the British; the French claimed it as a right-of-way to their Mississippi trading posts. The fort represented strategic access to the west, where the Ohio River forked to join the Allegheny and Monongahela Rivers in the vicinity of present-day Pittsburgh. While the French constructed a road and a chain of four forts from Presque Isle (now Erie, Pennsylvania) to what is now Pittsburgh, the English colonials, who had already claimed the same lands, sent a small group of Virginia traders to build a fort. Young George Washington, a surveyor and member of the Virginia militia, was sent with 120 soldiers to defend the fort and to inform the French that Virginia had prior claim. Before he got there a French army along with some 500 Indian

THE IROQUOIS CONFEDERACY AND ITS INFLUENCE ON THE U.S. CONSTITUTION

One of the interesting questions of American history is the degree to which the drafters of the American Constitution were influenced by their interactions with the Iroquois confederacy. The framers of the Constitution, after all, were European-trained lawyers. They knew a lot about monarchies; little about democracy. The model of Greece was 2,000 years distant; the model of the Iroquois, on the other hand, was nearby and available. Benjamin Franklin was a knowledgeable student of the Iroquois and he frequently quoted in his letters details of Iroquois politics and economics that he had learned in his Indian negotiations. He also, between 1736 and 1762, collected and published the precise contents of more than a dozen Indian treaties. George Morgan, George Washington's Indian aide, kept a diary which detailed his dealings with the Iroquois. Washington himself had fought side by side with Indians and acknowledged that it was the Indians of the Delaware that allowed his troops to survive the winter at Valley Forge.

The present-day Onondaga Chief Oren Lyons, a professor of American Studies at the University of New York, Buffalo, has observed that most historians and legal scholars do not research cultural diffusion. Whenever two cultures come in contact an immense amount of information changes hands. The Iroquois confederacy—a confederacy of six individual nations governed by a grand council of 49 chiefs who made policy decisions in regard to trade and exterior relations and who were governed in their deliberations by the Great Law of Peace, peace being the only condition under which justice was possible among nations—had a long history of meetings with white Europeans, years of complex interactions, formal and informal, meetings, discussions, agreements relating to war and peace. "Historians and anthropologists," writes Lyons, "who deny American Indian influence in this process [of inventing governmental forms] are proposing something not only unlikely, but probably unprecedented: that an independent invention occurred which was purely coincidental and entirely isolated from the indigenous societies at hand."

As the colonial Indian commissioner for Pennsylvania, Benjamin Franklin was among the colonial commissioners who met with the chiefs of the Iroquois League in Albany in 1754. The chiefs wanted the colonies to develop a union, an instrument by which the colonies could speak with one voice, instead of each colony's Indian commissioner dealing with the confederacy individually and undercutting the others. The failure to do so made it difficult for the chiefs to take the colonists seriously. The pro-British, 80-year-old Chief Hendrick of the Mohawks, one of the first Mohawk "kings" sent to London in 1710, expressed the distaste of many for how the English had debauched Indians: The English, he said, had "thrown us behind [their] back and disregarded us, [while the French], a subtle and vigilant people, [were] ever using their utmost endeavors to seduce and bring our people over to them." The English had become an increasingly difficult ally for the Iroquois to back. The chiefs detailed many grievances: land swindles, British bigotry against Indians, the slave trade, the liquor trade, which demonstrated the record of better treatment by the French.

In response to the chiefs' demands, Franklin brought to the Albany Congress a draft of a proposal in which the colonies would set up a central council while maintaining their own constitutions. Called the Albany Plan of Union, it was the beginning of the American federal system. It eventually formed the basis for the Articles of Confederation, which in turn influenced the U.S. Constitution. Although the commissioners at the Albany Congress voted to accept the plan, the colonies refused to ratify it. It was only when the colonies' revolt against England made a central governmental structure a necessity that it was used as the basis for the Articles of Confederation.

Franklin was not the only one of the Constitution's drafters who had wide experience with the Iroquois. John Rutledge of South Carolina was also known to be an "Indian buff." Iroquois ideas such as individual political freedom, free speech, equality, and rights of assembly had been recorded and discussed by many people — Franklin, Rutledge, and George Morgan among them.

Although Iroquois ideas about women's rights and communal property did not make their way into the founding fathers' thinking, Franklin's Albany Plan of Union was influenced by many Iroquois principles of confederation in which certain functions of governance were given up to a central authority. "It would be a strange thing," Franklin wrote, "if Six Nations of ignorant savages should be capable of forming a scheme for such an union, and be able to execute it in such a manner as that it has subsisted for ages and appears indissoluble; and yet, that a like union should be impracticable for ten or a dozen English colonies, to whom it is more necessary and must be more advantageous, and who cannot be supposed to want an equal understanding of their interests."

warriors from the upper Great Lakes (Hurons, Ojibwas, Abenakis, Ottawas, Algonquins, and Iroquois from the French missions) had forced the Virginians to surrender the post. Washington himself was subsequently attacked at a site called Fort Necessity. (It was an ancient Indian temple mound with high earthworks, which Washington adapted into a fort.) The French offered Washington honorable surrender terms, which he accepted. They renamed it Fort Duquesne for the French military commander in North America.

1755

Enlightenment ideas came from the New World. Rousseau, a French philosopher, published *Discourse on the Origin of Inequality Among Mankind*, in

1755

Molly Brant, a Mohawk, married Sir William Johnson, English superintendent of Indian affairs. Johnson's jurisdiction extended from New York which he first used the terms "noble savage" and "return to nature." This work was widely translated and read in Europe. Enlightenment ideas about justice and equality and freedom, used to critique monarchy and the entitlements of aristocracy, were based on a new concept of man in nature and often derived from French Jesuit descriptions of their missionary travels in Canada among the Huron. Voltaire's *The Huron or The Pupil of Nature* was another influential work in which the narrative structure of a critique of French aristocracy was based on the viewpoint of a Huron Indian.

to the Mississippi. Johnson was an Englishman who had grown rich in the New York colony and had previously married two Mohawk women. His third wife was Molly Brant, older sister of Joseph Brant, and niece of Chief Hendrick, the Mohawk *sachem*. The liaison was extremely beneficial for Johnson and the English, since her uncle, Chief Hendrick, brought Mohawk warriors to fight for the British side and kept the powerful Iroquois confederacy on the side of the British.

1755
Battle of Lake George. The French defeated. Mohawk Chief Hendrick, then over 70 years of age, brought 400 Mohawk warriors into the service of William Johnson to help fight the French at Lake George. On the eve of a battle against a large force of French and huge numbers of Indian allies, the old chief looked over his small army of Mohawk warriors and said, "If they are to fight, they are too few; if they are to die, they are too many." The British won the battle, but Hendrick and most of his Mohawk warriors were killed. William Johnson himself was wounded and when the wound would not heal, the Iroquois introduced him to the hot mineral springs of Saratoga, which were used by the Indians for healing. Johnson's wound healed. (In the 1800s Saratoga Springs became a great spa, and the springs are still used for relaxation and medicinal purposes.)

1755
A pan-Indian force of Ottawas, Ojibwas, Hurons, and Delawares allied to the French defeated British forces at Fort Duquesne. General Edward Brad-

dock's British army of 1,300 soldiers and eight Indians made its way into Pennsylvania from Virginia in November 1755 with orders from the king to take back Fort Duquesne (later Fort Pitt, now Pittsburgh) from the French. However, the garrison of 300 French soldiers and Canadian militia drew support from a multitribal army of over a thousand Indians, who trounced Braddock's forces. British losses included close to 900 casualties (two-thirds of his forces), as well as horses, provisions, and supplies. Braddock himself was mortally wounded. Indian tradition holds that the Huron and Potawatomi of Michigan acquired their first horses at Braddock's defeat.

1756—1763

The Seven Years' War in Europe. War was formally declared between France and England, although it had been going on for several years prior to formal declaration. Because of the extent of England's and France's colonial empires, this was the first European war fought on a global scale, with engagements in Europe, Africa, Asia, South America, and North America. It was about land, annexations, and the succession of royal lines in Europe. On one side were France, Austria, Sweden, and Russia; on the other, England and Prussia. The French and Indian War, as it was called by English colonials, was the American arena of the larger war in Europe which the French lost, largely through mismanagement of the French royal treasury.

1756—1760

Cherokee alliance with the British. Kanagagot (Standing Turkey), principal chief of the Cherokees, negotiated with the British to be a buffer against French-allied tribes in Kentucky, Tennessee, and Virginia. The Cherokee, descendants of the Mississippian culture, were one of the East's most powerful and largest Indian nations. Their lands extended across South Carolina, northern Georgia, Alabama, western North Carolina, Kentucky, Tennessee, and Virginia. They lived in centralized towns composed of well-constructed buildings arranged geometrically around a central ceremonial structure, and were governed by a combination of clan-based democracy and pre-Columbian Mississippian religious doctrine. Intelligent and disciplined, their relative isolation in the interior had protected them from the demoralization and disruption of the Atlantic Coast nations. In exchange for sending war parties to help defend Virginia's borders against the French, the Cherokee obtained an agreement from the British to build forts in the frontier country to protect them from their immediate enemy, the Shawnee. However, English abuses— atrocities by English settlers against the Cherokee as well as British officers' bigotry—soon cooled the Cherokee's enthusiasm for their new allies. They deserted the English in favor of the French; and Cherokee warriors eventually attacked the very forts, such as Fort Loudon, they had asked the English to build. Chief Kanagagot was mistakenly known to the English colonials as "Old Hopp of Chote" because, when he went to London in 1762 with other Cherokee leaders, and had his portrait painted, the artist misunderstood his name as Cunne Shote, a mispronunciation of the chief's name and the Cherokee capital, Echota.

1757

China restricted all foreign traders to Canton.

1757

In India Clive retook Calcutta from the Bengali for the British East India Company.

1758

In Paris Antoine Le Page du Pratz published *Histoire de la Louisiane* in three volumes, including his drawings and accounts of the Natchez, the largest and last of the intact Mississippian cultures. It remains the single best firsthand account of the culture that built the vast temple mounds in America and the rule of the Great Sun.

1758

The Delawares, allied with the French, left Pennsylvania to settle in eastern Ohio after the British recaptured Fort Duquesne. (The British renamed it Fort Pitt for William Pitt, their prime minister.) During a treaty council at Easton, Pennsylvania, with British representatives, the Delawares agreed to transfer their allegiance from the French to the British in return for an enforced boundary line between Indians and British settlers.

1759

Many Indian leaders in New York and Pennsylvania were divided on the issue of continued alliance with the French. As the British established military supremacy over the French in New York and on the Pennsylvania frontier, groups of French-influenced Mohawk, Onondaga, and Seneca sent war parties against the English. In Ohio the non-League Seneca and Mingo (Mingo was a term used for groups of Onondaga, Seneca, Mohawk, and Oneida who had migrated to Ohio and were not represented by the Iroquois League) aided George Washington and the colonists against the French. The Mohawk of upper New York State, under pro-British influence, actively joined the English campaign against the French in the Champlain Valley. The issues were often regional, but when the British won the war, all Indians lost. They lost their land, trading relationships, and political leverage. No longer could they threaten the British by dealing with the French. After the transfer of Fort Duquesne to the English, more than a thousand Indians held a council at Fort Pitt with British trading agents to determine what the new British trading terms and relationships would be. Included were the Mingo, Huron (henceforth Wyandot), Delaware, Shawnee, Ottawa, Ojibwa, Potawatomi, Miami, and Kickapoo.

1760-1820

George III became king of England. A member of the German Hanoverian family, he made a series of disastrous decisions regarding the colonies in America. For the last two decades of his life he was frequently insane from a hereditary illness, and his son acted as regent.

1760

Acquisition of the horse by all Plains nations. By this time all the Plains groups had acquired horses. Horses significantly changed life among the Plains peoples, making it easier to follow the buffalo and to transport goods. Horse ownership became a symbol of prestige and wealth within tribes; it also

1760
French defeat at Montreal. The terms of surrender included the capitulation of all military posts in French Canada to the English. Although the war in Europe lasted another three years, the Montreal surrender effectively marked the end of French domination in North America. The French also asked that the British respect the lands which the French had reserved for use by Indians.

1761
Spain drawn into the war in Europe on the side of France. A secret treaty between France and Spain conveyed some of French Louisiana west of the Mississippi to Spain.

1762
The British laid siege to Havana and claimed conquest of Cuba.

1762–1796
Catherine II (Catherine the Great) ruled Russia. She engineered the overthrow of her husband, warred against the Ottoman Turks, partitioned Poland, instituted administrative reforms, and was a patron of the arts.

1763
The Treaty of Paris. The end of the Seven Years' War. France relinquished to Britain all claim to Canada and ceded all parts of Louisiana east of the

changed the manner and organization of warfare among the Plains Indians. Warrior societies developed in which great horsemanship was the decisive attribute.

1760–1763
The message of the "Delaware Prophet" spread across the Old Northwest. A Delaware Indian named Neolin was proclaimed the Delaware Prophet in Ohio. He preached a militant vision of driving the Europeans off the continent and returning to the traditions of the ancestors. Only with a return to the old ways—without guns, trade goods, or European relationships—could Native Americans be restored to their former prosperous and harmonious state. His message greatly influenced the Ottawa leader Pontiac, who used it to mobilize the general Northwest uprising of 1763.

1762
Benjamin Franklin in Philadelphia collected 13 Indian treaties made between 1736 and 1762, and published them. He was known to be fascinated with the protocols of Indian treaty-making.

1763
Sir Jeffrey Amherst noted for his deliberate use of smallpox-infected blankets as a weapon against Indians. Amherst and his British lieutenants

Piegan encampment. Because of the paintings of Frederick Remington and the Hollywood western movie, the dominant image of the American Indian became that of the Plains Indian. Edward Curtis's photographs, like this one taken in 1900 on the Blackfoot reservation in Montana, established beautiful images of the Plains teepees against a timeless landscape.

Mississippi. Britain restored Havana to Spain. Spain ceded Florida to Britain. The treaty ended France's colonial aspirations in Canada and greatly weakened her hold on Louisiana.

1763

King George III made Sir Jeffrey Amherst the military commander of Britain's new territories in America. He also initiated a series of new taxes and tariffs to pay for the costs associated with administering the vast new lands acquired in North America, which enraged the colonies.

1763

George III issued the Indian Proclamation Line of 1763 in an attempt to contain westward expansion. It was a line of demarcation that ran along the

were a marked change from the French commanders at the forts throughout the Old Northwest and Canada. He made no effort to build goodwill with Indian peoples. He had no respect for Indian leaders, treated them contemptuously, and frequently described them as "wretched people." He put an immediate end to the traditional French practice of giving Indians ball and powder when they ran short; he also prohibited emergency provisions if game was scarce, and clothing or gifts of goodwill. Lord Amherst (for whom Amherst College is named) initiated a genocidal new policy: "Could it not be contrived," he wrote to one of his officers, "to send the smallpox among these disaffected tribes of Indians? We must on this occasion use every stratagem in our power to reduce them." Blankets were taken from crest of the Appalachian Mountains. It delineated Indian country as west of the line; colonists' lands as east of the line. The British Crown, shaken by the Indian uprisings and the effectiveness of Pontiac's rebellion, proclaimed this boundary line until land cession treaties could be negotiated. But the line proved unenforceable, and English colonists poured into western lands.

1765
The Stamp Act and Quartering Act passed by British Parliament in an attempt to pay for the war and underwrite new administrative costs in the colonies. Greatly resented in the colonies, it led to the Stamp Act Congress in New York and a declaration of grievances delivered to the British Parliament.

recent smallpox victims and given to healthy Indians, thus spreading the fatal epidemic.

1763–1766
Chief Pontiac's rebellion in the Old Northwest. Pontiac organized a pan-Indian alliance against the new British rulers. Pontiac, the highly respected war chief of the Ottawa, had fought in the principal theater of the war against the British. When the victorious British sent out agents to receive the surrender of all French forts, Pontiac blocked them at the southern margin of Lake Erie. Pontiac explained to them that although the French had surrendered, the Indians had not. Following a number of incidents with the new British military, Pontiac organized a pan-Indian confederacy to resist. By the end of 1763 only two of 13 French forts, Pittsburgh and Detroit, were under British control, and they were both under siege. The rebellion lasted until 1766 when Pontiac and his armies ran out of guns and ammunition. (See "Pontiac" on page 194.)

1765
The Paxton raids in Pennsylvania. Land-hungry settlers, impatient for the opening of western Pennsylvania lands, attacked Christianized Susquehannocks. The vigilantes murdered and scalped 20 Indians, including 14 who had been placed in jail for their own safekeeping.

1766
Pontiac's rebellion ended. Pontiac and 40 other chiefs concluded a formal peace with the British. The long Indian sieges at Fort Pitt and Detroit collapsed. One by one, individual tribes made peace with the English.

The original thirteen colonies. The Proclamation Line of 1763 would have prohibited white expansion beyond the Appalachian Mountains. But white settlers in Virginia and Massachusetts had already claimed land in the Ohio Valley and Kentucky and the area that would become the Old Northwest.

PONTIAC

Pontiac was still in the field with his army of more than 500 warriors when the French surrendered in 1763 (largely due to defeats in Europe) to the British. A 40-year-old war chief of the Ottawa nation, he had led a number of Indian armies in 10 years of battles against the British. He was the most prominent native leader in the most active theater of the French and Indian War, which centered on the line of forts running along the Great Lakes from Niagara to Detroit. At the southern margin of Lake Erie a large force of Pontiac's warriors intercepted the British troops sent out to receive the surrender of all French forts in the name of His Britannic Majesty. When the British major was brought before him, Pontiac explained that although the French had surrendered, the Indians had not.

Detroit was then a settlement of 2,500 people, including 120 soldiers and 40 fur traders, surrounded by Indian villages of three different nations—the Potawatomi, the Wyandot (Huron), and the Ottawa. Pontiac, who lived on the Canadian shore opposite Detroit, was the war chief of a loose confederacy of these nations and the Illinois tribes to the south. After four days of negotiations with Pontiac, the British agreed to recognize the delineation of Indian lands previously negotiated with the French, to uphold the trading practices previously in force, and to continue to supply the Indians with ammunition. Only after these agreements had been worked out did Pontiac allow the British to occupy the fort.

Relations between the British and the Indians deteriorated almost immediately. The farther west the English went, the greater the grievances: British traders cheated the Indians and debauched them with whiskey; British soldiers made no secret of their dislike of Indians and kicked and insulted warriors used to being well treated at French forts; the British prohibited the French practice of giving out ball and powder upon request; and the British eliminated the French practice of gift exchanges of clothing and food. The British wanted "subjects."

Pontiac, influenced by the vision of the Delaware Prophet, Neolin, sent out messages to the Wyandot, Potawatomi, the Seneca of the Iroquois confederation, and to nations far down the Mississippi for a rebellion against the English. He planned and organized a pan-Indian uprising against the British in which every tribe—Ottawa, Delaware, Ojibwa, Huron, Shawnee, and Seneca, among others—was to simultaneously attack the British fort nearest to it, some 13 forts strung out over a thousand-mile corridor. In May and June of that year, using various ruses, local warriors killed or captured all personnel at Fort Sandusky, Fort St. Joseph, Fort Miami, and Fort Ouiatenon.

The most notorious event of the war was the surprise attack at Michilimackinac in which the Ojibwa, during a game of lacrosse with visiting Sauk, lobbed a ball over the stockade wall and then rushed in to recover it with guns under their clothes. Once inside, they killed the commander and took prisoners. In Detroit, Pontiac had a similar plan to take Ottawa warriors with guns concealed beneath their blankets into the fort for a treaty council. It was betrayed before it could take place. Instead, Pontiac and his warriors surrounded the fort and subjected it to a six-month siege. The Seneca invaded forts in Pennsylvania. Delaware Indians attacking Fort Pitt (formerly Fort Duquesne, now Pittsburgh) were presented with "gifts" of blankets taken *from the smallpox ward of the fort's hospital. It started an epidemic that would rage through the Delaware villages and Shawnee towns of Ohio, decimating their populations. Still, by the end of 1763, eight out of 12 British posts had been captured and their garrisons massacred.*

Pontiac's War became a major topic of debate in Britain. The English enlarged Sir Jeffrey Amherst's powers to subdue the rebellion. (The smallpox blankets at Fort Pitt had been Lord Amherst's inspiration.) And Pontiac, who had been assured of help from the French, was astonished when he learned from the French commander in Louisiana that France had relinquished all her lands along the Mississippi and could not help resupply Pontiac and his men. Pontiac's troops were running out of ammunition and had no source of supply.

In 1766 Pontiac and 40 other chiefs concluded a formal peace with the British. Pontiac traveled to Oswego, New York, to formally declare his submission to the Crown in front of William Johnson, the British superintendent of Indian Affairs in America. Pontiac's defeat threw open the Ohio Valley to the English. Pontiac watched more and more huge, cumbersome, canvas-topped wagons roll into the rich valley. (The new settlers called these Conestoga wagons, after one of the Pennsylvania tribes, the Susquehanna, also called Conestoga, who had been relocated to lands farther west.)

In the spring of 1769 Pontiac was murdered at Cahokia, Illinois, stabbed in the back by a Kaskaskia Indian who had been bribed with a barrel of whiskey by an English trader named Williamson. Today, Pontiac, Michigan, north of Detroit, is named for him.

1766
Early investors and real estate developers in the Ohio Valley began to map and record the great temple mounds of the Ohio Valley. Henry Brackenridge, a Pennsylvanian who purchased lands in Ohio, was one of the first to write and publish about the Indian antiquity of his day, including the profusion of Indian mounds he found along the Ohio and Scioto Rivers. These included the mound complex at Newark, the great site at Chillicothe, Mound City, and countless other sites at Cincinnati and other places now called Liberty, Frankfort, Circleville, High Bank, Marietta, Anderson. Brackenridge was one of a circle of Ohio investors from Virginia

and Pennsylvania that included George Washington, Albert Gallatin, and Thomas Jefferson. He noted in one of his letters that "all of these vestiges invariably occupy the most eligible situations for towns or settlements." The Indian antiquities occupied high ground along a river, the same lands the new settlers were looking for and eventually purchased.

1766–1774

Indian leaders evaluated their future between the colonists and British Crown. With the end of hostilities between the French and British, Indian leaders realized they faced a markedly changed situation in which they had lost their negotiating leverage between two hostile powers. Although many Native American leaders knew that there was a rift between the British Crown and the English colonists in America, they were uncertain about what would be the best strategy should war come again. Some, like Joseph Brant and the Mohawks, favored alliances with the British. Others, like the Delawares and the Oneidas, favored alliances with the colonies. Others advocated neutrality. Many would again end up on the losing side. All were troubled by various colonial practices like those in Pennsylvania, where colonists offered bounties of 150 dollars for every captured male Indian over 10 years old, 134 dollars for every scalp of a killed Indian; 130 dollars for every captured woman or boy.

1768

The Liberty Affair in Boston. British troops had to quell a riot in Boston after they seized John Hancock's ship, *Liberty*, for illegal entry into the port.

1768
The first volume of the *Encyclopedia Britannica* issued in London.

1769
Shawnees captured Daniel Boone but freed him after confiscating his goods and gear. Daniel Boone opened a route from Virginia into Kentucky called the Wilderness Road, even though these western lands were clearly delineated as Indian lands. In defiance of the Appalachian boundary line of the Proclamation of 1763, settlers poured into the lands of the Shawnee and Cherokee, in western Virginia, Tennessee, and Kentucky. The Wilderness Road and Daniel Boone became a popular subject of American art and myth.

1769
First Spanish mission founded in California. The Spanish founded Mission San Diego as the first in a series of missions extending northward along the California coast. They built 21 missions, a day's journey apart, between San Diego and San Francisco. Thousands of Indians were Christianized and impressed for mission work. All tribal ties were suppressed and any Indians attempting to escape were brutally beaten, branded, or disfigured. Within the mission system, the Indians, or "neophytes" as they were called, were taught trades ranging from blacksmithing and candlemaking to farming. All traditional religious practices were forbidden. The Church in Spain considered the missions successful and profitable. The Indians resisted by poisoning priests, burning churches, and engaging in frequent uprisings. The mission at Santa Barbara alone recorded

4,000 deaths. The coastal California Indian population was reduced from an estimated 70,000 to less than 15,000 in 30 years. There were over 300 separate Indian bands in southern California, which were virtually eradicated by the Spanish mission system.

1770
Boston Massacre. First act of war between Britain and her colonies. British troops fired into a crowd gathered outside the Boston Customs House to protest British trade policies. The first victim of the colonies' rebellion was Crispus Attucks, a man of African American and Massachusetts Indian extraction. Britain subsequently repealed the duties on paper, glass, and paint, but left the tax on tea.

1770
First Spanish governor for Upper Louisiana took control from the French commander.

1771
First mechanized spinning mill produced in England by Sir Richard Arkwright.

1773
In China the opium trade developed. Addiction spread rapidly despite an imperial ban on its use.

1773
Patriots in Boston, dressed up as Mohawks, dumped 342 chests of tea into the harbor to protest the tea tax. Ironically, American colonists used the symbols of Indians to represent defiance and bravery while real Indian people, protecting their families and lands, were being attacked and murdered.

1773
Border wars intensified in Kentucky between settlers and colonists. The great intertribal hunting grounds of the Shawnee, Delaware, and Cherokee in Kentucky and Tennessee were invaded. The Creeks in the South were forced to cede territory. More settlers from Virginia moved west into the territory around the forks of the Ohio River. Although some of the Kentucky hunting lands had been ceded by the Six Nations of the Iroquois League, the Shawnee, who were the principal occu-

pants, refused to acknowledge either Iroquois authority or British possession. Settler-Indian relations deteriorated until the murder of the family of Chief John Logan, a Cayuga man married to a Shawnee woman, set off a series of violent Indian raids against white settlements. The Proclamation Line of 1763 was turning into little more than legal fiction.

1774
Committees of Correspondence established in every American colony. The purpose was to communicate regularly regarding the steps being taken to resist "the intolerable acts" enacted by the British Parliament. These committees were important in improving communications among the colonies and in the spread of consensus for independence.

1774
Passage of the Coercive Acts by British Parliament. These laws enacted in England to control the colonies were called the Intolerable Acts in America, and included the closing of the port of Boston, the right to try colonists for certain capital crimes in England, the right to tax the colonists directly, and the extension of British claims into the Ohio Valley.

1774
Cornstalk's resistance to Lord Dunmore's War against the Shawnee. Lord Dunmore, governor of Virginia, put 3,000 militia into the border lands of Virginia to protect white settlers from the Shawnee. With the Delaware Indians, the Shawnee organized a confederacy to resist white encroachment. Under the leadership of Cornstalk, a Shawnee leader, the confederacy raided English settlements in Virginia, West Virginia, and Ohio west of the Appalachian proclamation line. At Port Pleasant the Shawnee, Delaware, Wyandot, and western Iroquois (Mingo) fought the Virginia militia. The outnumbered Indians were finally forced to accept the settlement of their lands. Although defeated in Virginia, the Shawnee confederation continued to fight to keep settlers out of the trans-Appalachia West and remained intact until the War of 1812.

1774
The Quebec Act enacted in England legislated a boundary line between English colonies and Crown lands reserved to the Indians in Canada which extended as far south as Ohio. To the great alarm of the colonies, Parliament extended the boundary line of Quebec as far south as the Ohio River,

cutting into the land claims of Pennsylvania, New York, and Virginia in the Ohio Valley. Many of the founding fathers and the future leaders of the War for Independence had invested heavily in lands in Ohio.

1774
The First Continental Congress of representatives from all the colonies. The delegates committed 40,000 pounds to Indian affairs and appointed a Committee on Indian Affairs to negotiate terms of neutrality or support from the Indian nations. Indian relations were considered of critical importance to the success of the upcoming War for Independence.

1774
Yuma resistance led by Salvador Palma against the Spanish in Arizona along the lower Colorado River.

1775
Benjamin Franklin sent to England to represent the colonies' grievances before Parliament and the Ministry of Trade. When he returned he introduced his draft of the Articles of Confederation, based on the earlier Albany Plan, to the Second Continental Congress.

1775–1783
War for American Independence. First battles in Lexington and Concord, Massachusetts, and Fort Ticonderoga, New York.

1775
The Second Continental Congress established Indian commissioners for three departments. The Congress assumed centralized control over Indian affairs, not leaving it to the individual colonies, as the British had. They created Northern, Southern, and Middle departments of Indian affairs with commissioners to head each: Benjamin Franklin (Northern), Patrick Henry (Middle), and James Wilson (Southern). They were authorized to make treaties and to arrest British Indian agents. Franklin opened negotiations with the Six Nations to win their neutrality in the upcoming war. He was authorized to offer trade goods and blacksmith services. The Six Nations under Mohawk Joseph Brant declined his offer, but others supported the colonies.

1775

The *sachems* of the Six Nations met with the Indian commissioners in German Flats, New York, to negotiate a treaty of neutrality in case of war. The notes of the meeting taken by Charles Thomson (an adopted Delaware) show how well versed the commissioners were in the concepts of the Iroquois League. Responding to the Indian leaders' skepticism about the colonies' lack of organizational coherence, the commissioners answered: *"[We] have lighted a great Council Fire in Philadelphia and have sent Sixty-five Counsellors to speak and act in the name of the whole."* The commissioners explained why they had to fight Britain: *"We do not take up the hatchet . . . for Honor and Conquest, but to maintain our Civil constitution and religious privileges."* Benjamin Franklin proposed the Pine Tree Flag as the first flag of the U.S., the great pine being the symbol of the life and roots and strength of the Iroquois confederacy. The commissioners also adopted the symbol of an eagle clutching arrows, another Iroquois image, for strength and sovereignty. The *sachems* were concerned about who would be the colonists' chief. (At the Second Continental Congress in Philadelphia, George Washington was given the title of commander in chief.)

1776

Adam Smith in England wrote *Wealth of Nations.*

1776

Britain hired German mercenaries to put down the insurrection in the American colonies.

1776

The Spanish mission of San Juan Capistrano founded near present-day San Clemente, California. Its Indian population was 785.

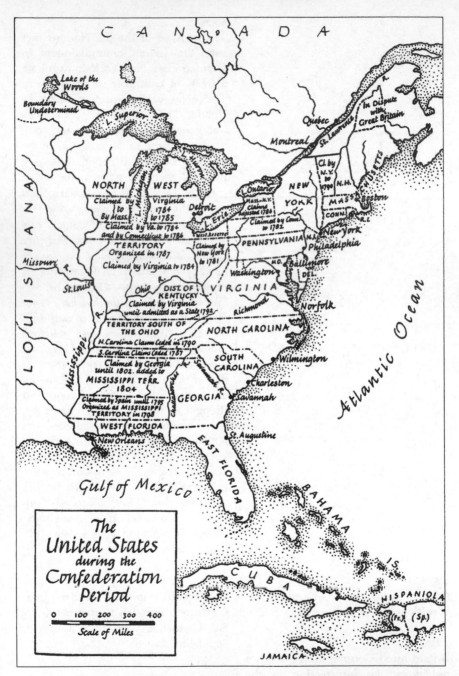

The United States during the Articles of Confederation.

1776

The Declaration of Independence adopted by the American colonies against England. Native American rights were ignored in the Declaration. One of the colonies' grievances against the Crown was its interference in Indian affairs.

1777

Articles of Confederation adopted as the first U.S. laws forming a governmental structure for the 13 colonies. Under the Articles, Native Americans were treated as sovereign nations. Benjamin Franklin and others drew on the concepts expressed in the Albany Plan of Union, his understanding of the workings of the Iroquois confederacy, and even some of the language of the Iroquois League. Article II of the Articles of Confederation stated that the *"Colonies Unite themselves so as to never be divided by any act whatsoever, and hereby severally enter into a firm League of friendship with each other . . ."*

1777

Battle of Saratoga. British defeated in a crucial engagement of the war at Saratoga, New York. As a result of the colonies' unexpected victory, France supported them with money, supplies, and troops. This was a critical defeat in which the colonists outmaneuvered the British General Burgoyne and his English troops on their way down the Hudson Valley from Canada. The terms of surrender required that Burgoyne and his 8,000 soldiers leave the country immediately.

1777

Shawnee leader Cornstalk killed while at Fort Randolph under a flag of truce after a raid in the area of Wheeling, West Virginia. He was taken as hostage and then murdered by whites.

1777

Oneida, Tuscarora, and Delaware Indians helped George Washington's cold and starving troops survive the winter at Valley Forge, Pennsylvania.

1777

The Six Nations of the Iroquois confederacy divided and then permanently dispersed, their council fire extinguished. The Mohawk, led by Joseph Brant, were determined to support the British Crown. The Seneca and the Onondaga favored neutrality. The Oneida and Tuscarora, because of local trade and friendship ties with settlers, sided with the colonies. The Iroquois central council, which was required to come to consensus to form a binding plan of action, was unable to do so. Individual nations and villages then made their own decisions about alliance or neutrality in the war, a policy which caused deep fissures within the Iroquois confederacy. At Onondaga, the home of the confederacy's council fire, an epidemic struck. The survivors sent a message to the new United States government: *"We have lost out of [our] town by death ninety, out of which are three principal [chiefs]. We the remaining part of the Onondagas do now inform our Brothers that there is no longer a council fire at the Capital of the Six Nations."* The council fire had been kept burning permanently as a symbol of the life of the League. When it was extinguished, the spirit of the confederacy dissolved.

The battle of Oriskany marked the final rupture of the Iroquois confederacy. At Oriskany Creek in New York a party of Mohawk under Joseph Brant, fighting for the British, ambushed Oneida troops fighting for the Americans. It was the equivalent of an Iroquois Civil War. (See "Thayendanegea, or Joseph Brant" on page 206.)

1778
France signed the Treaty of Commerce and Alliance with the new United States and sent military advisors to help in the war.

1778
Britain sent an offer of conciliation to the U.S., which was rejected by Congress.

1778
Captain James Cook landed on Vancouver Island and later claimed Oregon country (Oregon, Washington, Idaho, and parts of Montana and Wyoming) for the British.

1778
First U.S.–Indian treaty signed. The Delaware (the Turtle people) signed a peace treaty with the United States at Fort Pitt which gave them the potential right to send Delaware representatives to Congress in return for supporting the colonies against the British. Although the clause was never implemented, it established the idea of Indian representation in Congress. It also recognized the mechanism of the treaty as the primary legal instrument for federal policy toward American Indians. The practice of negotiating treaties continued until 1871, when Congress prohibited any further treaties with Indian tribes. Between 1778 and 1871, the Senate ratified 370 treaties with Indian peoples. After 1871 agreements with Indian groups were made by acts of Congress, executive order, or

executive agreement. The provisions of treaties were rarely kept. Once Indians were a minority population, they had little leverage in Washington.

1779
Sullivan's Indian Campaign. General Washington sent an American army of 4,000 troops under General John Sullivan to attack the villages of the Iroquois confederacy in western New York. Because of the dissension and division within the Iroquois nations, Sullivan's men devastated the area.

1779
The Oneida Indians as allies of the American forces helped to destroy Onondaga, capital of the Iroquois confederation.

1779
The Continental Congress passed a law asserting that only the federal government, not individual states, could transfer ownership of Indian lands.

1779
George Rogers Clark waged war in the Old Northwest and discovered the great temple mound city at Cahokia. The older brother of William Clark (of the Lewis and Clark expedition), he led a force of Virginians into the lands of the Old Northwest and accepted the surrender of the British commander at Fort Vincennes. He was also the first to report on the existence of Cahokia, the great temple mound city at the confluence of the Missouri and the Mississippi Rivers in Illinois.

THAYENDANEGEA, OR JOSEPH BRANT

The great pine tree whose roots were the five most powerful tribes of the Iroquois and whose tip pierced the sky was the symbol of the Great Peace of the Iroquois confederacy, and the chiefs of the central council were called Pine Tree chiefs. For 200 years the Iroquois confederacy had been able to keep the peace. They controlled lands from the St. Lawrence to the Great Lakes. Over the years they had brought into their alliances the Hurons to the northwest and the Susquehannas (Conestogas) to the south. When the English drove the Tuscaroras, another Iroquois people, out of North Carolina, the Iroquois gave them land in New York and the confederacy became Six Nations. Peace was conceived by the Iroquois as not simply an absence of war, but a dynamic relationship among nations in which war was viewed as an ill-conceived solution to conflict. With sophisticated agriculture, wide trading relationships, and abundant resources, the Iroquois had a way of life that was enhanced by peace and damaged by war.

One of the great Pine Tree chiefs was "King" Hendrick, half-Mohawk, half-Mohegan, who had been taken to England in 1710 by the first British governor in New York. He had been impressed by the size of London and the complexity of the British governing system. Subsequently, he developed strong ties with the English and encouraged his children to attend the British schools and learn English. He developed close ties with William Johnson, the English Indian agent in America, who had learned Iroquois and married three Mohawk women. When Johnson asked for Iroquois volunteers in the battle against the French at Lake George in 1755, Chief Hendrick, age 70, was among the several hundred warriors who stepped forward. The old sachems wanted to keep the neutrality of the League, but the English were persuasive. Supposedly Hendrick's nephew, young Thayendanegea, age 13, went along with his uncle but stayed out of battle.

Thayendanegea's older sister Molly, a full-blooded Mohawk, was William Johnson's third wife, a liaison that cemented the Iroquois friendship with the English. Her connections provided the English with invaluable intelligence about Indian alliances and movements throughout the series of French and Indian Wars. Johnson took an interest in the chief's nephew and his wife's brother and sent Thayendanegea to the Indian Charity School in Lebanon, Connecticut. There Thayendanegea took the name Joseph Brant. He was a brilliant pupil and started translating the Anglican prayer book into Mohawk.

When he graduated and returned to the Mohawk Valley in New York, he became secretary to Sir William Johnson (Johnson had received the royal title of baronet in 1755 because of his service to the Crown in securing the Iroquois volunteers against the French). As Johnson's secretary, Brant saw the humbling lessons of choosing the losing side: Chief Pontiac was among many of the French-allied chiefs who made the journey to Johnson Hall at Oswego, New York, to bow his head and formally seal his submission to the Crown. After Sir William's death Brant continued as secretary to Johnson's nephew, Guy Johnson, who took over as the Crown's representative in North America.

Brant went to England in 1775. He had tea with Boswell; he sat to have his portrait painted by Romney, the court painter; he delivered a speech before the secretary of state:

Brother, we have crossed the great lake and come to this kingdom with our superintendent, Colonel Johnson, from our Confederacy of the Six Nations . . .

that we might see our father, the great king. . . . Brother, the Mohawks . . . have on all occasions shown their zeal and loyalty to the great king; yet they have been very badly treated by the people in that country, the city of Albany laying an unjust claim to their lands. . . . We have only, therefore, to request that His Majesty will attend to this matter: it is very hard, when we have let the king's subjects have so much land for so little, they should want to cheat us in this manner of the small spots we have left for our women and children to live on. We are tired out in making complaints and getting no redress. We therefore hope that the assurances now given us by the superintendent may take place and that he may have it in his power to procure justice.

But Brant with the British, like Chief Pontiac with the French, was to choose the losing side. His request that the English guarantee the return of the lands his people had lost on the Mohawk and Susquehanna Rivers assumed that the British would never lose in the rebellion of the 13 colonies. Would Brant commit, the English secretary wanted to know, the resources of the Six Nations in support of the British government in the war against the American colonies? Although it was not in Brant's power to do so, he assured the British secretary that he would.

The subsequent debate within the Iroquois League on which side to support in the American War of Independence was to be its last. Action within the confederacy required consensus. But there was none. Under Brant's leadership, the Mohawks and Senecas supported the British; the Oneidas and Tuscaroras supported the colonies; the Cayugas and Onondagas wanted to remain neutral. When war came, they each supported opposing sides. Of Brant's behavior as a colonel in the British army, Indian author Frank Waters has written: "Wholly dedicated to the British Crown . . . he hurled himself into the Revolutionary War with savage ferocity. The frightful massacre at Wyoming [Pennsylvania] . . . Cherry Valley . . . the attack on Minisink . . . Oriskany . . . swift raids throughout the Mohawk Valley and on the New York–Pennsylvania border. And with everyone, his reputation for bloody violence and savagery increased until he became known as 'Monster Brant' to every settler on the frontier."

Brant's own nature seemed to be split into halves, one English, the other Mohawk. Putting aside the traditions of the Iroquois confederacy and his devout translation of the Gospels, he revenged himself for the colonists' greed. The raids of the Mohawks and Senecas were feared and "Monster Brant" was a terrifying figure on the frontier. The end came in the Battle of Johnstown when George Washington dispatched 4,000 troops to defeat the combined force of the English and Brant's Mohawks and Senecas. The American troops devastated the Mohawk Valley and all the Iroquois villages in it. They wiped out a sophisticated civilization, as one of Washington's generals wrote: "The Indians live much better than most of the Mohawk River farmers, their Houses very well furnished with all necessary Household utensils, great plenty of Grain, several horses, cows, and wagons."

When the war was over Brant went to Canada, where the British Crown gave him a grant of land in Ontario. A few years later the British also gave a land grant to the warriors who had fought with him. This would prove the background for the claims of two Six Nations confederacies, one in New York and the other in Canada.

1780

The French monarchy, although almost bankrupt, sent General de Rochambeau and 6,000 French troops to aid the U.S. cause.

1780

In California the Spanish expanded the Indian mission system. Spanish forts, or presidios, were established all along the California coast attached to missions at Santa Barbara, San Diego, Monterey, and San Francisco. Smaller military garrisons were established at Yuma and on the Colorado River at the main crossing for the land route into Sonora, Mexico.

1780–1782

A smallpox epidemic spread throughout the Great Plains. The disease spread northward from Mexico and affected all the villages on the greater Plains, killing off large numbers of Chippewa bands, Shoshoni, Siksika, Kainai, Peigan, Cree, Assiniboine, and Gros Ventre.

1781

Battle of Yorktown and the surrender of Cornwallis. French troops were crucial to the final victory at Yorktown, where Washington with French generals Lafayette and Rochambeau surrounded British General Cornwallis while the French fleet entered Chesapeake Bay. Although the definitive treaty of peace wasn't signed until 1783 in Paris, the surrender of Cornwallis at Yorktown marked the end of the War for Independence. The American commissioners disregarded their French allies and negotiated a separate peace with Great Britain.

1782

In Japan crops failed, causing widespread famine. Financial troubles plagued the shogunate.

1782

Indians living around Ventura, California, were dispossessed of their lands by the Spanish. In order to give large individual land grants to three

Spanish soldiers for their service to the Crown, the Mission San Buenaventura took huge tracts of lands. These were the first of the massive land grants that formed the basis of the California land system.

1783

Treaty of Paris signed between U.S. and Britain. It recognized U.S. independence and ceded British territorial claims. It made no mention of Indian rights within states. Britain recognized the U.S. claim to all lands from the Atlantic to the Mississippi and from the Great Lakes to the Florida border. Provisions relating to the northwest boundary led to later difficulties with the British; provisions relating to the southern boundary led to later difficulties with Spain.

1783–1790

U.S. Congress centralized control of Indian lands and took authority away from the states. Public lands were virtually the only asset available to the new government for purposes of raising revenue. In lieu of cash bonuses for veterans of the War for Independence, the new government gave them land. The U.S. claimed not only political sovereignty over the Indian lands surrendered by the British, but actual ownership of the land itself.

1783

Iroquois confederacy formally disbanded with the signing of separate U.S. treaties with the Tuscarora and Oneida and a British treaty with the Mohawk. The British awarded Joseph Brant and his Mohawk followers a land grant in Canada, where they formed their own Iroquois confederacy. The Iroquois remaining in New York were forced to cede most of their territorial lands, although the tribes supporting the colonists, the Tuscarora and the Oneida, were given larger land grants and treaties providing for education and the construction of a sawmill. By the 1800s two independent Iroquois confederacies emerged.

1784

Treaty of Fort Stanwix between the Iroquois Six Nations and U.S. government. The New York Iroquois, by means of hostages and threats, were forced to cede all their lands in western New York and Pennsylvania, as well as territories in Ohio and Kentucky occupied by their allied tribes, and to accept a small reservation in New York State for themselves. Other members of the Iroquois confederacy repudiated the provisions of this treaty.

1785

The Ordinance of 1785 created townships and took more land away from the Indians. The government called for the survey of public lands into "townships" of six miles square, divided into 36 sections of 640 acres each, costing 1 dollar an acre. This method of land management favored speculators with money to invest. The new government was able to raise considerable money by surveying and selling Indian lands in Ohio, Illinois, Indiana, Kentucky, and Tennessee to land companies and land speculators, who in turn sold to land-hungry settlers. The new U.S. government immediately began making treaties with small Indian groups to gain additional public lands. The Indian agents used bribery, threats, alcohol, hostages, and manipulation of unauthorized Indian "chiefs" to wrench land away from communally held tribal property. The Treaty of Fort Stanwix with the Iroquois and the treaty of Fort McIntosh with the Delaware were two such forced treaties.

1785

The Wyandot, Delaware, Chippewa, and Ottawa were forced to sign the Treaty of Fort McIntosh ceding certain lands in Pennsylvania, Ohio, Indiana, and Tennessee to the U.S. government. This was viewed as a "whiskey treaty," extracted by threats and alcohol. Since few Indian leaders recognized the treaty's legitimacy, they did not abide by its terms. Consequently, land struggles began almost immediately in those states, where white settlers bought lands from land companies, who had bought "public lands" from the government, who in turn did not have legitimate title to the lands they sold.

1786–1792

Grigori Shelikhov intensified conquest of Alaska for Russia. He established fortifications, imported cattle, and built a permanent settlement on Kodiak Island. He also enslaved Aleuts as hunters and domestic servants.

1787

Riots in Japan as economic and social problems sparked unrest. Population of Edo (Tokyo) put at one million.

1787

Constitutional Convention met in Philadelphia. The inability of Congress to raise money, the outbreaks of disorder on the frontiers, the problems with trade, and the need for a uniform commercial code required a stronger government than that allowed under the Articles of Confederation. After four months the Constitution was drafted, signed, and submitted to the states for ratification.

The Commerce Clause (Article 1, Section 8) empowered Congress to make all laws regarding Indian trade and to "regulate commerce with foreign nations and among the several states and with the Indian tribes within the limits of any states, not subject to the laws thereof." It prohibited the states from negotiating treaties directly and delegated all control of Indian lands to federal authorities. The legal relationship was to be executed through treaty-making.

1786

New Mexico's new governor Bernardo de Galvez inaugurated a policy of treaties and trade with the Navajos and Apaches.

1787

Northwest Ordinance passed by Congress. It called for the division of lands known as the Old Northwest (renamed the Northwest Territory) into not less than three, not more than five, districts which, after passing through territorial status, should become states. Slavery and involuntary servitude were prohibited. It organized the lands, provided for a governor, and delineated the process by which the districts would be divided into states. It also acknowledged that these lands were occupied by Indian nations: "*The utmost of good faith shall always be observed toward the Indians; their land and property shall never be taken away from them without their consent; and their property, rights and liberty shall never be invaded by Congress; but laws founded in justice and humanity shall from time to time be made for preventing wrongs to them, and for preserving peace and friendship with them.*" The principle of "ordinance," or ultimate statehood, became the basic and distinguishing feature of the American land policy of

1787
The French monarchy bankrupt. The nobles refused additional taxes. The Parlement of Paris demanded the convocation of the Estates General, precipitating the events of the French Revolution.

1789
Beginning of the French Revolution. The storming of the Bastille by a Paris mob. France was a prosperous country in 1789, with a bankrupt government unsuited to the needs of a large commercial and agricultural state. Once the Estates-General was called to remedy the bankruptcy, they took on a massive reform of the entire state.

the nineteenth century. The Northwest Territory was subsequently divided into Ohio, Indiana, Illinois, Michigan, and Wisconsin.

1788
Kentucky lands, which settlers called "a dark and bloody ground," had been ceded by the Iroquois. These were Shawnee hunting grounds, which the Shawnee defended fiercely, regardless of the Iroquois cession, which they considered illegal and invalid. By the end of the 1700s over 300,000 people had followed the Wilderness Road through the Cumberland Gap into Kentucky.

1789
Indian affairs were moved to the War Department. Secretary of War Henry Knox agreed that Indian nations held legal title to their lands "until the government by just negotiation—or a just war—extinguished that title." Because so many Indian nations had been allied with the British in the Old Northwest or with the Spanish in the South, the War Department took over as the site of Indian relations, with responsibility for negotiation of all treaties. The responsibilities of the U.S. Indian Department were to monitor Indian relations, regulate trade, and manage land cessions and settlement.

Thomas Jefferson stated: *"It may be regarded as certain that not a foot of land will ever be taken from the Indians without their own consent. The sacredness of their rights is felt by all thinking persons in America as much as in Europe."*

1789–1850
Over 450 million acres of Indian land taken by the U.S. government. Between 1789 and 1850 the U.S. acquired over 450 million acres of Indian lands for less than 190 million dollars (approximately 42 cents an acre). Revenues from the sale of public (Indian) lands were 80 percent of the new government's annual budget.

1790
In Paris the Estates-General adopted the Declaration of the Rights of Man, a bill of rights based on American documents of the Revolution, English precedents, and the theories of the French *philosophes*.

1790
First American cotton textile factory built in Rhode Island by Samuel Slater. The increased demand for raw cotton would motivate Southern cotton plantation owners to pressure the government to remove the southeastern tribes in order to open their lands for cotton cultivation.

1790
A confederation of Shawnees, Miamis, Chippewas, and other allied Indian nations of the Ohio country and lower Great Lakes under chiefs Blue Jacket and Little Turtle decisively defeated General Harmar's army in the Northwest Territory. Already outraged by frontiersmen and militia who came from Kentucky and sacked and burned Shawnee villages on the Miami River, the western Indian nations were particularly incensed by President Washington's decision to build a fort on the north bank of the Ohio River on land still claimed by the Miami Indians. The British, who had not yet left the Northwest Territory (citing American violations of the Treaty of Paris), supplied the western Indian confederation with arms, food, and other trade goods. The Miamis, under the command of their war chief Little Turtle, and the Shawnees, under the command of war chief Blue Jacket, began a campaign against all the white settlements in the territory. Secretary of War Knox approved a retaliatory campaign of some 1,450 men under the command of General Josiah Harmar. Little Turtle and Blue Jacket and their armies ambushed General Harmar and his troops, killed 183 Americans, and put the general's troops to flight.

1790-1799

Hundreds of visitors returned from the Ohio Valley with reports of the scale of Indian antiquities and the amazing earthworks of the Ohio Valley. Both George Washington and Thomas Jefferson constructed earthen mounds on their estates and Thomas Jefferson devoted the interior hall of Monticello to Indian artifacts sent to him from Ohio.

1790

Congress enacted the first Trade and Intercourse Act to regulate trade and to strengthen federal authority over states in regard to Indian relations. The goal was to establish direct federal control of trade and commerce with Indian nations. The act provided: *"That no sale of lands shall be made by any Indians, or any nation or persons, or to any state . . . unless the same shall be made and duly executed at some public treaty, held under the same authority of the United States."* It was the first in four such acts regulating all trade and intercourse with Indian tribes and placing all interactions between Indians and non-Indians under federal control. The basis of many present-day land claims by eastern tribes was the legal requirement, still in effect, that Indian land could not be sold by the tribe without federal consent.

1791

Vermont admitted as 14th state; the Bill of Rights ratified; the Democratic Republican Party founded by Thomas Jefferson to oppose the Federalist Party of Alexander Hamilton and John Adams.

1791

Blue Jacket and Little Turtle and 14 allied tribes routed General St. Clair, Harmar's successor, in one of the greatest defeats of the U.S. Army. Arthur St. Clair, governor of the Northwest Territory, and his force of 1,400 untrained militia, eight artillery pieces, and assorted

1791-1799

Slave rebellions in Haiti against the French. Led by former slaves Jean Baptiste Sans Souci and Toussaint l'Ouverture, more than 500,000 slaves fought the French colonial forces to a standstill, eventually taking the lives of 19 generals and as many soldiers as Napoleon would lose at Waterloo. The costs of the Haitian (Santo Domingo) rebellion influenced Napoleon to sell France's Louisiana to the U.S. All slaves were freed and the 40,000 whites either fled or were killed.

1792

Kentucky admitted as 15th state.

1792

Francis II of Austria succeeded his father as emperor of the Holy Roman Empire; he would be the last emperor.

1793-1794

The Reign of Terror in France. Louis XVI and Marie Antoinette guillotined. The government of the new Republic organized a 12-man Committee of Public Safety to put down rebellions throughout France and organize for war. The Committee quickly took the shape of a police state, setting up thousands of surveillance committees, courts, a Revolutionary Tribunal, and detaining and prosecuting more than 120,000 for crimes against the Republic. More than 40,000 people were guillotined (one out of every 700 people in France). Robespierre, the theoretician of the Terror, believed that it would cleanse the country of a corrupt aristocracy, but the Terror soon devoured its

camp followers arrived on an unprotected plateau of the upper Wabash River. A party of Indian scouts (which included Tecumseh, the Shawnee chief) had reported on the army's movements from the moment they entered the Northwest Territory. Attacking at dawn in a surprise assault, the Indian troops killed 623 soldiers and 24 civilians in one of the worst defeats in the history of the Indian wars. (Custer's loss at Little Bighorn was comparatively smaller, only 211 men.) Indian casualties were 21 killed and 40 wounded. The scale of the Indian victory temporarily panicked settlers and land development companies, and halted settlement in the Northwest Territory.

1793

Congress appropriated 1 million dollars to equip and train a new federal army, to be called the Legion of the U.S., to avenge St. Clair's defeat and subdue the Indians of the Northwest Territory. The cost of the new federal army was politically unpopular. Consequently, Secretary Knox made another highly publicized effort to reach a peace agreement with the tribes.

own. Robespierre was executed along with 100 "Robespierrists." In the reaction that followed, Napoleon emerged as a dominant figure.

1793

Eli Whitney introduced the cotton gin, which revolutionized the production of cotton in the South.

1794

Missionaries from the Russian Orthodox Church arrived on Kodiak Island, Alaska. Consequently, Christianity in Alaska followed the forms and teachings of the Eastern Orthodox Church.

1794

Jay's Treaty signed between Great Britain and the United States. It set out the new border between the U.S. and Canada, established terms and conditions of trade, and stipulated that the British would leave their forts in the Northwest Territory. The Indians were guaranteed freedom of movement between the two countries without the need to pay any duties. (See "Jay's Treaty" on page 219.)

1794

General "Mad Anthony" Wayne and the Battle of Fallen Timbers. When Secretary Knox's peace overture was not accepted, he sent General Wayne with 2,200 infantry regulars, 1,500 Kentucky militia, and a full cavalry with the best equipment. When Little Turtle learned that the British could not supply the western tribes with guns and ammunition (because of Jay's Treaty), he recommended negotiation, but the other chiefs wanted war. Wayne's cannon and numbers routed the Indian forces. The battle was over in an hour and the losses were relatively small (31 Americans dead; 40 Indians dead), but the Indians knew they were outnumbered and outgunned, and without British aid they could no longer hope to defeat the Americans. It was called the Battle of Fallen Timbers because the fight took place in a field where trees had been downed by a tornado.

1794

The Oneida, Tuscarora, and Stockbridge Indians made the first agreement concerning Indian education. Because they were tribes that had supported the American colonies during the War for Independence, the new U.S. government agreed to compensate them for any property losses (the total was 5,000 dollars) and to provide them with any form of education they requested, particularly training to operate the gristmills and sawmills that the government had agreed to build in the peace treaty of 1783.

1795

The Greenville Treaty of Peace signed by 1,100 chiefs of the western confederated tribes. The seven-foot-long document was signed by the chiefs of the Shawnee, Delaware, Ottawa, Potawatomi, Wyandot, Miami, Chippewa, Kickapoo, Wea, Piankashaw, and Kaskaskia. After the Battle of Fallen Timbers and the British agreement to withdraw from their forts, General Anthony Wayne imposed the treaty on all the tribes of the region. It extinguished Indian title to lands representing two-thirds of present-day Ohio, a section of Indiana, and the sites of Detroit, Toledo, Chicago, and Peoria. The treaty also fixed a firm boundary line between Indian lands and white settlements. Acting under orders from the War Department, Wayne insisted that all 1,100 chiefs individually sign the peace treaty, which was written on parchment seven feet long and three feet wide. The allied tribes gave up lands, and in return were promised a firm boundary between Indian territories and the U.S. The treaty also stipulated that lands could be ceded only by tribes as a whole, and not individually, and that they had a right to all remaining lands not specifically ceded to white settlers. Acting on Jefferson's orders, the new Northwest Territory governor, William Henry Harrison, violated the treaty almost immediately.

1797
Much of Italy fell to Napoleon. Revolt in Naples against the Napoleonic regime.

1799
Russian-American Company granted monopoly of fur trade in Alaska; many Russian missionaries died in a shipwreck.

1797
Senecas in upstate New York deceived into selling all their territories in western New York and northwestern Pennsylvania. The Mohawks, Oneidas, Onondagas, and Cayugas retained only small pieces of once vast territories.

1797
The American Philosophical Society in Philadelphia, founded in 1743 "to promote useful knowledge," expanded its mission to obtain accurate plans, drawings, and descriptions of the "western fortifications, tumili, and other Indian works of art." These included the archaeological ruins and temple mounds found in the Ohio Valley and along the Mississippi commonly called "Spanish forts" in public documents.

1799
Andrew Jackson's law partner found the remains of an 800-year-old village. Judge Overton wanted to build a new home six miles south of Nashville, Tennessee, and unknowingly chose a site in the midst of some Mississippi mounds. When he dug the foundation, he found that the earth was filled with ancient graves and stone coffins. When the site was finally excavated in the twentieth century it was found to be the site of a large village inhabited between 1000 and 1300.

1799
Handsome Lake, half brother to renowned Seneca war chief Cornplanter, had a vision that began the Longhouse religion. Handsome Lake was a Seneca Indian (New York) and a clan leader whose villages had been destroyed during Sullivan's raids through

JAY'S TREATY

Although the Americans succeeded to all British colonies in the United States, the Treaty of Paris had not taken into account the realities of the American-Canadian border, where Indian peoples crossed freely from Canada to the U.S, and where strategically located posts such as Oswego, Niagara, Detroit, and Michilimackinac were still in British hands, though they were technically owned by the Americans. In 1794 the governor-general of Canada, Lord Dorchester, gave a speech encouraging the Indians of the Great Lakes region to make war on the United States. He was supported in this by British merchants who engaged in the highly lucrative Indian fur trade (half of which came from below the border). In Washington there was an outcry and people called on George Washington to "do something." Knowing that the United States had neither the finances nor the inclination to engage in another war, Washington sent Chief Justice John Jay to London to seek a settlement of Anglo-American differences with the British foreign secretary, Baron Grenville.

The resulting treaty established a boundary line between Canada and the U.S., set a date by which the British would evacuate their posts on American territory, provided for the terms of trade across the border, and allowed for free movement of the Indian nations who lived and hunted on both sides of the border.

Article III of Jay's Treaty: ". . . It is agreed that [the border] shall at all times be free to His Majesty's subjects and to the citizens of the United States, and also to the Indians dwelling on either side of the said boundary line, freely to pass and repass by land or inland navigation, into the respective territories and countries of the two parties on the continent of America . . .

". . . No duty on Entry shall ever be levied by either party on peltries brought by land, or inland navigation into the said territories respectively, nor shall the Indians passing or repassing with their own proper goods and effects of whatever nature, pay for the same any impost of duty whatever. But goods in bales or other large packages unusual among the Indians shall not be considered as goods belonging bona fide to Indians . . ."

Although Jay's Treaty might be a dusty document to white people, it is a living treaty to Native peoples who live on both sides of the U.S.–Canadian border. In the pan-Indian magazine Akwesasne Notes (Spring 1995, p. 64), the editors pointed out that "the border-crossing issue has been a matter of contention for 201 years." It is also the basis of a suit before the Canadian Supreme Court. In 1957 Louis Francis, chief on the Canadian side of the Akwesasne reservation, bought a used washing machine from his brother-in-law who lived on the American side of the reservation. The government of Canada confiscated the washing machine because he had not paid customs duty. Louis Francis then brought suit against the Canadian government, claiming violations of Jay's Treaty. For over 33 years the case made its way through the Canadian court system, finally reaching the Supreme Court of Canada in 1994. Akwesasne Notes observed: "In 1994 we commemorated the 200th anniversary of the Treaty of Amity, Commerce and Navigation between the United States and Great Britain, more commonly known as the Jay Treaty of 1794. In 1995, the Native peoples await a Supreme Court decision . . ." The case is still pending.

Iroquois country. Relocated to lands on the Allegheny River on the New York–Pennsylvania border, he had taken refuge in alcohol and retreated from the cultural and political deterioration of his once great Seneca nation. In his sixties, when he was sick and dying, family and friends gathered to pay their last respects. Later he told them that in his illness his spirit had left his body and he had a vision of what had to be done to help the Seneca find their way in the new world. Instead of a funeral, his family and friends heard his first sermon, a description of his vision and the lessons the Creator had revealed to him. He had been transformed and his teachings, *Gaiwiio*, also called the Good Word, became the basis of the Longhouse religion and led to a cultural revival of the Iroquois. Among his teachings, which are still alive today as part of the Handsome Lake Church, is the idea that natives should live in peace with the United States, but they should spiritually and culturally remain Iroquois. He stressed peace within family and among peoples and based many of his tenets on the Great Law of the Peacemaker of the Haudenosaunee, the old Iroquois confederacy. The religion gathered many followers, ensured the survival of traditional beliefs and ceremonies, and still has many adherents. Just before he died he told his followers: "*I will soon go to my new home . . . whoever follows my teachings will follow in my footsteps and I will look back upon him with outstretched arms inviting him into the new world of our Creator. Alas, I fear a pall of smoke will obscure the eyes of many from the truth of Gaiwiio but I pray that when I am gone that all may do what I have taught.*"

1799

The third Trade and Intercourse Act passed. The first federal Indian agents named. The law carefully regulated who could have contact with Indians. It restricted anyone without a license from having "any trade with the Indians" and subjected unlicensed traders to a fine and/or imprisonment. The act also provided for the presidential appointment of temporary federal agents to the tribes, the first Indian agents. The act was designed to keep federal control over all aspects of Indian relations.

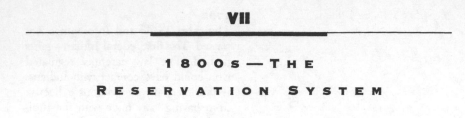

VII

1800s — THE
RESERVATION SYSTEM

"I know what the misfortune of the tribes is. Their misfortune is not . . . that they are a dwindling race; nor that they are a weak race. Their misfortune is that they hold great bodies of rich lands."

SENATOR EUGENE CASSERLY, 1871

During the 1800s the French, English, and Spanish pulled back and returned to Europe. The new players were the victorious colonists, greedy for land. For them land meant wealth, freedom, power; it defined the promise of the New World. To the Indians, land had a very different meaning—culturally, economically, and spiritually. Land belonged to everyone; it could not be owned. "Sell a country!" Tecumseh thundered at a meeting of the representatives of the Northwest Territory in 1810. "Why not sell the air, the clouds and the great sea, as well as the earth? Did not the Great Spirit make them all for the use of his children?"

At the beginning of the 1800s, white settlement was contained to the east of the Appalachian Mountains. Except for the eastern seaboard, more than 80 percent of what is now the contiguous 48 states was Indian land. The history of the 1800s in America is the story of how that land was taken away from its native inhabitants.

With the Treaty of Paris in 1783, Great Britain had relinquished all its claims to Indian lands east of the Mississippi. When the U.S. assumed the rights of conquest and moved to take control of western New York, Pennsylvania, and the Ohio River Valley, the Indian inhabitants—who had won almost every battle—informed them in no uncertain terms that although the British might have surrendered, they had not. Having neither the resources to pursue another war nor the ability to administer such vast lands, the new colonial government resumed the British practice of purchasing Indian lands and writing treaties. The treaties typically contained provisions concerning land use and the introduction of missionaries and teachers into Indian settlements. The policy of assimilation—which has continued to the present under the names of "allotment," "termination," or "abrogation"—was a way to get around the political reality that the new United States, founded on the principles of freedom and equality, was setting out to destroy Indian nations for the sake of real estate.

However, border-area skirmishes between land-hungry settlers and Indians were ongoing, and increased in both savagery and frequency. Abundance of land— which was central to Thomas Jefferson's political concept of an agricultural nation

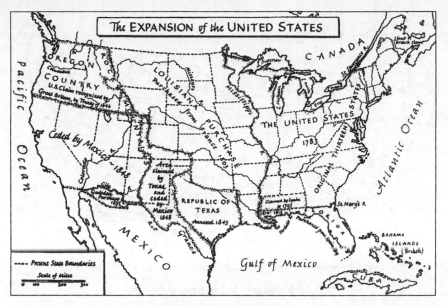

The expansion of the U.S.

of yeoman farmers—was dependent on the dispossession of the original inhabitants. Economist Steven Cornell has pointed out that the cotton economy of the South, which was the driving force of early American economic growth, expanded only as fast as acquisition of Indian lands would allow. From 1815 to 1830 cotton production in the South increased at exactly the same pace as Indian land cessions. The idea of southeastern Indian removal had been raised as early as 1803 when President Jefferson, after purchasing the vast acreage of the Louisiana Purchase extending from the Mississippi to the Rockies, proposed that all the Indians east of the Mississippi be relocated to "new lands" west of the Mississippi. It was a policy eventually executed by Andrew Jackson in the 1830s with the forced removal of the Five Civilized Tribes—the Chickasaw, the Cherokee, the Creek, the Choctaw, and the Seminole—from Alabama, Georgia, Florida, Louisiana, and Mississippi to what is now Oklahoma.

As the century progressed and white demand for land intensified, Indian removal to Oklahoma Territory or remnant land in other states became official policy, even when it took a war to accomplish it. The professional American military took shape in the West. By 1900, Indians had lost 95 percent of their 1800 holdings. At the same time the U.S. was beginning to emerge as the world's leading economic power. Land was the great untapped economic resource of America. Dispossession became essential to economic development. Capital and labor poured into America and fueled agricultural expansion, mineral development, and infrastructure construction.

Indians were systematically removed from their lands, beginning in western New

Tribal locations of Indian tribes of the U.S.

York State and the Ohio Valley. By the 1880s all the eastern Indian nations had been moved to reservations. Segregated within reservations, they were excluded from the American economy and political system. Consequently, Indians developed a unique relationship with the federal government. They couldn't vote; they had no elected representatives; they had no voice in the American political system. Yet they had a complicated series of treaties which had status in law.

Indian historian Francis Jennings has suggested that American historians have given undue attention to the Indian battles of the far West, that they were a repetition of patterns tried and tested in the East, and that western Indians never had a chance. "*After Tecumseh's death, government officials never had the slightest intention of honoring treaties with the tribes,*" Jennings wrote. "*Such arrangements were regarded as mere conveniences to keep the natives quiet until more resources could be mustered and organized ... racist conceptions negated established standards of morality.... Conduct condoned will be conduct repeated.*" The reality was that the government saw no reason to abide by treaty provisions. By the 1880s white penetration into the interior West, the building of the transcontinental railroads, and the discovery of rich mineral resources resulted in the imposition of severe administrative controls over Indian peoples already confined on Indian reservations. Traditional religious observances like the Sundance or the Ghost Dance were outlawed; Indian children were compelled to attend white-run boarding schools, cut their hair, wear "citizen" clothing, learn English, and adopt Christianity.

In 1887 the two strains of American Indian policy—assimilation and removal—converged in the Dawes Act, or the Indian Allotment Act. The act provided for the dissolution of the reservation system and the end of tribal landholding. It broke up the remaining reservation lands into 160-acre parcels, assigned them to individual families, and sold off the rest as "surplus lands." Intended to make Indians individual landowners, it was justified as the only way Indians would assimilate into white society. "It is doubtful," the commissioner of Indian affairs wrote in 1876, "whether any high degree of civilization is possible without individual ownership of land."

In 1881 Indians still held 155 million acres. By 1900 they held only 77 million acres. Land *was* wealth, power, freedom. The calculus of dispossession was inexorable.

1800s—THE
RESERVATION SYSTEM

WORLD HISTORY

1800
Eli Whitney invented interchangeable parts for musket manufacture. Arms manufacture changed to mass production. It became known as the "American system" and was the forerunner of industrial mass production.

1800
Thomas Jefferson was elected U.S. President. Jefferson believed in western expansion and adopted a federal policy of Indian land acquisition. He encouraged territorial governors to do all they could to acquire Indian land cessions, writing: *"To promote the disposition to exchange lands which they have to spare and which we want—we shall be glad to see the good and influential Indians among them in debt; because we observe that when these debts get beyond what the Indians can pay, they become willing to lop them off by a cession of lands."*
Congress divided the Northwest Territory into Ohio Territory and Indiana Territory. "Indiana" was a latinized form of "Indian," meaning "land of the Indians." Thomas Jefferson appointed fellow Virginian William Henry Harrison as territorial governor.

NATIVE AMERICAN HISTORY

1801
Spain ceded Louisiana back to France, a result of Napoleon's victories against Spain in Austria and Italy and the dissolution of the Holy Roman Empire. Jefferson began negotiations with France to purchase parts of the Louisiana Territory.

1802
Tlingit Indians destroyed New Archangel (Sitka, Alaska). The Russian-American Company, a Russian trading company hunting sea otter and fur-bearing sea mammals along the coast of Alaska and the Pacific Northwest, had established Sitka as a major post and conscripted Indians for labor. When the Russians returned to Russia with their furs, the Tlingit Indians rose up and destroyed the town.

1802
Birth of Osceola, Seminole tribal leader and leader of the resistance movement among the Seminole in Florida.

1802
Trade and Intercourse Act of 1802 passed by Congress, restricting sale of liquor to Indian nations. Trading posts ignored it.

1803
Napoleon sold all of Louisiana to the United States for 15 million dollars, providing the U.S. with more than 800,000 square miles of land and doubling its territory. France needed money to offset its military failures in Egypt and Haiti. The purchase, which cost three cents an acre, included lands stretching from the Gulf Coast to Canada and from the Mississippi to the Rocky Mountains. **President Jefferson**

proposed that these new lands be used to relocate the powerful Indian nations of the southeastern states. He commissioned Lewis and Clark to explore and map the region.

1804–1815

Napoleon proclaimed emperor of the French. During the papal ceremony he took the crown from the pope in the manner of Charlemagne and put it on his own head.

1804–1806

Jefferson's private secretary, Meriwether Lewis, and army officer William Clark, along with 28 soldiers designated as the Corps of Discovery, set out for St. Louis to explore as far as the Pacific Ocean. Spain tried to intercept the expedition four times, but failed.

1805

The first volume of the *Voyages of Humboldt and Bonpland* published in Germany. The 30 volumes contributed to the sciences of physical geography, meteorology, botany, and environmental theory about the relationship of habitat to flora and fauna. It included the first accurate maps and records of climate, geology, and measurements of the earth's magnetic field compiled in the Western Hemisphere. Baron Humboldt, a German geographer and explorer, and Aimé Bonpland, a French botanist, traveled over 6,000 miles in South America, Mexico, and Central America. They explored the Orinoco River, the headwaters of the Amazon, the Andes Mountains, and the Pacific Coast. The Humboldt Current in the Pacific is named for the explorer.

1805–1806

Sacajawea, a Shoshoni Indian woman, guided the Lewis and Clark expedition. Largely responsible for their success, she acted as guide, translator, interpreter, and diplomat. Kidnapped by Hidatsa Indians when she was 10 years old, Sacajawea had been raised in a Hidatsa village near what is now Mandan, North Dakota, and was purchased (or won) by a French fur trader, Toussaint Charbonneau, as a wife. In 1804–1805 Lewis and Clark wintered with the Mandan Indians and hired the couple to be guides and interpreters. Sacajawea's presence and that of her baby (born in February 1805) assured other Indians that this was a peace mission and not a war party. Their mission was to preempt the British claim to the Oregon Territory and to map and

1805

Napoleon became king of Italy. France dominated much of Europe. Austria ceded the Italian states of Parma, Piedmont, and Piacenza to France. Joseph Bonaparte, Napoleon's older brother, became king of Naples. Napoleon's younger brother became king of Holland. As a large part of Germany became the Confederation of the Rhine and came under French domination, it marked the end of the old Holy Roman Empire.

1806

First lighting of cotton mills with gaslight, marking the beginning of factory system and longer work days.

1806

Napoleon occupied Berlin. French troops captured Danzig. Russians agreed to aid Prussia in war against the French.

explore the lands between St. Louis, Missouri, and the Pacific Ocean, land uncharted by whites. (The map they were using had been drawn by a Siksika Indian for an employee of the Hudson's Bay Company and showed the entire Missouri River drainage system.) Sacajawea spoke Shoshoni, Siouan, and a number of dialects. Without her ability to gain information from local Indians about routes through the Rockies, as well as her knowledge of edible plants and berries to supplement their sparse rations, her aid in horse buying, river routes, and canoe travel, historians believe, the 7,689-mile-long expedition through uncharted land would have had a different outcome. Following the expedition, trappers began to move into the upper Missouri regions.

Two versions of Sacajawea's fate exist: one is that she died of fever in 1812 in St. Louis; the other that she lived among the Shoshoni on the Wind River Reservation and died in 1884. A Bureau of Indian Affairs (BIA) study in 1924 concluded that she was the woman known as Porivo and was buried in the white cemetery at Fort Washakie.

1805

Tlingit Indians destroyed Yakutat, another Russian post.

1806-1809

Tecumseh, a Shawnee warrior, emerged as the most significant Indian political leader of the Northwest Territory and William Henry Harrison's implacable enemy. It was Harrison's defeat of Tecumseh that eventually elevated him to the U.S. presidency. A Shawnee warrior who had fought in all the significant battles against the French, British, and

Americans, Tecumseh had concluded that the Americans wanted all Indian lands and that a powerful Indian military force was needed to hold the Americans back. His vision of forging an Indian alliance from the Great Lakes to the Gulf of Mexico was supported by the spiritual leadership of his brother, Tenskwatawa, who founded a religious revitalization movement. The two brothers came from the Shawnee village of Chillicothe on the Little Miami River (three miles north of the present-day Xenia, Ohio). Tenskwatawa's vision, offering hope to a demoralized people, spread from the Shawnee to other nations. The two brothers founded a new village, called Prophetstown, near the junction of the Tippecanoe and Wabash Rivers. It attracted Shawnees, Wyandots, Delawares, Ottawas and many others who saw in it a hope for the future. Traveling the country from Michigan to Florida Tecumseh gained a reputation as a great orator and spokesman for traditional Indians. (See "Tecumseh and Tenskwatawa" on page 233.)

1807
England abolished the slave trade by an act of Parliament. France, Spain, and Portugal followed suit within 10 years. Illegal slave trade continued in Africa.

1808
Spain invaded by France. Napoleon's brother Joseph became king of Spain. Britain went to war against the French in Spain and Portugal.

1809
Napoleon annexed the papal states in Italy. The pope excommunicated Napoleon, who in turn had the pope arrested and imprisoned near Genoa.

1809
Creek leader Hillis Hayo (called Josiah Francis by whites) in Florida heard of the Shawnee pan-Indian movement and invited Tecumseh

to meet with the Creeks in Florida and Louisiana. Trade between the Shawnees and the Creeks was conducted through the Mississippi Valley, a great corridor of communication and trade among the interior Indian nations. Its complex population included nationals of Spain, France, escaped slaves and free blacks, as well as Indians from many southeastern tribes. The Creeks were the most powerful of the southern tribes and maintained alliances with Spain, France, and England that could have been extremely valuable to the Shawnee resistance. The alliance of the Shawnees with the Creeks was an important part of Tecumseh's strategy.

1809
Treaty of Fort Wayne, Indiana. A "whiskey treaty" signed by "treaty chiefs" in Ohio and Indiana, including the Munsee and Delaware, ceded three million acres of Indian lands to William Henry Harrison, the governor of the territory. The signers were chiefs of dubious legitimacy. The price paid for the land amounted to approximately eight cents an acre. It established a pattern of fraud and double dealing by territorial governors with local chiefs, and broke the principle of the Greenville Treaty. The Shawnee traditional leaders were so alarmed by the Fort Wayne Treaty, they confronted Harrison. Tecumseh questioned how Harrison had gotten 11 debt-ridden, whiskey-soaked "treaty chiefs" to sign agreements for lands they did not own, including lands as far as the Wabash River and extending from western Ohio to what is now Wisconsin and Missouri. Potawatomi chiefs had signed away lands belonging to the Shawnee.

Tecumseh went to the territorial capital to tell Harrison that the Shawnee had not agreed to the treaty and would not abide by it, and that the Shawnee held these same lands by "right of occupancy." Harrison insisted the treaties were valid, and right of occupancy meaningless.

1810
Revolt in Mexico of Indians and mestizos against Spain. Napoleon divorced Josephine, married Marie-Louise of Austria, and added lands in Italy, Austria, and Spain to the French empire. He named his brother, Joseph, king of Spain and ruler of Mexico. Joseph put the revolt down and denied any consideration of Mexican independence from Spain.

1810
Tecumseh's address to Governor Harrison delivered at Vincennes, Indiana, August 12. Tecumseh was a powerful orator, his reputation for passion and truthtelling impressed everyone who heard him, including white traders, Indian agents, and government officials. His words to the council were recorded: "It is true that I am a Shawnee. My forefathers were warriors. Their son is a warrior. From them I take only my existence . . . The Being Within, communing with past ages, tells me that once, nor until lately, there was no white man on this continent; that it then all belonged to red men, children of the same parents . . . once a happy race, since made miserable by the white people who are never contented but always encroaching . . ."

1811
Tecumseh formed an alliance with the Creek in Georgia and Florida. The powerful interior nations of the South were the Creek, the Chickasaw, the Choctaw, the Cherokee, the Seminole, the tribes whites called the Five Civilized Tribes. The Creek, or Muskokee (called Creeks by whites because all their villages were on creeks or waterways), were descended from the Coosa and other Mississippian nations whom De Soto had encountered in the sixteenth century. They were powerful not

TECUMSEH AND TENSKWATAWA

Tecumseh came from the Shawnee village of Chillicothe on the Little Miami River. His father, a Shawnee chief, was killed fighting settlers in the Ohio Valley. Two older brothers had been killed fighting the Americans under the Miami chief, Little Turtle. His third brother, Tenskwatawa, was not a warrior but a seer who had had a vision of the spirit world and sparked a religious revitalization movement which spread throughout the Northwest Territory. Tenskwatawa's spiritual vision was the underpinning of Tecumseh's political strategy. It was the brothers' conviction that the current crisis affected not just the Shawnee, but all Native peoples, and that the unslakable American thirst for land required a new political organization on the part of all Indians.

"Hear me, O deluded people," Tenskwatawa preached, ". . . this wide region was once your inheritance; but now the cry of the revelry of war is no more heard on the shores of the majestic Hudson, or on the sweet banks of the silver Mohawk. The eastern tribes have long since disappeared—even the forests that sheltered them are laid low; and scarcely a trace of our nation remains, except here and there the Indian name of a stream or a village. And such, sooner or later, will be the fate of other tribes; in a little while they will go the way that their brethren have gone. They will vanish like a vapor from the face of the earth; their very history will be lost in forgetfulness; and the places that now know them will know them no more. We are driven back until we can retreat no farther; our hatchets are broken; our bows are snapped; our fires are extinguished. A little longer and the white man will cease to persecute us, for we shall cease to exist."

The fate of the eastern nations was well known. Coexistence with the American settlers had not worked out. Tecumseh wanted a boundary beyond which whites could not pass, a boundary enforced by the full weight of a confederation of tribes that spanned the continent. Despite sentiments of conciliation voiced in Washington, extermination seemed to be American policy on the ground. Indiana offered a bounty of 50 dollars for every Indian scalp, and many Indians were being shot by ruthless bounty hunters. To provide a base to build broader alliances, Tecumseh and his brother started a new village, Prophetstown, at the junction of the Wabash River and Tippecanoe Creek. Shawnees, Wyandots, Ottawas, Kickapoos, Ojibwas, and Delawares all settled there. Whiskey was forbidden; no European trade goods were allowed. Christianity was outlawed. Only traditional rituals and customs were allowed.

Tecumseh's vision was comprehensive, larger than Pontiac's union of tribes in the Great Lakes region or the powerful League of the Iroquois. He saw the need for Indian unity on a continental scale, a pan-Indian confederacy of all the western and southern tribes rooted in a native concept of land which precluded individual ownership. He traveled up and down the Mississippi, west along the Missouri, east along the Ohio River. To every tribal council his message was the same: "We will keep all that is left us. The Ohio shall be our border. Beyond that, the white men shall not pass." In short, he wanted to enforce the Ohio River as the last boundary for white settlers.

Tecumseh's message and his fame spread. To counteract his influence, in 1809 Governor Harrison made agreements with 11 separate tribes in Indiana, including the Delaware, Potawatomi, Miami, Kickapoo and Eel River tribes for three million acres of choice land along the Wabash River. The chiefs got 8,200 dollars in return. Tecumseh and his followers declared the treaty (Treaty of Fort Wayne) illegal. In the treaty council with Governor Harrison, Tecumseh proclaimed: "Sell a country! Why not sell the air, the clouds and the great sea, as well as the earth? Did not the Great Spirit make them all for the use of his children?"

Tecumseh argued that according to the principles of a prior treaty (Treaty of Greenville) only cessions of land from tribes acting in common were valid. The present treaty encompassed Shawnee lands and the Shawnee had not been included in the negotiations, and therefore the new treaty was illegal. The territorial capital of Vincennes, Indiana (formerly a French fort and trading post) was only 150 miles south of the Shawnee village on the Tippecanoe, so Tecumseh and his warriors made several trips there to protest the sale of Indian lands. His eloquent "Address of Tecumseh to Governor Harrison," recorded at Vincennes, on August 12, 1810, defined the Indian "right of occupancy" over the treaties of ceded lands by individual chiefs. Tecumseh, a great orator, also described the evil of the white people, "who are never contented but always encroaching."

While Tecumseh traveled south to Florida in 1811 in an effort to persuade the Creeks, Choctaws, and Chickasaws to join his great alliance, Governor Harrison decided that a bold stroke was needed to restore his popularity with land-hungry settlers. Using a minor struggle between Indians and neighboring white settlers on the Tippecanoe as a pretext for military action, Harrison led a force of 900 troops to the Shawnee village. Tenskwatawa the Prophet was neither a politician nor a strategist, and instead of playing for time, he ordered a hasty and ill-conceived battle. The Battle of Tippecanoe, as Harrison named it, effectively broke up the Shawnee nation, restored Harrison's popularity, and established his military reputation. (When Harrison ran for president along with John Tyler as vice president, his slogan was "Tippecanoe and Tyler, too.")

Tecumseh returned home to find his village in ruins, his people scattered, and their will broken, for they had believed in the vision of the Prophet, which said their spirit was stronger than white men's bullets. When war broke out between the Americans and the British—the War of 1812—Tecumseh led his warriors to Canada and enlisted in the British forces. He commanded 2,000 warriors of allied tribes in four major battles against the Americans. Like Pontiac, he won every battle, but he lost the war. He had chosen the losing side. His final battle at the Thames River in Ontario was against his implacable enemy Harrison, former governor, now major general, commanding the American army. "We are determined to defend our lands," Tecumseh said in his last speech to a council of British officers and Indian chiefs the night before the battle, "and if it is His will, we wish to leave our bones upon them."

It is said that at the end of the battle Tecumseh's warriors carried his body off the field so it would not be mutilated by the enemy. Harrison went on to become U.S. president. Three miles north of the present-day town of Xenia, Ohio, the Shawnee tribe has erected a stone monument to mark the site of Tecumseh's birthplace.

only for their numbers—they could call up 6,000 fighting men from 100 villages—but because of their diplomatic alliances with Spain, England, and France, important counterweights to the new American government. The Creek-Shawnee alliance was closely monitored by local agents who reported to Washington.

1811
Battle of Tippecanoe. Knowing Tecumseh was absent in Florida, William Henry Harrison took 900 troops to Tippecanoe Creek on November 7 to break up the growing allied Indian confederacy. His troops were caught at dawn in a surprise attack, but his superior guns carried the day. The Indians left the field of battle (partly because Tenskwatawa had told them that the Great Spirit would make them invisible before the bullets, a prophecy which did not come true) and Harrison held the field. Harrison declared victory, burned all the Shawnee log buildings and food stores, and forced the Shawnee and allied tribes into a treaty ceding vast amounts of land. The success helped carry Harrison into the presidency. Tenskwatawa was discredited.

1812
France invaded Russia with 600,000 soldiers under Napoleon's command, the largest army ever assembled. France, Italy, Poland, Switzerland, the Netherlands, Germany, Austria, and Prussia all contributed troops. The Russians burned the city of Moscow rather than allow a French victory, refused to negotiate, and harassed Napoleon's retreating armies in the snows of the Russian winter. Only 100,000 soldiers returned to Paris.

1812
Creek Civil War in Georgia and Florida. The Creeks (Muskokees) divided into two factions: Upper Creeks, anti-American traditionalists who wanted to preserve their culture and fight U.S. interference in their affairs; and Lower Creeks, who wanted to cooperate with the U.S. Indian agents who urged land cessions and schooling and Christianity for their children. Tecumseh had gained a great following among the Upper Creeks. Taking the name Red Sticks,

1812

The War of 1812 between the U.S. and England, an extension of the Napoleonic Wars in Europe. The U.S. declared war against England for illegal impressment of American sailors. The deeper impetus for war was Britain's failure to leave its forts in the West and its continued aid to western Indian tribes who resisted U.S. expansion. President Madison had to flee while the British burned Washington, D.C. The American politicians (war hawks) in the West wanted to invade Canada to end the British support of Indian forces.

1813

Robert Owen, an industrialist, philanthropist, and the first utopian socialist, founded New Harmony, Indiana, in one of his pioneer efforts to construct utopian communities to counter the effects of industrialization in Europe and the United States.

1813

American ships under Commodore Perry destroyed the British fleet on Lake Erie and severed British supply lines in the West. A massive American force under William Henry Harrison assembled to pursue the British and their Indian allies.

batons rouges, from the red painted sticks they took into battle, the Upper Creeks decided to push the Americans out of their lands.

1813

Tecumseh went to Canada and offered his services and the combined military force of allied Potawatomi, Kickapoo, Shawnee, and Delaware to the British. Bands of Wyandot, Chippewa, Sioux, Winnebago, Sauk, and Fox soon joined him. The British put him in charge of their allied Indian force. Governor Harrison was made a brigadier general in the U.S. Army. Tecumseh's forces defeated one American division and achieved the surrender of the Americans at Fort Detroit.

1813

Battle of River Thames and Tecumseh's death. Without telling Tecumseh that he had no plans to engage the Americans in battle (because of the defeat of the British fleet), the British commander, Colonel Henry Procter, withdrew from Fort Detroit into the interior of Canada, with Harrison's American force in swift pursuit. Finally at the Thames River, Ontario, Tecumseh forced the British general to stop, and confronted him in a full council of the British and Indian generals: *"Listen, Father! . . . You have the arms and ammunition. . . . If you have an idea of going away, give them to us and you may go and welcome. As for us, our lives are in the hands of the Creator. We are determined to defend our lands, and if it be His will, we wish to leave our bones upon them."* Harrison's 3,000 men outnumbered the British and their Indian allies. Procter's men fought, but not for long. The Indians stayed and fought and then melted into the woods. No white saw Tecumseh killed and no Indian ever revealed what happened to his body. Tecumseh's vision for the western tribes' struggle to hold on to their lands between the Ohio River and the Great Lakes was lost, but he remained a heroic symbol to both whites and Indians. General William Tecumseh Sherman was named for him; even Harrison wrote to the secretary of war that he was *"one of those uncommon geniuses which spring up occasionally to produce revolutions and overturn the established order of things."*

1813
The Upper Creeks (Red Sticks) in southern Alabama attacked the Americans at Fort Mims. More than 350 Americans killed. The Americans ordered a massive retaliation. (Baton Rouge, Louisiana, was later named for the Red Sticks.)

1813
Seminole villages in northern Florida invaded by Tennessee militia on the pretext of alleged slave raiding and cattle rustling by the Seminoles. These were still Spanish territories. Andrew Jackson was one of the leaders of the Tennessee militia.

1814

Britain defeated in War of 1812. Treaty of Ghent between the U.S. and Britain. Since different Indian tribes fought for either the British or the Americans, two months of negotiations in Europe between the U.S. and England were devoted to the status of Indian tribes, but without any Indian representatives present. The U.S. maintained that the tribes were subjects of the U.S. and no concern of the English king; England maintained that the U.S. contemplated the removal and "extinction of those nations." The treaty restored the prewar status quo among Indian nations who moved freely back and forth across the Canadian border.

1815

Congress of Vienna redrew the boundaries of Europe following the defeat of Napoleon. Reputed to be one of the most brilliant assemblies of modern times, its participants included Prince Metternich of Austria, the czar of Russia, Tallyrand of France, Lord Wellington of England, and Cardinal Consalvi for the papacy. During the negotiations, Napoleon returned from exile in Elba, assembled an army, reentered Paris, and provoked his final European war.

1815

Battle of Waterloo and the final battle of the Napoleonic Wars. Napoleon's 105,000-man army fought against the combined English-Prussian army of 113,000 under the command of the duke of Wellington. Napoleon, decisively defeated near the Belgian village of Waterloo, abdicated for the second and last time.

1814

In answer to the Creek attack at Fort Mims, an army of 5,000 troops led by Andrew Jackson retaliated at the Battle of Horseshoe Bend. More than 1,000 Creeks were killed and 20 million acres of Creek lands ceded. At the village of Tohopeka at Horseshoe Bend on the Tallapoosa River, Jackson's troops surrounded the Upper Creek forces, killing more than 1,000 Creek men, women, and children. Jackson then forced all the Creek leaders, even Lower Creeks who had helped him, to cede more than 20 million acres of Creek lands to the U.S. government. As a result, Andrew Jackson gained a reputation as an Indian fighter.

1815

American victory in the Battle of New Orleans aided by southern Indians, particularly the Choctaws. Although the battle took place after the War of 1812 was technically over and peace negotiations were under way, it was a highly publicized battle in which Andrew Jackson defeated the British forces in New Orleans with the help of a number of Choctaw Indian warriors. The victory gave Jackson a national reputation and helped pave his way to the presidency.

1815

Indian tribes were prohibited from ceding any lands to any power except the U.S. federal government. Under U.S. law and international treaties, Indian nations were to maintain diplomatic relations with the U.S. only and were *prohibited from forming alliances with any foreign powers*. The Treaty of Ghent explicitly prohibited alliances between Indian nations and European

1815

Beginning of the assembly of modern Germany from German states whose nationalism had been aroused during the Napoleonic Wars. The "Metternich system" organized a German confederation of 38 sovereign powers in a permanent diplomatic congress, the first German Diet.

1817

Extermination of aboriginal peoples in Australia. British convicts and soldiers were given land in Australia (convicts 30 to 50 acres; soldiers 80 to 100 acres) upon completion of their sentences or service. When Native peoples fought back against the white practices of kidnapping aboriginal women as wives and their children as laborers, the rapid and brutal extermination of Native peoples ensued. British convicts were shipped to Australia from Britain beginning in the early 1800s until 1867.

countries. They were to accept U.S. regulation of trade relations and to relinquish jurisdictional rights. Although the Treaty of Ghent required each of the Indian tribes allied with the British during the war to sign a separate peace treaty with the U.S., the overall treaty terms marked significant increase in federal presence in and control over Indian life.

1817

Cherokee lands in Georgia exchanged for lands in Arkansas Territory (present-day Oklahoma), a forerunner of American policy that would remove all the southeastern Indian nations from their lands in the South. Andrew Jackson coerced a treaty from several Cherokee leaders in which large tracts of Cherokee lands in Georgia were exchanged for lands in the West. By 1820 several thousand Cherokee had emigrated west of the Mississippi into Arkansas Territory (Oklahoma) because of relentless harassment from white settlers. They were the first to migrate to what would become the Indian Territory of Oklahoma.

1817–1818

First Seminole War. Osceola, still a teenager, fought against Andrew Jackson and U.S. forces in this war. The Seminole were one of the Five Civilized Tribes, which the leaders in southern states wanted removed from their rich lands to facilitate expanded cotton production. Jackson attacked a former British fort in northern Florida that was also the home of the Seminole chief, Neamathla. Jackson burned and destroyed Seminole villages and farms in northern Florida before retreating back into Georgia. The goal

Osceola, Seminole warrior and leader. Osceola was considered the most bold and able of the Seminole leaders who led the resistance to the U.S. government in what would become the most costly series of Indian wars in U.S. history. The Seminole refused demands to leave their lands in Florida to move to Indian country in Oklahoma. Osceola was captured only after being invited to a phony peace negotiation under a flag of truce. He died in prison the following year from uninvestigated causes. One newspaper editorialized that there was no glory in his capture: *"If practiced towards a civilized foe, [it] would be characterized as a violation of all that is noble and generous in war."* Catlin drew this portrait after Osceola's death from a pre-existing painting.

1819
Spain sold Florida and west Florida to the U.S. These lands included what is now Florida, Alabama, and lands in Georgia.

was to remove the Seminole from their fertile homelands on the border of Georgia and Florida, which were still Spanish possessions, and to force the Spanish to cede Florida to the U.S.

1818
Creek leader Josiah Francis (Hillis Hayo) killed in Andrew Jackson's raid on Pensacola, Florida. Jackson tricked him onto an American gunboat by flying a British flag, and then had him executed. Josiah Francis had accompanied Tecumseh throughout his travels to the Five Civilized Tribes in 1811 and 1812, spreading the message of Indian confederation and opposition to U.S. interference. During the Creek civil war, he led the Red Sticks against Jackson's forces. Well-educated, articulate, and a respected leader, he had gone to England in 1815 in search of support for the Creek cause.

1821

Mexico declared independence from Spain. Legal status of Indians abolished. Slavery outlawed. California became a Mexican state. The new Mexican Republic welcomed American colonists and gave free land under the *empresario* system, and many tax benefits. Mexico believed the new colonists would serve as buffers against American expansion. Stephen Austin brought white settlers to the northern Mexican province of Coahuila, which later became Texas.

1821

Hudson's Bay Company acquired the Northwest Company in Canada.

1823

Oneida Indians settled at Green Bay, Wisconsin. One of the six tribes of the Iroquois confederacy in upper New York State, the Oneida had tried to remain neutral during the Revolutionary War, but they were subjected to punitive measures applied to the other tribes of the Iroquois confederacy who had supported the British. Their reservation near Oneida Lake continued to shrink in size. In 1823 the Oneida were induced to sell their lands, and the first group relocated to Wisconsin. Over the next 10 years, all the Oneida left New York State.

1823

The Office of Indian Affairs created within the U.S. War Department. The office was created without congressional authorization. Thomas L. McKenney was appointed as its first head.

1824

Mexican Constitution adopted, guaranteeing equality of citizenship to all under Mexican jurisdiction, including Indian peoples in California.

1825

World population reached one billion, double the population of the planet in 1500. It had taken from 8000 B.C. to A.D. 1500 to reach 500 million.

1825

Erie Canal opened. It was the first great American civil engineering work.

1825

Seminole Wars continued. Osceola became a leader in the ongoing Seminole resistance to the U.S. government. Agents pressured the Seminoles to move to lands west of the Mississippi River. The U.S. claimed rights to all the Seminole lands east of the Mississippi.

1825

Creeks ceded lands in Georgia and Alabama by an illegal treaty. William McIntosh, a mixed-blood Creek chief, accepted a 25 thousand-dollar bribe to sign a treaty ceding all Creek lands in Georgia and vast tracts in Alabama. The Creek council, which had voted a death sentence for any member of the nation who sold communally held Creek land, had McIntosh killed. **President John Quincy Adams rejected the McIntosh Creek Treaty** but negotiated another one in which the U.S. retained some of the Creek lands.

1827

Path Killer, the influential principal chief of the Cherokee nation, died. The Cherokee constitutional convention adopted a new political system for the Cherokee, modeled on that of the U.S. government. Path Killer's strategy had been to restructure political and economic institutions so that the Cherokee could better resist U.S. pressures for removal to lands in the West, negotiate more successfully in Washington, and stop individual Cherokee leaders from selling off communally held lands.

1828

Andrew Jackson elected president of the U.S. When he succeeded to the presidency, he was supported by the

1828

The Georgia legislature passed a series of laws extending the state's jurisdiction over the Cherokee. The laws were richest men in the southern states, who wanted to expand their cotton plantations into the fertile lands held by the Creeks, Chocktaws, and the other tribes of the South. Jackson set in motion the removal to the West of all the southeastern tribes in Florida, Georgia, Alabama, Tennessee, and Louisiana, accomplishing from the White House what his armies in the field could not.

designed to break up the Cherokee nation and take its lands. Since legally only the federal government could have jurisdiction over Indians, the state laws were unconstitutional. But Jackson as president did not enforce the legal authority of the federal government over the state of Georgia because of the pending Indian Removal Bill in Congress. Georgia's senators and congressmen had introduced this legislation in order to make it federal policy to move all the tribes of the Southeast across the Mississippi.

1828
John Ross, Cherokee tribal leader and Path Killer's secretary, became principal chief under a new system of popular election. A successful merchant and slave owner, John Ross dressed in fashionable clothes, drove a handsome carriage, and was the equal of any of his white aristocratic southern neighbors. He inherited Path Killer's role as the leader of the conservatives in the Cherokee nation, who wanted to preserve the integrity of the Cherokee nation from U.S. demands for land cessions. Using the monies from annuity payments, he built a national capital at New Echota, with imposing buildings for different branches of Cherokee government. Between 1828 and 1866, Ross led the Cherokee conservative majority and worked unsuccessfully to preserve Cherokee national and territorial independence from U.S. encroachments.

1828
Sequoyah (also known as George Gist), who had invented a Cherokee alphabet and system of writing, used this new language to create a Cherokee newspaper.

1828–1835

Cherokee newspaper, the *Phoenix*, was published with columns in English and Cherokee. It was edited by Elias Boudinot, a Cherokee who had gone to school in Connecticut. The Cherokee also had their own system of schools, public roads, agriculture, mills, and a well-organized political system based on a written constitution. In many ways they were more advanced than the white settlers who wanted to claim their territory.

1829

Gold discovered on Cherokee lands. Violating treaties that preserved the integrity of Cherokee lands from white encroachment, thousands of whites poured into Cherokee lands searching for gold. President Jackson removed all federal troops and gave a free hand to the Georgia militia. State officials enforced the rights of the white trespassers over the Cherokees. The Georgia legislature passed laws making it illegal for Cherokees to mine gold, to testify against a white man, or to hold political assemblies.

1829

In Washington John Ross protested illegal treaty violations, the suspension of Cherokee civil rights, and the intrusion of Georgia laws on Cherokee sovereignty which made it impossible for the Cherokee government to function. He met with little success, as the Cherokee had no voice in democratic institutions and the public was ill-informed about Georgia's treatment of its Indian nations.

1830

The Indian Removal Law passed by Congress. President Jackson signed the Indian Removal Law requiring the removal of all southern Indians to new lands west of the Mississippi. The law created Indian Territory in what is now Oklahoma, Arkansas, and Kansas. Since little was known of what was called the "Great American Desert," it was assumed that no whites would ever want those lands and that the tribes could be safely relocated there. Indian Territory was the forerunner of the reservation system.

1830

The Choctaw removal and the Treaty of Dancing Rabbit Creek. The Choctaw had opposed Tecumseh's confederation, had fought on the American side during the War of 1812, and were one of the tribes who had helped Andrew Jackson save New Orleans from the British in 1815. They held huge tracts of lands in Alabama and Mississippi and were a prosperous people with rich farmlands; many had intermarried with whites and some lived in two-story plantation houses. They were considered a pro-American people, and ironically it was the U.S. Indian agents' familiarity with the Choctaw that made them the first subjects of the Indian Removal Law. Through bribes and coercion the Choctaw tribes "agreed" in the Treaty of Dancing Rabbit Creek to give up all their lands in Mississippi and move to western Arkansas (Oklahoma). The treaty also provided for Choctaw education: "... the U.S. agrees and stipulates that for the benefit and advantage of the Choctaw people, and to improve their condition, there shall be educated under the direction of the President and at the expense of the U.S., forty Choctaw youths for twenty years." Of the 13,000 Choctaws who migrated, 4,000 died of hunger, exposure, or disease. Another

7,000 refused to move and stayed in Mississippi, where they became subject to state laws and were legislated out of tribal existence.

1831

De Tocqueville, a French historian visiting the United States, observed the Choctaw on their Trail of Tears and wrote of the process of dispossession. His book, *Democracy in America*, became one of the most widely read books in Europe and the United States on the new Americans.

1831

Cherokee Nation v. Georgia. The Cherokee sued Georgia in the U.S. Supreme Court for an injunction against the execution of Georgia's laws against them. To establish jurisdiction they used the argument that since the Court had authority over cases involving foreign nations and a state of the U.S., it could rule over a dispute between an Indian nation and a U.S. state. The Supreme Court affirmed the sovereignty of the Indian nations but said they were not foreign nations, hence the Court had no jurisdiction and denied the injunction. Chief Justice Marshall described Indian nations as "domestic dependent nations" whose relationship to the U.S. resembled "that of a ward to his guardian."

1832

The Khedive of Egypt opposed British plans to construct a canal at Suez linking the Mediterranean and the Red Sea. The plans were put in limbo while he reorganized Egypt on the French administrative model and went to war against the Ottoman empire, acquiring new lands in Arabia, the Sudan, Khartoum, Crete, and Syria.

1832

Worcester v. Georgia. In this suit, brought by a white missionary, Samuel Worcester, on behalf of the Cherokee, Chief Justice Marshall actively ruled for the Cherokees. The Supreme Court found that treaties signed between the U.S. and the Cherokee nation recognized the Indians' right to self-government and the obligation of the U.S. to protect that right. The U.S. was legally bound to treat Indians "*as nations, respect their rights, and manifest a firm purpose to afford that protection which treaties stipulate.*" Marshall asserted that "*the acts of Georgia are repugnant to the Constitution, laws and treaties of the U.S. . . . . The whole intercourse between the U.S. and this nation [Cherokee] is by our Constitution and laws vested in the government of the U.S."* President Jackson took no federal action and encouraged Georgia to ignore the decision. He was reported to have responded: *"John Marshall has made his decision, now let's see him enforce it."*

1832
Black Hawk's War. Black Hawk, a Sauk chief living in what is now Rock Island, Illinois, returned home to plant corn after spending the winter in Iowa. He found his village and lands invaded by white settlers. The settlers refused to move, claiming the land was theirs, purchased from a land company. They called on the Illinois militia (which included Abraham Lincoln and Jefferson Davis), to drive the Sauk out. Pursued through Illinois and Wisconsin by 8,000 state militia and 150 federal troops, Black Hawk's troops were ultimately defeated after receiving heavy casualties from cannon mounted on a steamboat. When a 1,300-man federal army arrived at the same river Black Hawk's troops were caught between the two forces. Some tried to surrender under a white flag of truce and were massacred. Black Hawk was captured and forced to cede the eastern part of Iowa as punishment for war. The Sauk pledged never to live, hunt, fish, or plant on their previous homelands in Illinois.

1832
Creeks were forced to surrender all their lands in Alabama and were removed to Oklahoma.

1833
Black Hawk wrote his biography. This was the first "as told to" Indian

biography and was translated by Antoine Le Claire.

1833

The state of Georgia held a lottery of Cherokee land and property, declaring Cherokee ownership of land in the state of Georgia to be illegal. Georgia officials gave away Cherokee lands and government buildings at the Cherokee capital of New Echota to holders of winning lottery tickets. John Ross lost his plantation. The Georgia militia was sent to enforce the lottery. Cherokees throughout Georgia were forcibly evicted from their homes, and their fields and livestock were seized.

1834

Charles Babbage designed the forerunner of the computer, the "analytical engine," a large-scale digital calculator. Too advanced for the technology of the day, it did not evolve into the computer until the discovery of electricity.

1834

In France Alexis de Tocqueville published *Democracy in America*. Based on his personal observations and travel in America, it remains one of the most acute analyses of American democracy: *"Two things are astonishing about the United States: the great changeableness of most human behavior and the singular fixity of certain principles. . . . Men bestir themselves within certain limits beyond which they hardly ever go. . . . They love change but dread revolutions."*

1834

Spanish missions in California secularized by Mexico. The authority of the Catholic Church subordinated to Mexican government.

1834–1835

Treaty of New Echota. Another Cherokee leader, John Ridge, went to Washington. Although he represented only a negligible number of Cherokee, he negotiated a treaty selling off Cherokee lands for 5 million dollars and agreed to move west. The Cherokee national council unanimously rejected the treaty of New Echota but the U.S. Senate ratified it. (In 1839 Ridge and his son and nephew were assassinated by the Cherokee in Oklahoma.) The governor of Georgia shut down the *Phoenix*, the Cherokee newspaper, and prepared to enforce the treaty provisions. John Ross continued to meet with senators and congressmen, and even the president, to have the illegal treaty annulled. It was to no avail.

1834

Chumash enslavement ended. In California thousands of Chumash Indians who had been enslaved by the Spanish missions were set free. One of California's biggest tribes, they numbered

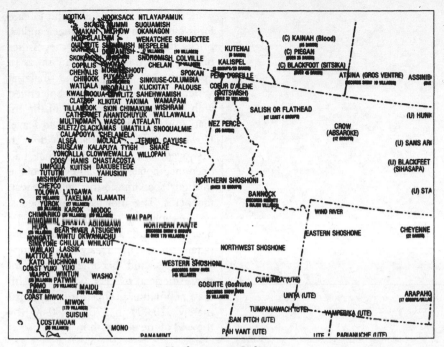

Northwest coast Indians.

almost 20,000 people and lived in villages that contained over 1,000 inhabitants each, in the area of present-day San Luis Obispo to Malibu Canyon. They spoke at least six dialects and inhabited lands as far inland as the San Joaquin Valley. The Chumash created some of the finest rock paintings in North America and were also the center of a thriving regional trading economy. Unable to recognize the complex religious underpinnings of the Chumash, the Spanish insisted they become Christians, and the missionaries sent out soldiers to the Indian villages to bring the Chumash, by force if necessary, into the missions. There they were dressed in blue uniforms, their families broken up, and men and women forced to live separately. They were ordered to work in the mission's fields and to care for livestock, tan hides, produce candles, bricks, tiles, shoes, and other necessities of life. They died by the thousands in epidemics of smallpox and malaria. When 65 years of enslavement ended with Mexico's secularization of the Indian missions, they were free to leave. However, their old villages had been destroyed, and their lands (that had been incorporated into land grants of the missions) soon transformed into Mexican rancheros. The Indians became peons, or the equivalent of feudal serfs, on the new rancheros, which in a few years (after 1848 and the Treaty of Guadalupe Hidalgo) would become property of new American owners. California's Indian population dropped from approximately 310,000 in 1769 to 30,000 by the end of the gold rush in 1860.

1835

Sarah and Angelina Grimke were the first American women to speak publicly against slavery and to advocate women's rights. The Protestant clergy of New England condemned the southern sisters as "unnatural women," claiming that the Bible "bade women to be silent." The sisters, who were from a slave-owning South Carolina family, countered by publishing the first tract calling for women's right to speak in public, to own property, and to have political voice.

1835–1842

Second Seminole War. The U.S. appropriated over 50 million dollars to fight the Seminoles. The war against the Seminoles was the most costly and least successful of all the American wars until Vietnam. For years the Seminoles forcibly resisted efforts of the U.S. Army and Indian agents to remove them from their lands in Florida and relocate them to the West. Between 5,000 and 10,000 U.S. troops were deployed in Florida against them. After Seminole leader Osceola led a party that ambushed the U.S. Indian agent working to gain Seminole compliance with the Removal Treaty of 1830, the second war broke out. Osceola was lured to a peace council under a white flag, then seized by American troops and put in prison. He died in prison the same year, 1837, at the age of 40. He was considered the most capable and the boldest of the Seminole leaders.

After Osceola's capture and death, Billy Bowlegs took over as leader. He led 200 Seminole warriors in an attack on a government trading post operating on Seminole land, killing most of the American troops. The Seminoles then retreated into the Everglades, where they hid during the day and raided at night. The U.S. Army pursued them through malarial swamps in a long, frustrating war. Bowlegs eventually fought for the North in the Civil War and died in 1864. (See photo of Billy Bowlegs on page 262.)

1836

Galvanized iron was introduced in France. Manufactured as barbed wire fencing, it found a huge market in the American West, where it was used to fence large tracts of cattle lands.

1836

Texas independence. Republic of Texas established by white *empresarios*, mostly southerners who had been given land grants by the Mexican government. Mexican soldiers captured the Alamo, inciting insurrection in Texas. Increasing military encounters between new Texas landowners and Mexican soldiers eventually led to war between the U.S. and Mexico.

1837-1885

Beginning of an explosion in warfare technology. New weaponry changed techniques of battle, organization of the military, and strategies of warfare. Improvements in metallurgy, machines, and explosives led to the development of shells instead of ball and powder, the

1836

16,000 Cherokee walked to Oklahoma from Georgia along the Trail of Tears. Seven thousand federal troops arrived in Georgia in December to enforce the final deadline for the Cherokee removal. They were backed up by the Georgia militia, who rounded up the Cherokee with bayonets. The ensuing migration of the Cherokee to Oklahoma in the dead of winter became known as the Cherokee Trail of Tears or "the Trail where they cried." The forced migration took six months and an estimated one out of four Cherokee died during the journey.

1837

Congress passed legislation ending direct payments to Indian tribes for lands they had ceded or sold to the U.S. Instead, proceeds were to be held by the Treasury "in trust" and used for the benefit of the Indians, a provision still in force. Over the years, suits by repeating rifle, the machine gun, and heavy artillery. France adopted the shell gun in 1837; the Prussian military adopted the breech-loading artillery manufactured by the Krupps in 1849; the U.S. invented the repeating rifle in 1860; the Gatling gun (a machine gun) was manufactured in England in 1861; the French *chassepot* in 1886; the Maxim gun in 1884; and smokeless powder in 1884. The new weaponry shaped the economic policies of governments, requiring them to raise huge amounts of money to finance wars. Competition among major powers led to the rise of a large armaments industry in both Europe and America.

various tribes have revealed many financial abuses in the administration of these "trust" funds: Indian trust accounts have been manipulated to show such irregularities as no interest over decades and declining revenues despite deposits. Tribes have sometimes even been refused the right to audit their own funds. (In a 1996 audit the BIA couldn't account for 2.4 billion dollars in trust account transactions.)

1837-1838
Smallpox epidemic destroyed the Mandan Indians in North Dakota. The Mandans were an agricultural people whose population of 10,000 was concentrated in nine villages along the Missouri Valley in North Dakota. They possessed lighter skin and fine features, and many whites, including artist George Catlin and explorers Lewis and Clark, commented on their fine appearance, dignity of manner, courtesy, sense of fun, and spectacular costumes. Although they had weathered a series of smallpox epidemics brought by early traders, the epidemic of 1837 was so devastating that only 130 survived; those survivors joined with the Arikara and Hidatsa peoples. George Catlin's paintings remain the best record of the Mandan.

1837-1838
Chickasaw removal from Mississippi and Alabama. The last of the southern Five Civilized Tribes, the Chickasaw were forcibly removed to Indian Territory from Mississippi and Alabama and their lands taken for cotton production.

1838
The Ogden Land Company purchased Seneca land in New York in a transaction characterized as "blatantly corrupt" by all participants.

1839–1842
First Opium War in China and the cession of Hong Kong to the British. Although the Chinese government had outlawed opium, British traders in Canton conducted a thriving trade in the illegal drug. When 20,000 chests of opium were confiscated by Chinese port officials in Canton from British ships, war broke out between British and Chinese troops, which China quickly lost. China was forced to cede Hong Kong to the British, pay a huge indemnity, and open five additional ports to British traders.

1840
Antislavery and Abolition movement gained momentum in the U.S. The Underground Railroad was organized in the border and northern states to help slaves flee the South. Thousands of escaped slaves reached the northern cities of Philadelphia, Boston, and New York and told of extraordinary brutality on the new plantations of Mississippi, Alabama, and Georgia. Narratives of runaway slaves became popular in the North as a means of dramatizing the condition of slavery, and made slavery a national issue. Debate centered around the opening of new lands in the West, and whether those new states would be "slave or free." Slaves by the thousands began risking escape from plantations in Virginia and the Carolinas rather than face being "sold south" to the new cotton plantations in Mississippi, Alabama, and Louisiana, created from the lands recently vacated by the southeastern Indians.

1841
George Catlin published *Letters and Notes on the Manners, Customs, and*

Conditions of the North American Indians, Written During Eight Years' Travel Amongst·the Wildest Tribes of Indians in North America. Catlin, an artist and pioneer ethnologist, traveled among the western tribes without government or private support, painting the Plains Indians. His paintings are some of the best records of nineteenth-century Plains Indian life. Catlin wrote: *"The history and customs of such a people are themes worthy of the lifetime of one man, and nothing short of the loss of my life, shall prevent me from visiting their country and of becoming their historian."*

1842
First law of thermodynamics presented. Julius von Mayer proposed that the total amount of energy in the universe is constant and that in natural processes, energy is never lost, but merely transformed from one kind to another.

1843–1845
First Maori War between the British and Maori tribes of New Zealand. The Maori, who were fierce fighters, objected to the British government's rapid acquisition of native lands.

1844
China allowed the first Catholic and Protestant missionaries into the country.

1844
In Wyoming the completion of an accessible pass through the Rocky Mountains led to the opening of the Oregon Trail. Thousands of white settlers began to arrive in wagon trains, traveling through Indian lands in Nebraska, Wyoming, and Idaho to reach Oregon.

1842
Seneca Indians moved to the Allegheny and Cattaraugus reservations.

1845

First mention of America's "Manifest Destiny" in an eastern newspaper. Manifest Destiny was the idea that Americans were destined by divine providence to expand their national domain. A popular slogan which expressed the general need for territorial expansion, the exact phrase was printed in the *Democratic Review* of July 1845 as a rationale for annexation of Texas from Mexico: "*. . . the fulfillment of our manifest destiny to overspread the continent allotted by Providence for the free development of our yearly multiplying millions.*" The concept was also used to justify the acquisition of Oregon, the purchase of California, Arizona, New Mexico, and Nevada. It was also attached to unsuccessful movements to acquire Mexico, Cuba, the Dominican Republic, and Canada.

1845

Texas admitted to U.S. as a state.

1846

Smithsonian Institution formed in Washington, D.C., at the behest of Englishman James Smithson for the purpose of the increase of knowledge in the U.S. His bequest was incorporated into law as an act of Congress. The Smithsonian became one of the principal repositories for artifacts, art objects, and anthropological matèrials relating to North American Indian peoples.

1846-1848

War between U.S. and Mexico over annexation of Texas. Henry David Thoreau went to jail after an act of civil disobedience against U.S. expansion into Mexican territory.

1846-1868

Apache Wars in New Mexico. Mangas Coloradas (known as Red Sleeves), a Mibreno Apache, joined Cochise, a Chiricahua Apache, in resisting the incursion of miners and the U.S. Army into Apache lands in New Mexico. The miners appealed to the U.S. Army for help against the Apache, who were renowned fighters. Skirmishes went on intermittently for years. In the 1850s, when Mangas Coloradas was over 60 years old, he was captured by miners, beaten senseless, and then released as an abject lesson for other Apache. After he recovered, he led a series of ongoing raids against the U.S. Army and miners that ended only with his death.

1848
Treaty of Guadalupe Hidalgo concluded the two-year war between U.S. and Mexico. The treaty awarded the United States Mexican territories in Texas, New Mexico, Arizona (the provinces of Sonora, Coahuila, Tamaulipas), and California.

1848–1849
Uprisings throughout Europe calling for constituent assemblies, and the rise of nationalism in France, Germany, Italy, and Austria. The Hapsburg monarchy in Germany and Austria fell; parliamentary assemblies were established in Frankfurt and Prussia. In France an uprising in Paris by workers and students caused King Louis Philippe to abdicate. In Italy the Italian wars for independence began with uprisings in Milan, Venice, and the Piedmont against Austrian rule.

1848
First Women's Rights Convention in the world held at Seneca Falls, New York, former home of the Seneca Indians. Organizers Elizabeth Cady Stanton, Susan B. Anthony, and Lucretia Mott demanded that women be given the right to vote and declared women's equality: *"We hold these truths to be self-evident, that all men and women are created equal."* Abolitionist and former slave Frederick Douglass chaired the convention.

1848
California gold rush. John Marshall, a mechanic at a sawmill on Sutter's Creek in California, found a nugget of gold in the stream where he was fixing equipment. The news of his find started

the California gold rush, with tens of thousands of people from all over the world pouring into California seeking gold.

1848

Karl Marx and Fredrich Engels wrote *The Communist Manifesto* for the Communist League in Germany. Considered the founder and premier theorist of modern socialism, Marx made his life's work a prodigious study of the principles of capitalism.

1848

In England, John Stuart Mill published the *Principles of Political Economy*, the single most influential work on classical free-market economics. He proposed some concessions to state intervention when market economics and private initiatives didn't work.

1849

The Department of the Interior was created to administer the vast new public domain lands in the interior western states. These lands were in aggregate approximately the size of western Europe.

1849

The Indian Service was transferred to the Interior Department from the War Department. As a consequence the Service became more politicized and corrupt. Appointments to the post of Indian trader or Indian agent were made almost entirely as a result of congressional patronage.

1849-1850

Pomo massacre in California. Five Pomo men killed two abusive American ranchers who had taken over a ranch from the previous Mexican owners. When soldiers were sent to arrest them, and couldn't find them, they killed an entire village of 130 Pomo men, women, and children who were fishing on a nearby lake. The Indian agent,

Adam Johnston, described the situation to Washington: *"The majority of the tribes are kept in constant fear on account of the indiscriminate and inhumane massacre of their people.... They become alarmed at the immence [sic] flood of immigration which spread over their country.... It was quite incomprehensible to them."* California Indians who had spent decades successfully resisting or evading Spanish mission soldiers were overwhelmed by the gold rush miners, who overran Indian hunting grounds, villages, and burial sites, and kidnapped Indian women as prostitutes and Indian children as slaves. Whites declared open season on California Indians and did not even attempt to stay within the law. Historian Alvin Josephy called the treatment of California Indians *"as close to genocide as any tribal people had faced, or would face, on the North American continent."*

1851
Foucault's Pendulum experiment. French scientist Jean Bernard Foucault used a pendulum to illustrate that the earth rotated on an axis even as it rotated around the sun.

1851
Isaac Singer invented the first domestic sewing machine.

1851
First Treaty of Fort Laramie. As thousands of white settlers poured across the Great Plains to the Oregon Trail, the U.S. military purchased Fort Laramie in the middle of Sioux lands in Wyoming. An estimated 5,000 settlers crossed the northern Plains every year on their way to Oregon or on the Mormon Trail to Utah. Fort Laramie (a former trading post), at the junction of the Laramie and North Platte Rivers, was a key stop on the migration route.

U.S. Indian commissioners negotiated the first Treaty of Fort Laramie with representatives of the Sioux, Cheyenne, Arapaho, Crow, Arikara, Assiniboine, and Gros Ventre, dividing the Plains into specific tracts for each of the signatory tribes with the larger purpose of securing peace among the tribes and protecting white pioneers. In the treaty the tribes defined the territories they would stay within and promised not to harass wagon trains. In return the U.S. promised to compensate them for damages done by settlers and to distribute annuities in exchange for ceded lands. The government promised that the Indian lands would be theirs forever, that they would be protected against white depradations, and that the government would distribute among the tribes 50,000 dollars in supplies and provisions during each of the next 50 years. The government also required that each tribe select a principal chief with whom the federal government could conduct business.

The different Sioux nations retained full range of their hunting grounds on the Great Plains, traveling to different locations to hunt bison, fish, find water sources, or locate special plants. They were nomadic only in that they moved seasonally. (Until they began to own horses, sometime after 1680 and the Pueblo revolt, the Plains Indians had not moved great distances.)

As eastern Indians moved west, they displaced the western tribes. (The Sioux originally came from Minnesota.) They had moved onto the Plains where they became known as Sioux, Crow, Cheyenne, Shoshoni, Arapaho, Assiniboine, Gros Ventre, Arikara, Pawnee, Kiowa, Comanche, Blackfoot. They lived in uneasy balance, speaking many dialects of different language families, although they learned sign language to communicate with each other. But tensions were high and Indians of the Plains began to war with each other. They developed a ritualized warfare in which the physical touching of an enemy, called "counting coup," represented higher bravery than actual killing. As white settlers moved into their lands, the situation became even more volatile.

The U.S. failed to comply with almost every treaty provision it negotiated, eventually precipitating 22 years of war on the Great Plains which culminated in the Battle of Little Bighorn in 1876. **The states of Colorado, Kansas, South Dakota, North Dakota, Montana, Nebraska, and Wyoming were eventually carved out of lands guaranteed to the Plains Indian nations in the Treaty of Fort Laramie.**

1851
Fort Defiance built in Navajo country. It was the first U.S. fort built in Arizona. Its purpose was to control the Navajo Indians, considered one of the "wild tribes." The Diné people, as they called themselves, had previously been under a distant Mexican authority. Now they were forced to negotiate with American authorities for their own land and water, as the U.S. Army's horses and mules were using the Navajos' best water sources and grazing lands. Like the Apaches, the Navajos were Athabascans from the north who had migrated into the lands of the Hopi and Zuni and Pueblo peoples sometime in the 1300s. A resourceful and adaptive people, they had taken up sheepherding from the Spanish, learned weaving from the Hopi, and tended gardens and orchards. Some of their headmen, known as *ricos*, were very prosperous. The intrusion of the army at Fort Defiance led to increasing skirmishes with Navajo headmen, particularly one named Manuelito, who had large livestock herds. In

1860, 1,000 Navajo attacked the fort, and although they were driven off, Fort Defiance was abandoned the following year.

1852–1870

The Second French Empire began in France with Napoleon III as emperor. Prince Louis Napoleon, a nephew of Napoleon I, became Napoleon III by virtue of a plebiscite which transformed the French Republic into an empire.

1852

Quechan Indians of southern Arizona rebelled against U.S. troops building Fort Yuma on their lands. They had successfully revolted against Spanish settlers in 1781—killing four Franciscan friars, 31 soldiers, and 20 settlers—and had remained free of European domination until the U.S. built the fort on their lands on the banks of the Colorado River. Under U.S. policy the lands surrounding the fort became the Fort Yuma reservation in 1884. The Quechan, popularly known as Yuma Indians, still live there today.

1853

Gadsden Purchase. Mexico sold its remaining lands in Arizona, California, and New Mexico to the U.S. It brought many southwestern Indian nations under U.S. jurisdiction for the first time.

1854

Japan was opened to western trade by American Admiral Matthew Perry. Ending Japan's isolation and forcing the weak Tokugawa shogunate to sign the Treaty of Kanagawa, Perry opened Japan to U.S. trade for the first time. Five years later the U.S. would negotiate another treaty opening five more ports to U.S. trade.

1854

The Egyptian Khedive granted Suez Canal concession to Ferdinand de Lesseps, a French diplomat. The canal was to be a commercial waterway

1854

The Gadsden Purchase completed U.S. acquisition of lands in Arizona, New Mexico, and southern California.

In Washington, D.C., the Omaha Indians signed the Missouri Treaty, which ceded more than 43 million acres of land in Nebraska and Kansas. It allowed the president to distribute communally held Indian tribal lands to individual Indians, a policy that would become widespread throughout the nineteenth century. The Omahas were allowed to keep 300,000 acres. The new treaty contained clauses that would be included in all future treaties with every connecting the Mediterranean Sea and the Red Sea, opening the east coast of Africa to trade. European banks loaned huge sums of money at high interest rates to the Khedive to carry out enormous public works projects, including irrigation canals, railroads, roads, bridges, dams, and primary schools. The usurious interest rates eventually bankrupted the Khedive.

1854

Henry David Thoreau published *Walden: or Life in the Woods*, an account of his solitary life and studies of nature.

Indian group: first, that the president had the power to survey the lands and allot parcels to individual Indians; second, the president had the power to build roads in Indian country without the tribe's consent; and third, the president retained complete control over the money paid to the tribe in annuities, including the power to withhold payment for a variety of reasons.

Billy Bowlegs, Och-Lochta Micco, Seminole warrior and chief. Billy Bowlegs took over leadership of the Seminole after Osceola's death. The Seminole never surrendered. Billy Bowlegs fought for the North during the Civil War and died in 1863. This portrait was published in Thomas L. McKenney's *History of the Indian Tribes of North America.*

1855–1858
The Third Seminole War. The third
and last Seminole War started when a
party of government workers vandalized
crops belonging to Billy Bowlegs. The
Seminole leader demanded an apology
or money and got neither. The Seminoles began another three years of raiding by night and retreating into the
Everglades by day. In 1857 some Seminoles accepted a cash payment to leave
Florida for western Indian Territory,
where another Seminole band had
created a traditional Seminole government. Others refused to move. Seminole descendants in Florida today take
pride that their ancestors could not
be beaten and never surrendered. The
Seminole Wars are estimated to have
cost the U.S. government from 40 to 60
million dollars.

1857
Major revolt in India by Indian troops
(sepoys) against British rule. The surviving puppet ruler of the Mughal dynasty was deported to Rangoon.

1857
Treaty with the Tonawanda band of
Senecas in New York State. The Senecas were authorized to buy back their
reservation land from the Ogden Land
Company with monies from the U.S.
government. A stipulation of the award
was that the attorneys appointed by the
Tonawanda tribal council be approved
by the secretary of the interior, since the
previous tribal attorneys had been working for the Ogden Land Company.

1858
Government of India Act reformed
rule of India. The British Parliament
revoked the charter of the East India
Company and transferred rule of India
to the British Crown. The governor-
general of India was given the title of
viceroy and made responsible for India
within the British cabinet.

1858
Manuelito, a Navajo headman, found
60 head of his livestock shot by U.S.
soldiers. Furious, he confronted the
major at Fort Defiance and told him
the water and the grass belonged to
him, not to the U.S. Army. Soldiers
from Fort Defiance, supported by 160
Zuni mercenaries, burned Manuelito's

1858—1870
Unification of Italy. Count Cavour of Piedmont, an admirer of British parliamentary reforms and an opponent of the pope's political leadership, proposed the need for agricultural, industrial, and economic reforms in Italy. To promote unification he conspired with Napoleon III to expel Austria from Italy.

1859
Age of oil began. First American oil well drilled in Titusville, Pennsylvania. The beginning of large-scale exploitation of petroleum in the U.S.

1860
Anglo-French forces in China burned the Imperial Summer Palace. Beijing was occupied, and new treaties forced the Chinese emperor to open all of China to westerners.

1860—1870
The Second Maori War in New Zealand. The Maori tribes tried to form a union under a Maori king to combat British domination and aggressive land acquisition. The fierce guerrilla war went on for 10 years. In 1865 a native land court was established; in 1867 four Maori chiefs were admitted to the legislative assembly. In 1870 British troops withdrew. The Maori lost most of their lands.

1860
Invention of the Winchester repeating rifle, the first firearm capable of repeated firings without reloading.

village and fields. Manuelito resolved to drive the white soldiers off their lands and began organizing other Navajo headmen for war.

1860
Navajo attack against Fort Defiance. Over 1,000 Navajos led by Manuelito, a wealthy headman, and Barboncito, a medicine man and war leader, attacked Fort Defiance. They almost completely overran it, until superior gunfire drove them off. This marked the beginning of the army's policy of "total war" against the Navajos. Although the outbreak of the Civil War the following year caused the withdrawal of the soldiers and the abandonment of Fort Defiance, the Navajo war was taken up by the new commander in Santa Fe, James Carleton. The Navajos, like the Apaches, were considered a grave threat to the Army of the West.

INDIANS AND THE CIVIL WAR (1861–1865)

The Indian nations most profoundly affected by the Civil War were the Five Civilized Tribes of Indian Territory (Oklahoma). Most Indians had little interest in the issues dividing the North and the South. However, each of the Five Civilized Tribes signed treaties with the Confederacy and sent men into battle for the South. Confederate Indian troops from Indian Territory numbered 6,435 men. Most of the Oklahoma nations agreed with John Ross, principal chief of the Cherokee nation, who at first called for neutrality, but then saw the future in terms of the Confederate states. Ross believed that a division of the U.S. into two separate governments was likely, and he believed the Cherokee would do better with the Confederacy. He asked the Cherokee council for authority to enter into agreements with the Confederate states "upon terms honorable and advantageous to the Cherokee nation." He argued that only such an agreement would assure the future of the Cherokee people.

The Chickasaw and the Creek had also negotiated separate treaties with the Confederacy and sent men to fight in the Confederate uniform. The Chickasaw, Cherokee, and Creek units were used to hunt down deserters, enemy scouts, and bands of Union sympathizers who were hiding in the mountains of the Carolinas and Tennessee. Stand Watie, a Cherokee, became the only Indian brigadier-general in the Confederate Army. However, many of the other of the Five Civilized Tribes' soldiers who began by fighting for the Confederacy became disillusioned, and abandoned it by 1863 to join the Union forces. Billy Bowlegs, a Seminole leader, was one of the well-known soldiers in the Union cause.

The Civil War had a less direct but equally profound impact on Indians in the West because it accelerated the political absorption of western territories into the northern political system. Lincoln strategically appointed pro-Union officials in the territories of Dakota, Colorado, Nevada, New Mexico, Utah, and Washington. When Congress organized the territories of Idaho (1862), Arizona (1863), and Montana (1864), Lincoln also made sure that not only did they have pro-Northern governors, but that they had viable political organizations loyal to the Union. There was a lot of pro-South sentiment in Arizona, Utah, and California. Arizona organized the Confederate Territory of Arizona and sent a delegate to the Confederate Congress, but only Santa Fe in New Mexico Territory was briefly captured by Texas soldiers for the Confederacy.

However, the newly appointed officials of the new western territories were ambitious for statehood and responsive to anti-Indian hysteria. Some of the worst excesses against Indians occurred during the Civil War period and were a prelude to the post–Civil War era. The withdrawal of regular army troops from the West left "protection" of the territories in the hands of volunteer state militia, often ill-trained soldiers with irregular supervision. In Colorado the volunteer militia guarding the road to Santa Fe also engaged in Indian raids. John Chivington, "the fighting parson" (and Congressional hopeful) led the infamous Sand Creek Massacre against Black Kettle while he was camped under a flag of truce. Chivington, a leader of the local militia, became a major by attacking a Confederate supply train on the Santa Fe Trail. In the Dakotas the volunteer militia battled the Sioux. In Minnesota the Santee Sioux were so mistreated by crooked Indian agents that they were brought to the *edge of starvation, which led to the Minnesota Uprising of 1862. Thirty-eight Sioux were publicly hanged, the largest public execution in U.S. history. In California, the volunteer Army of the Pacific under James Carleton traveled to Arizona where they fought Cochise and the Apache at Apache Pass. This engagement eventually led Carleton to a policy of "total war" against the Apache and the Navajo, and the imprisonment of 8,000 Navajo on a barren camp at Bosque Redondo. In the power vacuum created by the Civil War, Carleton exercised virtually unlimited authority in New Mexico and Arizona. In Nevada and Utah a California businessman, Colonel Patrick Connor, commanding a volunteer thousand-man California militia, warred aggressively and unmercifully against the Shoshoni, Bannock, and Ute Indians.*

The Civil War period in the West was a prelude to the Indian Wars of the 1870s and 1880s. Military historians point out that the professional military in the U.S. took shape in the West after the Civil War. Many officers and troops who were unable to find post-war careers joined the Army of the West, taking demotions in order to get a permanent assignment. The key Union generals of the Civil War, such as Generals William Tecumseh Sherman and Phil Sheridan, were transferred to the Army of the West; George Custer and Nelson Miles became colonels in the western military; and the smaller-scale skirmishes that had characterized the earlier period of white-Indian relations became full-fledged military campaigns.

1861–1865
Civil War in the U.S. Representatives of Mississippi, Florida, Alabama, Georgia, Louisiana, Texas, Virginia, Arkansas, Tennessee, and North Carolina seceded from the Union. A provisional government was formed in Montgomery, Alabama, taking the name Confederate States of America, with Jefferson Davis as president. Abraham Lincoln was inaugurated as the 16th U.S. president. The immediate cause of war was the southern states' secession from the Union. The underlying issues were economic: the extension or abolition of slavery in the new western territories; the imposition of tariffs to protect northern industrial goods (high tariffs) or encourage export of southern agricultural products (low tariffs); the scale of land ownership in the new states. Although the northern states were outgeneraled and out

fought by the South, the North won the war through superior communications and technology, mainly the railroads and the telegraph. (See "Indians and the Civil War (1861–1865)" on page 265.)

1861
Invention of the Gatling machine gun.

1862
Robert E. Lee became the Confederate commander in chief and decisively defeated the northern forces in the Battle of Fredericksburg. Great Britain recognized the Confederate States.

Little Crow, Sioux chief of the Santee Sioux in Minnesota. After being brought to the edge of starvation because of Indian agents who stole their rations, the Santee Sioux chiefs rose up against white settlers. Little Crow was one of the leaders and he was hanged along with 37 others in the largest public execution in American history.

1862
Apache resistance in Arizona against volunteer state militia. When the Civil War began, the Apache took advantage of the withdrawal of the regular army from New Mexico and Arizona. In southern Arizona Apache leader Mangas Coloradas and his ally, Cochise, attacked the California militia (126 soldiers of the First Infantry of California Volunteers) en route to New Mexico at a site renamed Apache Pass. Even though he was 70 years of age, Mangas Coloradas continued to press the attack. Howitzers and mounted cavalry finally pushed them back. Mangas Coloradas was wounded and his men took him to Mexico to be treated.

1862-1864
Santee Sioux uprising in Minnesota. The hanging of Little Crow. Migrations of the Plains Indians. The Kickapoo fled to Mexico. In June of 1862 the Santee Sioux, almost starving as a result of the incompetence and ineptitude of Indian agents, went to the Yellow Medicine Agency to collect their rations and annuities to which they were entitled by treaty. The Sioux were told that the food, which was stored in an agency warehouse, could not be released. The agents had been pilfering the rations. Under Chief Little Crow the Sioux began an uprising, attacking

1862

The Homestead Act and the Pacific Railroad Act passed by Congress, the two most influential laws in overturning Indian treaties and opening western Indian lands to settlement. The South's secession from the Union permitted passage of two bills previously blocked by southern Congressmen. The Homestead Act promised 160 acres of land to anyone (white) who claimed it and worked to improve it. The Pacific Railroad Act gave transcontinental railroad companies 174 million acres of public lands, land charters which eventually grew to encompass the combined acreage of California and Montana. Railroads and their land development subsidiaries became the major land-administering agencies in the West.

1862

New Mexico and Arizona supported the Confederacy. When Texas joined the South during the Civil War, a Texas militia under General Sibley invaded Santa Fe and claimed New Mexico Territory for the Confederacy.

1862–1890

Otto von Bismarck, prime minister who would become president of Prussia, began the reorganization of central Europe into what would become the nation of Germany.

white settlements in Minnesota. The uprising spread to other Sioux bands in the eastern Dakotas. More than 1,000 settlers were killed in raiding throughout Minnesota. Some of the Sioux fled from Minnesota into Hudson's Bay Company territory in Canada. More than 3,000 found refuge in Manitoba, Canada, where they were given a reserve. The rest were sent to reservations in Nebraska, South Dakota, and North Dakota. Little Crow and 37 warriors were publicly hanged in a mass execution in Mankato, Minnesota, the largest public hanging in American history. At approximately the same time, some 1,300 Kickapoo in Kansas, who had heard of the uprising and who also had endured corrupt Indian agents and crooked deals, migrated south to Mexico where they hoped for better treatment from the Mexican government. During their journey through Texas, the Kickapoo had to fight Texas Rangers who were in the process of fighting the Comanche and Kiowa, and who opposed any Indians even traveling through Texas.

1862–1863

Navajo-Apache Wars. The U.S. appointed General "Gentleman Jimmy" Carleton of California as head of the Military Department of New Mexico (which included Arizona), in order to take Santa Fe back from Confederate General Sibley and to "subdue the hostiles"—the Apache and the Navajo in Arizona and New Mexico. Carleton intended to remove all the Apache and Navajo from their homelands and place them on the Bosque Redondo reservation near Fort Sumner, in eastern New Mexico close to Texas. "There will be no negotiations with the Indians," Carleton announced and ordered that any Navajo or Apache men were to be shot on sight. His commander in the field was the famous Indian scout Kit Carson, who commanded an army of volunteers from New Mexico and Arizona.

1863
Battle of Gettysburg. Confederate General Lee began an invasion of the North by way of the Shenandoah Valley and southern Pennsylvania. The battle at Gettysburg, Pennsylvania, was the decisive battle of the war.
Although the Army of the North took tremendous losses, they were able to resupply their troops by railroads. Lee, unable to resupply men or ammunition, eventually had to fall back to Virginia. After this, the Confederate forces were on the defensive.

1863
The role of the railroads and the telegraph was so significant in the war that the U.S. Congress created the National Academy of Sciences as scientific advisor to the federal government and promoter of scientific research.

1863
Mangas Coloradas killed.
The U.S. government was so afraid of his abilities as a leader that in 1863 they invited him to a peace parley at Fort McLane. Although versions of events differ, the Apaches maintain he was murdered. U.S. authorities reported that he was killed while trying to escape.

1863-1864
The war against the Navajo. The Navajo Long Walk and imprisonment at Bosque Redondo.
Kit Carson drove the Navajo from their lands by destroying their means of survival. His army killed thousands of sheep, poisoned wells, burned orchards and crops, destroyed hogans and livestock shelters, and anything else that was of value to the Navajo. Manuelito, Barboncito, Ganado Mucho, and other headmen retreated into the most remote Navajo lands. Thousands of others went into hiding in the deep recesses of Canyon de Chelly, previously unexplored by white men and noted for its quicksand floor. By winter Carson's men set up a blockade at the entrance to the canyon, shot anyone trying to leave, and in March rounded up thousands of starving Navajo and sent them on the "Long Walk" to Bosque Redondo.

More than 8,000 Navajo—as well as some Mescalero Apache who had not fled south—were marched 350 miles through spring blizzards from Fort

Defiance to Bosque Redondo. Many of the Apache fled to Mexico rather than be captured. The soldiers shot anyone moving too slowly, raped women, and shot the elderly. (Oral histories of the Navajo recount that when they asked the soldiers to stop so a pregnant woman could give birth, the soldiers refused. "Not long after [we] moved on, we heard a gun-shot ...") Many froze to death. Others starved or became sick. At Bosque Redondo they grew ill from brackish water and inadequate food. Comanche came from Texas and raided the camp at will. Many of the women got syphilis from the soldiers at the fort and in turn infected the Navajo men. The story of the Long Walk is passed on by Navajo elders in the same way Jews talk about the Holocaust. (Kit Carson became an American hero. His gravesite in Taos, New Mexico, is marked with a special commendation by the Eagle Scouts of America.)

1864
French troops occupied Mexico City. Archduke Maximilian of Austria was named emperor of Mexico.

1864
After Ulysses S. Grant was victorious at the Battle of Vicksburg and other western campaigns, he was appointed commander in chief of all northern armies. Abraham Lincoln reelected president.

1864
First International Workingmen's Association founded by Karl Marx in London, then in New York. Its motto was "Workers of the world unite."

1864
Sand Creek Massacre. Gold discovered in Colorado. Gold discoveries on the South Platte River in Colorado triggered an invasion of white prospectors, violating the buffalo-hunting grounds of the Cheyenne, Arapaho, Sioux, Kiowa, and Comanche Indians. Although the governor of Colorado tried to keep the Indians away from the routes the emigrants were traveling, the prospectors were directly cutting through hunting grounds which had been guaranteed by the Treaty of Fort Laramie in 1851. At first the government tried to break the treaty and send the Cheyenne and Arapaho to barren reservations. The Indians, not surprisingly, refused to go.

During the negotiations, the governor of Colorado allowed Cheyenne Chiefs Black Kettle and White Antelope and their peaceful bands to camp near Sand Creek en route to Fort Lyon. Meanwhile, Colorado militia volunteers fanned rumors of imminent large-scale Indian wars that would isolate Denver and the Colorado mines from the rest of the country. Reverend John Chivington, a Methodist elder running for Congress, organized a militia of volunteers to save Colorado from the Indian uprising and to elect himself to Congress. "I have come to kill Indians," Colonel Chivington protested to the officers at Fort Lyon who told him that the Cheyenne and Arapaho camped at Sand Creek were peaceful and had been promised safe passage. Under perceived popular pressure to kill Indians whatever the occasion, Chivington deployed 700 troops and four howitzers of the Third Colorado Cavalry around the peaceful Cheyenne at Sand Creek. On the morning of November 29 he led the volunteer militia into an unprovoked attack against mostly elderly men, women, and children. Black Kettle, who believed he was under peace protection, was helpless as his people were massacred. White Antelope sang his own death song and the soldiers shot him, scalped him, and cut off his nose, ears, and testicles. Chivington claimed that 500 Indians were killed. The number was later revised down to approximately 30 men and 125 women and children. No disciplinary action was taken against him. The Colorado public believed that extermination of Indians was good policy, regardless of whether the Indians were peaceful or warlike. Black Kettle survived. Four years later he was shot down by U.S.

Colonel William Armstrong Custer on the Washita River in an almost identical raid.

1864
Gold discovered in Montana. The Bozeman Trail opened, cutting through the lands of the Teton Sioux guaranteed by the Fort Laramie Treaty. John Bozeman, a prospector, discovered gold in Montana and opened a wagon road extending from the North Platte River through Wyoming into Montana and across the Yellowstone River into the gold camps. The new series of wars that began on the Upper Plains involved every tribe along that route. The army built Forts Reno, Phil Kearny, and S. F. Smith (named for white army officers) to protect the prospectors and supply trains. The Sioux organized into several armies. Red Cloud and Spotted Tail were the most notorious leaders.

1865
The U.S. Civil War ended with General Lee's surrender at the Appomattox Courthouse in Virginia (April 9).

1865
President Lincoln was assassinated (April 14). The 13th Amendment to the Constitution, prohibiting slavery within the U.S., was passed by Congress and ratified by two-thirds of the states.

1865
The same three generals who had won the war for the North would eventually take over the war in the West: Ulysses S. Grant became president; William Tecumseh Sherman became general in chief of the U.S. Army; and

1865
War on the northern Plains. After the Sand Creek Massacre, the Cheyenne and Arapaho sent war pipes to their friends. Allied war parties of Sioux, Cheyenne, and Arapaho raided up and down the North Platte and South Platte Rivers burning stage stations, tearing up telegraph wires, halting supply trains, mails, and successfully cutting off Denver, Salt Lake City, and San Francisco from overland communications. The stream of white miners and settlers slowed to a trickle, then stopped. The Sioux moved north into Wyoming and then into the White River country of South Dakota, where they separated into two groups: the Arapaho and the southern Cheyenne followed Red Cloud, an Oglala Sioux

Phil Sheridan became commander of all the soldiers in the West.

1866

War of Prussia and Italy against Austria. Prussia (Bismarck) allied with Italy (Cavour) in a defensive alliance against Austria. When Austria tried to annex lands in northern Italy, it found itself in a war with Prussia. Italy received Venice from Austria.

war chief; and the Brulé Sioux and northern Cheyenne followed Spotted Tail, also known as Sinte Gleshka. The 3,000-man U.S. army followed Red Cloud into Powder River country in present-day Montana where they got lost, were surprised by inconclusive engagements with an elusive enemy, and encountered bitter weather. The soldiers threatened mutiny. No more than 30 Indians were killed. A military commission investigating the Sand Creek Massacre and its resulting Indian wars reported: *"No one will be astonished that a war ensued which cost the government 30 million dollars and carried conflagration and death to the border settlements."* It was estimated that the army on the northern Plains spent a million dollars for each Indian it killed.

1866

Red Cloud and other Sioux leaders were summoned to Fort Laramie for a peace council. The government decided to maintain the Bozeman Trail and ordered Colonel Carrington and 700 troops into Powder River country to open a chain of forts stretching from Wyoming to Montana. But first it tried to negotiate safe passage of the road with the Indians and called a peace council at Fort Laramie. Red Cloud stormed out of the treaty conference when he learned of the forts: *"Why do you pretend to negotiate for land you intend to take by force? I say you can force us only to fight for the land the Great Spirit has given us."* Then his warriors harassed the builders of the forts, the miners on the trail, wagon trains, emigrant parties, and soldiers. The Bozeman Trail was as unsafe as it had ever been. In the fall of 1866 Red Cloud lured 80 soldiers under Captain Fetterman from Fort Phil Kearny into an ambush and killed them all. *"If Indians continue their barbarities wipe them out,"* wrote the *Montana Post*. The Sioux renewed their attacks against work crews in the spring.

1867

Russia sold Alaska to the U.S. for 7.2 million dollars. It was called "Seward's folly," after the secretary of state who recommended the purchase (no Alaska natives were given voice in determining land ownership) until gold was discovered there in the 1890s.

1867

Washington provisioned the western cavalry with Springfield breech-loading rifles, a greatly superior firearm in its capacity for reloading and multiple firings.

1867–1894

Das Kapital was published in three volumes by Karl Marx, a German economist and philosopher living in London. His massive work formed the first systematic analysis of labor in capitalist systems and an elaborate analysis of economic and political history. He appealed to workers of all countries to unite against capitalist exploitation and proposed an analysis of "scientific" as opposed to "utopian" socialism. *Das Kapital* was later translated into more than a hundred languages. Marxist thought greatly influenced the radical political movements of the next century and formed a theoretical foundation for modern communist ideology, most notably in Russia, but also for socialist parties throughout Europe and Asia.

1867

The Northern Pacific railroad advanced west from Nebraska into the Dakotas and Montana on a route along the North Platte River in Sioux country. The railroads decisively altered control of the great tracts of Indian territories. The railroad financed its construction by selling land to settlers who did not know that the land was already occupied. In Washington, where congressmen and senators worked closely with the railroads, it was decided to force the Sioux out of their lands in the Platte Valley and onto new reservations in South Dakota. With the new route of the railroad, the Bozeman Trail became unimportant.

1867

Bill Cody, a 21-year-old sharpshooter working for the Kansas Pacific railroad, shot 4,000 buffalo in an eight-month period with a Remington repeater rifle. He became famous as "Buffalo Bill" Cody. Buffalo were killed at the rate of two million a year. By the 1880s the buffalo was virtually extinct.

1868

The Meiji restoration in Japan. With the installation of the boy-emperor Meiji, the power of the Japanese emperor was restored after centuries of rule by shoguns. A period of modernization and westernization followed. The city of Edo was renamed Tokyo and Japan began to develop industry and trade. The restoration lasted until 1912.

1868

General William Tecumseh Sherman called on George Armstrong Custer to join the Army of the West. Custer was on military suspension because of cruelty and negligence to troops under his command. Sherman was about to adopt a policy of total war against the Plains Indians.

1868

A victorious Chief Red Cloud signed the Fort Laramie Treaty of 1868, which marked the occasion of Indians winning a war against the U.S. and dictating the official terms of peace. (The U.S. government did not abide by the terms of the treaty.) The government agreed that securing the Bozeman Trail was not worth the expense of taking down the forts in Sioux country. General Sherman invited Red Cloud and the chiefs of his allied bands to a peace council at Fort Laramie. Red Cloud was not only a fine general, he was a good negotiator and made his victories 'in the field count at the negotiating table. He would not sign until the U.S. troops were gone and the Sioux had burned the hated forts. Then Red Cloud, accompanied by 125 war chiefs and headmen of the Oglalas, Hunkpapas, Sicangus, Sihasapas, and Sans Arcs divisions of, Sioux, arrived at the fort to sign the treaty. The treaty provisions included recognition of Indian lands—"absolute and undisturbed use and occupation," agreement by the government to keep whites out of their traditional hunting grounds, and permission for the Sioux to trade for firearms and ammunition at trading posts along the Platte River. Red Cloud realized that enforcement of the treaty might be problematic because he had learned that the government planned to establish a reservation in South Dakota west of the Missouri River for some Sioux bands.

1868
Black Kettle killed at the Washita River by Custer. Four years after Sand Creek the unlucky Black Kettle took his band of southern Cheyenne survivors to a new reservation set aside on the Washita River in Indian Territory. Many of the young Cheyenne men had refused to go on a reservation and had instead joined the warriors of the Kiowa, Comanche, or Cheyenne "Dog Soldiers" who fought the American invaders. Lieutenant-Colonel George Armstrong Custer, just brought West by General Sherman and on his first assignment, led the U.S. Seventh Cavalry to Black Kettle's village. Indian guides mistakenly told him the village was hostile. At dawn Custer's soldiers charged the sleeping village. Black Kettle and his wife tried to ride out in a snowstorm to meet Custer, carrying a white flag, hoping to stop the attack. Both were shot on sight. The regiment went on to kill another hundred Cheyenne; mostly women, children, and the elderly. It was Custer's first encounter with Indian people.

1868
Treaty of Bosque Redondo with the Navajo. Barboncito negotiated with General William Tecumseh Sherman for a return of the Navajo to their old lands. Sherman, hero of the Civil War, was given the position of commander in chief of U.S. forces in the West. The costs of Bosque Redondo, both in actual supplies and pilfered goods, had become so astronomical that Secretary of War Stanton had removed Carleton from

command and sent Sherman to negotiate a peace treaty with the Navajo and to relocate them to an Indian reservation. Sherman planned to send them to Oklahoma or Kansas. Barboncito refused to sign the treaty as written and insisted instead on returning to Navajo lands in Arizona and New Mexico. He skillfully and eloquently argued to be returned to their old lands: *"When the Navajos were first created, four mountains and four rivers were pointed out to us, inside of which we should live. That was to be our country and it was given to us by the First Woman of the Dineh. It was told to us by our forefathers that we were never to move east of the Rio Grande or north of the San Juan Rivers and I think that our coming here has been the cause of so much death among us and our animals. First Woman when she was created, gave us this piece of land and created it especially for us . . . I hope you will not ask me to go to any country except my own. . . . They told us this was a good place when we came, but it is not!"* (This translation was from Navajo to Spanish to English.) The negotiations concluded on June 1, 1868, and the treaty document, prepared by the Department of State, was signed by General Sherman and 29 Navajo headmen including Barboncito, Armijo, Manuelito, Ganado Mucho and Delganito. The new reservation was about one-tenth of the country the Navajos had previously claimed and excluded all the good eastern grazing lands and most of their water sources. In the five years of the Navajo captivity, white settlers had moved on to their best lands; their fields had been untended and their orchards destroyed. The reservation lands that Sherman finally agreed to were on the New Mexico–Arizona border, with sparse water supplies, and even at the time, were recognized as inadequate for the number of people to be resettled. In exchange for the Navajos' agreement to never make war against the U.S. again, the government agreed to give the Navajos 13,000 sheep (two per family), corn, flour, and food staples to get them through the first winters until they could reestablish a self-sufficient agricultural base. Not one treaty provision on the government side was fully met. Somewhere between Washington and the Indian agents in the field, most of the supplies and promised livestock disappeared. The Navajo observed the terms of the treaty they signed in 1868, which included agreeing to not possess firearms or conduct raids, and to send their children to white schools.

1869

Opening of the Suez Canal, connecting the Mediterranean and the Red Sea. Empress Eugénie of France attended. First performance of Verdi's opera, *Aida*, commissioned for the occasion.

1869

The Central Pacific and the Union Pacific lines met at Promontory Point, Utah. The continent had been joined; Indian lands were cut.

With the transcontinental railroad and the telegraph, the Army of the West could successfully outmanuever and resupply their troops in any engagement against the Indians.

1870

John D. Rockefeller formed the Standard Oil Company. Within nine years he controlled 95 percent of the U.S. oil industry.

1870

President Grant gave control of Indian agencies to Christian missionary denominations after Congress passed a law prohibiting army officers from holding the post of Indian agent. The U.S. Congress also appropriated

1870

Franco-Prussian War. The end of the Second French Empire. Three German armies invaded France. At the Battle of Sedan, Napoleon III was decisively defeated. German troops entered Paris. A provisional government was formed.

1870

Rome was annexed to Italy. As a result of the Franco-German war, French troops were withdrawn from Italy, and Rome, formerly under French control, became the new capital of Italy.

1871

The founding of modern Germany. With the Prussian victory over France, Bismarck was able to unify the states of northern and southern Germany. The new Germany contained four kingdoms, five grand duchies, thirteen duchies, and three free cities. Alsace-Lorraine was annexed from France.

1871

Rise of the Paris Commune. The end of the French empire. The Parisian populace invaded the Palais Bourbon and proclaimed the fall of the empire and a new French Republic. In Paris, France capitulated to the Germans and agreed to pay a five-billion-franc indemnity.

1872

Establishment of Yellowstone National Park in Montana and Wyoming, the first national park in the world. It marked public recognition that land in its natural state should be preserved.

100,000 dollars for American Indian education and to fund federal industrial schools for Indian education and training. The first schools were also contracted out to Christian churches.

1870

The Arikara, Gros Ventre, and Mandan Indians of the Dakotas were confined to a reservation at Fort Berthold in Dakota Territory and forced to relinquish all claims to all other lands which they had traditionally claimed.

1871

The end of Indian treaties as a means of agreement with Indian nations. Congress declared in an appropriations bill that no further treaties were to be signed with Indian nations or tribes. All further agreements were to be made by executive order or congressional act. The change in policy reflected new power realities.

1872-1874

The slaughter of buffalo destroyed the economic and cultural base of the Plains Indian nations. Buffalo hides were in great demand because of a new process of tanning the leather hides. The southern Plains filled with buffalo hunters equipped with new,

Buffalo Herds Crossing the Upper Missouri, 1832. When George Catlin arrived among the Indian villages of the Upper Missouri River in the early 1830s he reported that migrating buffalo herds stretched as far as the eye could see and sometimes it took three days for the entire herd to cross the river on its migration. *"The American bison,"* he wrote in his *Letters and Notes,* *". . . seems to have been spread over the plains of this vast country by the Great Spirit for the use and subsistence of the red men, who live almost exclusively on their flesh, and clothe themselves with their skins."*

high-powered rifles, who killed buffalo by the hundreds of thousands. They shipped the hides east and left the unused carcasses rotting on the ground. In destroying the buffalos, the hunters wiped out the Plains Indians' food supply, as well as the raw materials for their clothing, shelter, and other items used in their everyday life. The government realized that without the buffalo the Plains tribes would have no choice but to go onto reservations and accept government-issue rations. General Sherman made it army policy to encourage the buffalo hunters. In two years over four million buffalo were slaughtered. Within 12 years more than 20 million buffalo had been slaughtered, and the herds, which once covered the Plains from dawn to dusk as far as the eye could see, were exterminated. General Sheridan told the Texas legislature that the buffalo-hide hunters *"have done . . . more to settle the vexed Indian question than the entire regular army. . . . They are destroying the Indians' commissary. . . . For the sake of a lasting peace, let them kill, skin and sell until the buffalos are exterminated."* By the end of the 1880s more than 30 million buffalo had been slaughtered. Less than a thousand remained.

1873

Credit Mobilier scandal. Credit Mobilier was America's first holding company, formed as a separate construction company to build the Union Pacific railroad. Shares had been given at a low price to many members of congressional committees who had power over railroad routes, appropriations, and mineral-rich Indian lands. Credit Mobilier shares, which were also sold in Europe and run up by speculators, made many congressmen and senators millionaires before the scandal was exposed.

1874

The U.S. broke the 1868 Treaty of Fort Laramie by sending an army detachment under Lieutenant-Colonel Custer to prospect for gold in the Black Hills. Custer found gold. The discovery sent prospectors pouring into the Dakotas, lands that had been promised "absolute and undisturbed use and occupation" to the Sioux. War was the result. Red Cloud went to Washington to meet with President Grant.

1875
World population reached 1.5 billion.

1875
Britain purchased the Egyptian Khedive's share of the Suez Canal. The Egyptian ruler's near bankruptcy resulted in Anglo-French domination of Egypt. France and England formed an Anglo-French controller's office to supervise debt service. This European control provoked one of the first nationalist resistance movements in Africa.

1876
Korea declared its independence from China.

1876
Alexander Graham Bell patented the telephone.

1875
Comanches in Texas surrendered after war with the U.S. Army and Texas Rangers.

1875
Black Hills gold rush. Sitting Bull was chosen head chief of all the Teton Sioux. The unprecedented selection of a central leader for many diverse Sioux bands was believed to be necessary to meet the crisis of survival facing the Sioux. Sitting Bull was a holy man as much as he was a war chief. His followers attributed his success to the strength of his visions. Sitting Bull himself believed his powers came from harmony with the mysterious powers of the universe.

1876
The struggle for the Sacred Paha Sapa or Black Hills of South Dakota. Battle of Little Bighorn. Custer was killed along with 211 soldiers under his command. After Custer had illegally invaded the Black Hills, which were both sacred to the Sioux and protected by treaty, and the gold rush to the Black Hills began, Red Cloud asked the U.S. government to enforce the treaty provisions signed at Fort Laramie in 1868 and to evict the miners. The white miners in turn asked the government to evict the Sioux from their own lands. Instead, the government offered to buy the Black Hills for six million dollars, which the Sioux chiefs refused. This initiated a vacillating government policy that alternated between trying to meet the treaty obligations and forcing the Indians to leave their hunting lands for the great Sioux reservation. Red Cloud refused another offer of six million dollars for the Black Hills and asked instead for

sixty million dollars. The government refused. President Grant then issued an order that all Sioux bands must come into their assigned agencies by January 31, 1876, or be considered hostile and subject to capture or killing. The government believed that once the militant Indians were subdued at the agencies the remainder of the Sioux could be induced to sell the Black Hills at a reasonable price. Red Cloud realized that the government was not only refusing to honor the Fort Laramie Treaty, it would go to war to force his people onto reservations.

To fight the new policy, all the off-reservation (nontreaty) Sioux bands organized in a massive encampment at the Little Bighorn River in Montana. They were joined by reservation Indians. Seven thousand Lakota, Yankton, Santee, northern Arapaho, and northern Cheyenne were camped in a three-mile stretch along the river-banks. To force the Sioux bands back onto lands supervised by the Indian agencies, General Phil Sheridan organized a three-pronged campaign under General Crook, General Custer, and Colonel Nelson Miles. Crazy Horse, an Oglala Sioux warrior with 1,000 men, stopped the first prong under General Crook at the Rosebud River in Montana on June 17. A second prong, which included George Custer's regiment, crossed to the valley of the Little Bighorn River on June 25. Advancing ahead of the main column, Custer sighted a small portion of the camp, and perhaps remembering Black Kettle's defenseless village on the Washita River, he issued a highly unusual order for his men to charge. (It was noon, and attacks on Indian villages always took place at dawn.) Met in battle by Sitting Bull's warriors, Custer and all 225 soldiers with him were killed in less than half an hour. Ignoring all evidence, the newspapers called it a massacre. Seeing a second army coming up the valley of the Little Bighorn, Sitting Bull disbanded the encampment, fearing massive retaliation after the battle with Custer. Subsequently, every band of Sioux Indians was pursued by Colonel Miles and General Crook. Cut off from supplies and facing starvation in winter, the Sioux bands eventually "came in" to the reservations in the Dakotas. There, their horses and guns were taken from them. Government commissioners met with the Sioux chiefs at the agencies and with threats to cut off their rations forced them to sell the Black Hills. The choice for the Sioux chiefs was "sell or starve." The chiefs sold. The Black Hills were opened to miners and settlers.

GERONIMO AND THE APACHE RESISTANCE

Geronimo was a war leader with strong spiritual powers who had fought with Cochise as well as the great Apache chief Mangas Coloradas, first against the Mexicans and then the Americans. In fact, 25 years earlier, Geronimo had lost his mother, his wife, and three children to Mexican soldiers. In 1886 the U.S. government put General Nelson Miles and 5,000 troops into the field in Arizona to capture Geronimo and 24 "renegade Apache." These were the last holdouts of the Chiricahua Apache resistance, and the army spared no effort or expense to capture them. The troops were also assisted by 500 Apache scouts, thousands of civilian militia, and over a thousand Mexican volunteer troops. Both the Santa Fe railroad, which planned a southern transcontinental route across New Mexico and Arizona into California, and the U.S. Army did not want Apaches roaming Arizona Territory at will.

The history of the Apache was one of constant struggle with army troops, who first entered the Southwest in the 1850s after America's assumption of the territory from Mexico.

In 1874 the great war chief Cochise extracted a promise from the army that his people would be allowed to live in peace on their own lands around Apache Pass, but when he died that same year the promise died with him. By 1877 the American government had ordered the confinement of all Chiricahua Apache to the San Carlos reservation in southeastern Arizona. The Apache hated it. As a nephew of Geronimo described it, San Carlos was amazingly harsh and barren: "The Creator did not make San Carlos . . . He just left it as a sample of the way they did jobs before He came along . . . Take stones and ashes and thorns and, with some scorpions and rattlesnakes thrown in, dump the outfit on stones, heat the stones red-hot, set the United States Army after the Apaches, and you have San Carlos."

Although many Apache, tired of being harassed and hungry, went to the reservation, many others refused. They followed Cochise's son, Nakai, and Geronimo into the mountains of northern Mexico. For the next 10 years they were hunted by Mexican troops and by the American army. Their numbers dwindled as more and more left to settle on the reservation, but Geronimo refused to leave. However, Geronimo and his men seemed able to enter and depart the reservation lands at will. In 1882 he led a raid on the reservation and then left. In 1884 he returned to the reservation and left again in 1885. In March of 1886 he met with General George Crook at Canyon de los Embudos in Mexico, but did not like Crook's terms and left with his band in the middle of the night. Six months later General Nelson Miles had taken over; he met Geronimo at Skeleton Canyon near Apache Pass in Arizona. On the basis of Miles's promise that members of his band would be held as prisoners of war for only two years and then allowed to live peacefully on the reservation, Geronimo surrendered.

General Miles, unfortunately, did not have a good record in keeping promises. He was the same general who had taken Chief Joseph's surrender nine years earlier, promising him that his people would be returned to their country in the Northwest Territory. Instead the Nez Perce and Chief Joseph spent years being transferred around the military prisons of the West. Larger pressures were also bearing down on Miles: President Cleveland himself recommended that Geronimo be hanged.

Geronimo and several hundred of his followers, even those who had peacefully settled on the San Carlos reservation (but who were deemed to be sympathizers), were rounded up and shipped by train to Fort Marion in Florida. The children were taken from their parents and sent to the Carlisle Indian School in Pennsylvania, where a third of them died. Over a hundred of the prisoners died in Florida. Some were transferred to Alabama, others to Carlisle, Pennsylvania, and later to Fort Sill, Oklahoma. For 23 years Geronimo was held as a prisoner of war. Teddy Roosevelt requested that Geronimo be released for a day to ride in his inaugural parade in 1902. He died in 1909 at Fort Sill, Oklahoma. The rest of the Chiricahua Apache were held until 1913, and there are Apache elders alive today who were born as prisoners of war as late as 1913. Many of them were settled in Oklahoma rather than being returned to their lands in Arizona.

1876–1886

The Apache Wars. The U.S. government decided to relocate the Chiricahua Apache tribe to an Indian reservation on the Gila River known as the San Carlos agency. Geronimo refused to be relocated, and for the next 10 years led raiding parties throughout Arizona and New Mexico, and into Mexico. Whenever he became fatigued he would surrender, only to renew his raids as soon as reservation life became too oppressive. In 1886 the U.S. government put 5,000 troops into the field under General Crook, and Geronimo finally surrendered in 1887, under terms that later were not honored. (See "Geronimo and the Apache Resistance" on page 284.)

1877

The queen of England was proclaimed the empress of India at a ceremony in Delhi.

1877

Congress passed the Desert Lands Act. It encouraged development of irrigation by private companies in arid areas.

1877

The great Railroad Strike, America's first general strike. The walkout began in Baltimore when the Baltimore and Ohio railroads tried to make up for reduced profits by a 10 percent wage cut. The strike spread spontaneously to railroads in Pittsburgh, Chicago, St. Louis, Kansas City, and San Francisco where workers in other industries joined the walkout. The railroads recruited police and local militia to protect their property and President Rutherford Hayes called out federal troops against the strikers. Over a hundred strikers died and millions of dollars of railroad property was destroyed. As a consequence the War Department constructed armories in every major city and instituted a standing "National Guard" to deal with domestic emergencies.

1877

Sioux resistance broken. Colonel Nelson Miles (a former crockery-store clerk from Boston) continued the campaign. Many Sioux bands returned to their reservations. Crazy Horse surrendered. Sitting Bull fled to Canada. Crazy Horse, one of the great Sioux warriors, led many of the last of the free Oglala Sioux, some 900 members of his own band of Oglalas, into the Red Cloud agency on May 6, 1877. Four months later he was asked to attend a meeting with General Crook. Instead he was taken to prison. When he resisted being jailed, he was bayoneted and then killed by an Indian in a policeman's uniform. His captors said he was killed trying to escape. He was 35 years old. His likeness was never captured by photographers or artists. **Sitting Bull refused to surrender and led his band of Hunkpapa Sioux to Canada.** Under U.S. pressure, Canada would not give them a reserve. Sitting Bull remained there, eking out a living for the next four years. Although many of his people returned to the U.S., Sitting Bull remained an eloquent voice of the Sioux people and was frequently interviewed by white reporters and often quoted in the white press: "*When I was a boy the [Lakotas] owned the world;*

Sitting Bull

the sun rose and set on their land. . . .
Where are the warriors today? Who slew
them? Where are our lands? Who owns
them? . . . What law have I broken? Is it
wrong for me to love my own? Is it wicked
for me because my skin is red? . . . be-
cause I was born where my father lived
. . . because I would die for my people and
my country?"

1877
Chief Joseph's 1,400-mile campaign
across Oregon, Idaho, Wyoming, and
Montana. Chief Joseph and several
other nontreaty Nez Perce refused to relocate to a reservation in Oregon that
was one-tenth the size of their original
lands. After a fraudulent treaty in 1863,
the "thief treaty," which illegally ceded
six million acres of Nez Perce lands,
Chief Joseph, who was Christianized
and friendly with white leaders and missionaries, returned his Bible and took
up again the traditional religion of his
own people. Finally in 1877 he and
other nontreaty chiefs were pressured to
go on a reservation. Wanting to avoid
war, he agreed. But an altercation with
white troops, started by a few young
warriors, developed into a full-scale
war. When U.S. soldiers shot a negotiating team of Nez Perce riding out with a
white flag, Chief Joseph and 750 people,
including the chiefs of other bands, began what General Sherman called "one
of the most extraordinary Indian wars of
which there is any record." They outwitted over 2,000 soldiers aided by Indian
scouts, and 1,000 auxiliary soldiers of
other tribes for almost four months
across 1,500 miles of territory in a campaign still studied at West Point. They
were surprised in the open plains 40
miles from the Canadian border by

General Nelson Miles, who had been notified by telegraph. Chief Joseph's speech of surrender is one of the most quoted in all of Indian oratory. (*"From where the sun now sets, I will fight no more forever."*) The surrender terms he negotiated with General Miles (recently promoted) were reversed by General William Tecumseh Sherman, who instead of returning them to their old lands in Idaho after two years, sent them to Fort Leavenworth, Kansas, and then to Oklahoma, where they spent eight years as prisoners of war. Only after extraordinary efforts were they allowed in 1885 to return to the Northwest.

1878

John Wesley Powell published the *Report on the Lands of the Arid Regions of the United States,* a landmark study of the lands and water of the American West. It was largely ignored.

1878

Hampton Institute in Virginia expanded to educate Indians. The first off-reservation Indian boarding school in the U.S., it reflected the new federal policy of Assimilation and Civilization. Educating vanquished Indians was believed to be the solution to the "Indian problem." Founded by Samuel Armstrong, a former missionary and leader of a black regiment in the Civil War, the school expanded its mission from the education of black students to the transformation of Indians from "pagan wanderers" to farmers, ministers, seamstresses, millers, and lawyers. The first students were five Kiowa, eleven Cheyenne, and one Arapaho, hostages from Fort Marion in St. Augustine, Florida. Taken as prisoners of war near the Red River during the war on the southern Plains, they had been sent first to Florida and then transferred to Hampton. Booker T. Washington was a "housefather" to the Indian men. Hampton Institute's program was the forerunner of a system of off-reservation

Kill the Indian, save the man. With the conclusion of the Plains wars, policymakers viewed the solution to the "Indian problem" as educational rather than military: with education Indians would assimilate into American society and disappear. These Indian students arrived at the Hampton Institute in Virginia from the Dakota Territory in 1881. Their families were left behind on reservations at Fort Berthold and Standing Rock. *Standing on the porch, left to right*: Jennie No Ears (Sioux), age 15; Thomas Goodwood (Sioux), 14; John Tiaokasin (Sioux), 16; Deluska (Mandan), 15; Frank Black Hawk (Sioux), 15; Mary Walker (Gros Ventre), 12; Louis Agard (Sioux), 17; *sitting on steps left to right*: Charles Many Birds (Mandan/Gros Ventre), 13; Joseph Archambeau (Sioux), 14; Fidelia Walking Medicine (Sioux), 15; Frances White Cow (Sioux), 14; Josephine McCarthy (Sioux), 12; Rosa Bear Face (Sioux), 17; Susie Nagle (Mandan), 9; *standing near steps*: Cracking Wing (Mandan), 14; White Back (Gros Ventre), 15.

boarding schools designed to assimilate Indians into the dominant white society. English was the only language allowed; the Indians were to follow Christian teachings; to have their hair cut; wear "citizen" clothing; adopt Christian practices; and learn to schedule their day by the quasi-military regimen.

"It was ironic," wrote historian Rayna Green, *"that a society that declared the education of blacks and slaves illegal insisted on teaching Indians to read and write, often sending military units to separate them from their parents and homes."*

1878

Washakie, a Shoshoni chief, accepted a silver saddle from President Ulysses S. Grant in recognition of his service and cooperation with the U.S. government. Washakie had become chief of the eastern Shoshoni in 1843 and had determined early on that the interests of his people would be best served by co-operating with whites. With the Treaty of Fort Badger in 1863, he had promised not to molest travelers through Wyoming in return for 10,000 dollars in supplies each year for 20 years. In 1876 he led a group of 200 braves to the Bighorn Mountains in response to a request from General George Crook to join the campaign against the Sioux. (The battles were over before he got there.) In 1878 federal Indian agents persuaded him to "share" the Wind River reservation with 1,000 northern Arapaho, although it was 50 years after his death before the government got around to compensating the Shoshoni for their hospitality to the Arapaho. Although Washakie was often held up as an example of an "enlightened" Indian chief, he himself had no illusions about the true nature of the relationship with whites: *"Our fathers were steadily driven out, or killed, and we, their sons, but sorry remnants of tribes once mighty are cornered in little spots of the earth all ours by right."*

1878

Satanta, a Kiowa patriot known as the Orator of the Plains, who spent much of his life fighting the government's efforts to remove the Kiowa and Comanche to reservations in Oklahoma, died in a fall from a prison hospital window at Huntsville, Texas. He had been imprisoned for violating parole. Prison authorities said he had committed suicide. The Kiowa, who were not allowed to investigate, believed he had been murdered.

1879

Thomas Edison "invented" the light bulb, improving existing bulbs so that the filament would glow consistently.

1879

Carlisle Indian School founded in Carlisle, Pennsylvania, as the first exclusively Indian boarding school. Many of the first students were recruited by missionaries in Dakota Territory following the war on the northern Plains. Its first headmaster was Captain Richard Pratt, who coined the motto "Kill the Indian and Save the Man." The goal of the school was to eradicate "Indianness" and substitute white values and white thinking. To that end Indian students had their hair cut, their blankets and clothes taken away and replaced by military uniforms. Corporal punishment was administered, Bible reading and vocational skills were emphasized. Many students ran away; some became sick and died; a few became "model citizens." Within three years it was followed by another Indian school at Lawrence, Kansas, and plans for dozens more. By 1880 there were more than 7,000 Indian children enrolled in federally financed, missionary-run Indian boarding schools.

1880

Beginning of the "green revolution" and worldwide application of chemical fertilizers to increase agricultural production. Sodium nitrate beds in Chile exploited; use of potash as an inorganic fertilizer.

1881

The first hydroelectric plant in America went into operation on the Fox River in Wisconsin.

In New York Thomas Edison, backed by J. P. Morgan, opened the first central electric power plant, the Pearl Street station, which illuminated 85 buildings.

1883–1885

French war in China. Beginning of French Indochina. At the conclusion

1881

Sitting Bull and the remainder of his band of Hunkpapa Sioux crossed the Canadian border and came into Fort Buford, Dakota Territory. They were removed to the Standing Rock Reservation. For five years Sitting Bull traveled with Buffalo Bill Cody's Wild West Show, returning to the reservation only intermittently.

1881

A *Century of Dishonor* published. Written by Helen Hunt Jackson, it was an indictment of U.S. Indian policy and the treatment of American Indians in U.S. society.

1882

By executive order, President Chester Arthur removed some 4,000 square miles of land in northern Arizona from the public domain and made it a reservation for "the Moquii [Hopi] Indians and such other Indians that the President should decide to settle thereon ..." The intent of the order was to prevent Mormon settlers from claiming the lands under the Homestead laws. The Mormons had built settlements next to the Hopi mesas. The land was believed to hold valuable mineral deposits as well as a large coal reserve. The order formed the legal basis of the present-day Navajo-Hopi land conflict.

1883

Sitting Bull guest of honor at opening ceremonies of Northern Pacific. The of the war, China ceded to France regions formerly under Chinese domination—Vietnam, Laos, Cambodia, and other adjacent areas. The region became known as French Indochina.

1883

The railroads imposed four "standard time zones" on the United States. This was done without act of Congress, president, or the courts. Railroads had been operating within their own private universes of time and with as many as 50 different time zones according to the railroad line. Railroad stations often displayed several clocks, each telling the time on other lines and one declaring the presumed local time. Railroad clock towers were the most influential source of time in the cities. With "standard time zones" the entire country adopted railroad time.

1883

Buffalo Bill Cody's Wild West Show began to tour Europe. It was a popular show-business extravaganza that replicated buffalo hunts, wild Indian battles, and frontier exploits, and anticipated Hollywood's depiction of the frontier West.

1883

The Northern Pacific transcontinental railroad completed, following a route through Montana, Idaho, Oregon, and Washington, and opening those lands to settlers.

1883

Rise of nationalist sentiment in India. The Indian middle class promoted a bill to allow Indian judges to prosecute Europeans. Although defeated, it resulted

Northern Pacific railroad executives invited Sitting Bull to Bismarck, North Dakota, for ceremonies celebrating the completion of their transcontinental route. Sitting Bull rode at the head of the parade and sat with the dignitaries on the speakers' platform. When it was his turn to speak, he rose and began in Sioux: *"I hate all white people. You are thieves and liars. You have taken away our land and made us outcasts."* The army officer assigned to translate was stunned but then recovered and told the audience how happy Sitting Bull was to be there and how he looked forward to peace and prosperity between the whites and the Indian people. The audience gave Sitting Bull a standing ovation and the railroad executives invited him to another ceremony in St. Paul. Sitting Bull had great public acceptance and popularity.

in the formation of all-Indian associations to promote legislative reforms and to agitate for the Indianization of the British-controlled Civil Service. These ideas were vigorously promoted at the annual Indian National Congress.

1885

In Germany Karl Benz produced the first prototype of an automobile using an internal combustion motor. His company became known as Mercedes-Benz.

1886

First major hydroelectric installation at Niagara Falls.

1885

Indian police units were established by the Bureau of Indian Affairs at 48 out of 60 Indian agencies. Responsible to the BIA Indian agents, the tribal police, recruited from among reservation men and paid by the U.S. government, were used to enforce BIA regulations and bypass traditional shamans and leaders. They were often informers and became enforcers of a surrogate "assimilationist" government.

1886

Geronimo and his "army" of twenty-four renegade Apaches was hunted by General Nelson Miles and 5,000 U.S. soldiers (about one-third of the combat strength of the U.S. Army). Geronimo, who had hidden in the Sierra Madre mountains, was eventually found by two Apache scouts working for Lt. Charles Gatewood. He agreed to surrender on condition that he and his people would be allowed to return to the San Carlos reservation after two years. Instead, President Cleveland recommended he be hanged and the harshest treatment be given to the Apaches as an example to other tribes. Geronimo and all the Chiricahuas were sent to Ft. Marion in Florida. There over a hundred died in the moist, humid Florida climate. All the children were taken from them and sent to the Carlisle Indian school in Pennsylvania where more than 50 died and few of the survivors ever saw their families again. Even the "friendly" Apache who had worked for the army and had led the troops to Geronimo's hiding place lost their lands and livestock and were shipped to the Florida prison. It was said that the Chiriacahuas had fought too hard, for too long, and were marked for extinction.

1887

The great flood of the Yellow River in China killed 1.5 million Chinese. The river broke a massive dike and flooded 10,000 square miles.

1887

The Dawes Act, or General Allotment Act, passed by Congress. The intent of the act was the dissolution of tribal landholdings and the systematic destruction of tribal leadership. During the 40-year period of allotment (1887–1934), more than 86 million acres, over 60 percent of the remaining Indian land base passed into non-Indian hands. As applied to most Indian reservations, the act authorized the division of Indian reservation lands into 160-acre parcels to individual families who were to be listed on government-administered tribal roles. "Surplus lands" were to be put up for sale to white settlers or development companies. Proceeds from land sales were to be held in trust by the government "for the benefit of the tribe." Sponsored by Senator Dawes of Massachusetts, with the assistance of Alice Fletcher, a Harvard-trained anthropologist, the act reflected the political convergence of the ideas of humanist reformers with the designs of eastern railroad interests who wanted access to larger landholdings in the West. (Even today the largest landholders in the West are the federal government and the railroads.) The designation of "federally enrolled member" was resisted by many individual Indians and continues to be a matter of contention among those who are of Indian parentage and culture but not registered on tribal membership rolls. Many whites found spurious Indian blood ties, got themselves listed on tribal rolls, and received land.

1888

George Eastman in Rochester, New York, perfected a hand camera which he called a Kodak, a name that he thought (correctly) would have international market appeal.

1889

Susan La Flesche, an Omaha Indian from Nebraska, became the first female Native American physician. Following graduation from the Hampton Institute, she went on to the Women's Medical College of Pennsylvania, where she graduated at the head of her class in 1889. She interned in Philadelphia and then was appointed physician for the Omaha agency from 1889 to 1893. She later married, settled in Nebraska, raised two sons, and continued practicing medicine, even building the first Indian hospital in Waltkill, Nebraska.

1889

The Ghost Dance Revival. Wovoka, a Paiute holy man in Nevada, spread the beliefs of an earlier Paiute spiritual leader whose followers danced the traditional circle dance of the Plains and sang divinely revealed songs in which departed ancestors mingled with the dancers. Called the Ghost Dance, it promised that its practitioners would be reunited with the spirits of the dead, death would cease to exist, and whites would disappear. The Indians of California and Nevada, where the dance originated, were largely unimpressed. But in the Plains, where warfare had recently devastated the people, it spread like wildfire among the Sioux, Cheyenne,

Comanche, Arapaho, Assiniboine, Shoshoni, and others. It had its greatest impact on the Teton Sioux, where its mythology expanded to include a return of the great bison herds. The Sioux were people who had seen in a mere 20 years the annihilation of the buffalo, defeat in warfare, confinement on reservations, and epidemic disease. For them the dead outnumbered the living. As the dance was taken up among the Sioux, it spread panic among neighboring white communities, and the consequent call for army intervention led directly to Sitting Bull's death and the massacre at Wounded Knee.

1889-1890

First Oklahoma land rush. Indian Territory in what is now Oklahoma, which in the Indian Removal Act of 1830 had been promised to the Five Civilized Tribes in perpetuity—"for as long as the grass grows and water runs"—was opened as a result of the Allotment Act and sale of "surplus lands" to Oklahoma settlers. President Benjamin Harrison authorized the opening of unoccupied lands to white settlement, and the first of several "runs" were held. More than 50,000 whites claimed two million acres of land. A few months later Congress established the Territory of Oklahoma. Thomas Morgan, commissioner of Indian affairs, justified the policy of allotments, detribalization, and sale of surplus lands as the necessary adjustment of Indians to American life: *"The Indians must conform to the white man's ways, peaceably if they will, forcibly if they must. . . . The tribal relations should be broken up . . . and the family and the autonomy of the individual substituted."*

Burial of the dead at Wounded Knee. Contrary to the title on the photo, Wounded Knee was not a battle. Chief Big Foot and his band of Minneconjou Sioux were moving to a more protected area of the Pine Ridge agency and had surrendered to 500 soldiers of the U.S. Army's seventh Cavalry. Under a flag of truce Big Foot's men were giving up their guns when a gun accidentally went off (no one knows the source). Four army howitzers fired into the center of the unarmed camp killing 146 men, women, and children and wounding another 51. Because of a blizzard it took five days for a burial detail to reach the site of "the battle." The first man at the scene was George Trager, a photographer from Omaha, Nebraska, who made a series of eleven photographs of the trail of bodies frozen into grotesque shapes in the snow. This photo of the mass burial with all military and civilian participants formally lined up around (and in) the burial trench was widely distributed and reproduced.

1890–1898

The great European powers—England, France, Germany—divided China into "spheres of influence" for purposes of trade and economic exploitation. China's weakened rulers were unable to resist. By 1898 the scramble for concessions involved Britain, Germany, Russia, France, and Japan.

1890

Sitting Bull's death. After touring with Buffalo Bill's Wild West Show, Sitting Bull returned to live at the Standing Rock agency where he remained a powerful leader and outspoken critic of the U.S. government and its agents. During the Ghost Dance movement, the Indian agent was afraid Sitting Bull might lead another great rebellion and sent a

Village of Brulé near Pine Ridge, South Dakota. Within six months of the Wounded Knee Massacre, John Grabill took this bucolic photo of a Sioux camp, calling it "the great hostile Indian camp on the river Brulé near Pine Ridge." The figure in the lower left appears to be a cavalry officer. At a time when Indians were living in near-starvation conditions on reservations with no viable economies, the public became interested in images of authentic Indians.

1890

U.S. Sherman Antitrust law passed in response to formation of the Standard Oil Trust and other industrial monopolies.

detail of Indian police to arrest him. The police arrived at dawn. After a fight, Sitting Bull, his son, and six bodyguards were killed. Six policemen were also dead. The remaining policemen said Sitting Bull had died resisting arrest.

1890

Massacre of Chief Big Foot's Sioux at Wounded Knee. Hearing of Sitting Bull's death, Chief Big Foot decided to move his band to a more protected area of the Pine Ridge reservation in South Dakota. U.S. troops had been given orders to eradicate the Ghost Dance among the Plains Indians and were patrolling the plains with vague instructions on how to do this. Big Foot, ill with pneumonia and riding in a wagon that flew the white flag of truce, surrendered to the U.S. Seventh Cavalry and agreed to have his warriors surrender their arms the following morning before traveling to the Indian agency at Pine Ridge. When the troops were sent to disarm the warriors the following day, an altercation arose and a gun went off. The 500 troops opened fire with four howitzers into the center of the unarmed encampment. Some 250 women and children and the warriors who had not been killed fled down adjacent ravines. The soldiers chased them down, killing more than 146 men, women, and children, and wounding 51, leaving a trail of bloodied Sioux bodies that stretched for miles. The Wounded Knee Massacre ended the Plains Indian Wars.

1890
U.S. Indian population fell to its lowest. The prevalent theory in the U.S. was that Native Americans were "vanishing Americans" and would soon disappear entirely, assimilated into the larger population. By the 1900 census, the total Indian population in the U.S. was 237,196. (In 1300 it was estimated to have been as high as 10 million.) By 1990 it had climbed to 1,959,234.

1891
With the construction of the Trans-Siberian railway across Russia, European and American banks began to have greater influence in Russian affairs. The intrusion of foreign influence was greatly distrusted by those outside the Russian aristocracy.

1892
British expansion in Africa. Britain conquered the Anglo-Egyptian Sudan.

1892
The Chiricahua Apaches and Geronimo transferred from Florida to the

Given the mission to secure Egypt's water supply, General Kitchener conquered all the lands surrounding the headwaters of the Nile in the Sudan. He effectively stopped further expansion by France from French Equatorial Africa and by Belgium from the Belgian Congo.

1892

Invention of the gasoline tractor for farming.

1892

First great organized strike at the Homestead Steel Mills owned by Andrew Carnegie. For the first time Pinkerton detectives were used to break the strike.

1893

The last year free land was available under the Homestead Act.

1893

Historian Frederick Turner read "The Significance of the Frontier in American History," in Chicago at a meeting of the American Historical Association. It became one of the most influential essays on American history. Exploring the formation of the American national character as one that was distinct from the European, he suggested that America had been uniquely shaped by the availability of land and the dynamics of the frontier. Turner, who was from Wisconsin, had written his doctoral dissertation on the "Indian Trade in Wisconsin" in which he considered the fur-trading post a civilizing institution. His book, *The Frontier in American History*, was not published until 1920.

Mount Vernon Barracks in Alabama. All were without due process of law and treated as prisoners of war.

1894-1899 \ NATIVE AMERICAN HISTORY

1894-1899

The Dreyfus affair in France. Dreyfus, a Jew serving in the French army, was charged with treason and sentenced to Devil's Island in French Guiana. French author Emile Zola wrote a famous public letter accusing the French general staff of collusion, conspiracy, and treason within the aristocratic class. Zola himself was tried and convicted to a year in prison. Subsequent revelations of forged documents, a suicide, and an unraveling scandal brought the affair to the very center of French politics, where socialists and republicans were known as Dreyfusards and the monarchists and Catholics as anti-Dreyfusards. The Dreyfus case was not resolved until Dreyfus was retried, pardoned, decorated, and raised to the rank of major.

1894

Japan and China at war. After 10 years of competition in Korea, the Japanese seized the Korean queen and appointed a regent. The Korean regent then declared war on China. When China sent troops to Korea, they were attacked by the Japanese. Japan and China declared war on each other. China lost and was forced by Japan to accept a punitive treaty and the cession of territory.

1896

Alfred Nobel established the Nobel Prize. The Swedish inventor of dynamite and a pacifist, Nobel endowed prizes for outstanding achievements in peace, literature, physics, chemistry, physiology or medicine. (The Nobel Memorial Prize in Economic Science was established in 1968 by the Central Bank of Sweden.)

1894

Geronimo and the surviving Apaches transferred from Alabama to Fort Sill in Oklahoma. General George Crook and others who knew the true circumstances of Geronimo's surrender and imprisonment worked to have the Apaches returned to the San Carlos reservation as originally promised. But the white citizens of Arizona refused to allow the Apaches back in the state. The Kiowas and the Comanches then offered the homeless Chiriacahua Apaches, their old enemies, part of their reservation in Oklahoma. Geronimo died at Fort Sill in 1909, still a prisoner of war.

The Snake Dance at Walpi, 1897. Ceremonial dances by real Indians were among the most sought after attractions for the tourists lured to the West by the railroads. The snake ceremony in which priests dance with a variety of desert snakes was and is a dance for rain, a ceremony about nature's regenerative power. (Visitors to contemporary dances often remark that rain always falls at some point during the ceremony.) Ben Wittick was a freelance photographer on contract to the railroads who moved around the Southwest taking scenes of the pueblos and photographing famous chiefs like Nachee and Geronimo. Ironically, he died from a rattlesnake bite in Arizona.

1898

America declared war on Spain and invaded Cuba. The Philippines, Puerto Rico, Cuba, and Guam were ceded to the United States. Theodore Roosevelt's role as a Rough Rider in Cuba propelled him to the presidency.

VIII

1 9 0 0 s — "W E A R E S T I L L H E R E" :
I N D I A N A C T I V I S M

By the 1900s the violent wars to contain Indians on reservations were over. The transcontinental railroad had cut the open plains of the West into three parallel corridors; the buffalo herds had vanished. But land was still an issue. In 1881 the Indians still held 155 million acres. By 1900 they held only 77 million acres. Between 1900 and 1910 another 18 million acres were taken by the U.S. government through the policy of forced allotments and the subsequent sale of "surplus lands" to development companies. The land development companies were frequently associated with the railroads, which, once Indian lands were opened, advertised in Europe promising emigrants a free railroad ticket to their own farm. From 1887, when the Dawes (Allotment) Act became law, until 1934, when allotment policy was officially abandoned, 86 million acres passed into non-Indian hands. Much of it was sold off under the surplus lands provision; the rest was taken through debt, fraud, and deception. The single most important instance of Indian land loss in the twentieth century was the dissolution of Indian Territory and its transformation into Oklahoma.

At the turn of the century many people felt the "Indian problem" was over. The total Indian population was at a historic low. Indians simply weren't visible in the larger American society, except in the art of the romantic West and dime novels of cowboys and Indians. But in 1928 the reality of poverty and suffering on Indian reservations caused Congress to authorize a comprehensive study of Indian issues. The result was the Meriam Commission and a new consensus for reform. The years 1934 to 1949 brought what was called the Indian New Deal. In 1934 Congress passed the Indian Reorganization Act, a reform bill which recognized the terrible failures of the allotment policy and the fact that the Indian reservations had no self-sustaining economies. Indians had been relegated to the worst areas, usually lands that no whites wanted. Facilities for health, education, and employment were virtually nonexistent. As America became the richest country in the world, Native Americans were destitute.

The Indian Reorganization Act (IRA) proposed the reorganization of tribal governments and the institution of efforts to resuscitate reservation economies with special programs to build roads, water facilities, and develop small-scale industries. Its provisions were based on the Meriam Report of 1928, a scathing indictment of the allotment policy which called for structural reforms in land management, support for a policy of communally held tribal lands, and investment in schools and hospitals. Although the intent of the Reorganization Act was excellent—it had

Hopi snake priest. Although the Snake Dance confirmed nineteenth-century white opinion about primal Indian paganism, it was so compelling a tourist attraction that hotel owners like Fred Harvey hired local Indians to perform some versions of the Snake Dance with harmless snakes in their mouths. Knowledgeable westerners traveled hundreds of miles by train, wagon, and buckboard to witness the Hopi's sixteen-day Snake Dance in August. Before photography was banned in 1901, Jennie Hammaker, a missionary teacher at Zuni, was believed to have taken this photo of the Hopi snake priest with a live rattlesnake in his mouth. (All whites were banned from attending in 1971.)

been promoted by a coalition of Indian organizations and white reformers like John Collier—the actual bill was severely blunted by congressional conservatives. The land reform provisions that the new tribal governments were to supervise were eliminated. Powerful assimilationist forces—a combination of eastern railroad interests and western ranchers—succeeded in undercutting the proposed reforms. In 1945 they forced the resignation of the most visible white reformer, John Collier as commissioner of Indian affairs, and replaced him with Dillon Meyer, the former director of the Japanese internment camps.

By the late 1940s the "Indian problem" was back in a new form. By the end of World War II it had been discovered by the government—although not yet by the tribes—that over a third of America's mineral resources lay under Indian reservations in the West. Uranium on the Navajo reservation; coal on the Crow reservation; oil on the Fort Berthold reservation; coal on the Hopi and Navajo reservations; gas on the Jicarilla Apache reservation; uranium and coal on the Laguna pueblo; oil, gas, and coal on the southern Ute reservation. During the years 1948 to 1960 western Republicans led an effort to dismantle the reservation system entirely. (Utah's Senator Watkins argued in 1950 that while America was spending billions of dollars to fight communism, it was fostering socialist environments on Indian reservations. It was a point of view reiterated in the 1980s during the Reagan administration.) During these twelve years, which came to be known as the termination period, 13 tribes were terminated, the largest being the Menominees in Wisconsin and the Klamaths in Oregon, along with more than one hundred bands, communities, and rancherias (California Indian communities). Termination meant that tribes lost federally recognized status, and lost federal annuities and services. In 1961 the National Congress of American Indians (NCAI) met in Chicago and declared termination to be the greatest threat to Indian survival since the military campaigns of the 1800s. The NCAI position led the Kennedy administration to review and eventually overturn the termination policy.

By the end of the 1960s a new national Indian resistance had asserted itself. Indian actions included the occupation of Alcatraz, the takeover of the Bureau of Indian Affairs offices in Washington, D.C., BIA sit-ins throughout the country, the armed confrontation on the Pine Ridge reservation, the trials of Indian activist Leonard Peltier, the founding of the American Indian Movement, the protests at Pyramid Lake, the formation of Women of All Red Nations, and the founding of the Native American Rights Fund. Indians organized their own programs to deal with problems of alcoholism on reservations and prison rehabilitation. And a number of Indian youth groups formed—National Indian Youth Council, Young American Indian Council, Organization of Native American Students—showing that Indian youth were determined to have a hand in shaping their future. By the 1970s tribes knew the value of the mineral resources that lay under their lands. They terminated disadvantageous leases negotiated by the Bureau of Indian Affairs, hired their own lawyers, and formed the Council of Energy Resource Tribes to better manage their own resources. At the same time there were reversals. The removal of 12,000 Navajos from stripmined lands in northern Arizona was the largest Indian removal since the 1800s.

The 1990s has marked what author James Welch *(The Indian Lawyer)* has called an Indian renaissance, with the success of many Indian writers using European-American narrative forms to tell Indian stories and old myths. These have found a broad audience in America and worldwide. The true discovery of the past decade might have been a growing recognition by white America of Native American culture, of America's deep history, best expressed by Gros Ventre activist George Horse Capture: *"We are here now, have been here for thousands of years, and we will always be here. We have fooled them all!"*

1900s — "WE ARE STILL HERE": INDIAN ACTIVISM

WORLD HISTORY

1900-1995
The century of war. Over 160 million people killed in wars between 1900 and 1995.

1900
Hawaii was declared a U.S. territory.

1900
The Boxer Rebellion in China. Resentment against foreign influence in China led to the formation of secret military societies called Boxers. When a rebellion broke out in Beijing, the Boxers began burning foreign embassies and churches, and killing missionaries. A combined force of 18,000 British, French, and German soldiers put down the rebellion and compelled the Chinese to pay 739 million dollars in gold, and to open more Chinese cities to foreign trade.

1901
Theodore Roosevelt assumed the U.S. presidency. Having been a Dakota rancher (for less than three years), Roosevelt was dedicated to western development, water reclamation, and land conservation. His "cowboy cabinet" included easterners with a penchant for the West: Owen Wister (Harvard graduate and author of *The Virginian*); Frederic Remington (Yale graduate, failed

NATIVE AMERICAN HISTORY

1900-1910
Over 18 million acres of tribal Indian lands were taken by the U.S. government through the policy of forced allotments and sales of "surplus land." Indian economies were destroyed and traditional tribal leadership devastated with the enforcement of individual ownership over communally held lands. Although the allotment policy was later condemned, a complex administrative system of government trusteeship was set up to administer the lands "in trust."

1901
Geronimo transferred from Carlisle Indian prison to Washington, D.C., to ride in Roosevelt's inaugural parade.

Kansas rancher, and artist of the American West), Hamlin Garland, George Bird Grinnell, Charles Lummis, and Francis Leupp.

1902

British sovereignty in South Africa. Population 95 percent black. The Boer War ended in South Africa between the British and Dutch. For over 50 years the British and the Dutch (known as Boers) had vied for control of the territories of South Africa. With the discovery of diamonds (1867) and gold (1886), dominance passed from the Dutch to British mining interests led by Cecil Rhodes, owner of De Beers Diamonds and Consolidated Gold Mines. Rhodes financed a revolutionary movement against the Dutch. By the end of 1902 the British had sent 300,000 troops to South Africa to deal with 75,000 Dutch settlers. In the Treaty of Vereeniging, the Boers accepted British sovereignty in South Africa.

1902

Founding of the U.S. Reclamation Service in the Department of the Interior. Its mission was to "reclaim" arid lands in the West, build dams, reservoirs, and implement flood control. Its first project, initiated by Teddy Roosevelt, was the Roosevelt Dam on the Salt River in the mountains above Phoenix, Arizona. By the 1970s there was not one undammed, free-flowing river left in the West.

1902

Opening of the Aswan Dam in Egypt, first of the great water storage reservoirs on the upper Nile.

1902

The Five Civilized Tribes dissolved and the Territory of Oklahoma was formed. The Five Civilized Tribes owned approximately half of what is now eastern Oklahoma, lands rich in oil, coal, and natural gas. When their governments refused to administer the allotment policy and sell off energy rich surplus lands, Congress passed the Creek Land Allotment Act, the Cherokee Land Allotment Act, and the Choctaw and Chickasaw Land Allotment Acts. These acts broke up communally held tribal lands, forced the sale of "surplus lands," and selected the disposition of town sites in the new Oklahoma Territory. As they had been promised these lands in perpetuity when they left Georgia, Alabama, Mississippi, and Florida in the 1830s, the tribal governments had resisted the provisions of the 1887 Dawes Allotment Act, saying that its purpose was to destroy Indian tribes as territorial, economic, and political entities.

Since 1893 the Dawes Commission had tried to dissolve the Oklahoma tribal governments and implement allotments, but, except for the western Seminoles, had not succeeded. The Cherokee and other "civilized" tribes had developed strong governments, schools, and newspapers, and had even designed plans for their own railroad routes through Indian territory. But in 1902 the U.S. ignored the tribal governments and took over the task of drawing up tribal membership lists for distribution of individual land allotments. Thousands of whites, aided by attorneys, got themselves listed on tribal rolls. To be an "enrolled member" served as documentation for federal recognition of tribal membership and eligibility for a land allotment. The Choctaws and Chickasaws hired their own law firm, challenged the lists, and got 3,200 people removed, but litigation over tribal membership continues to the present day. The Department of the Interior removed all mineral-rich lands from the allotments. This land was later leased to the railroads or mining companies. Individual Cherokees were given two allotments, "a homestead" assignment and "away land," intended to reflect actual land use patterns. But often they found white settlers already living on their "away lands." The white courts appointed guardians for Indian minors. This created a class of bankers, lawyers, and businessmen trustees who took the incomes of their Indian wards and sometimes even murdered them to get it. (Linda Hogan's contemporary novel *Mean Spirits* explores this phenomenon.) Indians with oil income from their lands were frequently declared incompetent by the courts and assigned guardians who then took all their wealth. Within 30 years of Oklahoma's "land rush" the rich, verdant valleys of eastern Oklahoma had been detimbered and ploughed under by white "boomers," and Indian Territory was on its way to becoming the arid dust bowl of the 1930s.

1903

Lone Wolf, a Kiowa of southern Oklahoma, fought the allotment policy all the way to the Supreme Court. In *Lone Wolf v. Hitchcock* the Court articulated the principle of "plenary powers" of Congress for the first time. Lone Wolf, a Kiowa leader, filed suit to prevent the breakup of Kiowa lands according to allotment policy. He based his case on the preexisting Treaty of Medicine Lodge of 1867, which provided that *"no part of the Kiowa Comanche reservation could be sold to the U.S. without the approval of three-fourths of the adult male tribal members."* In its 1903 ruling against Lone Wolf, the Supreme Court got around the legal precedent of the prior treaty by creating the new concept of "plenary powers," which gave Congress the power to abrogate, ignore, or change Indian treaties without interference from the courts. This decision was a critical blow to Indian treaty rights and was often cited as justification for exempting congressional disposition of Indian lands from judicial review.

1904

War between Russia and Japan. Russian interference in northern Korea and the occupation of Manchuria provoked Japan to war. Japan decisively defeated Russia on land and sea. Korea became a Japanese protectorate.

1904

U.S. acquired a French canal company in Panama and began design for a canal connecting the Atlantic with the Pacific Ocean. President Roosevelt announced the "Roosevelt Corollary" to the Monroe Doctrine, proclaiming U.S. intent to intervene anywhere within the Western Hemisphere to protect U.S. interests. It shaped future U.S. policy in Central and South America.

1904

The government began allotting lands to the Sioux in South Dakota.

The government outlawed the Sun Dance among Plains Indians in clear violation of the Free Exercise clause of the First Amendment to the U.S. Constitution.

1906

J. P. Morgan, one of America's wealthiest financiers, agreed at the urging of Theodore Roosevelt to support the

travels of a young photographer, Edward Curtis, throughout the reservations of Indian tribes in the West and
Northwest. Morgan, whose investment
in northwest railroads required the acquisition of Indian lands, had financed
the government bond used to pay the
troops during the hunt for Chief Joseph
and the Nez Perce. Morgan's interest in
Indian culture was such that he (and after his death his son) spent a million
dollars over a 20-year period to support
and publish Curtis's work, which was
then made available to a minuscule audience of 500 collectors and libraries.
Curtis's photographs were not widely
known among the American public until the 1960s. Morgan also purchased
Thoreau's original journals, of which
12 out of 22 are devoted to writings
about Indians.

1906

Congress amended the Allotment Act,
eliminating the 25-year trust period.
With the new amendments the secretary of the interior had the power to
issue fee-simple titles to any Indian allottee deemed "competent and capable
of managing his or her affairs." Once
the allottee had received title, "all re-
strictions as to sale, incumbrance, or
taxation of said land [were] removed."
This eliminated the 25-year waiting period and made more Indian land available for sale or lease.

1907

Oklahoma admitted as 46th state.
More than 50 tribes lived in eastern
Oklahoma. Oklahoma white settlers
had established themselves in western
Oklahoma. The two areas were politi-
cally diverse.

Four Hopi Women. As America became increasingly industrial, the romantic photographs by Edward Curtis of "a vanished race" and a more innocent America gained the support of powerful people. Curtis took this photo of unmarried Hopi women wearing their hair in squash blossom coils and making bread in 1906. That same year President Roosevelt invited him to photograph his daughter's wedding and also introduced him to financier J. P. Morgan, who became Curtis's financial sponsor for the next 24 years. This image inspired a number of imitations. Unlike his imitators, Curtis caught the personality of his subjects like the young woman who looked up at the camera.

INVENTING THE IMAGE OF THE INDIAN

The visual images of American Indians organized by Edward Curtis in the twentieth century came out of a complicated tradition of Indian portraiture.

In 1821 the superintendent of Indian trade under President James Monroe, Thomas McKenney, began to commission portraits of the Indian chiefs who came to Washington, D.C., to negotiate with "the Great White Father." He commissioned Charles Bird King, a Washington portrait painter, to do the studio portraits and James Lewis in St. Louis to do the field portraits. More than a hundred Bird portraits hung in McKenney's office and became known as the "Indian Gallery." McKenney's goal was to record the appearance of the most powerful of the western chiefs in their proud and gorgeous costumes. Both McKenney and Bird believed in "the noble savage." In 1828 McKenney moved the "Gallery" to Philadelphia for safekeeping and began a three-volume series of lithographs of Bird's paintings along with histories of the chiefs and their tribes. It was published as a History of the Indian Tribes of North America *(1834–44).*

Many Goats Son. This image of a young Apache man caught the public imagination. By 1904 when it was first published, General Nelson Miles had put 5,000 soldiers into the field in Arizona to catch Geronimo and 24 "renegades." At the same time, public imagination was captured by the operations of the Suez Canal in the Middle East. America's nomadic natives of the southwestern desert were often compared to Arabs and Curtis posed his Apache in an Arab-like pose.

At approximately the same time the young Pennsylvanian, George Catlin, who was studying law in Connecticut, began painting sketches of relatives and his law professors. In 1821 he decided to leave the law and move to Philadelphia to study painting. By 1824 he was admitted to the Pennsylvania Academy. There he encountered the notion of an expanded tradition of the artist as scientist. In Philadelphia Charles Wilson Peale promoted the synthesis of natural history (science) with the fine arts. Out of this original aesthetic vision came the idea of the traveling artist-naturalist. Among its followers were Peale himself, Jefferson's friend William Bartram, and ornithologist and illustrator Alexander Wilson. Catlin was greatly influenced by this ideal of the artist in nature. He later attributed his motivation to move West and paint Indians to having seen a delegation of western Indians en route to Washington in Philadelphia, (date unknown) who walked like "lords of the forest" through the city streets "in silent and stoic dignity." However, it is also likely that his imagination was stimulated by McKenney's Indian Gallery and he realized these exotic chiefs still existed in their native habitat. In 1830 Catlin traveled to St. Louis and began to sketch and paint the Missouri River tribes, the southern Plains Indians, and later the Minnesota and Wisconsin tribes, staying near the forts and trading posts. He did thousands of sketches and hundreds of paintings which he assembled into his own Indian Gallery. Repeatedly and unsuccessfully he tried to sell his gallery to the U.S. government. In 1841 he published Letters and Notes on the Manners, Customs and Conditions of the North American Indians, filled with illustrations. After he took his Indian exhibition to Europe, where it was a great success, an English publisher put out a portfolio of 44 Catlin lithographs of Plains Indians (which in turn were bootlegged by Currier and Ives and sold widely in the U.S.).

Although we don't know if George Catlin met Karl Bodmer, their paths were similar. As a 23-year-old, Karl Bodmer, a Swiss artist, accompanied Prince Maximilian of Germany, an amateur anthropologist, along the same route as Catlin in 1832–1833 along the Missouri River. While the prince wrote up his notes of some 400,000 words in the best tradition of romantic anthropology, Bodmer painted ceremonial scenes and portraits. (It was Prince Maximilian who proposed that the Mandan Indians were descendants of the blue-eyed Welsh Prince Modac who sailed from Wales in 1170 west over the Atlantic.)

By the 1890s the heir to the documentary tradition articulated by Catlin and Bodmer was photographer Edward Curtis who began "his Indian project" photographing the Indians of his home city of Seattle. Although photography began in the 1850s, it was not until the late 1880s that celluloid film came into use permitting what we now call documentary photography. Up until that time daguerreotype and wetplate camera exposures were so long that subjects had to be posed in stillness sometimes for as long as three minutes. The photographic documentation of Indian treaty delegations that came to Washington was always done in a photographer's studio, both to serve as a historical record of the treaty, and because the War Department wanted a file of the chiefs' likenesses in case war broke out again. By the advent of true documentary photography, coherent traditional Native American cultures had almost ceased to exist. The "real" Indians were also the starving Indians who lined up at Indian forts for food rations, they were prisoners of war who had their hair cut and were forced into work gangs, or the drunk Indians who were a common sight in towns in the West. Forbidden by law from wearing traditional dress, they often wore a ragged combination of missionary handouts and traditional attire made from whatever materials they could find.

However, by the 1880s the railroads had opened the West to tourism, and romantic ideas of beauty, grandeur, the picturesque and the exotic required documentation. In 1899 the great railroad baron E. H. Harriman (Union Pacific) took a trip to Alaska. En route he hired the local Seattle society photographer, Edward Curtis, to be the photographer for the expedition. Curtis got along well with the millionaires and men of letters of the expedition and accepted an invitation extended by George Bird Grinnell to go with him to the Blackfoot encampment for the Sun Dance the following August in Montana. Like Catlin, upon whom Curtis deliberately modeled himself, he wanted to record the existing tribes before they "vanished." Curtis's trademark in Indian photography was a soft focus sepia print, learned in society photography, which won him awards and an Indian photography exhibit in New York. His first national award was for his photo of "Princess Angelina" in Puget Sound gathering

Winter—Absaroka Woman. Although Curtis was criticized for posing his subjects and dressing them in clothes from museums, some of Curtis's photography had an eloquence that portrayed the harmony of nature and landscape that was the essence of native beliefs. In this photo of an Absaroka woman in the Montana/Wyoming woods, taken in 1908, he achieves the timeless quality that he was striving for. "I do not see or think photographically," Curtis said about his work, "hence the story of Indian life . . . will be presented as a broad and luminous picture."

mussels. *The Princess Angelina was actually the toothless and poverty-stricken daughter of Chief Seattle. (Chief Seattle had died the same year the Seattle City Council passed a law forbidding Indians to live within the city limits.) In 1901 President Roosevelt, who had a special interest in the West, hired Curtis as the official photographer for his inauguration. (Roosevelt also had Geronimo taken out of prison in Pennsylvania to ride in the inaugural parade.) Roosevelt introduced Curtis to financial baron, J. P. Morgan as an underwriter for his "Indian project." For the next 24 years Morgan and his son underwrote Curtis's work, spending over a million dollars to subsidize his travels. The Curtis publishing enterprise, which eventually produced 20 volumes, was called the North American Indian Publications Office with quarters at 437 Fifth Avenue, New York City.*

The powerful Indian image that Curtis created as an art form was that of "the vanishing American," the title of one of his most famous photographs. It presented an image with a historical subtext, that indigenous cultures were disappearing because of an innate inferiority, a melting away in the glare of superior European culture and technology. Onondaga poet, artist, and photo historian Gail Trembly has suggested in an article in Views ("Constructing Images, Constructing Reality: American Indian Photography and Representation," Winter, 1993) that this was propaganda: "This bloodless description of genocide as a natural process of Social Darwinist evolution hides the real nature of the historical encounter between settler and indigenous culture—one that can only be described as invasion and rape if one is honest." Cameras, like guns, were in the hands of the European Americans. (It was not accidental that J. P. Morgan was Curtis's financier and sponsor.)

The message of Indians as a vanishing race was promoted in less subtle ways by other photographers and artists hired by railroad interests. These images often showed Indians standing at the edge of a picture "amid wild nature" looking out in awe on a vista that includes telegraph poles, wires, and the railroad. (In fact, "real Indians" fought back, removing railroad ties, setting fires around the tracks, and derailing trains with a variety of imaginative techniques.)

Curtis produced some 40,000 glass plate slides and 20 volumes of images of North American Indians. Like Catlin he also collected their songs, legends, and biographies and published this ethnological material with his photographs. President Roosevelt wrote the introduction for his first published volume (only after appointing a commission to refute Franz Boas's criticisms of Curtis's ethnography. Although Boas's academic training was in physics, he was in the process of establishing his reputation as the dean of American anthropology.) The 20 volumes received a limited public circulation—fewer than 500 complete sets were published and sold—although Curtis became widely known as the preeminent Indian photographer. After 1930 Curtis became a still photographer for Cecil B. DeMille in Hollywood and died in 1952. His images were not discovered by the American public until the 1960s and 1970s.

Recent historians like Christopher Lyman (The Vanishing Race and Other Illusions) have pointed out that Curtis doctored and posed the subjects of his photographs. However, Catlin and Bodmer did the same. Documentary objectivity in the matter of American Indian images is not to be found. Gail Trembly's conclusion is more to the point, that "the highly romanticized images [came from] photographers like Curtis who dressed Indians in traditional clothes from museums and private collections and posed them as cultural artifacts—last survivors—in an effort to record their images before their cultures vanished. What the real record in various native photographic archives demonstrates is that while native people were forced to adapt their dress to the policies of forced assimilation, their cultural institutions were maintained even under terrible duress. The majority of Indians refused to 'vanish' regardless of the punishment and oppression imposed upon them."

1907

Theodore Roosevelt appointed his friend Francis Leupp as Indian affairs commissioner. Leupp accelerated the pace of allotments and the distribution of Indian lands. Congress gave him the power to sell allotments belonging to "noncompetents." Although the law implied that he would apply it only to those with specific disabilities, Leupp interpreted it to include all those Indians who had shown "bad judgment" in "failing to develop" their land. Instead of waiting for Indians to apply for an allotment, Commissioner Leupp set up competency commissions that toured the Indian agencies. He wrote: "Not until the surplus spaces in their country are settled by a thrifty, energetic, law respecting white population, can the red possessors of the soil hope to make any genuine advancement."

1908

Gifford Pinchot, director of the National Forest Service, convened the first conference on the conservation of natural resources. Chaired by President Roosevelt, the Governors' Conference on National Resources was held in Washington. Its leaders were widely condemned as "saboteurs of progress."

1910

Japan annexed Korea following the murder of Japanese Prince Ito by a Korean.

1912

Arizona admitted as a state. Roosevelt Dam opened. With 22 Indian tribes and 70 percent of its land under federal control, Arizona had the largest concentration of Native Americans of any state except Alaska.

1912

The British Empire comprised 25 percent of the earth's surface.

1908

Long-term sugar beet leases negotiated on the Fort Belnap, Uintah, and Wind River reservations with white farmers. The leases were to run for 20 years.

1910

Over 30 reservations in the West were opened to allotment and sale at the request of state congressional delegations.

1912

Apaches were used as workmen to build the Roosevelt Dam in Arizona, the first big federal dam and water reclamation project in the West, named for its original sponsor Theodore Roosevelt. Financed by 50-year, interest-free federal loans (later repaid in 1955 dollars), it was the first of what would be known as "cash register dams." Chained at night so they wouldn't run away, the Apaches were the only workers capable of negotiating the narrow, mountainous routes into

1912
First Balkan War. Bulgaria, Serbia, and Greece went to war against Turkey for additional territory. Turkey made alliances with Italy and Austria.

1913
Second Balkan War. Serbia invaded Albania to gain an outlet to the sea. Italy and Austria adamantly opposed Serbian access to the Adriatic. When Serbia and Greece went to war against Bulgaria, Italy and Austria supported Bulgaria.

1913
Henry Ford introduced the assembly line for production of Model-T Fords. By breaking down automobile machinery manufacture into its constituent parts, he invented mass production techniques and revolutionized manufacturing. Up until that time, unit production was the standard.

1914
Opening of World War I. Archduke Ferdinand, crown prince of Austria, was assassinated by a Serbian revolutionary in Sarajevo. The Third Balkan War escalated into world conflict, with 16 powers declaring war on each other. Austria declared war on Serbia. Germany and Italy were pledged to support Austria. (Although Italy was a member of the Triple Entente she ultimately fought on the allied side.) The war eventually involved Britain, the countries of the British Empire, France, and Russia on one side with Germany, Austria-Hungary, Turkey, and their allies on the other. The United States entered the war in 1917. More than 10 million were killed and 20 million wounded. The war was fought in Europe, the Middle East, Africa, and at sea.

the dam site. The road from Phoenix to Roosevelt Dam is still called the Apache Trail. Many of the Apaches and other Indians whose lands lay in the way of future irrigation routes lost their lands through fraud or theft.

Nez Perce in automobile. By 1916 the assimilation of Indians into white society was taken for granted. In the preceeding 30 years they had lost 87 million acres of land. Frank Palmer was a resort photographer based in Spokane, Washington, who posed these Nez Perce Indians in an automobile, suggesting the erasure of Native culture in the face of white technology. His Indian images were immensely popular and sold tens of thousands of postcards.

1915

German submarines sank the liner *Lusitania* off the Irish coast, killing 1,145 civilians. **The Germans introduced chemical warfare for the first time at the Battle of Ypres.** Anti-German sentiment was high in the U.S.

1916

Battle of Verdun in France. France and Germany fought for control of Verdun in northeastern France, sustaining staggering losses in a single battle, estimated at almost 700,000—330,000 German casualties to 350,000 French casualties. (The victorious French general, Marshall Pétain, later became head of the collaborationist French Vichy regime in 1939 and an ally of the German Nazis.)

1916
The National Park Service created in the United States, the first park system in the world to make wildlife protection a goal.

1917
U.S. entered World War I.

1917
The Russian Revolution and the overthrow of the Czar. The October Revolution brought the Bolsheviks to power and created the world's first communist state, which became the Union of Soviet Socialist Republics. Lenin and Trotsky returned to Russia from Paris. The first Workers and Soldiers Soviet was formed in St. Petersburg. Russia withdrew from the European war theater.

1917
Indians, who were still not allowed to vote in the U.S., were encouraged to enlist in the armed services. "Citizen Indians" were those who had taken up their allotment lands and held them for the 25-year trust period, or who had received a "certificate of competency" from the secretary of the interior and were subject to conscription. After draft registration for all Indian males took place in June 1917, protests broke out on a number of reservations, including Fort Hall in Idaho, the Navajo agencies in Arizona, and the Goshiute reservation in Utah. The Goshiute protest was so militant that federal troops were sent into Utah. The Goshiutes said (correctly) they were not citizens because they could not vote, and that only "citizen Indians" were subject to the draft. Although there was an Indian draft registration, there was no draft. However, there were considerable pressures to enlist. **More than 10,000 Indian men enlisted.** Many came from the Indian boarding schools, which were already military-style institutions. The Five Civilized Tribes sent more than 4,000 men into the armed forces. The war created increased job opportunities for Native Americans—cotton picking in Arizona and migratory farm labor—but offered little employment in war industries. It also curtailed BIA services in education, health, and agriculture. Wartime agricultural policy encouraged the "Great Plowup," a campaign to grow more food for the war effort and to put more land into agricultural production.

To support that policy the BIA administered large-scale leasing of Indian lands to white farmers.

1917
Large-scale leasing of Indian lands for wartime agricultural production. The Crow reservation was asked to lease 5,000 acres to the Great Western Sugar Company for sugar beets. The Shoshoni, Blackfoot, and Crow reservations were asked to lease 200,000 acres to the Montana Farming Corporation, a New York company connected with the Great Northern railroad, which continued large-scale farming on the Crow reservation until the 1930s. The Pine Ridge reservation leased lands to white farmers.

1917
Cato Sells, a Texas banker appointed commissioner of Indian affairs by Woodrow Wilson, issued the "Declaration of Policy in the Administration of Indian Affairs" and set up competency commissions. Competency commissions toured the Indian agencies and issued fee patents (titles to land) to qualified allottees. The commissions issued titles without waiting for Indians to apply for them. Not surprisingly, Indians who received a fee patent for 160 acres and full control of individual monies from the tribal treasury soon lost both. Sells declared that this was *"the dawn of a new era in Indian administration . . . the competent Indian will no longer be treated as half ward and half citizen. It means reduced appropriations by the Government and more self-respect and independence for the Indian. It means the ultimate absorption of the Indian race into the body politic of the Nation. It means, in short, the beginning of the end of the Indian problem."*

Blackfoot in the Rockies. While Indians fought to hang on to their lands, Hollywood began the production of cowboy and western movies which placed Indians in the great "wild" landscapes of the American West while American pioneers and homesteaders prevailed over Indian savagery. Film producers reproduced images by photographers such as Roland Reed, a Minnesota photographer who attempted to re-create Plains Indians in original dress and settings. In this photo taken in 1912 he tried to reproduce a Blackfoot hunting party of the mid 1800s.

1917
Peyote religion adopted by the Native American Church in Oklahoma. Formally incorporating peyote, a hallucinogen, as part of their religion, they adopted its use as a right under constitutionally protected freedom of religion. Peyote meetings were intertribal, conducted in English, and gave Indians a sense of identity with a larger pan-Indian community. Whites reacted in fear and alarm, just as they had to the Ghost Dance religion of the 1880s.

1918

World War I ended with Germany's surrender.

1918

Czar Nicholas and his wife and five children were executed by a firing squad. Many of Russia's upper classes, called "White Russians," emigrated to Paris and New York City.

1918–1920

Worldwide influenza epidemic; almost 22 million dead.

1919

Treaty of Versailles. Treaty provisions were drawn up by the U.S., Britain, and France against the defeated powers of Germany, Austria-Hungary, Turkey, and their allies. Germany was forced to accept responsibility for the war, relinquish its vast land holdings in Poland, limit its armies, and pay huge monetary reparations. The treaty also provided for the establishment of the League of Nations, forerunner of the United Nations. Germany had little say about the treaty provisions. The following year the Nationalist Socialist (Nazi) Party was founded in Germany.

1918

Arizona Congressman Carl Hayden introduced a bill outlawing peyote use by all Indians under BIA jurisdiction. The bill did not pass. Hayden served in Congress for 57 years (until 1969) and had more influence over Indian legislation than any other member of congress until Barry Goldwater.

1918–1919

Virulent influenza epidemics swept the Indian reservations and boarding schools in Arizona, New Mexico, and the Rocky Mountain states, killing tens of thousands. The U.S. government offered little medical assistance since Indian health services had been drastically curtailed for the war effort. Some agencies had no doctors, and health staffs had been cut to the bone. Although wartime inflation had reduced the BIA budget to half, Commissioner Sells asked for no additional monies. No steps were taken to check the epidemics.

1919

All Indians who had served in the Armed Forces were granted full citizenship by Congress.

1920

U.S. Senate refused to ratify the Versailles Treaty. President Wilson was paralyzed by a stroke, the government allegedly carried on by his wife.

1920

Noncooperation movement in India. Mahatma Gandhi organized protest movements involving the boycotting of British goods and nonsupport of British institutions. It marked the beginning of *satyagraha*, nonviolent protest against British domination of India, and the beginning of widespread civil disobedience.

1921

Adolf Hitler, an Austrian, reorganized the German Workers' Party in Bavaria into the Nazis, National Socialist German Workers' Party. As a nationalistic, paramilitary party, it grew rapidly because of massive unemployment in post-war Germany. Hitler focused on widely held prejudices against Jews, intellectuals, pacifists, homosexuals, communists, socialists, and liberals as the cause of Germany's troubles. Promising a revived, heroic Germany, an Aryan nation purified of Jewish elements and rooted in the traditions of Teutonic heroism, he attracted large numbers of adherents to the Nazi Party.

1922

Rise of Fascist Party in Italy. Supported by business and clerical elements who feared communism, fascism spread throughout Italy. After the "March on Rome," the king called on Mussolini to organize a government, and granted him dictatorial powers.

1920

American Indian population began to come back from its lowest point of 250,000 at the turn of the century. The life expectancy rate on a reservation was 43 years; in Alaska and Arizona it was 33 years. Infant mortality was twice that of the rest of America. A student graduating from a BIA high school had the equivalent of an eighth grade education elsewhere in America. Unemployment was as high as 75 percent on many reservations.

1922

Oil discovered on Navajo reservation. The BIA appointed a Navajo "business council" to sign leases. Standard Oil of California wanted access to the oil, but the U.S. government, as trustee, could not lease Navajo lands without tribal consent and there was no tribal entity that could legally sign. The Navajo tribe had no governing body, and leadership was

Maricopa women. The Maricopa were an agricultural people who lived along the rivers of central Arizona. (The Maricopa reservation is outside Phoenix.) Edward Curtis photographed these women gathering fruit from the giant saguaro cactus and transporting it on their heads.

decentralized among many different local headmen. A meeting of influential headmen was called at the San Juan agency in May 1922. The headmen rejected all leasing applications. The secretary of the interior, Albert Fall of New Mexico (later implicated in the Teapot Dome oil scandal), invented a series of legal fictions to facilitate leasing. He created a Navajo "business council" to sign and approve the oil leases; he placed all "executive order" reservation lands—nontreaty Indian lands designated after 1871—under the provisions of the General Leasing Act; he appointed a New Mexico crony, Herbert Hagerman, to take charge of leasing arrangements on Indian lands.

1922
The first Pueblo confederation formed as the All-Pueblo Council in response to Secretary Fall's treatment of Pueblo lands. Since the revolt of 1680, there had been no unified Pueblo political entity. For the first time twenty Pueblos organized and joined with white reform organizations to defeat a Senate bill that would have given non-Indians the rights to Pueblo lands and water. Senator Bursum of New Mexico introduced the bill under the direction of Secretary Fall, who owned ranch lands adjacent to the Pueblo reservations and wanted access to their lands and water rights. Opposition came from reformist organizations in New Mexico, which included transplanted wealthy New Yorkers like Mabel Dodge Luhan, humanist groups in California, and the All-Pueblo Council. The coalition defeated the bill and obtained the resignation of Secretary Fall from the cabinet on the basis of conflict of interest. The lobbying campaign

focused on the Pueblos' loss of autonomy under the proposed bill, its bias in giving title to whites, the unfairness of compensating Indians with worthless public lands, and the fatal loss of water rights. The campaign produced a new generation of Indian activists and whites engaged in Indian policy reform, and led to the drafting and passage of the Pueblo Lands Act and eventually to the Indian Reorganization Act of 1934.

1922

Herbert Hoover, a mining engineer from California and secretary of commerce, negotiated water rights to the Colorado River. The Colorado River Basin Compact, an interstate compact dividing up the waters of the Colorado River, has been called the Constitution of the American West. Although article VII said, "*Nothing in this compact shall be construed as affecting the obligations of the United States of America to Indian tribes,*" Indian water rights were almost completely ignored. The compact formed the basis of water politics in the West for the rest of the century and has greatly affected the Indian tribes in the six signatory states and Arizona, a nonsignatory state. The compact formed the legal structure for the building of the Boulder (later renamed Hoover) Dam, the largest civil engineering project undertaken by the U.S. government, which propelled Hoover to the presidency in 1928.

1923

Navajo tribal council reformed. The U.S. government made an effort to organize a more representative Navajo tribal council for purposes of mineral leasing. BIA superintendents supervised the election of delegates from a larger geographical area to sit in what would be called the Navajo tribal council. The new council authorized the interior official (Hagerman) to negotiate all future oil and gas leases. The question of Indian rights to revenues from oil and gas leases raised issues of Indian title to the land itself, and formed the basis of a new round of land struggles.

1924

Indian Oil Leasing Act passed by Congress. The act dropped the 10-year limit for leases and allowed them to run as long as the oil did. It also **allowed states to tax production on the reservation.** Senator Carl Hayden introduced an amendment which gave states 37.5 *percent* of revenues, with the provision that the monies be spent on Indian education or roads. Since most tribes had no centralized authority to take charge of leasing revenues, the expectation that states would spend money on Indian education or roads was disingenuous. In most instances, state taxes on mining production on Indian reservations were higher than the royalties received by the tribes.

1924

American Indians made U.S. citizens with passage of Indian Citizenship Act. It marked the first time Indians could vote in national elections. In many states, like Arizona and New Mexico, Indians were not allowed to vote in state or local elections based on their federal trust relationship and special status under federal law.

1924

U.S. attorney general ruled on the status of reservations that contained both

treaty lands and executive order lands. Executive order lands covered 22 million acres of Indian lands in Arizona and New Mexico. Most westerners believed that Indians should have no title to these areas and that they resided there only at the sufferance of the government. In 1921 Interior Secretary Fall had made all executive order lands subject to the terms of the General Leasing Act, in which revenues from exploration or development of oil, natural gas, or other minerals found on public lands accrued to the federal government as public domain lands. In 1921 the U.S. attorney general ruled that the executive order lands were no longer public domain lands, but stated that neither Congress nor the courts had made distinctions among Indian lands designated by executive order, by treaty, or legislation. He warned that the issue would remain unresolved until the courts or Congress acted.

1924

Pueblo Lands Act set up a three-man Pueblo land board to determine the validity of contested claims to Pueblo lands and to fight for clear title in federal district court. **John Collier emerged as a national voice for Indian reform legislation.** Mabel Dodge Luhan had persuaded Collier to come to New Mexico to help with the Pueblo Indian land struggles and shape a legislative strategy. Unlike previous reformers, Collier did not focus on individual incompetents and corrupt appointees in the Interior Department and Bureau of Indian Affairs, but took a systemic view of Indian policies. Collier said that allotment was a ruinous policy and must be repealed. He linked Indian cultural survival to the re-

1925

World population reached two billion.

1925

Navigable Rivers and Harbors Act passed. Congress authorized a survey of all rivers in the U.S. to determine their potential for hydroelectricity, navigation, flood control, or irrigation. Under the act, Indian lands which bordered rivers or were in a floodplain appropriate for a reservoir became prime targets for appropriation by the Bureau of Reclamation.

1928

The Boulder Dam Authorization Act passed. Following Herbert Hoover's election to the presidency in November 1928, legislation authorizing federal dam construction on the Colorado River, which had been before Congress for 20 years, passed both houses of Congress. It allocated funds for what would become the largest civil engineering project ever undertaken by the U.S. government. The structure would change the face of the American West.

tention of their land base, and became an outspoken opponent of assimilationist policies. His ideas would form the basis of the Indian Reorganization Act of 1934.

1926

Native American organizations began lobbying for a presidential commission to review Indian policies. They wanted an audit of the execution of treaty obligations, a review of trust accounts, and recommendations to curb the worst abuses and the institution of reforms. The appointed commission was funded by the Rockefeller Foundation and became known as the Meriam Commission for Louis Meriam, its chairman.

1928

The Meriam Report issued, after a three-year study of the economic and social conditions of the American Indian. Considered the most significant inquiry into Indian conditions in the twentieth century, the Meriam Report investigated the status of Indian economies, health, education, and the government's administration of Indian affairs and trust funds. It labeled the allotment policy a staggering failure, advocated support for Indian community life, strong protection of Indian property rights, and new initiatives in the areas of education and health. The most comprehensive survey of national Native American conditions ever conducted, it remains the standard for clarity and comprehensiveness. Implementing the report's recommendations became the focus of a movement of Indian organizations and white social reformers for Indian policy reform.

1929-1939

Stock market crash and the Great Depression. Black Thursday (October 24) marked the beginning of a prolonged stock market fall that caused massive failures of American businesses and the rise of vast unemployment in both the U.S. and Europe. The Great Depression became a worldwide phenomenon and full economic recovery did not occur until the beginning of World War II. The American president, Herbert Hoover, a Republican conservative, did not believe in government intervention to stimulate the economy. By 1932 over 75 billion dollars in market value had been lost since the 1929 crash began. Hoover was not reelected.

1930

Emergence of Hitler's Nazi Party as a major German party. In a single election Nazis gained 95 seats in the Reichstag, going from 12 seats to 107.

1930-1936

Bureau of Reclamation issued the specifications for bids for the building of Boulder Dam. The job was won by a consortium of six western construction companies including Bechtel, Morrison Knudsen, Henry Kaiser, and Utah International. For the next five years the building of Boulder Dam

1930

U.S. Senate Investigating Committee confirmed the systematic kidnapping of Navajo children to put them in boarding schools. The church denominations which ran the schools authorized the kidnappings in order to fill their quotas.

created jobs and infrastructure in the West. It also gave rise to the founding of Las Vegas as the gambling capital of America, and it marked the first time a major dam was built on any large river in the world. The dam provided the water, irrigation systems, flood control, and hydroelectricity to transform the West. But because of the large amount of silt carried by the Colorado, engineers feared that the dam might soon silt up. In response, a new dam was planned upstream at Glen Canyon and a livestock reduction plan instituted for the Navajo reservation.

1932

Persia (Iran) canceled the oil concession given to the Anglo-Persian Oil Company in 1909. Britain brought the matter before the League of Nations and was able to negotiate a new agreement, but with higher royalties and a smaller lease area. Two years later Persia granted a lease concession to Standard Oil Company of California, opening the way for American domination of the Middle East oil industry.

1932–1936

More than 250,000 Navajo sheep and goats were destroyed by federal agents under the stock reduction policy. The policy was implemented by the BIA in coordination with the soil conservation service, and the Navajo had no say in its adoption. In fact they were never told the rationale behind it. Although Navajo women actually owned the sheep, the five BIA Navajo agencies held meetings only for Navajo men, instructing them in the concept of "carrying capacity" of the land. An acre could "carry" no more than six sheep. At first federal officers paid the Navajo for the sheep and goats and loaded them onto trains to sell in cities. But logistics soon broke down and in subsequent stock reductions, the federal officers simply shot thousands of sheep and left the carcasses to rot. Since sheep were the mainstay of the Navajo economy and culture, the difference between one dozen and two dozen sheep often meant the difference between starvation and survival. The stock reduction was viewed by the Navajo as a monstrous act, and contributed to their refusal to adopt an IRA reform government in 1934.

Stringing the bow. Navajo. Reed realized he could never compete with Edward Curtis and stopped trying to re-create Plains Indians scenes. With this photo of a young Navajo man evoking Greek and Roman classic statuary, he achieved great success as an artistic photographer. At a time when the Navajo were being subjected to a ruthless livestock reduction, this image was widely popular.

1932

Black Elk Speaks was published. Black Elk was an Oglala Sioux holy man who told his life story to poet and writer John Neihardt. Born in northeast Wyoming, he was a cousin of Crazy Horse and fought as a young teenager in the Battle of The Little Bighorn. His published story remains the most frequently taught work about American Indians and has sold millions of copies throughout the world. Black Elk's life encompassed some of the major events of Sioux (Dakota) history, including the Ghost Dance religion and the massacre at Wounded Knee. He began his story with his childhood among the Plains people in the 1860s, when he first received a powerful mystic vision. He wrote of his sacred practices, his participation in the Battle of Little Bighorn, and his subsequent travels through Europe with Buffalo Bill's Wild West Show. He returned to the reservation in 1889 in time to witness the army's suppression of the Sioux and the Wounded Knee Massacre. Black Elk was one of the last living Sioux to possess full knowledge of the metaphysics and practice of the Sioux religion. Scholars have noted that the book omitted the fact that Black Elk was also a Christian and took pride in many of his accomplishments in the white world. (See "Black Elk, A Holy Man of the Oglala Sioux" on page 334.)

1933

Franklin Delano Roosevelt inaugurated as president. He appointed Harold Ickes secretary of the interior and John Collier commissioner of Indian affairs.

1933

Indian Emergency Conservation Work Program. Collier's immediate agenda was to implement the Indian Emergency Conservation Work Program, an Indian version of the Civilian Conservation Corps. He received 6 million dollars for emergency projects to be

BLACK ELK, A HOLY MAN OF THE OGLALA SIOUX

"Then I was standing on the highest mountain of them all, and round about beneath me was the whole hoop of the world. And while I stood there I saw more than I can tell and I understood more than I saw; for I was seeing in a sacred manner the shapes of all things in the spirit, and the shape of all shapes as they must live together like one being. And I saw that the sacred hoop of my people was one of many hoops that made one circle, wide as daylight and as starlight, and in the center grew one mighty flowering tree to shelter all the children of one mother and one father. And I saw that it was holy."

Black Elk
from Black Elk Speaks: Being the Life Story of a Holy Man of the Oglala Sioux
(as told through John G. Neihardt)

executed on 33 reservations in road building, dam construction, and building repair. When BIA employees resisted designing new projects, buying equipment, and recruiting Indian teams, Collier put new men in charge. (Author Edward Hall's memoir, *West of the Thirties*, recounts his experience working on the Navajo reservation as part of Collier's conservation work program.) The program received great criticism from conservative assimilationists, who branded it "socialistic" and dangerous to the individualist work ethic that they said Indians needed to develop to succeed in American society.

1933
Adolf Hitler became chancellor of Germany and Germany became a one-party state under Nazi rule. A suspicious fire in the Reichstag was blamed on communists. Emergency decrees were enacted, including the Enabling Act. Hitler suspended constitutional guarantees of free speech and

free press. The Enabling Act gave him dictatorial powers, allowing him to liquidate all opposing political parties, and completely overhaul German legal, administrative, and governmental systems. April 1 was declared official Anti-Semitic Day and concentration camps for Jews were made legal institutions. It is believed the Nazis were supported by big industrial interests as a last bulwark against communism. The Nazi revolution proved to be one of the great overturns in European history.

1934

The United States experienced its greatest drought in history. Entire counties in Oklahoma, north Texas, and Arkansas became known as the **Dust Bowl.** Dust storms blew away tens of thousands of acres of topsoil. A mere 30 years after the Oklahoma land rush, destitute "Okies" migrated west from Oklahoma to California as agricultural laborers. Deforestation and destructive farming techniques had denuded fertile Oklahoma lands and helped to worsen the drought's effects. In reaction Congress passed the Taylor Grazing Act, regulating grazing on federal lands, and created the Soil Conservation Service in 1935.

1934

The Indian New Deal and the introduction of the Indian Reorganization Act. John Collier proposed a thorough reform of federal Indian policy, ending allotment, consolidating Indian land holdings, creating tribal governments, and instituting Indian courts. Collier believed in cultural pluralism rather than assimilation, and lobbied the Indian Reorganization Act through Congress. Unfortunately, the legislation that passed, the Wheeler-Howard Act, was not the bill originally drafted. Historians note that the "Indian New Deal" did not fundamentally change the relationship between Indians and larger American society, although it did curb some of the worst abuses. **Its greater influence was the creation of Indian tribal governments with rights and responsibilities vis a vis the federal government. The act gave tribes one year to hold referenda to decide if they wanted to adopt a constitution and set up tribal councils. Collier concentrated on getting key reservations to approve the act, in an attempt to create a bandwagon effect.**

THE INDIAN REORGANIZATION ACT OF 1934

The Indian Reorganization Act was an outgrowth of the recommendations of the Meriam Report in 1928. The initial impetus behind the act was to end the breakup of Indian lands through the allotment system and encourage Indian land reform policies. A group of reform organizations met in Washington in 1933 to discuss the need to link Indian land reform with Indian self-government. Indian Affairs Commissioner John Collier and Interior Secretary Harold Ickes attended the meetings and Lewis Meriam presided. They drafted a series of policy resolutions to end allotment, consolidate land holdings, create tribal governments, and replace existing Indian courts. They then translated their resolutions into legislative language, which became known as the Indian Reorganization Bill. They sent it to the chairs of the Senate and House Committees on Indian Affairs, chaired respectively by Senator Wheeler and Representative Howard, for whom the final bill would officially be named.

It was a 50-page bill with four titles. Title I permitted Indian groups to establish tribal governments that could charter business corporations and secure loans; Title II endorsed the ideas that Indian education should have as its goal the preservation of Indian heritage, and that Indians should take jobs held by whites within the Bureau of Indian Affairs; Title III repealed the General Allotment Act and outlined a complicated system for land consolidation; Title IV called for the creation of special Indian courts to exercise original jurisdiction on reservations. By far the most controversial provisions of the bill dealt with allotments, land reform, and how to resolve the issue of reservation lands already broken into thousands of individual allotments. The bill allowed the secretary of the interior to force the sale of allotments and to implement exchanges to consolidate land.

Opposition was swift, vocal, and aggressive. Conservative white assimilationists said that the only future for Indians was "Christian assimilation into American life." Business interests that had leasing rights on the reservations opposed the land consolidation provisions. Indians themselves saw the tribal council system of government as another top-down imposition from Washington that would displace traditional leaders and give an advantage to English-speaking Christian Indians. Others saw Collier's concepts of cultural pluralism as naive and elitist. Collier held a series of public hearings in towns near the major reservations in an attempt to overcome tribal opposition.

The bill that passed in 1934 had been considerably changed by the House and Senate committees and virtually eliminated Titles III and IV. The special courts were gone; education, self-government, and the land provisions were much abbreviated. Alaska and Oklahoma were excluded from most provisions. Tribes could constitute themselves as legal entities (the equivalent of federal municipalities) only by drafting a constitution and adopting it through tribal referendum. Collier's plan for Indian land use had been decimated. The repeal of the General Allotment Act, the extension of federal trust over allotted land, and the return of surplus lands to the tribes all had been successfully opposed as fundamentally unworkable, and deleted from the bill. Too much land had been allotted; too many Indians had fee patents; too many white settlers were living on "surplus lands." What survived were the provisions for adopting constitutions and tribal councils. What would become known as IRA govern-

ments proceeded, but without the land reforms that had originally been envisioned to accompany them.

The act gave the tribes one year to hold referenda to decide whether or not they wanted to adopt a tribal council form of government. If they did, they then became eligible for enlarged federal aid. If not, they had no way of negotiating improved services in education and health care. Collier proceeded as though the original bill had survived. He launched a series of campaigns to persuade many reservations to adopt the new constitution. Since many of the tribes undertook action only by consensus and did not believe in majority vote, the rules of parliamentary procedure were foreign to them. Many tribal elders viewed the old treaties as binding and believed that no changes could be made without three-quarters of the tribe's approval. Factions developed in almost every tribe, based on relationships to the federal government. The old designations of "hostiles" and "friendlies" gave way to "traditionals" and "progressives." The Klamath, Crow, Fort Peck, Sisseton Sioux, Turtle Mountain Chippewa, and Navajo rejected the IRA government. The Hopi and Sioux adopted it, but with tremendous internal divisions among tribal cultures. Within the allocated time, 358 elections were held in which 181 tribes voted to accept the IRA provisions while 77 tribes rejected it. The remainder had a somewhat ambiguous status because they voted to accept the act but then refused to organize under it.

1935

The Arabian peninsula was recognized as one of the world's potentially most important oil-producing regions. It today includes the countries of Saudi Arabia, Yemen, Oman, Kuwait, United Arab Emirates, Qatar, and Bahrain.

1935

John Maynard Keynes published *The General Theory of Employment, Interest and Money*, advocating government intervention in the face of large-scale unemployment. "Keynesian economics" and monetary policy were widely adopted by many government economists in free-market economies around the world.

1935

Tribes held IRA elections: 181 tribes accepted it; 77 tribes rejected it. The Klamath of Oregon, the Crow of Montana, the Fort Peck, Sisseton Sioux, and Turtle Mountain Chippewa all rejected the IRA provisions. The Navajo defeated it by 518 votes out of 15,876, saying it conflicted with the provisions of their 1868 treaty. They were also still angry over the stock reductions associated with Collier's administration. On the Pine Ridge reservation the Sioux approved the reorganization by a vote of 1,169 to 1,095 out of 4,075 eligible voters. Nonvoting Sioux mistakenly thought that boycotting the election would defeat the act's application. Consequently, Pine Ridge developed two rival political organizations: Old Dealers who were separatist, full-blooded Sioux; and New Dealers, who formed the new tribal council and who were often mixed blood, English-speaking and assimilationist. The Old Dealers regarded the tribal council as an illegitimate institution forced upon the Sioux by the BIA. Instead they fought for federal recognition of the "treaty council" formed after the Fort Laramie Treaty of 1868. This struggle between the full-blooded traditionalists (also known as hostiles) and the Christianized mixed bloods (progressives) repeated itself on many reservations with increasing friction.

1936-1939
Spanish Civil War. In a dress rehearsal for World War II, Hitler and Mussolini sent "volunteer" soldiers to support the army, clericals, and monarchist forces against the republican government in Spain. The conflict began with a revolt of the army generals in the south against the newly elected Popular Front government, composed of republicans, socialists, syndicalists, and communists. The war soon became a battleground of rival ideologies and foreign intervention. Russia supplied the new government with equipment and advisors. Hitler put 10,000 troops in Spain to support the army. The war ended in 1939 with the surrender of Madrid and the victory of the rightist forces under General Francisco Franco.

1936
Germany reoccupied the Rhineland. Hitler denounced the Locarno Pacts and announced his intention to reoccupy the territories taken under the Versailles Treaty. Britain unwilling to invoke sanctions.

1936
The Hopi divided into two factions over IRA reforms. John Collier focused on the Hopi, one of the oldest and most traditional peoples still living on original ancestral lands, as a test case for the IRA reforms. Thinking it would hold great weight with other tribes if the Hopi adopted a constitution and tribal council form of government, Collier hired novelist, anthropologist, and socialite Oliver La Farge to go to the Hopi reservation to help them write a constitution. La Farge had spent time on the Hopi and Navajo reservations as a young man and had written a successful novel about the Navajo. He was typical of the paternalistic, Harvard-educated anthropologist reformer of the era. The traditional Hopi were unenthusiastic about La Farge's arrival. Like the Pueblos of New Mexico, the 12 separate Hopi villages, each with its own leaders and clans, had functioned for centuries as independently as Italian city-states. The idea of a Hopi tribe existed only in Washington. Their leaders drew their authority from hereditary rights, tradition, and knowledge. (One village retained its Tewa language from its days in the 1600s as a Rio

Grande pueblo.) Majority vote was an alien concept. The Hopi who cooperated with La Farge were largely the boarding-school, English-speaking, and missionary converts, the Mormon and Mennonite Hopi, who saw possibilities in a new balance of power. The traditionals felt the basic assumptions of government policy toward Indians remained unchanged: namely, that Indians had to become more like whites, especially in terms of government. "We have had democratic self-government for a thousand years," said one Hopi leader. La Farge redefined Hopi identity to reflect patriarchal Euro-American culture by requiring Indian paternity in order to qualify as a voting Hopi. Up until that time a Hopi mother was the only blood lineage required. When the vote was taken, the Hopi expressed their disapproval by refusing to vote. Over 90 percent of the eligible Hopi voters stayed home. Even though La Farge (by then back in New York) tried to explain to Collier that absenteeism was a traditional Hopi way of expressing a negative, the Bureau of Indian Affairs ruled that the ayes had it. The imposition of the IRA government reforms set up a dual structure of governance between the tribal council and the traditional priests, a struggle which continues to the present.

1936
Congress passed the Alaska Native Reorganization Act extending certain provisions of the Wheeler-Howard Act to the Territory of Alaska. It was designed to assist Native peoples in setting up tribal corporations.

1937–1945
Sino-Japanese War. In an undeclared war, Japan invaded China, occupied Shanghai, bombed Chinese cities, and organized a naval blockade. Japan eventually controlled the north of China and installed its own governments in Canton and Hankow. China declared war against Japan in 1941. Although Chiang Kai-shek was elected president of a new Chinese Republic (1943), it was Mao Tse-tung's forces that were most effective against the Japanese in the north of China.

1937
Josef Stalin instituted government by terror with widespread treason trials in Moscow, putting on trial generals in his army, bureaucrats administering his programs, and loyal members of the diplomatic service. The defendants were executed regardless of guilt or innocence.

1939
The insecticide DDT was first synthesized.

1939
Opening of the Trans-Iranian railway from the Caspian Sea to the Persian Gulf. Constructed entirely with Iranian

1937
The Navajo tribal council was formed. The reservation was known to hold large reserves of oil, coal, and natural gas. Even though they had not adopted an IRA government, the BIA "created" a tribal council for them. A Catholic priest who spoke Navajo toured the reservation, getting the names of 250 authentic local headmen. He then reduced the list to 70 and gave it to the BIA superintendent, who declared them a Navajo tribal council and pressured these headmen to meet.

1938
Indian Lands Mining Act passed. Congress gave the secretary of the interior broad powers over mineral development on Indian lands, including the right to issue 10-year leases on lands of various status—any unallotted Indian lands, any Indian lands under federal jurisdiction, and any lands owned by any tribe. This was a direct result of the ambiguities in the 1924 General Leasing Act.

1939
Pueblo members of the All-Pueblo Council met in New Mexico to address the right of Indians to vote. Despite the Indian Citizenship Act of 1924, Indians in Arizona and New Mexico were still not allowed to vote in state elections. The states justified

capital, it was the major accomplishment of Reza Shah Pahlavi in his efforts to modernize Iran.

1939-1945
World War II. Hitler invaded Poland. Britain and the Allied powers responded by declaring war on Germany. To recover German lands taken by the Treaty of Versailles, Hitler occupied the Rhineland and Czechoslovakia, and annexed Austria. The participants in World War II assumed roughly the same configuration as World War I with Germany, Austria, Italy and Japan as the Axis powers; England, France, the British Commonwealth countries, the U.S., and the U.S.S.R. (after 1941) as the Allied powers.

1939
Igor Sikorsky, a Russian émigré, flew the first helicopter of his own design and founded Sikorsky aircraft.

1941
Japan bombed Pearl Harbor. U.S. entered World War II.

denying Indians the vote by claiming that they did not pay state taxes (even though that was not a requirement for white voters), by disputing their status as wards of the federal government, or claiming their residence on a reservation did not constitute state residency. **The Pueblo leaders rejected a proposal to take legal action to obtain the vote because they were reluctant to get involved in New Mexico state politics.**

1941-1945
All Native American men were required to register for the draft, although in many states they could not vote. A total of 24,521 Native American men served in the U.S. armed services during World War II. Many southwestern Indians served in a National Guard unit sent to the Philippines (the 200th Coastal Artillery Regiment), which was captured by the Japanese and sent on the infamous Bataan death march. Others refused to register on the basis of religious or political grounds: a few Papagos, some Utes, six Hopis from Hotevilla, some Iroquois, and a number of Seminoles. The Seminoles refused to register on the grounds that they were still at war with the U.S.; the Iroquois objected

because they did not consider themselves citizens of the U.S.; the Papagos because they followed a religious leader who prohibited killing. The conservative Pueblos resisted sending their young men to the draft. In all, however, more than 70,000 native men and women left the reservations to enter military service or work in defense industries.

1941
Felix Cohen's *Handbook of Federal Indian Law* was published, a definitive work on Indian court decisions, laws, and administrative practices. A lawyer and solicitor general in the Department of the Interior, Cohen wrote the *Handbook* as a manual for government lawyers. He summarized past court decisions, federal legislation, and administrative practices to provide Interior Department lawyers with background material not taught in law schools. However, legal scholars Vine Deloria and Clifford Lytle point out in *American Indians, American Justice*, that Cohen's handbook did not provide much context in which to understand the circumstances and conditions which produced this body of Indian law.

1942
The beginning of the nuclear age. The first self-sustaining nuclear chain reaction was achieved at Stagg Field, Chicago, by Enrico Fermi, an Italian physicist.

1942
Many military training bases were located in Arizona, Nevada, and southern California, close to West Coast bases and staging areas for the war in the Pacific. More than 40 billion federal dollars were spent in the West.

1942
More than 400 Navajo were recruited for special code unit, "Navajo codetalkers." They developed a code in the Pacific which the Japanese could not break. After the Marines had successfully used Indian languages as code for wartime training operations in Louisiana, nine Navajos were recruited to demonstrate the possibilities of a code based on the Navajo language. The code used real Navajo words for military references: the Navajo word for "chicken

The West's colonial status changed forever. As great demands were put on expanding western infrastructure for water and power, it set up a new round of legal actions to obtain Indian water rights, lands, and mineral resources.

hawk" meant a dive bomber; "two stars" meant a major general; "whale" meant a battleship. The Navajos memorized the code and became radio operators for units in the Pacific islands. They were in direct combat, participated in assaults on island beachheads, and in several instances were threatened by other Marines because they looked like Japanese. By the end of the war 420 Navajos had served as Navajo codetalkers, developing a communications code that the Japanese could not decipher. The Japanese were never able to break the code because the Navajo language was then unwritten. The Navajo code is said to be the only Allied code never broken during the course of the war. Here is a sample of the word to be encoded, followed by its English translation and the Navajo pronunciation:

minesweeper: beaver—*cha*
destroyer: shark—*ca-lo*
transport: man carrier—*Dineh-nay-ye-hi*
amphibious: frog—*chal*
anti-aircraft: bird shooter—*chy-ta-gahi-be-wol-doni*

1942

Japanese internment camps were located in the West primarily in Arizona on lands taken from the Pima and Mohave Indian reservations. The War Relocation Authority under Milton Eisenhower coordinated with John Collier's BIA to establish Japanese relocation camps. The Pima on the Gila River reservation and the Mohave on the Colorado River reservation were asked by the BIA to give up thousands of acres for the internment of Japanese American citizens. Collier argued that the BIA was uniquely qualified to deal with cultural minorities. Collier's New

Deal Indian policies were overtaken by the demands of the war effort.

1942

An estimated 900,000 acres of Indian lands were taken in Alaska and 16 Indian reservations in the West to use as air bases, gunnery ranges, nuclear test sites, training installations, or internment camps for Japanese Americans. On the Pine Ridge reservation 300,000 acres were taken as a gunnery range. The government gave the Sioux 75 cents an acre and 30 days to move. It took another 12 years for each individual Sioux to get 3,500 dollars in compensation.

1942

The Iroquois Six Nations declared war on the Axis powers, asserting its right as an independent sovereign nation. This allowed Iroquois men to enlist and fight in World War II on the side of the Allied powers.

1942

The Seminole sued the U.S. for failure to pay trust fund monies and to fulfill its fiduciary responsibilities. In *Seminole Nation v. the U.S.* the Supreme Court ruled for the Seminole on the responsibilities of the federal government in regard to the management of Indian lands and assets in trust, calling its trust responsibilities "a moral obligation of the highest order."

1943

In a survey of the location of America's mineral resources, the Office of War Preparedness found that over one-third lay under Indian reservation lands in the West. The three largest owners of mineral-rich lands in the

U.S. were the federal government, the railroads, and more than 30 Indian tribes. This discovery would influence the adoption of termination as the Indian policy of the post-war era.

1944

Franklin Delano Roosevelt was elected for an unprecedented fourth term. Although he was extremely ill, the public was not aware of it and popular sentiment did not want a change of war leaders.

1944

Founding of the National Congress of American Indians. D'Arcy McNickle, a Salish Indian and a writer and historian, brought together tribal leaders from more than one hundred reservations to found the National Congress of American Indians. An Indian leader who had worked for John Collier in the BIA, McNickle was also a writer of history (*They Came Here First*, 1949; *Indian Tribes of the U.S.*, 1962) and fiction (*Wind from an Enemy Sky*, 1978). Later, he served as the first director of the Newberry Library Center for History of the American Indian in Chicago. The National Congress of American Indians (NCAI) took as its mission the advancement of Indian rights, the preservation of native culture, and the safeguarding of tribal lands. Their successful lobbying on behalf of Native American land claims led to the formation in 1946 of the Indian Claims Commission.

1945

First nuclear bomb exploded in test near Los Alamos, New Mexico (July 16), at the Alamogordo test site.

1945

Germany signed unconditional surrender near Reims, France, May 7, 1945. Hitler committed suicide.

1945

First atomic bomb dropped on Hiroshima (August 6); second bomb

1945

Ira Hayes, a full-blood Pima of Arizona, was one of the five soldiers photographed raising the flag at Iwo Jima. A member of an elite paratrooper unit in the Marines, Hayes became a widely publicized hero, but returned to the state of Arizona where he could not vote and racism against Indians was strong. Unprepared for the intense publicity surrounding the photo and unable to reenter the life of the Pima reservation, he became one of many Indians dropped on Nagasaki, Japan (August 9). An estimated 110,000 to 150,000 Japanese were killed outright and another 200,000 died from radiation-related sicknesses within five years. Japanese emperor surrendered on August 14.

1945
End of World War II. More than 55 million lives were lost, 20 million of them Russian civilians. The San Francisco Conference was held to write the United Nations Charter. The Potsdam Conference rearranged boundary lines of Europe. Nazism was outlawed in Germany. Soviets were given control of East Germany. A new Japanese constitution was promulgated. French troops entered Hanoi, the capital of French Indochina, and expelled the Japanese. Japan was prohibited from retaining any of its possessions in China or Southeast Asia.

1945
The nationalist All-India Congress met in Bombay, calling on Great Britain to "quit India."

1946
In China a truce between the nationalist forces of Chiang Kai-shek in the south and Mao Tse-tung's Red Army in the north.

1946
Philippines independence recognized by the U.S. Congress.

1946
Atomic bombs were exploded over the Bikini Atoll in the Marshall Islands, contaminating islands as far as 200 miles downwind. The U.S. Atomic

whose experience in war left them psychologically unable to re-adjust— culturally, economically, or personally—to post-war life. (The experience of such a veteran from the Laguna Pueblo of New Mexico and the sacred ceremony that subsequently allowed him to "regain the balance of his mind" is the story of Leslie Marmon Silko's *Ceremony*, 1979, considered one of the great contemporary American novels.)

1945
John Collier resigned. End of the "New Deal" for Indians and the transition to the policy of termination. Collier's administration of the BIA had come under increasing criticism from Congress, especially western conservatives and business interests who charged he was resisting assimilation policies. The new thrust in Indian policy would soon be termination of Indians' special status with the federal government and the end of federal supervision of Native American affairs. This policy was especially favored by those interested in dam building or mineral development on Indian lands.

1946
National Congress of American Indians (NCAI) lobbied for and achieved legislation setting up a national Indian Claims Court. Under the U.S. Constitution no state or federal court had jurisdiction over Indian land claims. Each individual case had to be authorized by a specific act of Congress and then brought to the U.S. Court of Claims. The average case took 15 years to wend its way through the system. The NCAI made the case for setting up a federal tribunal for the express purpose of providing Indian tribes the

Energy Commission was formed to regulate the development of civilian and military nuclear power.

opportunity to obtain damages for loss of tribal lands either through fraud, illegal allotments, railroad charters, or state annexation without federal oversight. The Indian Claims Commission Act provided that *"the Commission [composed of three appointed commissioners] shall hear and determine the following claims against the United States on behalf of any Indian tribe, band, or other identifiable group of American Indians residing within the territorial limits of the U.S. or Alaska."* Among the claims considered valid were those *"which would result if the treaties, contracts, and agreements between the claimant and the U.S. were revised on the grounds of fraud, duress, unconscionable consideration . . . claims arising from the taking by the U.S., whether as the result of a treaty of cession or otherwise, of lands owned or occupied by the claimant without the payment for such lands of compensation agreed to by the claimant."* The Claims Commission provided for Indian-initiated legislation. Although the act did create a tribunal for the express purpose of providing Indians with the opportunity to obtain redress for the loss of tribal lands, the tribes could only receive money, not actual land, based on the value of land at the time it was taken. During the existence of the commission from 1946 to 1978, over 852 claims were filed. (The commission's life was extended four times.) The proceedings of the commission resulted in the unearthing of a vast amount of information and documentation on the histories of individual people and bands. Many Indians went to law school as a result of Indian-initiated suits. Over 800 million dollars was awarded. Historians give the Claims Commission a mixed evaluation. Indian leaders wanted land. They frequently said that their lawyers had misrepresented the possible outcome of a legal suit and told them filing a claim was a way to get their lands back. Often they didn't realize until they received a check that the claims settlement meant a massive and final buyout of disputed land claims at nineteenth-century prices. Many, like the Hopi and Sioux, never cashed the checks they received. In 1978 the commission went out of business and all its remaining cases were transferred to the U.S. Court of Claims.

1946

Setting up of the law firm of Wilkinson, Clagun and Barker, which would handle more tribal claims than any other law firm in the country. Ernest Wilkinson, a Mormon attorney from Utah working for the Interior Department, had drafted the legislation setting up the Indian Claims Commission. (In the Interior Department the Claims Commission reports are called the "Wilkinson file.") Soon after passage of the law Wilkinson left government to set up his own Washington law firm, Wilkinson, Clagun and Barker. Wilkinson wrote the Claims Commission law in such a way that *the tribes could receive no land, only financial compensation, based on the price per acre at the time the land was taken.* Wilkinson had also provided for legal fees of 7 to 10 percent of the total award to be paid by the Interior Department. In Salt Lake City Wilkinson set up a partnership with John Boyden, another Mormon attorney, to handle Indian claims cases. Wilkinson's firm signed up the Ute, the Shoshoni, the Goshiute, the Paiute, the Klamath, and the Hopi, among others. The Indian Claims Law made both Wilkinson and John Boyden multimillionaires. Wilkinson ran for the Senate, lost, and became president of Brigham Young University. His law firm also represented the Mormon Church in Washington, D.C. Boyden became the Hopi tribal lawyer for 30 years.

1946

Mining companies petitioned the secretary of the interior to clarify title to the mineral estate on Black Mesa, Arizona, underlying Hopi and Navajo reservation lands. The 4,000-square-mile area was known to hold the largest coal deposit in the U.S., over 20 billion tons of coal. Government documents showed that the lands were considered to be owned by both the Hopi and Navajo. Although the Navajo lived on the lands and had been granted grazing licenses, an executive order of 1882 under President Chester Arthur had designated the lands "for the Moquii [Spanish name for the Hopi] and other such Indians as the secretary should decide to settle thereon." Consequently, the energy companies could not get valid leases because title to the lands was not clear. Felix Cohen, solicitor general of the Department of the Interior, was asked to prepare an opinion for the secretary.

1946

Creation of the Bureau of Land Management. The General Land Office and the Grazing Service (140 million acres of federally owned grazing lands) were merged to form the Bureau of Land Management, administering millions of acres of public land in 15 western states.

Ute Delegation, Washington, D.C., 1868. One of the first claims filed before the Indian Claims Commission was by the Utes of Utah for violations of their 1868 treaty. They had come to Washington in 1868 to sign a treaty ceding some of the lands they controlled in Utah, Nevada, and Wyoming. The treaty was never upheld and the federal government and the state of Utah took vast amounts of land. This photograph was taken in order to document the treaty negotiations between the chiefs and the government's representatives, as well as to provide the War Department with a likeness of the Indian chiefs in case war broke out again.

1947

Independence of India. Britain divided the country in two, with Pakistan as the Moslem country and India the Hindu country.

1947

Partition of Palestine into Israel and an Arab state. The UN General Assembly voted for the partition of the country into Jewish and Arab states, Jerusalem to be under UN trusteeship. War broke out immediately between the Jews and the Arabs.

1947

The U.S. government survey of mineral resources was completed. The principal mineral-rich reservations were the following:

Blackfoot—coal, oil, gas;

Crow—coal, oil, gas;

Fort Berthold (Mandan, Hidatsa, Arikara)—coal, oil, gas;

Fort Peck (Assiniboine and Sioux)—coal, oil, gas;

Hopi—coal, oil, gas;

Jicarilla Apache—coal, oil, gas;

Laguna Pueblo (Keresan)—uranium, coal;

Navajo—uranium, coal, oil, gas;

Northern Cheyenne—coal, oil;

Osage—oil, gas;

Southern Ute—coal, oil, gas;

Spokane—uranium;

Uintah and Ouray (Ute)—coal, oil, gas, uranium;

Wind River (Arapaho and Shoshoni)—coal, oil, gas, uranium.

1947

Felix Cohen, solicitor general of the Interior Department, ruled on the matter of the mineral estate of the Hopi and Navajo reservations, saying that both tribes had equal rights in regard to minerals. *"The rights of the Navajo within the area are coextensive with those of the Hopis with respect to the natural resources of the reservation."* The energy companies immediately appealed to the secretary of the interior for a review of the opinion, stating the need for a single tribal ownership so they could commence mineral development.

1947

Dams on the Columbia, Snake, and Missouri Rivers wiped out the major salmon fishing sites and inundated lands of the Fort Berthold reservation, the Standing Rock Sioux, and the Cheyenne River reservation. Post-war reclamation projects proliferated throughout the West, threatening many reservations with the loss of water rights or access to tributary rivers. The National Congress of American Indians supported the long but ultimately unsuccessful attempt of the three affiliated tribes of the Fort Berthold reservation in North Dakota to stop construction of the Garrison Dam, which eventually flooded one-quarter—154,000 acres—of their richest bottom lands. Previously self-sufficient economically, the Fort Berthold tribes had a post–Garrison Dam unemployment rate of 60 percent. The Yankton reservation also lost lands to dam construction and reservoirs.

1948

Arizona Indians were granted the right to vote as a result of their suit. In *Harri-*

son v. Laveen disenfranchisement was declared illegal.

1949
People's Republic of China proclaimed in Beijing with Mao Tse-tung as chairman and Chou En-lai as premier and foreign minister. In the previous year Mao Tse-tung's Red Army had succeeded in defeating the nationalist armies of Chiang Kai-shek and pushing them off mainland China to the outlying islands of Taiwan and Formosa.

1950
World population reached two and a half billion.

1950
Hydrogen bomb developed. The U.S. Atomic Energy Commission was ordered by President Truman to conduct hydrogen bomb tests.

1949
Termination and urbanization proposed as a new federal Indian policy. The Hoover Commission under former president Herbert Hoover recommended that Native Americans be "integrated economically, politically as well as culturally" into the American mainstream and proposed that the federal government "terminate" its responsibility for Indian affairs. A former mining engineer whose first million had been made working for mining companies around the world, Hoover wanted the federal government to urge Indians to leave the reservations for urban areas and enter the economic and cultural mainstream. To that end the Hoover Commission recommended removal of all Indian lands from trust (nontax) status, the repeal of the Indian Reorganization Act, and the outlawing of 100 tribal constitutions. Termination had much to recommend it as a policy to those energy corporations who wanted to exploit the vast mineral resources hidden under reservation lands. Only four years later, termination would be adopted as official policy.

1950
Dillon Meyer, former head of the Japanese internment camps and a supporter of termination, appointed commissioner of Indian affairs.

1950
The Sun Dance was openly revived among the Sioux. In 1904 when the Sun Dance was outlawed by the U.S. government, it was practiced by at least 26 Plains tribes and generally took place in

1950–1953
Korean War. North Korean troops crossed the 38th parallel. UN forces under U.S. General Douglas MacArthur intervened to support South Korea. The first of a series of wars in "client countries" of the U.S. and the U.S.S.R. in which the noncommunist West was pitted against the communist East.

June or July in connection with communal spring hunts. It was the only religious ritual in which the entire political unit also acted as a ceremonial unit. Organized by the shamans, or medicine men, and involving every member of the tribe, it began with an individual's vision or vow of personal sacrifice for the good of his people. The ceremony lasted a week and the actual dance, during which the dancers fasted, was four days long. After it was outlawed, many tribes continued the ceremony disguised within Fourth of July celebrations. In 1950 the Sioux openly revived the Sun Dance in its original form and meaning and began to train medicine men to pass it on to other tribes and groups.

1950
Congress passed the Navajo Hopi Rehabilitation Act, making the Navajo and Hopi reservations test cases for the ideas of the Hoover Commission on urbanization and termination. The Rehabilitation Act provided money to build roads and infrastructure on the reservations and to lure families away from the reservation into employment in the cities. Navajo and Hopi men found jobs in the border towns of Arizona, working for the railroads or doing agricultural work. But they behaved differently than government policy makers had expected. Although they took jobs in the city and brought their families, many returned to the reservation, which remained "home." From 1950 to 1968 more than 200,000 Indians from all tribes moved to cities, but many kept ties to their reservations. Urban America made Indian Americans more aware of what reservation life had that greater American society did not—land, conti-

nuity, roots, a shared sense of community. Urban Indians would become the Indian militants of the 1960s and 1970s.

1951
Mohammad Mossadegh, an Iranian nationalist, was elected premier of Iran. He nationalized the Iranian oil industry. Britain and the U.S. contested the abrogation of their oil leases.

1951
First electricity produced from atomic power in the U.S. Beginning of the government-sponsored "atoms for peace" campaign, a program advocating the peaceful uses of atomic energy.

1951
Uranium discovered on the Navajo reservation. Rich deposits of uranium were found on the Navajo reservation in New Mexico and Arizona. Navajo miners were put to work without protective clothing, without information about the nature of the material they were mining, or the possible effects on their families. They worked in unventilated mines and drank radioactive water. Many became violently ill. As soon as they got sick they were dismissed. Any questions about the nature of uranium were considered unpatriotic because of the defense-related nature of the nuclear industry and Cold War attitudes. The sole purchaser of uranium was the U.S. government.

1951
John Boyden was appointed Hopi tribal lawyer. The Hopi progressives, which included the Mormon and Christianized Hopi, agreed to hire attorney John Boyden as Hopi "claims counsel." Although the purpose was to file a Hopi claim before the Indian Claims Commission, the Hopi entered into a 30-year relationship with Boyden. Many called the post-Boyden Hopi tribal government "Boyden's puppet council." Boyden traveled the Hopi mesas with a BIA official who confirmed that it was the will of the Hopi to reconstitute the tribal council. The Hopi tribal council had gone out of business in 1939 after the Hopi traditionalists refused to vote, attend meetings, or send representatives to any council meetings. The council never had a quorum. Boy-

I

den implied that by filing a land claim the Hopi could reclaim lost land. Even the progressive Hopi tribal council members were shocked when they received a check for 5 million dollars in lieu of land. They agreed to not cash it. (The money continues to sit in a bank in Utah, gathering interest.) Boyden received a million-dollar fee. He went on to work with the Hopi tribal council to open Black Mesa to stripmining, even though mining was clearly contrary to Hopi traditional religious beliefs.

1953
Coup d'état in Iran. Mossadegh was overthrown by Iranian royalists with the help of British and American intelligence services. Shah Mohammad Reza Pahlavi returned to the throne. Agreement was reached with American and British oil companies for resumption of their oil leases in Iran.

1953–1962
Termination became official American Indian policy. During the official period of termination (1953–1962) 13 tribes were terminated, the largest being the Menominees in Wisconsin and the Klamaths in Oregon; and over a hundred bands, communities, and rancherias (California mission Indians) were terminated or lost many federal protections and services. In practice termination meant that the tribes lost trust status and had to start paying taxes, often selling off land to meet tax obligations, and providing their own education and health services. In 1961 the National Congress of American Indians met in Chicago and declared termination to be *"the greatest threat to Indian survival since the military campaigns of the 1800s."* It was officially outlawed in 1962 by the Kennedy administration.

1953
Arthur Watkins, senator from Utah, passed legislation making termination the official new Indian policy. He argued that while the U.S. was spending billions fighting communism, it was promoting socialism on Indian reser-

vations. He set out to dismantle the reservation system, the programs and services that supported it, and the federal bureaucracy that administered it. Calling his new program the "Indian Freedom program," he translated it into legislation that provided for the general termination of "certain tribes, bands, and colonies of Indians in the state of Utah" as well as a dozen tribes in other states. Watkins was also a fervent promoter of reclamation. One of the first tribes to be terminated was the Klamath of Oregon, who lived in the way of a great dam and reservoir project favored by Watkins.

1953
The Flatheads of Montana, Menominees of Wisconsin, Potawatomis of Kansas and Nebraska, and Chippewas of North Dakota were targeted for termination. Their tribal communities were to be disbanded and their assets and lands distributed among tribal members. Dillon Meyer, commissioner of Indian affairs, immediately began withdrawing federal programs on the targeted reservations. Federal services such as health and education were turned over to the states. The goal was to get rid of the reservations. (The termination mentality survives into the present. The new term is "abrogation" but the rhetoric is the same: Indians should be given equal status with other Americans and assimilated into the mainstream.)

1953
John Boyden, attorney for the Hopi, petitioned the secretary of the interior for a review of Felix Cohen's opinion regarding ownership of the mineral estate of Black Mesa.

1954

In *Brown v. Board of Education of Topeka, Kansas,* the U.S. Supreme Court reversed the "separate but equal" doctrine of racially segregated public schools in America. Thurgood Marshall, the young NAACP lawyer who argued the case before the Court, eventually became the first black justice on the U.S. Supreme Court.

1954

French defeated by the Vietnamese in the historic battle of Dienbienphu. With losses of more than 50,000 soldiers, France withdrew from French Indo china. America, a French ally, considered using tactical nuclear weapons to prevent a communist victory. Instead, a peace conference was held in Switzerland and under the Geneva Accords, the parties agreed to the artificial division of the country into North and South Vietnam, pending an election for reunification.

1955

Construction of the first nuclear-powered electrical generating station in the world, in Illinois. Disposal of nuclear waste was an unresolved issue.

1954

The Menominee Termination Act. The Menominees, who had won an 8.5-million-dollar claims settlement, were blocked from receiving the monies unless they agreed to termination. The tribe at the time was doing well economically because of a forest products industry. Under the termination legislation tribal assets were put under the control of a corporation in which individual Menominees held shares. Previously untaxed lands became subject to state and local taxes. The tribal hospital, financed by the BIA, was shut down. Other services were ended. The corporation tried to raise money by leasing timber lands to non-Indians. They sold off other lands to pay taxes. The result was a predictable replay of what had happened under the policy of allotment: accelerated land loss, deepening poverty, economic chaos, and no economy for Menominees to move into.

1954

A series of acts designed to speed termination were introduced: Fort Peck Reservation Fee Patents Act; Lower Brulé, Crow, Cree, Sioux, and Yankton Sioux Act; Indian Health Care Transfer Act; Klamath Termination Act; Western Oregon Indians Termination Act; Alabama and Coushatta Termination Act; Fee Patent Allotments for Mission Indians Act; Ute Tribe Termination Act; Certain Utah Indians Termination Act.

1955

Termination policies slowed when Democrats gained majorities in the House and Senate. Senator Watkins was defeated. President Eisenhower

1956

First airborne H-bomb was exploded. A new series of atomic tests began in the Pacific.

1957

The first commercial U.S. nuclear reactor came on line in Shippingport, Pennsylvania.

1957

The space age began with Sputnik I, the launching of the first satellite by the Soviet Union.

1957

President Eisenhower sent federal troops to Little Rock, Arkansas, to enforce a federal court desegregation order. Civil Rights Act passed to protect black peoples' voting rights in the U.S.

appointed Watkins head of the Indian Claims Commission.

1956–1958

Senator Barry Goldwater, freshman senator from Arizona, introduced S.231, a bill to set up a special three-judge court to decide the status of the mineral estate on Black Mesa and the so-called boundary dispute between the Hopi and Navajo. Written by John Boyden after he received no response from the secretary of the interior, the purpose of the bill was to allow the Hopi to sue the Navajo in a "friendly" suit to clear title to the mineral estate of Black Mesa so leasing could proceed. The bill was opposed by the U.S. attorney general, many Hopi and Navajo, and was defeated in 1956 and 1957. It passed in 1958.

1957

A series of encroachments on upstate New York reservation lands led to increased militancy among the Iroquois tribes, including the Mohawk, the Tuscarora, and the Seneca. Tuscarora Chief Clinton Rickard refused permission to the New York Power Authority to take soil tests on the Tuscarora reservation lands in New York State. The Tuscarora had learned that 1,383 acres of their lands were to be condemned and taken by eminent domain for development. The Tuscarora resisted nonviolently. Women lay down in the road in front of the surveyors' trucks and state police vehicles.

1957

The Seneca learned that 10,000 acres of their reservation lands, which were ensured by a treaty with George Washington, were about to be lost to flooding by the proposed Kinzua Dam. The Seneca hired their own engineers, who proved that the dam could be built more cheaply and more effectively 30 miles downstream. The Army Corps of Engineers refused to consider the alternative site. In planning the relocation of a Seneca town the U.S. government gave the best lots to Christian Senecas and saved the most isolated lands for the Handsome Lake Senecas, followers of the Longhouse religion, who were most vocal in opposing the dam.

1958

The Great Leap Forward in China. A campaign to increase agricultural and industrial output by reorganizing the entire population into communes, it was spectacularly unsuccessful and caused massive disruption in Chinese society.

1958

First jet-powered transatlantic service, inaugurated by BOAC and Pan-American Airways.

1958

In California 48 rancherias, Indian lands of Spanish origin, were terminated. The BIA withdrew special Indian programs such as college scholarships, vocational education, economic development programs, and water and sanitation projects. Medical services were curtailed.

1958

The Lumbees of North Carolina drove off a Ku Klux Klan rally in Robeson County. The Ku Klux Klansmen were attempting to intimidate the Lumbee people, who had protested sending their children 35 miles away to a state-run Indian school. They asked for an Indian school closer to home. When the hooded Klansmen invaded their lands, they drove them off with shotguns.

1958

The Miccosukee of Florida resisted the Army Corps of Engineers' Everglades Reclamation Project, a proposed project to straighten the river running through the Everglades. The U.S.

Army Corps of Engineers proposed transforming the 103-mile Kissimmee River into a 56-mile canal, draining 40,000 acres of land for residential development and range land.

Since both the Seneca of New York and the Miccosukee of Florida were subject to the U.S. Army Corps of Engineers projects, and since neither tribe was able to gain a review of the projects within the appropriate agencies of the U.S. government, the Miccosukee and the Iroquois Six Nations joined together to send a delegation to Cuba at the invitation of Fidel Castro. They asked the Cuban leader to sponsor their membership in the United Nations as indigenous nations. (The Everglades Reclamation Project, now considered to have been responsible for killing off the Everglades' natural flora and fauna by changing water temperatures and flow patterns, is currently the subject of a billion dollar federal project to return the river to its original channel in order to save the Everglades.)

1958

The Tuscarora were awarded 13 million dollars in federal appeals court for the lands improperly taken by the New York Power Authority by eminent domain. The Tuscarora appealed the award, wanting land rather than money.

1959

Alaska admitted as a state, the largest in the Union, with more than 580,000 square miles. The major groups of indigenous peoples are Eskimos, Aleuts, the Athabascans, and the Tlingits.

1959

Alaska natives made land claims for more than 300 million acres. Although the federal government granted the state of Alaska the right to select 102 million acres from the public domain, Alaska native villages made their own land claims, which conflicted with those of the state.

1959

Pope John XXIII ordered the French worker-priest movement to cease operation and to stop all involvement in political causes. The worker priests had a powerful influence in the "liberation theology" movement that developed in Central and South America as well as the anti-Vietnam movement in the U.S.

1960

World population reached three billion.

1960

Nixon-Kennedy debates. First presidential election in which television played a significant role.

1961

Yuri Gagarin, Russian astronaut, first man in space, orbited the earth in *Vostok I.*

1961

Bay of Pigs. The CIA-sponsored invasion of Cuba became an international embarrassment for the U.S.

1961

Berlin Wall erected through the middle of Berlin by East German government to stop the flow of refugees to the West.

1961

Kinzua Dam completed, flooding Seneca lands in New York and destroying the burial place of Cornplanter, a great Seneca leader who had negotiated with George Washington to secure Seneca lands. The Seneca had asked for a halt to the construction of the dam on the basis of a 1794 treaty that gave the Seneca rights in perpetuity to these same lands in New York. President Kennedy refused an additional investigation into the project on grounds that all procedures had been followed. When the lands were flooded, much of the reservation was destroyed.

1961

National Congress of American Indians met in Chicago and declared termination the greatest threat to Indian survival since the 1800s military actions. It was the largest multitribal gathering in decades and marked the beginning of a new Indian consciousness and militancy. The National Indian

Youth Council was founded. Formed by members who were dissatisfied with the mainstream Indian leaders' reluctance to confront major issues in Indian affairs, their centrist approach to legislative action, and their failure to take an activist stance, the new organization called for an activist and national orientation on Indian issues.

1961

President Kennedy appointed a task force on Indian affairs headed by Phillips Petroleum Company executive W. W. Keeler, who recommended the end of the policy of termination. Philleo Nash appointed commissioner of Indian affairs under Secretary of the Interior Stewart Udall of Arizona. Responsiveness to the needs of energy companies continued to be the overriding policy of the BIA.

1961

Janet McCloud, a Puyallup of Washington State, was one of many women who maintained a river vigil after the state police arrested Nisqually Indian fishermen for net fishing. It was the first of a series of "fish-ins" designed to draw attention to the abrogation of Washington Indians' fishing rights. Treaty rights stipulated Nisqually fishing rights and the Nisqually claimed they had the right to traditional net fishing rather than the hook-and-line fishing dictated by Washington State game laws. The vigil marked the beginning of new militant tactics and national media attention to Washington's suppression of Indian fishing rights in order to protect fish, particularly salmon, for sportsmen and private companies. Dick Gregory's arrest in 1966 with the Nisqually fishermen and subsequent six-week hunger strike focused national attention on the fish-ins. It marked the first incidence of the militant tactics of the Red Power movement which became prominent in the 1970s.

1962
Rachel Carson published *The Silent Spring*, a monumental investigation of the effects of DDT and other pesticides on the global environment.

1962
Linus Pauling won the Nobel Peace Prize for opposing nuclear warfare. He also had won the Nobel Prize in chemistry in 1954 for his theory of chemical bonding.

1962
New Mexico Indians finally gained the right to vote in state elections. The case of *Montoya v. Bolack* forced New Mexico to allow its Indian population to vote. The court ruled against the state's arguments that Indians living on reservations or in the pueblos were not technically state residents.

1962
Institute of American Indian Art founded in Santa Fe. Students and teachers included Fritz Scholder (Luiseno), Allan Houser (Apache), T.C. Cannon (Caddo).

1962
A special federal three-judge court ruled in *Healing v. Jones*, the suit of the Hopi against the Navajo. The court ruled that the Hopi tribe had exclusive title to an area known as District Six (a land unit measured by the BIA as a grazing district), that both tribes had "joint, equal, and undivided rights" to 1.8 million acres of the 1882 executive-order reservation outside of District Six, and that both tribes had equal interest in subsurface minerals. The court renamed the disputed area the Hopi-Navajo Joint Use Area and charged the two tribal councils with negotiating a land management plan. The negotiations broke down when Abbott Sekaquaptewa, chairman of the Hopi negotiating committee, at the direction

of John Boyden, refused to meet with the Navajo committee. Legal analysts believe that Boyden did not want to give away in negotiation what he had already won in court.

1963
South Vietnam premier, Ngo Dinh Diem, assassinated in Saigon (November 1).

1963
U.S. President Kennedy assassinated in Dallas, Texas, November 22.

1964
Beginning of large-scale U.S. military intervention in Vietnam with the Gulf of Tonkin resolution passed in Congress. After subverting the elections meant to unify Vietnam, the U.S. supported a series of puppet rulers in South Vietnam propped up by the U.S. military. Over the next 10 years a million American troops would be sent to Vietnam in an unsuccessful attempt to block the success of Ho Chi Minh's North Vietnamese communist regime. American soldiers called the Viet Cong–controlled territory "Indian country."

1964
U.S. passed the Civil Rights Act, which prohibited discrimination based on race, religion, or sex in all institutions receiving federal funds.

1963
Arizona v. California decided. After a 30-year legal battle, Arizona's claim to a larger share of the water of the Colorado River was approved in the U.S. Supreme Court; Indian water rights along the Colorado River were affirmed. The decison paved the way for the Central Arizona Project.

1963
State of Washington ruled against the Indians' right to fish with nets, regardless of prior treaties, and mandated that all Indian fishing had to be done with hook and line according to Washington fish and game laws. The Indians appealed.

1964
The American Indian Historical Society was founded in California and began publication of *The Indian Historian*, a journal of articles on Indian history primarily from an Indian perspective.

1964
The Office of Economic Opportunity created an Indian desk and gave anti-poverty funds directly to tribes. For the first time Indian tribal governments gained direct access to federal funds that were not administered through BIA officials. This model for direct grants to tribal governments became the model for self-determination starting in the 1970s.

few realized that this photograph was from a movie he made called *In the Land of the Head-hunters* in which he translated the Montagues and Capulets of Shakespeare's *Romeo and Juliet* into the Bear and Eagle Clans of the Kwakiutl Indians of the Pacific Northwest. He showed the movie once in New York to rave reviews, but could get no backers and no distributor. (The film did serve as the model for Robert Flaherty's classic *Nanook of the North*.) Curtis's film was restored in 1974.

1965

Alaska Natives created the Alaska Federated Natives, a statewide organization empowered to pursue land claims for Native peoples of Alaska.

1965

In California 33,000 Native people received 900 dollars each in compensation for ceded lands that represented two-thirds of the entire state. After decades of hearings, the descendants of the original plaintiffs voted to accept an award of 29 million dollars for 64 million acres of land, approximately 47 cents an acre.

1966

The Hopi and Navajo tribal councils signed coal-mining leases with the Peabody Coal Company and its parent, Kennecott Copper, for stripmining on the newly declared Hopi-Navajo Joint Use Area. The leases also included the sale of the first Indian water rights in the country. In both tribes the leases were signed quietly, without any public referendum. Hopi tribal attorney John Boyden, whose law offices were in the Kennecott Building in Salt Lake City, also listed Peabody Coal Company as one of his law firms' clients. The BIA, which had to approve the leases, saw no conflict of interest. A later investigation by the Indian Law Resource Center showed that the tribes agreed to a royalty of 15 cents a ton, no rights of renegotiation, and no environmental assessments. The royalty rate was less than a third of what government charged for mineral extraction on public domain lands. BIA experts had told them that nuclear power was soon going to make their coal worthless and they should sign while they could. The Indians did not know that three massive coal-powered plants had already been planned for construction on the Colorado Plateau by a consortium of 23 utility plants of the western states. Interior secretary Udall of Arizona hailed the leases.

1967

Arab-Israeli Six-Day War. Egypt blocked Israeli access to the Gulf of Aqaba. Israel retaliated by capturing Sinai, the West Bank, and Golan Heights.

1968

Rev. Martin Luther King, Jr., leader of the U.S. civil rights movement,

1968

Kiowa novelist N. Scott Momaday received a Pulitzer Prize for his novel, assassinated in Memphis, Tennessee. Rioting erupted in American cities.

1968
Robert F. Kennedy assassinated in California while campaigning in the Democratic Party presidential primary.

1968
Riots in Paris. Student uprisings sparked a national political crisis. General de Gaulle was given an absolute majority in the assembly.

1968
Prague spring. A program of reforms and liberalization in Czechoslovakia crushed by invasion of Soviet troops.

1969
Nuclear arsenals of the Soviet Union and the U.S. said to be capable of

House Made of Dawn. It was a critical work in opening mainstream publishing to Native American writers.

1968
American Indian Movement (AIM) founded in Minneapolis. Dennis Banks (Anishinabe), Clyde Bellencourt (Ojibwa), Mary Jane Wilson, George Mitchell, and other Indian community activists started a new organization to represent urban Indian goals, protect the traditional ways of Indian peoples, hire legal counsel, and intervene in cases relating to treaty and aboriginal rights to hunting, fishing, trapping, and gathering wild rice.

1968
The Mohawk of the Akwesasne Reserve blocked the International Bridge between the U.S. and Canada to draw attention to the violation of Jay's Treaty of 1794 by the government of Canada. Mohawk ancestral lands were in both the U.S. and Canada, and Jay's Treaty guaranteed the Mohawk free movement over the border and exemption from any border taxes or custom duties from both the U.S. and Canadian governments. The precipitating incident was the insistence by the Canadian government that the Mohawk chief in Canada pay custom duties on a used refrigerator he bought from his brother who lived on the U.S. side of the reservation. The Canadian marshals confiscated the refrigerator until he paid the duties. The case was appealed through the Canadian court system.

1969-1971
Indians of All Tribes, a pan-Indian group, occupied Alcatraz Island in

destroying every person on the planet. The two countries began SALT (Strategic Arms Limitation Talks) negotiations on arms limitation.

1969

U.S. astronauts walk on the moon.

San Francisco Bay under an 1868 Sioux oral agreement granting Indians first rights to government surplus lands. Fourteen activists occupied the island and offered to purchase it for 24 dollars in glass beads. (The prison of Alcatraz had been closed and the island was declared surplus land.) The occupiers sought to draw attention to the treatment of Indians throughout the United States. The occupation grew until it involved hundreds of Indians and minority college students who took up permanent residency in the cell blocks, defying federal demands to leave the island. The occupation lasted 20 months. During the period of the occupation the Nixon administration announced a policy of Indian self-determination and signed legislation that returned the sacred Blue Lake to the Taos Pueblo.

1969

Standing Rock Sioux Vine Deloria published *Custer Died for Your Sins,* the first contemporary book to force a rethinking of the traditional narratives of Native American history in the context of the myths of the settling of America. Deloria, a writer, lawyer, and professor of political science, published many other books on Indian history, law, and religion, including *God Is Red, The Nation Within,* and *American Indians, American Justice.*

1970

First Earth Day. Celebrated in Washington, D.C., and cities throughout the United States, it inaugurated the American phase of a global environmental movement. Congress passed the National Environmental Policy Act (NEPA), requiring an environmental

1970

The Paiutes of Nevada protested the draining of Pyramid Lake and sued the Interior Department. They were supported by the Alcatraz demonstrators. Pyramid Lake was drying up at the rate of 50 inches a year as prosperous ranchers and farmers in California and impact statement for every large project funded by a federal agency.

1970
The undeclared war of the U.S. in Vietnam escalated with the secret invasion of Cambodia.

1970
Riots on college campuses throughout the U.S. in response to the Cambodian invasion. In Ohio, where Governor James Rhodes had called anti–Vietnam War protestors "brownshirts" and vowed to "eradicate" them, the National Guard was called onto the Kent State campus. Four students and youths were shot and killed, an event which marked a turning point in both opposition to the war and civil disobedience throughout the U.S.

Nevada dammed its tributary rivers and feeder streams. Contrary to federal laws and prior Paiute treaties, the California-Nevada Compact of 1969 subordinated Indian water rights to those of the states and added more dams and water diversion projects. The Paiute protest was joined by the Indians of All Tribes from Alcatraz, whose caravan of cars from San Francisco to Nevada attracted press attention throughout California. They demonstrated that tribal grievances were not isolated, that pan-Indian support was available. As a result of the media attention, Nixon's secretary of the Interior, Walter Hickel, California Governor Ronald Reagan, and Nevada Governor Laxalt met with the Paiutes and agreed on a level of stabilization for Pyramid Lake.

1970
Return of Blue Lake to the Taos Pueblo and passage of the Taos Land Bill. In 1956 the Indian Claims Commission confirmed the rights of the Taos Pueblo in New Mexico to 130,000 acres of land (taken by President Roosevelt in 1906 and given to the Forest Service) including the 48,000-acre Blue Lake watershed, a lake sacred to the Taos. The tribe refused to accept a financial settlement in lieu of land. The return of the land was proposed in the Taos Land Bill but had been opposed over the years by various New Mexico senators and timber interests who wanted access to the virgin forest. The Taos land bill that finally passed in 1970 returned title to the Taos of the entire Blue Lake watershed under perpetual trust status, in one of the few significant land returns to Indians in this century.

1970

Sit-ins took place at BIA offices throughout the country. The BIA office in Littleton, Colorado, was occupied, as were BIA offices in Chicago and Cleveland. Another demonstration took place at a BIA warehouse in Gallup, New Mexico. Fort Lawton in Washington State and Ellis Island in New York harbor were occupied by Indian demonstrators who wanted recognition of Indian rights based on treaties, protection of traditional ways, and a curbing of abuses by BIA offices.

1970

Iroquois resurgence. Two hundred members of the Iroquois confederacy met in Geneva, New York, to discuss proposals for regaining political power lost to state and federal governments.

1970

Mount Rushmore in the Black Hills of South Dakota reclaimed by Indians. A pan-Indian coalition of 50 Indians climbed to the top of Mount Rushmore and announced their takeover of the historic site. They wanted the return of 123,000 acres of Sioux lands taken as a gunnery range during World War II.

1970

Thanksgiving declared a national day of mourning. AIM members Dennis Banks and Russell Means seized control of the Mayflower II in Plymouth Harbor, Massachusetts, and declared Thanksgiving a day of national mourning. This was AIM's first national protest.

1970

The Mohave Generating Station opened in Nevada. Fueled by coal mined on the Hopi and Navajo reservations, it was the only plant in the country to be run by a coal slurry pipeline, the Black Mesa Pipeline. Few Indians of either tribe knew that the tribal councils had sold water rights along with coal mining rights to the Peabody Coal Company (owned by Kennecott Copper). The slurry line used over a billion gallons of water a year in order to transport crushed coal through a 275-mile pipeline to the Nevada power plant. Within two years water levels began to drop and springs and water holes began to dry up. The electricity generated by the plant was sold to urban populations in Los Angeles, Las Vegas, Phoenix, and Tucson. Fewer than half of the Hopi or Navajo families had electricity. Struggles over the water used in the pipeline continue to the present. Despite repeated protests, the Office of Surface Mining refused to review the lease terms.

1970

President Nixon formally brought the termination policy to an end. Announcing a new federal policy of Indian self-determination without a termination of federal services, he also signed the bill recognizing the return of Blue Lake to the Taos Indians.

1971

The Alaska Native Claims Settlement Act. Following the discovery of oil on Alaska's North Slope, the state of Alaska leased lands to private oil companies for over 1 billion dollars in fees. Native people, organized as the Arctic Slope Native Association, claimed in a legal suit against the state that its selection of 76,000 acres of oil-rich lands of northern Alaska that the Eskimo had occupied, used, and "exercised dominion over" for centuries violated native land rights. Other native claims resulted in settlement legislation proposed in the U.S. Congress, giving Alaska natives a land grant of 44 million acres and 962 million dollars in compensation for giving up claims to nine-tenths of Alaska. *The land was to be divided among some 220 native village corporations and 12 regional corporations established by the act specifically for the purpose of doing business for profit.* The regional corporations were to receive 462.5 million dollars over an 11-year period and an additional 500 million dollars in mineral royalties. Although the Alaska Federation of Natives approved the act, it remains controversial among Alaskan Natives who see it destroying their traditional lands and lifestyle organized around hunting and fishing.

1971

Founding of Native American Rights Fund, providing legal assistance to tribes. It is the oldest and largest Indian public interest lawfirm in the United States.

1971

Sixty-two traditional Hopi religious leaders, represented by the Native American Rights Fund, sued to stop the stripmining on the Hopi reservation. They claimed that the leases were illegal, having been signed by the tribal council at a time when it did not have a quorum. They also charged excessive secrecy by the tribal council about terms as well as violations of the Hopi constitution because the council had not held a public discussion or tribal referendum about the leases. The court refused to hear the case on the Catch-22 grounds that only the tribal council could represent the Hopi in court. John Boyden, who also represented the Peabody Coal Company, was still the Hopi attorney.

The Five Civilized Tribes petitioned the Bureau of Indian Affairs for the direct election of their own chiefs. It marked the first time since 1902 that the Five Civilized Tribes had the right to elect their own leaders and reconstitute their own governmental systems.

1972–1974

Watergate scandal. In Washington, D.C., the arrest of burglars in the Watergate office complex who had connections to the White House began a coverup which ended in President Nixon's resignation in August 1974.

1972

Richard Oakes, an organizer of the Puyallup-Nisqually fishing rights movement, found murdered. Tacoma, Washington, police claimed he had shot himself in the stomach. His murder was denounced in a press conference in Seattle held by Russell Means and other AIM members.

1972

AIM's Trail of Broken Treaties Caravan and occupation of the BIA offices in Washington, D.C. The caravan traveled from San Francisco to Washington, D.C., to highlight the U.S. history of broken treaties. Joined by vehicles from many reservations as it crossed the country, it was a four-mile procession of cars and trucks by the time it reached Washington. AIM developed a 20-point position paper on Indian rights to present to the Nixon administration. After an unsatisfactory meeting with Assistant Secretary Harrison Loesch, AIM eventually took over the federal BIA building for six days, in which 600 to 800 people took part. Because it was two days before the presidential election, the administration negotiated the end of the occupation rather than conducting a military assault. But the FBI expanded its counterintelligence program (COINTEL PRO) to include AIM, and 32 AIM leaders were later indicted for grand larceny and arson on charges growing out of the BIA occupation. The occupation brought Indian rights to the national agenda.

1972

The Paiute of Nevada won their suit against the Department of the Interior for unlawful water diversion at Pyramid Lake.

1973

Arab oil embargo. As oil reached 40 dollars a barrel, it created an energy crisis in America, Europe, and Japan resulting in a great increase in coal exploration, natural gas development, and research in alternative energies, along with expansion of nuclear power facilities.

1973

Nixon administration formally rejected the Twenty Points that had been presented during the Trail of Broken Treaties demonstration.

1973

Siege at Pine Ridge and the occupation of Wounded Knee. AIM leaders Russell Means and Dennis Banks returned to the Pine Ridge reservation after the BIA occupation in Washington. Richard (Dicky) Wilson, chairman of the Pine Ridge tribal council, banned AIM activities, called for U.S. marshals to protect the BIA building, and used federal highway funds to equip and train his own paramilitary police force, Guardians of the Oglala Nations (which became known as "goon" squads). Both Means and Banks were arrested.

Because of the violence of the tribal police and the invasion of the reservation by federal marshals (according to the Major Crimes Act of 1885, the federal government has jurisdiction on reservations only in cases of major felonies, and none had been committed), the Sioux Civil Rights Organization (a group of Sioux traditionalists) drew up a petition to impeach Richard Wilson. More than 200 AIM protestors congregated at the site of the 1890 Wounded Knee Massacre to demonstrate support for the traditionalists. They publicly charged that the tribal government of Richard Wilson was corrupt, rife with nepotism, and in collusion with paramilitary federal police. They were quickly surrounded by the FBI, the U.S. Marshal Service, and the BIA police. Between February and May more than 2,000 Indians went to Pine Ridge to support the siege, which lasted 71 days and involved more than 300 federal marshals and FBI agents equipped with guns, armored personnel carriers, and other military weapons. The head of the U.S. Army's 82nd Airborne Division was called in for military attack preparations. Two Indians were killed in the 10-week standoff, which finally ended in a negotiated release with 185 people indicted on charges of arson, theft, assault, and "interfering with federal officers."

1974

Richard Nixon resigned, the first U.S. president to resign under threat of impeachment.

1974

Communist buildup of supplies and men in South Vietnam. South Vietnamese forces began to desert.

1974

International Treaty Council founded by representatives of 40 Indian nations to gain United Nations representation for Native peoples in the U.S. and Canada.

1974

Russell Means, leader of AIM, ran for chairman of the Oglala Sioux tribal council against Richard Wilson. Although Means did not campaign because he was on trial in Minnesota, he almost won the election. The vote was 1,709 to 1,630. Charges against Chairman Wilson of corruption and illegal vote counting followed the election.

1974
Mohawk activists occupied Eagle Bay in the Adirondacks in upper New York State.

1974
WARN, Women of All Red Nations, was founded as a pan-Indian organization of Native American women activists. WARN was formed in affiliation with AIM to focus on the traditional leadership roles of women in Native cultures.

1974
The Northern Cheyenne of Wyoming and Montana succeeded in having their coal leases canceled. Secretary of the Interior Rogers Morton agreed to cancel the leases because the BIA had not negotiated favorable or responsible terms for the tribe. New guidelines required that all leases meet federal environmental protection standards, follow a revised royalty schedule, and obtain the joint approval of the tribe as well as the mining company. The problems with the Peabody leases on the Navajo and Hopi reservations had focused attention on BIA collusion with the mining companies. The Crow, the Northern Cheyenne, and the Blackfoot all had large coal reserves and were in the midst of negotiations with large mining companies, including Peabody Coal, Fluor, and Newmont Mining.

1974
Congress passed the Hopi Land Settlement Act (also called the Navajo Relocation Act), which eventually forced the relocation of more than 12,000 Navajo who lived over the coal deposits in the Hopi-Navajo

GEORGE WASHINGTON AND
THE PASSAMAQUODDY, 1776–1976

In 1777 the Passamaquoddy saved most of eastern Maine (then part of Massachu-, setts) from the British. George Washington's agents had promised them their "ancient tribal haunts" in perpetuity if they chose the Revolutionaries over the Loyalists. Colonel Allan of Massachusetts reported to Washington about their campaign and the exceptional discipline of the Passamaquoddy in fighting: "Their Zeal & attention during the war . . . is so well known in that Country that it needs no comment. Their uniform conduct both in respect of humanity, as well as in submitting with patience under every difficulty was not inferior to the most disciplined troops, & even when Imposed on at a time of Intoxication & fleeced of the little they had, they always sat down contented and resigned without any appearance of resentment or malice . . ," In 1794 Colonel Allan and other officials of the Commonwealth of Massachusetts signed a treaty with the Passamaquoddy tribal leaders granting them some 30,000 acres of lands in perpetuity, a tiny amount of land in comparison to the vast hunting grounds that had been theirs. By 1970 the Passamaquoddy had been reduced to 200 acres and the 800 people living on the Passamaquoddy reservation were no longer considered a federally recognized tribe. The tribal leaders sued the secretary of the interior Rogers Morton for the illegal annexation of Passamaquoddy lands by the state governments of Maine and Massachusetts. In 1975 in Passamaquoddy v. Morton the federal court of appeals upheld a lower court decision and ruled that the federal government did indeed have an obligation to defend the Passamaquoddy against illegal land seizures by the states of Massachusetts and Maine. Eventually a landmark settlement gave the Passamaquoddy both land (taken from federal forest lands) and a large financial settlement. They could point to a long and patriotic history and a special commendation from George Washington during the Revolutionary War:

"I am glad to hear by Major Shaw, that you accepted the chain of Friendship which I sent you last February from Cambridge, and that you are determined to keep it bright and unbroken. . . . Brothers, I have a piece of news to tell you which I hope you will attend to. Our enemy, the King of Great Britain, endeavored to stir up all the Indians from Canada to South Carolina against us. But our brethren of the six Nations & their allies the Shawnees & the Delawares would not hearken to the advice of his Messengers sent among them, but kept fast hold of the ancient convenant chain. The Cherokees & the Southern tribes were foolish enough to listen to them and take up the hatchet against us. Upon this our Warriors went into their country, burnt their houses, destroyed their corn and obliged them to sue for peace and give hostages for their future good behavior.

"Now Brothers never let the king's wicked counsellor turn your hearts against me and your brethren of this country, but bear in mind what I told you last February and what I tell you now. In token of my friendship I send you this from my army on the banks of the Great River Delaware, this 24th day of December, 1776."

George Washington to the Passamaquoddy, December 24, 1776

Joint Use Area. It became the largest Indian removal since the 1800s. Harrison Loesch, assistant secretary of the interior, testified that only 800 families would be affected by the law. Although the bill was ostensibly to settle a land dispute between the Hopi and Navajo, it removed the people who lived over the coal and who were in the way of stripmining. The Peabody Coal Company opened a second mining site after the passage of the act. Loesch left the interior department to become vice president of Peabody Coal.

1975
World population reached four billion.

1975
The U.S. quit Vietnam. North Vietnamese forces captured Saigon. The last Americans were evacuated. The country was reunited under communist rule.

1975
Pasamaquoddy v. Morton resolved in the Indians' favor with the Pasamaquoddy being given financial compensation and a large tract of land taken from the national forest lands in Maine. (See "George Washington and the Passamaquoddy, 1776–1976" on page 377.)

1975–1977
Shoot-out at Pine Ridge, South Dakota. Leonard Peltier jailed. Peltier, a Sioux-Chippewa, was one of the AIM activists involved in a shoot-out of undetermined cause, which left one AIM member and two FBI agents dead. Peltier was convicted in 1977 of the agents' deaths, although the record showed the government had falsified evidence. Other AIM activists who were tried earlier were all acquitted. (In 1983 author Peter Matthiessen wrote an account of the Pine Ridge conflicts, the subsequent trials, and Peltier's imprisonment, *In the Spirit of Crazy Horse*. Although first published in 1983, it was withdrawn from publication until 1991 when a legal suit brought by FBI agents and a South Dakota state official was resolved.) Peltier continues to

serve two consecutive life sentences for murder of the two agents. In the Matthiessen account Peltier was singled out for having drawn attention to the uranium resources in the Black Hills, the dangers of nuclear mining and milling, water depletion, and other environmental problems associated with the nuclear industry. Peltier supporters charge that it was the planned uranium mining and development in the Black Hills that had made Pine Ridge central to FBI operations for the previous five years. In Europe and other countries, Peltier is considered a political prisoner.

1975
Council of Energy Resource Tribes (CERT) founded in Denver, Colorado, to help protect tribal mineral resources. Tribal leaders from 25 reservations containing oil, coal, gas, shale, uranium, and other energy sources established the council to gain expert information independent of the BIA, and to better manage their energy resources. Navajo tribal chairman Peter MacDonald was elected its first chairman.

1977
The Alaska oil pipeline opened.

1979–1981
Iran hostage crisis. Muslim militants seized the U.S. embassy in Teheran and held 52 American hostages for 15 months to humiliate the U.S. The hostages were not released until Jimmy Carter was defeated and Ronald Reagan elected president in 1981.

1979
Largest nuclear accident in the United States (including Three Mile Island) at a United Nuclear Company milling plant on the Navajo reservation in Church Rock, New Mexico, (July 16). More than 1,100 tons of uranium wastes gushed through a ruptured Tailings Mill dam, releasing more than 100 million gallons of radioactive water into the Rio Puerco. Livestock grazing near the river got untreatable sores, soon became ill and died. Navajos were

forbidden to drink the water or sell their livestock. When tested, the Rio Puerco showed 6,000 times the allowable level of radioactivity. The river, which flows from New Mexico into Arizona, showed radioactive groundwater spreading through the geologic layer known as the Rio Puerco Alluviam. The cleanup still continues as a Superfund Site of the Department of Energy.

1979

American Indian Religious Freedom Act became law, stating that Indian religion was protected under the First Amendment. *"It shall be the policy of the United States to protect and preserve for American Indians their inherent right of freedom to believe, express, and exercise the traditional religions of the American Indian, Eskimo, Aleut, and native Hawaiians, including . . . access to sites, use and possession of sacred objects, and the freedom to worship through ceremonials and traditional rites. . . ."*

1979

Activists staged the Longest Walk from San Francisco to Washington, D.C., symbolic of the forced marches of Indians. More than 2,000 joined the march.

1979

Act of Congress passed to allow burial of Turkey Tayac, a Piscataway chief and the last native speaker of the Piscataway language. He was interred in Piscataway burial grounds, now national park lands, opposite Mount Vernon on the banks of the Potomac River in Maryland.

1979

**William Janklow, South Dakota's attorney general, ran for governor as an "Indian fighter." When he won, he abolished the state's Department of Environmental Protection, placing its functions in the Department of Natural Resources. From 1983 to 1988 Governor Janklow was one of the plaintiffs in the suit against publication of *In the Spirit of Crazy Horse*. His case was dismissed.

1979
White environmental groups and Indian activist groups, including Women of All Red Nations, formed the Black Hills Alliance in South Dakota. The group's mission was to educate the people of South Dakota, white and Indian, about the dangers of nuclear mining and milling, water depletion and contamination. It also supported the Lakota claim to the Black Hills, hoping to tie the uranium leasing arrangements up in court.

1979
The Archaeological Resources Protection Act was passed, which strengthened the 1906 Antiquities Act: *"The purpose of this Act is to secure ... the protection of archaeological resources and sites which are on public lands and Indian lands and to foster increased cooperation [regarding] archaeological resources and data which were obtained before the date of the enactment of this Act ..."* It was designed to slow the destruction of archaeological sites, such as had occurred in the 10-year stripmining of Black Mesa, which had destroyed an estimated 4,000 Anasazi cliff houses and archaeological sites.

1979
Navajo uranium miners and families were found to be part of an epidemic

of lung cancer. The disease had been unknown on the reservation before World War II. One Navajo miner testified before Senate hearings held in Farmington, New Mexico saying, "We were treated like dogs. There was no ventilation in the mines." (The mining company, Kerr McGee, which had operated many of the mining sites on the Navajo reservation, issued a press release saying that lung cancer deaths among Navajo miners were all allegations.)

One uranium tailings pile was 70 feet high and a mile long. Radioactive dust from the pile had been blowing through the air for years, affecting families and residents of the area. The mining companies were under no legal obligation to clean up the toxic sites. As soon as the Navajo asked for cleanup of the uranium mines, the reservation subsidiaries of the uranium mining companies declared bankruptcy and left the cleanup to the government. The Tuba City uranium mine was cleaned up after a grassroots effort refused to let the matter rest.

1980

Worker strikes in Poland. The independent unions formed a national federation, Solidarity, led by Lech Walesa.

1980

First global effort to measure world deforestation. Estimates projected that the planet had lost one-fifth of its forests from pre-agricultural times, affecting carbon dioxide levels, wildlife habitat, and biological and plant diversity. Massive extinction of species was predicted by 2050 because of the destruction of habitats.

1980

U.S. federal census reported almost 1.5 million Native Americans.

NATIVE AMERICAN WRITERS: TWENTIETH CENTURY VOICES

When Kiowa poet and novelist N. Scott Momaday won the Pulitzer Prize in 1969 for his novel House Made of Dawn, *some critics cited the event as the beginning of a Native American renaissance in literature. In fact, Native American writers had been writing and publishing for years. What had changed was the willingness of white audiences to accord value to Indian stories. For decades, writers like D'Arcy McNickle and Frank Waters had been publishing novels and nonfiction books about America and Native Americans with complex themes of landscape, Native people, and history. But recognition went to writers like Oliver LaFarge, a white author and anthropologist, who won the Pulitzer Prize for literature in 1927 for* Laughing Boy, *a Navajo story told from the perspective of a Navajo man. In many ways the recognition given* House Made of Dawn *marked the acknowledgment of Native American storytelling on its own terms rather than filtered through the sensibility of a non-Indian writer. The following is an outline of a few of the better-known contemporary Native American writers and brief mention of their best-known work. Almost all are poets and, as writer James Welch has observed, "Indians have something to say about their culture and society and it's harder to be political and polemical in fiction." Obviously, a complete list would have to contain dozens more writers and poets and I refer the interested reader to* Notable Native Americans, Native North American Literature *(Gale Research Inc.), and* Smoke Rising: The Native North American Literary Companion *(Joseph Bruchac, Editor).*

D'Arcy McNickle (1904–1977) is considered by many to be among the founders of contemporary Native American literature and ethnohistory. A Cree-born Salish-Kootenai, McNickle was a novelist, short-story writer, biographer, and anthropologist who attended Oxford and who wrote several acclaimed novels, including Wind from an Enemy Sky (1978), *as well as groundbreaking works of anthropology, including* The Indian Tribes of the United States *(1962) and* They Came Here First: The Epic of the American Indian *(1949). His themes center on the conflicts between white and American Indian cultures, particularly the Anglo-European concept of property ownership and the white transmutation of land into money in opposition to the Native American belief in land as sacred, as the repository of all history and the source of life.*

Frank Waters (1902–1995) was nominated five times for the Nobel Prize in literature. Born and brought up in Colorado, his best-known novel is The Man Who Killed the Deer, *which has remained in print for 40 years; his best-known nonfiction is the* Book of the Hopi. *His lifetime body of work includes over 20 novels and nonfiction works about the landscape and people of the West, with themes that range from the cultural mix of whites and the Pueblo peoples, to nuclear testing and the invention of the atomic bomb. Before he died he published a book of profiles of Indian heroes, which he dedicated to his father, who was part Shawnee. Vine Deloria, Jr. , wrote the introduction.*

Vine Deloria, Jr., (1933–), a lawyer, theologian, and educator, is considered one of the most outspoken writers and radical thinkers in contemporary Native American affairs. A Standing Rock Sioux born in South Dakota, Deloria studied religion before he studied law, as his father was an Episcopal clergyman. He combines the two perspectives in his highly original nonfiction writing. Custer Died for Your Sins: An Indian Manifesto is both a fierce indictment of white America's treatment of Indians and a manifesto for the goals of Indian activists. God Is Red: A Native View of Religion breaks new ground by presenting the central concepts of Native American religious beliefs as well as the American legal system's efforts to deny Native American religion. Historian Dee Brown described Deloria's status among the Sioux as "similar to that of Sitting Bull's leadership for the Sioux tribes a century ago." An activist and an organizer, he served as an expert on Indian treaties as the first witness for the defense in the Wounded Knee trial of 1974.

N. Scott Momaday (1934–), a poet, playwright, and novelist, is one of the most widely respected and successful contemporary Native American literary figures, often compared with William Faulkner. Born in Oklahoma of Kiowa, white, and Cherokee background, he has a doctorate in literature from Stanford University and has taught literature at the University of California and Stanford. House Made of Dawn was the first work by a Native American to win the Pulitzer Prize and has greatly influenced other native writers. His other best-known work includes a book of poetry, In the Presence of the Sun, and an autobiographical book of nonfiction, The Way to Rainy Mountain (1969). He is also the author of a film script based on Frank Waters's The Man Who Killed the Deer.

Gerald Vizenor (1934–) is a prolific writer whose published work includes 29 books of poetry, fiction, stories, songs, autobiographical stories, and historical narratives such as The People Named the Chippewa: Narrative Histories. A mixed-blood Chippewa (Anishinabe), he was raised in Minnesota by a succession of caretakers including his grandmother, an alcoholic stepfather, and a series of foster parents. The poverty, violence, and capriciousness that shaped his own early life underlie his writing. The trickster figure is prominent in his work and his characters encourage people to follow the trickster and shamans with their visions and dreams in order to rediscover traditional tribal values. Vizenor is controversial because he challenges conventional generalizations about Indians (pure blood is not better than mixed blood, according to Vizenor). In his acclaimed novel The Heirs of Columbus he rewrote the myth of Columbus from a Native American perspective.

Paula Gunn Allen (1939–) is a poet, essayist, novelist, and editor of Native American literature and legend, who draws from the traditions of the Sioux and the Laguna Pueblo, both of which are part of her family ancestry. She particularly focuses on the feminine in Indian traditions, ritual, and stories. Her best-known books are The Sacred Hoop: Recovering the Feminine in American Indian Traditions (1986), a collection of 17 essays on women's rituals and stories in folklore and legend; and Spiderwoman's Granddaughters: Traditional Tales and Contemporary Writing by Native American Women (1989), an edited compilation of stories, legends, and interviews by and about Native American women.

James Welch (1940–) is part Gros Ventre and part Blackfoot and lives in Montana, where much of his fiction and poetry is placed. His best-known novels are Fools Crow, a historical novel set in Montana Territory in the 1870s, about the transformation of a restless warrior, Fools Crow, into a powerful medicine man of his tribe;

and The Indian Lawyer, *a contemporary novel of Sylvester Yellow Calf, a lawyer and congressional candidate who also serves on the Montana prison parole board. One critic remarked that Welch's real subject is the American Indian's search for identity in his native land.*

Simon J. Ortiz (1941–) *of Acoma Pueblo is one of the most widely read Native American writers. In his poetry, short stories, and edited works he maintains that the survival of all people is dependent on their relationship to land and their connection to each other. In* Fight Back: For the Sake of the People, for the Sake of the Land, *a poetry collection published in 1980, Ortiz celebrated the 300th anniversary of the successful Pueblo revolt against the Spanish in 1680 and focused on the uranium mining by Pueblos, Navajos, and whites in New Mexico's "Uranium Belt." In* From Sand Creek: Rising in This Heart Which Is Our America *he drew parallels between the massacre at Sand Creek and America in Vietnam. His themes focus on the interlaced destinies of the Indian and the white man, suggesting that the fate of the Indian will inevitably become the fate of all.*

Michael Dorris (1945–) *is the author of fiction and nonfiction, notably* The Broken Cord, *a first-person chronicle of the effects of fetal alcohol syndrome on his adopted son Adam, which also deals with the larger impact of alcoholism on Native American communities. His fiction,* A Yellow Raft in Blue Water, *takes place in Washington, where he spent part of his childhood. Part Modoc, he was born in Washington, grew up in Kentucky, and now divides his time between New Hampshire and Montana. He has also co-authored a novel with his wife Louise Erdrich.*

Linda Hogan (1947–) *is a Chickasaw poet, novelist, short-story writer, playwright, and essayist who has played a prominent role in the development of contemporary Native American poetry. Born in Denver, Colorado, of Chickasaw parents from Oklahoma, she weaves Chickasaw familial and tribal history in her work. Her verse collection* Daughters, I Love You *is an indictment of nuclear proliferation. Her critically acclaimed novel* Mean Spirit, *published in 1990, is a mystery story based on the U.S. government's annexation of oil-rich Osage land during the 1920s. In all of her work she combines a spiritual attitude toward nature with an activist political stance.*

Leslie Marmon Silko (1948–), *a novelist and a poet, was born in New Mexico into a family from the Laguna Pueblo. Her celebrated novel* Ceremony *is about a World War II veteran who has lost his sanity in a prisoner-of-war camp. After his unstable return from a veterans' hospital to his Pueblo reservation, he joins other mixed-blood veterans in wasted days of drinking. Eventually he meets a traditional Indian who teaches him that ceremony is not merely a formal ritual, but a means of conducting one's life, a way of experiencing the power of timelessness, of connecting to primal ways of seeing and knowing that relate to all of life.* Ceremony *is considered one of America's best contemporary novels. Silko has also published a volume of poetry, a book of short stories and poems,* Storyteller, *and a second novel,* Almanac of the Dead. *She lives in Tucson, Arizona.*

Joy Harjo (1951–) *is a Creek poet and film-script writer. Born in Oklahoma of Creek (Muskogee) parents, she was raised in New Mexico, and she often uses Creek myths, legends, and images in poems that are set in the Southwest. She also draws on the contemporary traditions of feminist poetry and of personal and political resistance. An accomplished musician, she sometimes reads her poetry accompanied by a* *traditional Indian drum and flute.* She Had Some Horses, *her first volume of poetry, is known for its use of prayer chants and animal imagery;* Secrets from the Center of the World *(with Steven Strom) combines photography with poetry. Her best-known work,* In Mad Love and War, *is concerned with tradition, memory, politics and, in her words, "the transformational aspects of language."*

Mary Brave Bird, also Mary Crow Dog *(1953–) Mary Brave Bird's autobiographical writing focuses on political events in which she participated and the traditions of family and ancestral traditions that sustain native women. She was born on the Rosebud reservation in South Dakota, and her autobiographical* Lakota Woman *(with Richard Erdoes) recounts the hard reality of a woman on the present-day Sioux reservation and offers a firsthand portrayal of the American Indian Movement in the 1960s.* Lakota Woman, *which won the American Book Award in 1991, recounts her struggles with poverty and alcoholism, domestic hardships, her marriage to Sioux activist Leonard Crow Dog, and her experience of the siege of Wounded Knee in 1973. A second book,* Okitika Woman, *continues her autobiographical account. By the time of publication she had divorced Leonard Crow Dog and changed her name to Mary Brave Bird (her grandfather's name).*

Louise Erdrich *(1954–), poet, novelist, and essayist, was raised on the Chippewa reservation in North Dakota by German-American and Chippewa parents who worked at the Bureau of Indian Falls boarding school. Her four interrelated novels, which trace two extended families of Chippewa origin as well as some of their white neighbors, have all been national best-sellers. Her first novel,* Love Medicine, *won the National Book Critics Circle Award in 1984. Her highly regarded volume of poetry,* Jacklight, *is one of several volumes of poetry, essays, and short stories dealing with life and contemporary issues on modern Indian reservations. She has recently published a fifth novel,* Tales of Burning Love. *She has also co-authored a novel with her husband Michael Dorris.*

Sherman Alexie *(1966–) is a young poet from Washington State who is Spokane and Coeur d'Alene and who has found a national audience. In his first collection of fiction and poetry,* The Business of Fancydancing, *his comic sensibility drew a large audience of whites as well as Indians. In his second collection of poetry and fiction,* The Lone Ranger and Tonto Fistfight in Heaven, *he received wide acclaim for his gritty, realistic, and wonderfully humorous treatment of contemporary reservation life. His writing is also highly political, targeting events such as the nineteenth-century Sand Creek Massacre, Hollywood's treatment of Native Americans, as well as corrupt tribal council members working for the government.*

1981

Anwar Sadat, premier of Egypt, assassinated in Cairo while reviewing a military parade. Muslim fundamentalist soldiers in the Egyptian military dismounted from a parade vehicle and sprayed the reviewing stand with automatic weapons. Ten others were killed.

1982

National Navajo Codetalkers Day declared by President Ronald Reagan to commemorate the cadre of Navajo servicemen who had relayed defense communications during World War II.

1982

Jim Thorpe's medals restored. Thorpe, a Sauk Indian, was an Olympic gold medal winner in 1912. His two gold medals were taken from him in 1913, ostensibly because he had played a season of semi-pro baseball. It had taken 69 years to have the medals returned, 29 years after his death in 1953.

1984

The Union Carbide plant in Bhopal, India, released a toxic cloud of methyl isocyanate gas into the air, killing more than 2,000 people immediately and an estimated 4,000 within months. Another 200,000 were injured.

1985

First confirmed observation of the "ozone hole" over Antarctica, an opening in the atmospheric layer that screens ultraviolet rays from the sun.

1985

Wilma Mankiller sworn in as principal chief of the Cherokee nation in Oklahoma. The first woman in modern history to lead a large tribe, she had previously served as deputy chief. Her autobiography, *Mankiller*, tells the story of her education and rise to leadership. The Cherokee tribe is the second-largest in the U.S. after the Navajo, and is headed by a 15-member council.

1986

State of emergency declared in South Africa. As unrest in black communities continued, more than 2,300 blacks were killed by white police. The U.S. and British Commonwealth countries imposed economic sanctions. More than

1986

The final deadline for the Navajo removal from the Hopi-Navajo Joint Use Lands. Purchase of nuclear-contaminated lands as a place of relocation. Despite the legally mandated removal deadline of July 1986, thousands

200 U.S. companies were forced to withdraw because of U.S. boycotts.

1986
World's worst nuclear accident at the Chernobyl plant in Russia. The number four reactor at the plant failed and released a radioactive cloud, forcing the evacuation of 450,000 people living within a 30-mile zone around the plant. Milk and agricultural products within a 500-mile radius in eastern Europe were banned. Months later they were found to still have unacceptably high radiation levels. Breast and thyroid cancer rates in the area are exceptionally high and still being monitored.

of Navajo remained on their lands because there was no place to move them to. The U.S. government extended the relocation deadline and allocated funds to purchase "New Lands" on which to resettle the Navajo, a series of contiguous ranches on the southern edge of the Navajo reservation. It was widely believed that the reason the ranchers were anxious to sell was because the Rio Puerco, whose radioactive waters (from the 1979 nuclear accident at the United Nuclear uranium milling plant) ran through a portion of these lands, had contaminated the groundwater supply. The government appropriated monies to test the water supply.

1986
The Mashantucket Pequot tribe opened a high stakes bingo operation on their reservation in Connecticut. After the Pequot War of 1637 the remaining Pequot (some 2,500 out of 15,000) were split into two groups: the Pawcatuck Pequot who were placed under the Narragansetts; and the Mashantucket Pequot who went to live under the Uncas and Mohegans. Eventually the Mashantucket Pequot were allowed to return to their old country and in 1666 were given a 2,500 acre reservation. By 1983 they were reduced to 214 acres and 55 tribal members on the rolls. With the help of the Native American Rights Fund the Pequot filed suit to regain the lands taken from them and gain federal recognition. They hired members of the Penobscot tribe in Maine to train them to run a high stakes bingo game. It was the forerunner of the Foxwoods High Stakes Bingo and Resort Casino, now the largest gaming resort in the country. Between 1986 and 1996 the number of the resort's employees grew

from 100 to 11,000, making the Pequot tribe one of Connecticut's largest employers and taxpayers.

1987
Montreal Protocol signed by 24 industrial nations to cooperate in protecting the ozone layer. The increase in ultraviolet light entering the atmosphere because of ozone depletion is known to increase skin cancer risks.

1987
Ben Nighthorse Campbell, Northern Cheyenne from Colorado, elected to the U.S. Congress. A former member of the U.S. Olympic team in judo, he was only the second Native American elected to the Colorado legislature, where he served from 1983 to 1986.

1988
Termination resolution of 1953 officially repealed by Congress.

1989
The largest oil spill in history occurred when the *Exxon Valdez* ran aground off the coast of Alaska, spilling 37,000 tons of oil, polluting Indian lands and wildlife around Prince William Sound. An estimated 50,000 birds and fish were killed. Subsequent events showed that despite laws, Exxon had no emergency cleanup plans in place for such an accident.

1989
Upheaval in the communist world. One million demonstrators in Tiananmen Square, China, called for more democratic freedoms. The Chinese government responded with a crackdown. After mass demonstrations in East Germany, two million Germans crossed into West Berlin. The Berlin Wall was dismantled. Fall of the communist regime in Czechoslovakia; Vaclav Havel elected interim president.

1989
Congress appropriated funds to establish a National Museum of the American Indian in New York and in Washington, D.C., as part of the Smithsonian. The collections of the Heye Foundation of Native American art formed the basis of the new museum with a special facility for storage and preservation to be built in Maryland. In 1994 the Museum of the American Indian opened in the former Customs House in New York. A second museum is being designed for the Mall in Washington, D.C. It marked the first national museum to present exhibits from the native point of view.

1990
World population reached 5.3 billion.

1990
Congress passed the Native American Graves Protection and Repatriation

1990
In South Africa Nelson Mandela was released from prison after 20 years, elected deputy president of the African National Congress, and began formal talks with the government of South Africa.

1990–1991
The Gulf War. Iraq invaded Kuwait. The U.S. launched the Persian Gulf War to expel Iraqui soldiers from Kuwait.

Act. It required universities and museums receiving federal funds to return Indian bones, human remains, and sacred objects to any tribes that requested them.

1990
The Supreme Court ruled that states could outlaw religious practices (such as peyote) of the Native American Church. It was considered a major setback to First Amendment protections of Indian religious freedom. The origins of the Native American Church were in Mexico (peyote comes from the Aztec word *peyotl*) and spread through Texas and New Mexico to the Kiowa and the Kiowa Apache in the southern Plains following the suppression of the Ghost Dance religion in the 1890s. Religious practice focused on the ritual consumption of peyote (a cactus button) in the form of tea or in food. According to Huston Smith and Reuben Snake (*One Nation Under God: The Triumph of the Native American Church*, 1996, Clear Light Press): "*Peyote is regarded as a gift from the creator. It counters the craving for alcohol . . . It is not taken to induce visions or hallucinogenic experiences but because it heals and teaches righteousness.*" It is estimated that today over a quarter of a million people attend meetings of the Native American Church.

1990
U.S. Congress passed a compensation bill for Navajo uranium miners. After 35 years the government took responsibility for the inhumane conditions of uranium mining on the Navajo reservation. More than a thousand miners' families applied for benefits. Less than a third received awards because of a difficult bureaucratic process requiring docu-

mentation, such as pay stubs from 20 years earlier, that few Navajo families could meet. Former secretary of the interior Stewart Udall had represented the Navajo miners in their suit.

1990
Mohawks protested the expansion of a golf course on tribal burial lands near Oka, Quebec. Kahnawake Mohawks erected barricades. Many members of AIM and other American Indians joined the Mohawks in their protest.

1991
START treaty signed by U.S. President Bush and Soviet Premier Gorbachev, calling for a historical first-ever reduction in long-range nuclear arms, to amount to 30 percent of stockpiles by 1998.

1991
Collapse of the U.S.S.R. and the creation of the Commonwealth of Independent States. The Soviet republics declared independence. The Communist Party was dissolved; Gorbachev was out of power.

1991
Indian groups succeeded in having the Custer Battlefield National Monument in Montana renamed the Little Bighorn Battlefield National Monument.

1991
Foxwoods gambling casino opened in Ledyard, Connecticut, by the Pequot Indians. It eventually became the single most profitable casino outside of Las Vegas. Indian tribes throughout the country, whose reservation lands are exempt from state laws prohibiting gambling, were approached by professional gambling operations like Bally's to open casinos with the profits shared between the tribe and the professionals. By 1995 more than a hundred Indian reservations had opened casinos as an economic measure to provide jobs and income for poor reservations.

1992
Rigoberta Menchu, a native indigenous leader of Guatemala, awarded the Nobel Peace Prize. In *Voices of Indigenous Peoples* she said: *"The recognition of the ethnic and cultural diversity of this world is an essential element in the progress of humankind . . .*

1992
Columbus Quincentennial recast to highlight Indian contributions to the world and the injustices of Spain during the period of conquest. The second voyage of the *Niña, Pinta,* and *Santa Maria* ended up bankrupt in New York harbor.

such as the concept we [indigenous peoples] possess of the world and our relationship with nature."

1992

Earth Summit in Rio de Janeiro. In what was believed to be the largest international gathering in history, hundreds of heads of state, representatives of thousands of governmental organizations, and indigenous peoples around the planet gathered in Brazil under the auspices of the United Nations to discuss issues of environment and industrial development.

1992–1996

The Balkan War. The breakup of former Yugoslavia brought war in the Balkans among Serbs, Croats, and Muslims. When Croatia and Slovenia declared independence, the government troops, Serbs, attacked them to establish sovereignty over their territory. Bosnia declared independence. More than one million people were forced to leave their homes. Bosnia, Slovenia, and Croatia became members of the UN. Serbia and Montenegro were expelled from the UN. The war marked the final spasms of the Ottoman Empire and the Hapsburg monarchy, begun at the turn of the century.

1992

Ben Nighthorse Campbell elected to the U.S. Senate, the first Native American to serve there.

1992

The Native American Council of New York City hosted a meeting of indigenous leaders for the United Nations official opening of the Year of Indigenous Peoples in 1993. More than 250 delegates came from all over the world: aboriginal peoples of Australia, the Saami of Norway, the Mapuche from Chile, the Nanaentz from Russia. The North American nations were represented by Haudenosaunee (Iroquois), Lakota (Sioux), Diné (Navajo), and Cree delegates.

1993

Native American Free Exercise of Religion Act introduced in Congress to negate the Supreme Court ruling regarding interference in the Native American Church and to strengthen religious rights as set out in the earlier American Indian Religious Freedom Act.

1994

Everglades Restoration Project and the Kissimmee River restoration. The government began a 400-million-dollar project to reverse the effects of the 1958 Everglades Reclamation Project and the straightening of the Kissimmee River by the U.S. Army Corps of Engineers, which had occurred despite the objections of the Miccosukee Indians. The draining of the Kissimmee River had taken 10 years, dried up 40,000 acres of marshland, and straightened the 103-mile river into a 56-mile concrete canal. The loss of the marshes caused the disappearance of 90 percent of the fish and wildlife, altered the wetlands, and changed the water flow into Lake Okeechobee, changing water temperature and causing a buildup of algae, water weeds, and deformed wildlife. The reversal proposed to eliminate the canal and restore the oxbows in the natural river course, which the Miccosukee had insisted was the necessary water cycle in the Everglades.

1994

Mescalero Apache signed a nuclear-waste storage planning agreement with the federal government, the only tribe in the country to do so. They were one of more than 50 tribes who were approached by the U.S. government offering multimillion-dollar contracts to locate waste disposal sites on their reservation lands. Despite a tribal referendum that defeated the proposed nuclear-storage dump, a second referendum passed by a narrow margin. According to Wendell Chino, Mescalero Apache tribal president for the past 30 years, the nuclear-waste storage complex would provide jobs and economic benefits to the tribe. The governor of New Mexico announced the state's opposition to the nuclear-waste dump due

Roberta Blackgoat. Navajo elder and chair-woman of the Big Mountain nation.

to the health and safety concerns of New Mexico residents.

1994

The Indigenous Environmental Network, an international alliance of grassroots native groups, publicly opposed the Mescalero nuclear decision, citing the lack of accountability from the nuclear industry and the documented increases in cancer deaths in native communities.

1994

Roberta Blackgoat, Navajo, was named "America's Unsung Woman" by the National Women's History Project for her 20-year leadership in the environmental and human rights struggle on Black Mesa and the ongoing removal of 12,000 Navajo. Mrs. Blackgoat, a 77-year-old grandmother and Navajo elder, had traveled to the United Nations in Switzerland and New York to present the case of the Navajo relocatees. In addition to presenting the human rights case of the Navajos, she had drawn attention to the environmental issues surrounding stripmining, the pollution of the Grand Canyon from power plants, the contamination of the water supply, and the larger issues of ecocide on Native American reservations. By attending a stockholders meeting of Hanson's Ltd. in London, the new multinational parent company of Peabody Coal, she drew attention to the absentee ownership of the stripmines on Black Mesa. The export of environmental issues to third world areas is an internationally recognized issue under review by several UN commissions.

1994

James Bay Project delayed and Matthew Coon Come, a Cree, received the Goldman Environmental Prize in San Francisco for 15 years of fighting the James Bay Hydro Quebec project. The entire project would flood thousands of miles of Cree lands in northern Quebec and affect an ecosystem the size of France. Although the first phases of the project had been completed, damming three rivers with 27 dams for hydroelectricity, the third phase was delayed when Hydro Quebec found its buyers in New York and New England backing out of their contracts.

1995
Yitzhak Rabin, prime minster of Israel, assassinated by a fundamentalist Jew bent on stopping the peace negotiations with Palestinians.

1995
A White House commission on nuclear experiments issued a public report acknowledging nuclear-related experiments and government-sponsored nuclear projects affecting indigenous peoples, particularly native villages in Alaska (nuclear storage) and radiation exposure to residents of the Marshall Islands in the Pacific (nuclear testing) in the 1940s and 1950s. The report also acknowledged the effects of radiation on "downwinders" at nuclear test sites in Nevada in the 1960s and 1970s.

1995-2005
The United Nations inaugurated the Decade of Indigenous Peoples to run from 1996 until the year 2005. The Declaration of Indigenous Peoples was presented to the United Nations General Assembly. In announcing the new decade, Secretary General Boutros Boutros-Ghali said: ". . . *on the eve of the year 2000 the number of lanugages and*

dialects spoken throughout the five conti-
nents [is] only half what it had been in
1900. The modern world [has] been a great
destroyer of languages, traditions, and cultures. The latter are being drowned by the
flood of mass communications, the instruments of which all too often remain in the
service of a handful.... Today, cultures
which do not have powerful media are
threatened with extinction.... Allowing
native languages, cultures, and different
traditions to perish through 'nonassis-
tance to endangered cultures' must
henceforth be considered a basic violation of human rights."

1996
World population reached 5.75 billion, surpassing estimates for the year
2000. More than half the people in the
world live in India or China.

1996
For the first time in an Indian suit
against a multinational energy company, a federal judge in Arizona ruled
for the Navajo traditionalists of Black
Mesa and against the London-based
Hanson's Ltd., owner of Peabody Coal
Company, America's largest coal pro-
ducer. In denying the company a permanent operating permit until they were in
compliance with the law, the federal
judge agreed with the Navajo plaintiffs,
saying that Peabody's Kayenta coal strip-
mine polluted the air, contaminated
groundwater, affected the health of Indians in the area, killed their sheep, and
destroyed Indian burial sites. In the landmark ruling the judge said the Office of
Surface Mining had not been stringent
enough in insuring that the mine met
permit requirements and observed that
the agency had too high a "tolerance ...
to the adverse effects mining has upon
the lives and well-being of Native Americans." The suit was initiated by the
Diné Alliance, a Navajo organization of
more than 500 traditionalist Navajos
from Black Mesa, in cooperation with a

Phoenix-based environmental group called Don't Waste Arizona. The coal mined at the Kayenta site supplies electricity for greater Phoenix, Los Angeles, and Las Vegas, as well as power to run the department of the interior's water project known as the Central Arizona Project, often described as the most expensive water project in the world.

1996
Missing funds in tribal trust funds. The Native American Rights Fund filed a class action lawsuit against the secretary of the interior (Bruce Babbit) and treasury secretary (Robert Rubin) for mismanagement of tribal trust funds. In an audit completed by the Arthur Andersen accounting firm the BIA couldn't account for 2.4 billion dollars in transactions involving those funds. *"They [the BIA] have no idea how much has been collected from the companies that use our land and are unable to provide even a basic, regular statement to account holders,"* said John Echohawk who brought the lawsuit. In 1837 Congress ended direct payments to tribes for lands they had ceded or sold and stipulated that the monies be held in trust. Dozens of auditors over the years have criticized BIA management of the tribal accounts and cited problems in poor accounting systems, lack of security controls, and incompetent personnel.

1996
Chief Joseph and the return of the Nez Perce. The white residents of the Wallowa Valley in Oregon, from which Chief Joseph and his Nez Perce were expelled in 1877, have invited the Nez Perce to return and are in the process of building a Chief Joseph Interpretive

Taos Pueblo.
"We have lived upon this land from days beyond history's records, far past any living memory, deep into the time of legend. The story of my people and the story of place are one single story. No man can think of us without thinking of this place. We are always joined together."
A Taos Pueblo man quoted by Alfonso Ortiz.

Center. One of the prime tourist attractions in Oregon is the burial site of old Chief Joseph in the Nez Perce cemetery in the town named for him. (The National Park Service maintains the Nez Perce National Historic Trail, an 1100-mile route, which commemorates the 1877 war.) After his 1500 mile march in which he outwitted the U.S. Army and won 21 separate military encounters, Chief Joseph and his band were surprised in the open plain 40 miles from the Canadian border and forced to surrender. They were never allowed to return to their homelands in Oregon. It is said that Chief Joseph died of a broken heart. White residents hit on the idea of developing tourism as the timber industry shut down and cattle prices fell. They have raised money to return some of the lands to Chief Joseph's Nez Perce descendants (all of whom live in other places) and to build a Chief Joseph Interpretive Center. The visitor brochure for the Wallowa Valley reads, "Gateway to the Land of Chief Joseph."

LIST OF ILLUSTRATIONS

Allen, Paula Gunn. *The Sacred Hoop: Recovering the Feminine in American Indian Traditions*. Boston: Beacon Press, 1986.

Bataille, Gretchen M., ed. *Native American Women: A Biographical Dictionary*. New York: Garland Publishing, 1993.

Berkhofer, Robert E. *The White Man's Indian: Images of the American Indian from Columbus to the Present*. New York: Knopf, 1979.

Berrin, Kathleen, and Esther Pasztory. *Teotihuacán: Art from the City of the Gods*. London: Thames & Hudson and the Fine Arts Museum of San Francisco (exhibition catalogue), 1994.

Brain, Jeffrey, and John Grimes. "We Claim These Shores: Native Americans and the European Settlement of Massachusetts Bay." Salem, Massachusetts: Peabody Museum paper, 1992.

Brown, Dee. *Bury My Heart at Wounded Knee: An Indian History of the American West*. New York: Holt, Rinehart and Winston, 1970.

Bruchac, Josephy, ed., with Sharon Malinowski. *Smoke Rising: The Native North American Literary Companion*. Detroit: Visible Ink Press, 1995.

Catlin, George. *North American Indians, Notes and Letters*. Edited with introduction by Peter Matthiessen (reprint of 1841 text). New York: Viking, 1989.

Champagne, Duane, ed. *The Native North American Almanac: A Reference Work on Native North Americans in the U.S. and Canada*. Detroit: Gale Research, Inc., 1994.

Coe, Michael D. *Mexico*. London: Thames & Hudson, 1984.

Coronado, Hernando. *The Journey of Coronado, 1540–42: The City of Mexico to the Grand Canyon of the Colorado and the Buffalo Plains of Texas, Kansas, and Nebraska*. Translated and edited by George Parker Winship. New York: A.S. Barnes & Company, 1904.

Cornell, Stephen. *Return of the Native: American Indian Political Resurgence*. New York: Oxford University Press, 1988.

Crosby, Alfred W. *The Columbian Exchange: Biological and Cultural Consequences of 1492*. Westport, Connecticut: Greenwood Press, 1972.

Davies, Nigel. *The Toltecs Until the Fall of Tula*. Norman and London: University of Oklahoma Press, 1977.

Deloria, Vine, Jr. *Custer Died for Your Sins: An Indian Manifesto*. New York: Avon, 1969.

Deloria, Vine, Jr., and Clifford M. Lytle. *American Indians, American Justice*. Austin, Texas: University of Texas Press, 1983.

———. *The Nations Within: The Past and Future of American Indian Sovereignty*. New York: Pantheon Books, 1984.

De Vaca, Cabeza de. *Adventures in the Unknown Interior of America*. Translated by Cyclone Covey. Albuquerque, New Mexico: University of New Mexico Press, 1983.

Diaz del Castillo, Bernal. *The Bernal Diaz Chronicles: The True Story of the Conquest of Mexico*. Translated and with introduction and notes by A. P. Maudsly (1908). New York: Farrar, Strauss & Cudahy, 1956.

Fleming, Paula, and Judith Luskey. *The North American Indian in Early Photographs.* New York: Harper & Row, 1986.

——. *Grand Endeavors of American Indian Photography.* Washington, D.C.: Smithsonian Institute Press, 1993.

Flexner, James Thomas. *Mohawk Baronet: Sir William Johnson of New York.* New York: Harper Bros., 1959.

Freeman-Grenville, G.S.P. *Chronology of World History: A Calendar of Principal Events from 3000 B.C. to A.D. 1973.* London: Rex Collings, 1975.

Goodman, James M. *The Navajo Atlas: Environments, Resources, People, and History of the Diné Bikeyah.* Norman: University of Oklahoma Press, 1982.

Grinde, Donald A., and Bruce E. Johansen. *Ecocide of Native America: Environmental Destruction of Indian Lands and Peoples.* Santa Fe: Clear Light Publishers, 1995.

Grun, Bernard. *The Timetables of History: A Horizontal Linkage of People and Events.* New York: Simon & Schuster/Touchstone, 1991.

Hoyle, Russ. *Gale Environmental Almanac.* Detroit: Gale Research, Inc., 1993.

Hoxie, Frederick E. *A Final Promise: The Campaign to Assimilate the Indians, 1880–1920.* New York: Cambridge University Press, 1984, 1989.

Hutchinson Dictionary of World History. Oxford, England: Helicon Publishing, 1993.

International Encyclopedia of Population. 2 vols. New York: The Free Press, 1982.

Jane, Cecil, ed. and trans. *The Four Voyages of Columbus.* New York: Dover Publications, 1988.

Jennings, Francis. *The Founders of America: From the Earliest Migrations to the Present.* New York: W.W. Norton, 1993.

——. *The Invasion of America: Indians, Colonialism, and the Cant of Conquest.* Chapel Hill, North Carolina: University of North Carolina Press, 1975.

Josephy, Alvin, Jr. *500 Nations: An Illustrated History of North American Indians.* New York: Alfred A. Knopf, 1994.

Kappler, Charles J., ed. *Indian Treaties, 1778–1883.* New York: Interland Publishing, 1972. (Originally printed as vol. 2 of *Indian Affairs: Laws & Treaties,* U.S. Government Printing Office, 1904.)

Kennedy, Roger G. *Hidden Cities: The Discovery and Loss of Ancient North American Civilization.* New York: The Free Press, 1994.

Lame Deer, John, and Richard Erdoes. *Lame Deer, Seeker of Visions.* New York: Simon & Schuster, 1972.

Langer, William L. *Encyclopedia of World History.* Boston: Houghton Mifflin, 1972.

Lamar, Howard, ed. *The Readers Encyclopedia of the American West.* New York: Thomas Crowell, 1977.

Le Page du Pratz, Antoine Simon. *Histoire de la Louisiane,* 3 vols. Paris: DeBure, 1758. (Translated from the French, Louisiana State University, Louisiana Bicentennial reprint series, 1975.)

——. *Handbook of North American Indians,* v. 9. Washington: Smithsonian Institution: for sale by the Supt. of Docs., U.S. Govt. Print Off., 1978.

Leon Portilla, Miguel, ed. *The Broken Spear: The Aztec Account of the Conquest of Mexico.* Boston: Beacon Press, 1962, 1992.

Lyons, Oren. *Exiled in the Land of the Free: Democracy, Indian Nations and the U.S. Constitution.* Santa Fe: Clear Light Publishers, 1993.

Matthiessen, Peter. *In the Spirit of Crazy Horse.* New York: Viking, 1983, 1991.

——. *Indian Country.* New York: Viking, 1984.

McNickle, D'Arcy. *They Came Here First: The Epic of the American Indian.* New York: J. B. Lippincott Company, 1949.

Merchant, Carolyn. *Ecological Revolutions: Nature, Gender and Science in New England*. Chapel Hill: University of North Carolina Press, 1989.

Meyer, William *('yonv'ut'sisla:* Burning Bear). *Native Americans: The New Indian Resistance*. New York: International Publishers, 1971.

Morgan, Lewis H. *League of the Iroquois.* 2 vols. New York: Burt Franklin, 1901. (Facsimile reprint of 1851 version.)

Nabokov, Peter, and Robert Easton. *Native American Architecture*. New York: Oxford University Press, 1989.

Parman, Donald L. *Indians and the American West in the Twentieth Century*. Bloomington and Indianapolis: Indiana University Press, 1994.

Prucha, Francis Paul. *The Great Father: The United States Government and the American Indian.* 2 vols. Lincoln: University of Nebraska Press, 1984.

Sahagun, Fray Bernardino de. *Florentine Codex. General History of the Things of New Spain*. Books I–XII, translated from Nahuatl into English by Arthur J. O. Anderson and Charles E. Dibble. Santa Fe: School of American Research, 1950–82.

Sauer, Carl. *Man in Nature: America Before the Days of the White Man.* Berkeley, California: Turtle Island Foundation, 1975 (1939 reprint).

Sturtevant, William, ed. *Handbook of North American Indians*, 9 vols. Washington, D.C.: Smithsonian, 1978 85.

Tainter, Joseph A. *The Collapse of Complex Societies*. London: Cambridge University Press, 1988.

Tanner, Helen Hornbeck, ed. *Atlas of Great Lakes Indian History*. Norman: University of Oklahoma Press, 1986.

——. *The Settling of North America: The Atlas of the Great Migrations into North America from the Ice Age to the Present.* New York: Macmillan, 1995.

Thornton, Russell. *Holocaust and Survival: An American Indian Population History Since 1492*. Norman: University of Oklahoma Press, 1987.

Trenton, Patricia, and Patrick Houlihan. *Native Americans: Five Centuries of Changing Images.* New York: Harry N. Abrams, 1989.

Truettner, William H., ed. *The West as America: Reinterpreting Images of the Frontier, 1820–1920*. Washington, D.C.: Smithsonian Press and National Museum of American Art, 1991.

United Nations Environment Program. *The World Environment, 1972–82*. Dublin: Tycooly International Publishers, 1982.

Waldman, Carl, and Molly Braun. *Atlas of the North American Indian.* New York: Facts on File, 1985.

Wallace, Paul A. W. *White Roots of Peace: The Iroquois Book of Life.* Foreword by Chief Leon Shenandoah. Santa Fe: Clear Light Publishers, 1994.

Waters, Frank. *Brave Are My People: Indian Heroes Not Forgotten*. Sante Fe: Clear Light Publishers, 1994.

Weatherford, Jack. *Indian Givers: How the Indians of the Americas Transformed the World*. New York: Crown Publishers, 1989.

Weeks, Philip, ed., *The American Indian Experience: A Profile: 1524 to the Present.* Arlington Heights, Illinois: Forum Press, Inc., 1988.

Wettrau, Bruce. *World History: A Dictionary of Important People, Places, and Events from Ancient Times to the Present.* New York: Henry Holt, 1994.

Weyler, Rex. *Blood of the Land: The Government and Corporate War Against the American Indian Movement.* New York: Everest House, 1982.

Willey, Gordon R., and Jeremy Sabloff. *A History of American Archaeology*. San Francisco: W. H. Freeman and Co., 1974.

World Population: An Analysis of Vital Data. Chicago: University of Chicago Press, 1968.

INDEX

Malacite Indians, 76
Maliseet Indians, 170
Malleus Maleficarum, 68
Mandan Indians, 176, 228, 252, 279
Mandela, Nelson, 390
Mandingo Empire, 52
Manhattan Indians, 117, 132, 140
Manhattan Island, 109
Manifest destiny, 255
Manioc, 69
Mankiller, Wilma, 387
Manuelito, 260, 263–64
Maori tribes, 254, 264, 346
Mao Tse-tung, 340, 352
Maricopa Indians, 326
Marie Antoinette of France, 215
Marie-Louise of Austria, 232
Marquette, Jacques, 109, 152–54
Marshall, John, 20, 246, 247
Marshall, Thurgood, 357
Marx, Karl, 257, 270, 274
Maryland, 103, 135–36, 141
Mascouten Indians, 165, 166, 169
Mashantucket Pequot Indians, 388–89
Mason, John, 137
Massachusetts, 10, 17, 87, 109, 126–28, 132, 150, 153, 154, 160
Massachusetts Bay Colony, 128, 133–37, 145
Massasoit, Chief, 110, 125–29, 150
Mathematics, 16, 18
Mather, Cotton, 133–34, 137–38
Mather, Increase, 136
Matthiessen, Peter, 378, 379
Maximilian of Austria, 270
Maya civilization, 5, 15, 28, 46
Mayer, Julius von, 254
Mayflower, 125
Mayflower Compact, 110
Mazarin, Cardinal, 149
McCloud, Janet, 362
McIntosh, William, 242
McKenney, Thomas L., 241, 262, 313, 314
McNickle, D'Arcy, 345, 383
Means, Russell, 370, 373–75
Mean Spirits (Hogan), 310
Membertou, Chief, 114
Menchu, Rigoberta, 391–92
Menendez, Lucas, 146
Menendez de Aviles, Pedro, 102–3
Menominee Indians, 165, 306, 355, 356, 357
Meriam Commission, 304, 330–31, 336
Mesa Verde, 29, 45, 95
Mescalero Indians, 40, 393
Mesoamericans, 19, 24, 29, 32, 36, 39, 43
Mesopotamia, 5, 6, 11, 13, 15, 16, 18
Mesquackie (Fox) Indians, 165–67, 169, 175

Metacomet, 127, 150, 154, 156
Metternich system, 239
Mexicas, 51–52
Meyer, Dillon, 306, 352, 356
Miami Indians, 159, 165, 166, 178–80, 189, 213, 217
Miccosukee Indians, 359–69, 393
Michelangelo, 78
Michigan, 12, 65, 136, 145, 153, 163, 166, 167, 212
Micmac Indians, 76, 77, 90, 113–14, 121, 170
Migration routes, 10, 11, 40, 41
Miles, Nelson, 266, 283–86, 288, 294, 314
Military service, 321, 324, 341–42, 387
Mill, John Stuart, 257
Mimbres culture, 29, 30, 41
Mingo Indians, 189, 199
Miniconjou Sioux Indians, 149, 298
Minnesota, 60, 139, 149, 163, 164, 167, 265, 267–68
Minnesota Uprising of 1862, 266
Minuit, Peter, 132
Mission system, 197–98, 201, 208–9, 248–50
Missisauga Indians, 165, 166
Mississippi, 65, 73, 92, 223, 252, 253
Mississippian culture, 21, 25, 37, 42–44, 50, 59, 64–66, 92, 98, 187
Mississippi River, 42–43, 98, 109, 154, 161
Mississippi Valley, 18–19, 23, 25, 38
Missouri, 65
Missouri Treaty, 261
Mitchell, George, 367
Mithras, 30
Miwok culture, 18, 104
Mobile Indians, 74, 94
Moctezuma I, 66
Moctezuma II, 76, 81–84
Mogollon peoples, 16, 25, 29, 30, 41, 46
Mohave Indians, 343
Mohawk Indians, 53, 55, 117, 136, 141–43, 147, 148, 151, 153, 165, 168, 185, 186, 189, 196, 203, 204, 207, 209, 218, 358, 367, 376, 391
Mohegan Indians, 154, 156
Mohican Indians, 117
Momaday, N. Scott, 366–67, 383, 384
Monetary system, 74, 81
Mongols, 55
Monroe, James, 313
Monroe Doctrine, 311
Montagnais Indians, 117
Montana, 149, 204, 260, 265, 272, 273
Montesinos, Antonio de, 78
Montesquieu, Baron de La Brède et de, 178, 179
Moors, 67–69

ABOUT THE AUTHOR

JUDITH NIES is the author of *Seven Women: Portraits from the American Radical Tradition*, a book of biographies of women in American radical political and social movements. Her writing has been featured in the *New York Times*, the *Boston Globe, American Voice*, and *Harvard Review*. In 1994 her essay on Navajo elder Roberta Blackgoat won the national essay contest sponsored by the National Women's History Project. She was a recipient of a Bunting Fellowship at Harvard Radcliffe. A former speechwriter in the U.S. Congress and assistant secretary of environmental affairs for the state of Massachusetts, she has also co-edited (with Erwin Knoll) two books on public policy. She was graduated from Tufts and Johns Hopkins Universities.